Centred on a study of the early archives of the Venerabile Collegio
Inglese in Rome, the predecessor of the English College of today, this
book is more than a study of the beginnings of English institutions in
Rome. It attempts to place the English community there between 1362,
when the first English hospice for poor people and pilgrims was
founded, and 1420 in its political, commercial and religious setting. It
includes a description of a group of English merchants, with their wives
and widows, as well as members of the papal curia in Rome (from 1376),
including a study of Cardinal Adam Easton, a well-known scholar and
opponent of John Wycliffe. The book also uncovers a notable although
unsuccessful attempt to forward English participation in commerce with
Rome before 1420, revealing important links between the English laity
in Rome and the city of London.

MARGARET HARVEY is Senior Lecturer in History, University of
Durham. Her previous publications include *Solutions to the Schism: A
Study of Some English Attitudes, 1378–1409* (1983) and *England, Rome and
the Papacy, 1420–1464: The Study of a Relationship* (1993).

Cambridge Studies in Medieval Life and Thought

THE ENGLISH IN ROME, 1362–1420

Cambridge Studies in Medieval Life and Thought
Fourth Series

General editor
D. E. LUSCOMBE
Leverhulme Personal Research Professor of Medieval History, University of Sheffield

Advisory editors
R. B. DOBSON
Professor of Medieval History, University of Cambridge, and Fellow of Christ's College

ROSAMOND MCKITTERICK
Professor of Early Medieval European History, University of Cambridge,
and Fellow of Newnham College

The series Cambridge Studies in Medieval Life and Thought was inaugurated by G. G. Coulton in 1921; Professor D. E. Luscombe now acts as General Editor of the Fourth Series, with Professors R. B. Dobson and Rosamond McKitterick as Advisory Editors. The series brings together outstanding work by medieval scholars over a wide range of human endeavour extending from political economy to the history of ideas.

For a list of titles in the series, see end of book.

THE ENGLISH IN ROME
1362–1420

Portrait of an Expatriate Community

MARGARET HARVEY

CAMBRIDGE
UNIVERSITY PRESS

PUBLISHED BY THE PRESS SYNDICATE OF THE UNIVERSITY OF CAMBRIDGE
The Pitt Building, Trumpington Street, Cambridge, United Kingdom

CAMBRIDGE UNIVERSITY PRESS

The Edinburgh Building, Cambridge CB2 2RU, UK   http://www.cup.cam.ac.uk
40 West 20th Street, New York NY 10011–4211, USA   http://www.cup.org
10 Stamford Road, Oakleigh, Melbourne 3166, Australia

First published 1999

Printed in United Kingdom at the University Press, Cambridge

Typeset in 11/12pt Bembo   [CE]

A catalogue record for this book is available from the British Library

Library of Congress cataloguing in publication data
Harvey, Margaret (Margaret M.)
The English in Rome, 1362–1420 : portrait of an expatriate community /
Margaret Harvey.
p.   cm. – (Cambridge studies in medieval life and thought: 4th ser.)
Includes bibliographical references and index.
ISBN 0 521 62057 0
1. British – Italy – Rome – History – To 1500.
2. Italy – Foreign relations – Great Britain.
3. Great Britain – Foreign relations – Italy.
4. Rome (Italy) – History – 476–1420.
I. Title.   II. Series.
DG807.8B75H37   1999
920′.009w22–45632 – dc21   99–23256   CIP
[B]

ISBN 0 521 62057 0 hardback

CONTENTS

ACKNOWLEDGEMENTS

The debts I have accumulated whilst working on this subject are legion. The most important is to the Rector and staff of the Venerabile Collegio Inglese in Rome who provided hospitality beyond the call of duty over many weeks. I most particularly thank Mgr Toffolo, the Rector, for allowing me to stay and Sister Amadeus Bulger for providing splendidly for my comfort. A whole series of student Archivists gave up their leisure to look after me also. I likewise thank Frau Dr Ingrid Schwarz of Collegio S Maria dell'Anima in Rome who not only answered queries but supplied much needed photographs very quickly when I was unable to come to see for myself.

Others who have helped are mentioned in footnotes, but I must in particular thank Professor Richard Sharpe for his kindness and encouragement and Dr Joan Greatrex for her generosity; both supplied me with material on Adam Easton which I would certainly not have noticed. Dr Ian Doyle in Durham has been a constant source of generous help too.

Several others have also been of great assistance. Professor Barrie Dobson read the entire first draft and supplied heartening correctives and encouragement. Professor Richard Britnell also read the entire first draft, having earlier urged me to think more deeply about economic matters (doing some of the thinking for me); he and his wife Dr Jennifer Britnell supplied encouragement, both material and otherwise, at various important points. Mr Alan Heesom cheerfully ferried me to and fro for several weeks at the end of the writing when I was in plaster; to him, to Dr Judith Turner, Mrs Cherry Dowrick and Dr Mary Watts is owed the fact that the book was finished more or less on time.

To Dr Anne Orde I owe warmest thanks for constant encouragement, coffee, wine, food and taxi-service which made the whole task much easier. This book is offered to her with gratitude.

ABBREVIATIONS

AC	Rome, Archivio Capitolino
AFP	*Archivum Fratrum Praedicatorum*
AHP	*Archivum Historiae Pontificiae*
AS	Rome, Archivio di Stato
ASV	Vatican, Archivio Segreto Vaticano
AVB	*Analecta Vaticano-Belgica*
BIHR	*Bulletin of the Institute of Historical Research*
BJRL	*Bulletin of the John Rylands Library*
BL	British Library
BRUC	A. B. Emden, *Biographical Register of the University of Cambridge*
BRUO	A. B. Emden, *Biographical Register of the University of Oxford*
CCCC	Cambridge, Corpus Christi College
CCR	*Calendar of Close Rolls*
CH	*Pseudo-Dionysius, Celestial Hierarchy*
CPL	*Calendar of Papal Letters*
CPP	*Calendar of Papal Petitions*
CPR	*Calendar of Patent Rolls*
CYS	Canterbury and York Society
DBI	*Dizionario Biografico degli Italiani*
DCN	Dean and Chapter of Norwich
DRGS	*Documents Relatifs au Grand Schisme*
EETS	*Early English Text Society*
EHR	*English Historical Review*
JEH	*Journal of Ecclesiastical History*
Le Neve (followed by name of diocese)	J. Le Neve, *Fasti*, new edn, with diocese
m.	followed by a number, *membrana* (deed) from

	Rome, Venerabile Collegio Inglese. In *Venerabile* they have dates, but they are now numbered
NRO	Norfolk Record Office
PL	*Patrologia Latina*
QFAIB	*Quellen und Forschungen aus Italienischen Archiven und Bibliotheken*
RG	*Repertorium Germanicum*
RS	*Rolls Series*
Rot. Parl.	*Rotuli Parliamentorum*
SS	*Surtees Society*
V	Vatican Library, MS Vat.Lat. with a number
VCH	Victoria County History
Venerabile	with no number, Sexcentenary issue, 21 (1961) other issues numbered
WAM	Westminster Abbey Muniments
X	Decretales of Gregory IX, with numbers of parts and chapters following

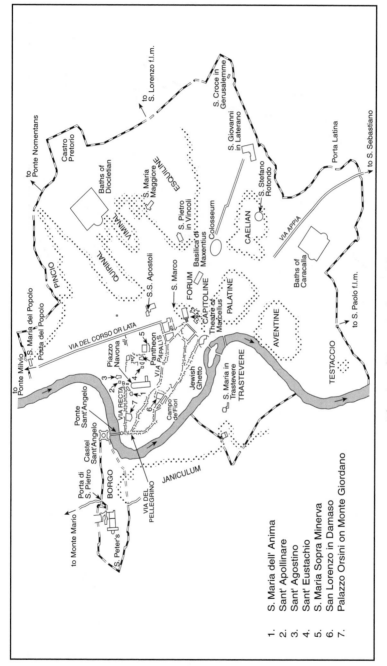

1 The city of Rome in the Middle Ages.
Only selective sites are shown.

1. S. Maria dell' Anima
2. Sant' Apollinare
3. Sant' Agostino
4. Sant' Eustachio
5. S. Maria Sopra Minerva
6. San Lorenzo in Damaso
7. Palazzo Orsini on Monte Giordano

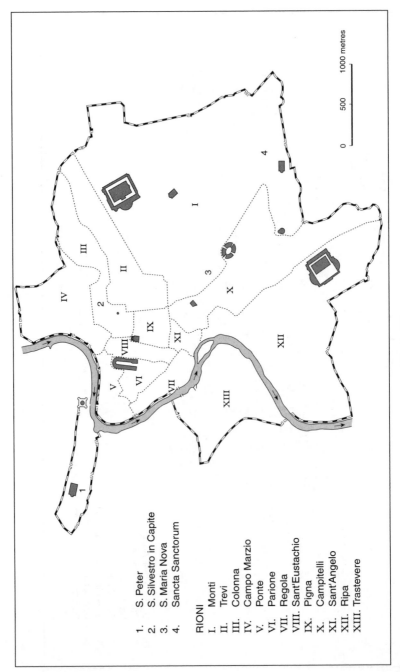

1. S. Peter
2. S. Silvestro in Capite
3. S. Maria Nova
4. Sancta Sanctorum

RIONI
I. Monti
II. Trevi
III. Colonna
IV. Campo Marzio
V. Ponte
VI. Parione
VII. Regola
VIII. Sant'Eustachio
IX. Pigna
X. Campitelli
XI. Sant'Angelo
XII. Ripa
XIII. Trastevere

2 *Rioni* of Rome.

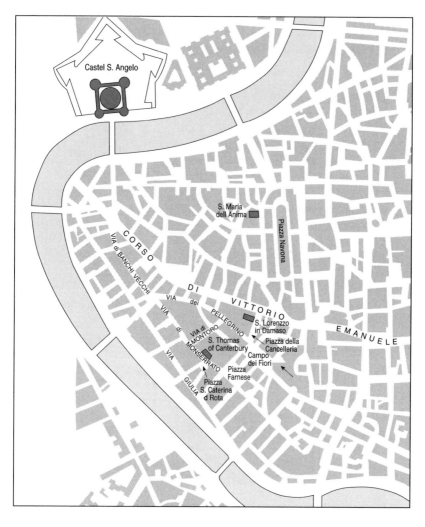

Castel S. Angelo

CORSO

VIA di BANCHI VECCHI

S. Maria dell'Anima

Piazza Navona

DI VITTORIO

VIA dei PELLEGRINO

VIA al

VIA di MONTORO

MONSERRATO

VIA

GIULIA

S. Thomas of Canterbury

S. Lorenzzo in Damaso

Piazza della Cancelleria

Campo dei Fiori

Piazza Farnese

Piazza S. Caterina d Rota

EMANUELE

3   Modern Rome round former S Thomas's hospice.

INTRODUCTION

It was the original intention of this study to describe a group of Englishmen who founded and then gathered round the English hospices of S Thomas and S Chrysogonus (later S Edmund) in Rome. The dates 1362 to 1420 were chosen because the first was the year when S Thomas's was founded and the second when the papacy under Martin V returned to Rome at the end of the Great Schism, in effect refounding the papal curia, and so making considerable changes in Rome itself. The scope of the study soon had to enlarge, however, to include the whole resident English community in Rome in the period, involving members of the papal curia not concerned in the hospices, because from 1376 they constituted an important element in the English group in the city.

There is no history of an English expatriate community in this period, though there were similar English groups in other places, for instance Bruges and Danzig. There are excellent studies of the Germans in Rome, for example by C. W. Maas for the whole group in the later Middle Ages and by C. Schuchard specifically for the Germans in the papal curia from 1378–1447.[1] But though the English founded what proved to be a significant centre in the hospice of S Thomas, which has an excellent archive, its early history has not been considered in depth by recent historians. In 1962 the students of the Venerabile Collegio Inglese, the successor of S Thomas's hospice, produced a volume of their house journal, *Venerabile*, devoted to the history of the hospices themselves up to 1579.[2] This remains the most authoritative account of earlier history of the institutions, superseding all that preceded it. But it

---

[1] C. W. Maas, *The German Community in Renaissance Rome, 1378–1523* (= Römische Quartalschrift für christliche Altertumskunde und für Kirchengeschichte, Supplementheft 39), Rome 1981; C. Schuchard, *Die Deutschen an der päpstlichen Kurie im späten Mittelalter (1378–1447)* (=Bibliothek des deutschen historischen Instituts in Rom 65), Tübingen 1987.

[2] *Venerabile*: The English Hospice in Rome, *Venerabile* (Sexcentenary Issue), 21 (1962).

is very much an institutional history, not very concerned with the wider scene nor with the standing of the founders or their successors and the writers had limited access to archives beyond their own. There is also an excellent account of the later history of S Thomas's, as a college for clerical students, by M. E. Williams, which, however, sketches the early history only briefly.[3]

Readers will realise, however, how much the present work is indebted to the labours of the students in 1962, who, for instance, compiled chronological lists of officers of the hospices and of names of English people present in Rome found in the deeds (*membrane*) and other manuscripts of the College. This work, however, needed redoing in the light of modern historical research, particularly on notaries' archives and on the history of Rome in the period.

The history of the city of Rome is inextricably linked with the presence in it of the relics of S Peter and therefore with the papacy.[4] But for a large part of the fourteenth century the papacy was not resident in the city. The pope had moved to France in 1309 and from then onwards Avignon was the centre of papal administration. The whole papal court, with its armies of bureaucrats and resultant trade, moved also. The fate of Rome thereafter seemed uncertain. It had no industrial specialism but had relied on the commerce resulting from the many people coming to do ecclesiastical business as well as on pilgrimage and so it suffered without the popes. With its famous shrines, however, especially S Peter's and S Paul's outside the Walls, it remained a pilgrim centre, though frequently its papal overlords did not control it, so that it became neglected. The city and the area around it, the papal states, were largely in the hands of great lords, ostensibly under papal over-lordship exercised usually by a papal legate who could seldom control them. Pope John XXII (1316–34) famously quarrelled with one of the aspirants to the throne of the Empire, Ludwig IV of Bavaria, who supported against him a schismatic group of Franciscans who objected to the pope's attitude to Christian poverty. Ludwig entered Rome in 1328. Though he could not hold it and failed to sustain his own anti-pope, he ravaged the papal states and John's successor Benedict XII (1334–42), spent money attempting restoration. Pope Clement VI (1342–52) even considered controlling Rome with the help of a strange charismatic local demagogue, Cola di Rienzo, who led an attack against the local nobles in 1347. But Cola had very little practical sense and in

---

[3] M. E. Williams, *The Venerable English College, Rome, 1579–1979. A History*, London 1979.

[4] For what follows, E. D. Theseider, *Roma dal comune di popolo alla signoria pontificia, 1252–1377* (=Storia di Roma 11), Bologna 1952; P. Partner, *The Lands of St Peter. The Papal State in the Middle Ages and the Early Renaissance*, London 1972.

any case frightened the pope by proclaiming a commune independent both of the nobles and the papacy. The short-lived attempt at complete independence failed, but not without local damage from the resultant fighting. The pope proclaimed 1350 a 'Year of Jubilee' or of special indulgences for pilgrimage to Rome, celebrated in the aftermath of Rienzo's fall, and seems to have attracted large crowds to the still very unsettled city. The pilgrims found a ruinous place, ill-equipped to house the thousands seeking lodgings. This may have been one reason for the foundation of hospices; several seem to have been begun in the aftermath of the Jubilee.[5]

Pope Urban V (1362–70) made the first serious attempt to bring the papal curia back from Avignon and actually succeeded briefly (1367–August 1370) with the aid of Cardinal Gil de Albornoz, his legate, who cajoled, bribed and fought the various local magnates and the mercenaries in their pay, re-organising local government in an attempt to bring the unruly magnates under papal control. But by late 1370 a local revolt, which the Romans joined, accompanied by a renewal of the Hundred Years War between France and England (the pope and most of the cardinals were French), convinced Urban that Rome was too unsafe and he returned to Avignon, leaving the citizens considerably disappointed. His successor Gregory XI (1370–8) spent the majority of his pontificate attempting to produce the local and international pacification which would allow him to return to Rome in safety, but he did not succeed until 1376. Gregory returned to Rome but even then the papacy was facing serious opposition from the Florentines, who were trying to persuade the Romans to join a revolt. There was also considerable scepticism about living in Rome among the members of the papal court itself, especially the largely French college of cardinals.

Against this background a question arises about the attraction of Rome to anyone who did not have to live there. The opening chapter of this study therefore considers the physical and social setting for the hospice of S Thomas and includes discussion of why an English group would have wanted to found institutions in 1362 in the apparently unpromising city of Rome. It concludes that the care of pilgrims and of English residents, with a desire to expand commerce to the Mediterranean, were among the motives.

The study then continues with a sketch of the history of Rome and of the papacy between 1376 and 1418 to explain what happened after the papal administration returned to the city. The death of the returned

---

[5] See below p. 21.

pope Gregory XI in 1378 led to a disputed election and the resultant Great Schism, with two and later three rival popes, each with his own administration, one section remaining in Avignon. The 'Roman' papacy, which is the one of concern here, was not always in Rome and its bureaucrats often had to follow its journeyings. When the papacy returned in 1376 the predominantly lay group of Englishmen which had founded the new hospice in 1362 was joined by men serving the papal curia and from then on the English group became more and more clerical.

Having outlined the history of the city and of the papal curia, the study then traces to 1420 the story of the hospice of S Thomas and follows with that of S Chrysogonus and of other unsuccessful attempts to found English hospices. It then describes the lay group up to 1420. A further chapter discusses English women who lived in Rome from 1362 to 1420. I know of no other study of an expatriate group of women in Italy.

The original English lay group (of merchants and artisans) was not replenished after 1400, or at least not visibly round the hospices of S Thomas and S Chrysogonus. The papal curia became more and more important in attracting Englishmen to become resident in Rome. I have therefore explored the careers of major English members of curia from 1376 to 1418, whilst noting how far, if at all, they played any part in the English hospices. I have studied in detail the careers of one high-ranking English curial, John Fraunceys, and that of Adam Easton, the last resident English cardinal for one hundred years, to show the problems facing such people during the schism and in Easton's case to discuss what a curial career might mean to a scholar.

This is not a history of the city of Rome; the city's history is included only so far as needed to understand the lives discussed. It has also been necessary to give an account of the curia, not synonymous with Rome, since many members of the English group worked for it, even though it was often not in Rome in this period. In all cases I have attempted to link the people with their English background, to discuss patrons and career patterns and to ask whether a stay in Rome helped or hindered a career in England. I have tried to describe the economic background, not merely because some of the Englishmen were merchants but also because some of the most bitter complaints about the curia were prompted by prevailing economic conditions.

Events in England would have had an influence on any expatriate English group. For laymen such as those who first began S Thomas's hospice a predominating factor must have been the state of the English economy, which in the fourteenth century was itself dominated by relations with France and by the Hundred Years War. From the outbreak of war with France in 1337 the English crown needed to raise unprecedented sums and did so by loans largely from Italian merchants who recouped themselves from trade in English wool. Tensions were caused in England by the manipulation of trade for money-raising; besides, from 1360 onwards, even though the English looked victorious they began to be less so. The king, Edward III, who had been very successful at first, grew old and his son, the Black Prince, was increasingly ill from 1371. As the papacy returned from Avignon the English were facing a minority. In June 1376 the Black Prince died, followed the next year by Edward III, leaving the eleven-year-old Richard II as ruler. As the old king was dying, intrigue and accusation gathered momentum; the so-called Good Parliament of 1376 was marked by accusations about government corruption and attacks on 'aliens', thought to be making vast sums at English expense. The Avignon papacy was included among the institutions and persons accused of corruptly milking England of money. The pope needed money too, for the control of the papal states and the return to Rome. Papal bureaucracy, particularly when appointing to benefices, charged large sums for its services and taxed benefices both directly and when they changed hands by its intervention. The loss of money out of England and the litigious quarrels which the papal benefice system was thought to entail, had already by 1351 involved English legislation by statute (against papal appointees, provisors). The English government regularly refused to allow direct papal taxation of the clergy and shared anything the pope was allowed to collect; statutes against provisors (1351) and praemunire (1353) were intended to control litigation in the papal court and to regulate the flow of papal bulls into the country as well as the flow of English money out. The clergy, being asked for money both by crown and pope, tried to resist constant demands but were in no position to do so, and many of the laity were convinced that the rich church was not paying its fair share to the needs of the country. John Wyclif, the reformer, was employed by the English government from 1371 to complain about clerical and papal greed and to resist the claims of the pope to collect money or to appoint to benefices, even taking part in a mission to Bruges in 1374 to discuss papal appointments. In the circumstances it was not surprising that to one Englishman in Avignon, Adam Easton, Wyclif appeared as the latest in a long line of persons attempting to undermine the whole basis of ecclesiastical power. Nor is it surprising that it became more and more difficult for Englishmen to evade the statutes against provisors. By 1420, although the English group in Rome was much more clerical, English or foreign clerics were much less likely than their predecessors to be able to obtain from the pope, and to keep, notable English benefices as a reward for faithful service.

The sources for this study were in the first place the early deeds or *membrane* of the Venerabile Collegio Inglese in Rome, the successor of the two English hospices, together with a few of its manuscripts (indexes and early lists of properties owned for instance). These were supplemented from notaries' protocols, some printed and some in manuscript in Rome in the Archivio di Stato and the Archivio Capitolino, as well as in the Vatican Library.[6] In medieval Italy notaries were employed to record in writing a multitude of everyday transactions: buying, selling and letting property, making loans, buying wine or planting a vineyard, seeking arbitration, making a will, organising the whole transaction of marriage, from the agreeing of a dowry to its investment in property, but also the actual exchange by the couple of 'words of present consent' which were, in the eyes of the church, the actual marriage. The notary advised the client on the form of the document (Roman law was the basis). The client took an original and the notary kept books with his copies. The archive of a dead notary could therefore be consulted, if documents got lost, to confirm that a transaction had occurred. When a house changed hands all the existing deeds about it were transferred too, including any documents concerning arbitration about its environs, documents about alterations which had been allowed by the street magistrates (*magistri stratarum*) and information about which members of the families of past owners had consented to the change of ownership. Rome is only unusual in having preserved less of this information for the fourteenth century than many Italian cities. But deeds such as those of the Venerabile Collegio Inglese exist also for other foundations, so that for example the archives of the German hospice of S Maria dell'Anima, situated on its original site just off the present Piazza Navona, proved unexpectedly interesting from an English viewpoint too.[7]

The *membrane* largely concern houses bought and sold, but also describe repairs agreed and include wills. Deeds of sale of houses always included a description of the kind of house: *domus terranea* for a basic house built on the soil, *domus solarata* for a house with an upper storey, and often have descriptions of marble steps, porticoes, gardens, wells and so on. The deeds also gave the names of the property-owners on all sides: 'on one side holds so and so, on the other the heirs of so and so,

---

[6] Below note 8.

[7] Inventory by F.-X. Nagl, *Urkundliches zur Geschichte der Anima in Rom* (= Römische Quartalschrift für christliche Alterthumskunde und für Kirchengeschichte, Supplementheft 12), Rome 1899.

behind is a vacant space and before is the public street', thus allowing one to reconstruct the setting for some houses. Documents also often contained the names of guarantors, friends and supporters who pledged that the seller would truly sell or that the money would truly be produced. Transactions also involved named witnesses, with as the minimum the witness' name and the district of Rome in which he lived, but often with an occupation and sometimes a place of origin. These documents therefore are excellent sources for tracing persons and reconstructing neighbourhoods.

Some of the documents belonging to the College are duplicated in existing notaries protocol books but these last are more useful for the extra documents they have concerning the individuals occurring in the *membrane* and in adding a very few other English names to the lists compiled by the student historians for *Venerabile* in 1962. Most of all, however, protocols can be used to trace further the Italians whose names appear in the *membrane*. In recent years some of the earliest Roman protocol books have been printed and these have proved most useful for this study.[8]

The history of Rome in the period is still to be written but apart from the sources described above there are two main chroniclers after 1400: Antonio Pietro dello Schiavo and Stefano Infessura.[9] These main sources of names of laymen in the early years of the study could be followed up, sometimes, in England; some problems involved are discussed in the chapter on Laymen.

One topic however needs emphasis here, that of surnames. In any Roman notarial document men were identified as their father's son followed by the city district in which they were now living and sometimes the area from which they had come. Hence English names emerge as *Robertus olim Roberti olim de Anglia nunc de urbe de regione Pinea*[10] (Robert, son of the late Robert, late of England now living in the city in the Pigna district). This identifies Robert de Pigna, one of the founders of the English hospice of S Thomas, Robert atte Pine as John Stow later called him.[11] Such methods of naming indicate that one was identified as one's father's son or daughter, or, if a woman, as

---

[8] For the fourteenth century the material is surveyed in I. L. Sanfilippo, 'I protocolli notarile romani del trecento', *Archivio della società romana di storia patria*, 110 (1987), pp. 99–150, with lists. The printed volumes used can be found in my bibliography under the names: Astalli, P.; Caputgallis, F. de, Goioli, A.; Johannes Nicolai Pauli; Staglia, L.; See also Paulus Nicolai Pauli; Nicolaus Johannis Jacobi and Johannes Paulus Antonii Goyoli.

[9] A. P. Schiavo, *Il diario romano di Antonio di Pietro dello Schiavo*, ed. F. Isoldi (= Rerum Italicarum Scriptores 24/5), Bologna 1917; S. Infessura, *Diario della città di Roma di Stefano Infessura, scribasenato*, ed. O. Tommasini (= Fonti per la storia d'Italia 5), Rome 1890.

[10] *m.* 38.   [11] J. Stow, *Annales or General Chronicle of England*, London 1631, p. 335.

someone's wife as well as a daughter. Only in the case of the upper classes would a family name be certainly included. Hence Italian notaries had problems with English names and one cannot always be sure what they meant. Robert atte Pine for example may have been called Robertson but probably was not. The 'founder' of the hospice of S Thomas, whose surname we do know, appears as *Johannes Petri Pecorarii paternostrarius dudum de Anglia et nunc habitator Urbis in regione Arenula.* That is 'John son of Peter Shepherd seller of beads lately of England now dwelling in the city in Arenula district'.[12] In his will however he was called simply John, son of Peter. He was certainly not known as Peterson.[13] The problems of tracing many of these individuals in the English records, when so many share Christian names and they were certainly identified in England with surnames, are insurmountable. Fortunately the curia identified people by surnames in its documents and the only problem there usually is making sense of Italian and other scribal versions of English names. In the case of Italians I have used the Latin version of their name unless they are well known under an Italian version; hence Cola di Rienzo is not called Nicolaus Laurentii, whereas Johannes Nicolai Pauli the notary is not referred to as Giovanni di Nicola di Paolo, though he may have been known as that.

Clerics can also be traced in the Vatican Archives and then followed up in England. The main problem there is the relative lack of sources for the schism period, partly caused by loss of archives in the Napoleonic era but partly because during the schism curial bureaucracy was in disarray.[14] The Vatican archives contain almost no supplication registers for the period[15] and the records of the Penitentiary begin only in about 1411 and then very scrappily. The letter book of William Swan (Oxford, Bodleian Library, MS Arch. Seld. B 23), who was a proctor in the curia from about 1404, in contact with many laymen and clerks, is extremely illuminating.[16] This can be supplemented a little with other letter collections and formularies but there still remain annoying gaps in the careers of individuals. The *De scismate* and *Nemus unionis* of the

---

12 *Venerabile,* p. 40; *m.* 37. 13 *Venerabile,* p. 42 (Johannes Petri).

14 The best introduction to the archives is now F. X. Blouin et al., *Vatican Archives. An Inventory and Guide to Historical Documents of the Holy See,* New York and Oxford 1998. For the losses mentioned here, see pp. xx–xxi. For the disarray see for instance J. Favier, *Les finances pontificales à l'époque du grand schisme d'occident, 1378–1409* (= Bibliothèque des écoles françaises d'Athènes et de Rome 211), Paris 1966, pp. 136–7.

15 Exceptions are BL Cotton Vitellius F II, a formulary, with some supplications from the period; ASV Reg. Suppliche 104A, for Boniface IX, formerly in Eichstadt.

16 His second volume, BL MS Cotton Cleop. C IV covers the period after 1420 for the most part.

leading curial, Dietrich of Niem, gives considerable insight into the experience of following the curia.[17]

An introductory chapter ought to admit what has not been attempted. The modern historian might suppose that this study of many individuals would lend itself to statistical analysis. I have attempted no such thing, partly being temperamentally unsuited to such a task, but largely because gaps in the records mean that the results would almost certainly be fatally distorted. Information on most of the careers I looked at was scrappy, that for laymen even scrappier than for clerics. Many individuals are merely names who appear only once. The result has had to be impressionistic rather than rigorously scientific. Nor have I attempted to trace the coming and going of all Englishmen known to have been in Rome; Édouard Perroy did this in 1933 for the diplomats up to 1399 and in 1983 I studied diplomatic relations from 1399–1409.[18] This is not a history of Anglo-papal diplomacy, so diplomats paying fleeting visits are encountered only as they meet the resident English group. The emphasis has been throughout on residence in Rome for some length of time.

To see the English group in their setting one must begin with a sketch of Rome about 1362, with the papal curia still in Avignon and the numbers of Englishmen very small, to place the first English enterprise in a context and ask why anyone would have thought of founding a hospice in the city.

[17] Niem, *De scismate* ed. G. Erler, Leipzig 1890; *Nemus unionis* was published as volume IV of *De scismate. Historiae Theodorici de Niem qua res suo tempore durante gestae exonuntur*, ed. S. Schardius, Basel 1566.

[18] E. Perroy, *L'Angleterre et le grand schisme d'occident. Étude de la politique religieuse d'Angleterre sous Richard II, 1378–1399*, Paris 1933; M. Harvey, *Solutions to the Schism. A Study of Some English Attitudes, 1378–1409* (=Kirchengeschichtliche Quellen und Studien 12), S Ottilien 1983.

Chapter 1

THE SETTING I: ROME IN THE LATER FOURTEENTH CENTURY, 1362–1376

This study begins in Rome in 1362 largely because that year a significant English institution was begun. It is also, however, a reasonable starting point because the year afterwards the city of Rome received a new constitution, intended to mark a decisive shift from the aristocratically dominated politics of the previous period; a new era was about to begin, dominated by the *popolo*.

Nowadays if one wanders along the via Monserrato from the direction of S Peter's, one comes eventually to a large building on the left side, not far from Piazza Farnese. There is a sizeable church and two large entrances, with inside a complex of buildings of different ages, including a courtyard and a garden, with a smaller chapel. All this and formerly much more is now the Venerabile Collegio Inglese, once the site of the English hospice of S Thomas, now in rione Regola, then called Arenula. The object of this chapter is to answer a few questions about the physical and economic setting in which the new enterprise was undertaken in 1362 and to sketch the background to its first fifty years. By 1420 the enterprise was important and the English had even founded a second hospice, in the Trastevere district, both operations involving substantial ownership of property and a considerable turnover of money.

The documents which record the first foundation of 1362 concern John Shepherd, beadseller (*paternostrarius*) of England, resident in Arenula district in Rome, buying a house from Antonio Smerucci, woolman (*lanarolus*) formerly of Camerino now of the same Roman district. He very shortly sold it again to William Chandler of York who received in his own name and for the community and *universitas* of the English of Rome.[1] Alice wife of John Shepherd then renounced her claims on the house; William Chandler was invested with it and Alice

---

[1] *mm.* 34, 36, 37, printed *Venerabile*, pp. 37–41.

and John then offered their goods and service to run it as a hospital. As well as Chandler, Robert de Pigna, proctor (*syndicus*) and John son of William, from *Maxigam* (?Massingham) goldsmith (*aurificus*), called treasurer (*camerarius*) of the English community, acted together to receive Alice Shepherd's statement and the offer from the couple. The witnesses included Simon son of John Barber, *paternostrarius*, William son of Richard, *paternostrarius*, Simon son of John Sparo, Robert, son of John, oblate of the church of S Maria in Julia and Henry son of John from Trastevere region, all of whom we know were English and several of whom were important in their small community. The Italians included Matthias Paccia, when Shepherd bought his house, Lellus de Narnia, weigher (*ponderator*), when Alice renounced her claims on it, Jacobellus Cafagi, builder (*murator*), Paulus Alisii, notary, and Lellus domini Johannis *cavalerii*, when Chandler was invested. All these were substantial neighbours, who appeared in other documents concerning the region.

The number of known Englishmen resident in Rome at this date was wider than the group founding the hospice. At least eleven households can be traced and there were probably several more; certainly some existed before 1362. What were these English people doing in Rome and why did some of them think it worth spending money founding a hospital? What was their relationship to the Italians among whom they were living?

First of all it will be necessary to look at the physical setting in which these English people lived. Rome in 1362 was probably very under populated. Before the Black Death there had been famines and Rome had probably lost significant numbers in the plague itself and thereafter from further outbreaks of plague and other diseases.[2] There is little evidence for the effect of the Black Death in the city but the oldest Roman notary's note-book, of Johannes Nicolai Pauli, who worked in the Monti region, stretched from precisely 1348 (to 1379).[3] Beginning on 15 June 1348, this recorded eighteen wills to 14 September.[4] The greatest number came in June and July. All the testators were said to be 'sick in body but sound in mind' (*infirmus corpore mente tamen sanus*). Of those recorded making wills Petrus Johannis Martini did so on 18 July,

<hr>

[2] For some evidence see G. Villani, *Nuova cronica*, ed. G. Porta, 3 vols., Parma 1990–1, XI/76, pp. 612–13, XI/118, pp. 669–10, XI/119, pp. 670–3, for instance about Louis of Bavaria in 1328. 1328/9 is recorded by Villani as a year of exceptional hardship.

[3] Johannes Nicolai Pauli, *I protocolli di Johannes Nicoli Pauli, un notaio romano del'300 (1348–1379)*, ed. R. Mosti (= Collection de l'école française de Rome 63), Rome 1982 (hereafter called Johannes Nicoli Pauli).

[4] Johannes Nicolai Pauli, nos. 18, 19, 21, 22, 23, 24, 25, 26, 27, 28, 30, 31, 32, 36, 37, 41, 50, 65.

altered it on 21 July, and was dead by about 23 July.[5] Johannes Mei Gratiani Muti, making his on 21 July, was dead by 19 September.[6] In other years Johannes Nicolai Pauli made far fewer wills; in 1354 for instance only one is recorded. Antonius Goioli Petri Scopte, who lived and worked in the Arenula district, by comparison, recorded only four wills for 1365.[7] The number in 1348 thus looks very unusual; the death rate was probably very great. Even in 1400, after the return of the papacy from Avignon, the population of Rome was at most 25,000.[8] In 1362 the figure could have been as low as 17,000.

Though the city walls enclosed a large area, much of the area within was uninhabited, consisting of open spaces, vineyards and gardens. Some deeds for the hospice of S Thomas concern a complex of property bought in 1371 in Parione region.[9] The earliest go back to 1332 when it was described as having on one side *vacans de communitate* and on the other *vacans et ortus*. In the earlier period, as we shall see, the English, in common with many other inhabitants, owned land (*stirps*, ?cleared areas), within the city walls. A deed concerning the buying of a house and garden in Trastevere region by John White, founder of the second English hospice of S Edmund, in 1404, recorded that the chapel of the hospice was built in the garden, where the original deed described fruit trees.[10] Andrew Alene, a Welsh priest, left vineyards within the city walls to the German hospice he helped to found in the place called Testacio *(infra menia urbis in loco qui dicitur Testacio).*[11]

Water supply was uncertain in some places and most inhabitants lived at the bend of the Tiber, even though that was subject to flooding. In the notarial protocols houses were described carefully as 'with a well in it' (*cum puteo existente in eo*) or as 'with a free well in it' (*cum puteo in se libero*)[12] added as an extra value.[13] Some houses which the English hospice of S Thomas later acquired were similarly described.[14] An English will made in Rome in 1401 left something to 'Agnes who is wont to carry the water' revealing a necessary though lowly urban task.[15] The mother of the great popular leader, Cola di Rienzo, as well as being a washer-woman, was also a water carrier, from the Arenula

---

[5] Ibid., nos. 25, 21, 33.   [6] Ibid., nos. 31, 70.

[7] Goioli, A., *Il protocollo notarile di 'Anthonius Goioli Petri Scopte' (1365)*, ed. R. Mosti, Rome 1991 (hereafter called Goioli).

[8] Maas, *German Community*, p. 2; R. Krautheimer, *Rome, Profile of a City 312–1308*, Princeton 1980, pp. 231–2; D. Herlihy, 'The Tuscan towns in the Quattrocento: a demographic profile', *Medievalia et Humanistica*, new series 1 (1970), pp. 81–109.

[9] *m.* 60.   [10] *m.* 165.

[11] Archives of Collegio di S Maria dell'Anima, Instr. Litt. B. tom. I, ff. 102–103v.

[12] Caputgallis, F. de, *Un notaio romano del trecento. Il protocolli di Francesco di Stefano de Caputgallis (1374–1386)*, ed. R. Mosti, Rome 1994, p. 216 (hereafter called Caputgallis).

[13] Goioli, p. 158.   [14] *mm.* 27, 43, 45, 51 (wells).   [15] *m.* 158.

region.[16] The original house which the Shepherds bought and then sold had no well (at least none mentioned in its deed) but in 1406 a deed mentioned that the English group had built a conduit to bring water for the next house which it had now bought.[17] Another case concerning English property, heard before the masters of the streets (responsible for settling disputes and later for policing building regulations)[18] in 1407, concerned the building of a dividing wall to show whose was the water in a shared well between a house owned by the hospice and that of a Florentine. The houses, in the Parione region, were described as having a well 'with shared water' (*cum aqua communi*) with 'a wall raised a little to show the division of this well and the part belonging to the hospital' (*paries aliquantulum in altum relevatum ad hostendum divisionem ipsius putei et partem dicti hospitalis*).[19]

Public roads were few but there is evidence of alleyways between houses. The house of the English *paternostrarius* William son of Richard, in the Parione region, was described as having a common lane running between it and the next house.[20] But very often houses leaned against one another, allowing quarrels about walls and boundaries and of course nuisance. In 1412 the hospice of S Thomas quarrelled seriously with a neighbour of one of its properties in Parione because a branch of a tree in his garden was damaging the roof of the hospice house 'it comes down strongly upon the roof of the said house' (*ascendit super tectum dicte domus cum vigore*). The neighbour had to cut the branch.[21] In 1428 Petrus Lei, a neighbour of a house owned by S Chrysogonus' hospice, complained that smoke from the house's kitchen was so noxious that he could not live in his house nor keep his cloths clean (it sounds as if he was a clothier). There was a common way between his house and that next door and the officials of S Chrysogonus' equally complained that water from the roof and elsewhere from Petrus' house was falling into their garden. Arbitrators decreed that Petrus must bar the windows on the hospice side and repair

the tunnel or ditch which was formerly in the said sluice. Petrus and anyone else from his house are not to throw nor cause to be thrown anything unclean or unsuitable through the windows of Petrus' house into the kitchen or garden of the hospice house.

---

[16] G. Porta, ed., 'Anonimo romano', *Cronica*, Milan 1979, p. 143: *la quale visse de lavare panni e acqua portare*.

[17] *mm.* 175, 178.

[18] C. Carbonetti Vendittelli, 'La curia dei *magistri edificarum urbis* nei secoli XIIIe e XIVe e la sua documentazione', in E. Hubert, ed., *Rome au XIIIe et XIVe siècles* (= Collection de l'école française de Rome 170), Rome 1993, pp. 3–42, esp. pp. 9, 13.

[19] *m.* 180.   [20] *m.* 96.   [21] *m.* 187.

One shudders to think what feud had preceded the case. The hospice likewise had to repair the chimney so that smoke did not injure Petrus' house and, if the parties wished, rulings were made about a conduit (*canalis*) they could build in the common lane between the houses.[22] In the inhabited area the houses were of all types, with towers, hovels, re-used ancient remains (*grypta*) and what are described as palaces, cheek by jowl, so there was no 'fashionable quarter', although there were certainly very different social classes in the city.

For residents of Rome an important territory was the *rione* in which they lived. There were thirteen in the fourteenth century, responsible for some aspects of local government, particularly the citizen militia from 1363.[23] Men were identified by their *rione*. It was the major subdivision of the city by 1362 and these areas elected representatives for the commune which was the ruling organisation until 1398.[24] But within that area there were subdivisions. When describing a property many deeds give the parish in which it lay[25] and often the *contrada* or subdivision of the *rione*.[26] The house which became the hospital of S Thomas was described in 1362 as in Arenula region, in the parish of Ss Maria and Caterina (now S Caterina della Ruota).[27] In 1375 a house which later belonged to S Thomas's hospice was described as in *rione* Ponte in *contrada* Pizzomerle.[28] This is the area near the present Sforza Cesarini palace, on modern via Vittorio Emmanuele. For many residents these divisions must have made up the whole world without need to go very far even outside the city walls. In 1395 an Englishman striving to explain how thoroughly a fellow country-man had vanished put it thus:

---

[22] *mm.* 194, 195: *gripta seu fossa quod primitus erat in dicto sciaquatorio . . . ipse Petrus et alius de domo ipsius Petri non proiaciat nec proicere debeat aut faciat aliquos immundos seu ineptitudines per fenestras domus dicti Petri in coquina et orto domus dicti hopitalis.*

[23] Krautheimer, *Rome, Profile*, p. 156.

[24] A. Esch, 'La fine del libero commune di Roma nel giudizio dei mercanti fiorentini. Lettere romane degli anni 1395–1398 nell' archivio Datini,' *Bulletino dell'istituto storico italiano per il medio evo e archivio muratoriano*, 86 (1976–7), pp. 235–77; Esch, *Bonifaz IX und der Kirchenstaat*, Tübingen 1969, chapter 4.

[25] S. Passigli, 'Geografia parrochiale e circonscrizioni territoriali nei secoli XII–XIV: istituzioni e realtà quotidiana', in E. Hubert, *Rome aux XIIIe XIV*, pp. 45–77 for the whole topic; also *Pievi e parrochia in Italia nel basso medioevo (sec. XIII–XV)* 2 vols. (= Italia sacra. Studi e documenti di storia ecclesiastica 36, 37), Rome 1984, especially for E. Petrucci, 'Pievi e parochie del Lazio nel basso medioevo: note e osservazione', I (36), pp. 892–1017.

[26] For these see Krautheimer, *Rome, Profile*, pp. 155–6; E. Hubert, *Espace urbain et habitat à Rome du Xe siècle à la fin du XIIIe siècle* (= Collection de l'école française de Rome 135), Rome 1990, pp. 365–8.

[27] *Venerabile*, p. 37; *m.* 34; U. Gnoli, *Topographia e toponomastica di Roma medioevale e moderno*, Rome 1939, pp. 217–18.

[28] *m.* 78.

about twelve years ago he left the city and wandered through the world and has not been found, and this is true and proved and is manifest and is commonly and publicly acknowledged in *riones* S. Angelo, Arenula and Parione among those who know John.[29]

The city was also of course divided into parishes. It probably came as a surprise for Englishmen to find that the *rione* rather than the parish was the administrative centre. Differences in the way Italians and English related to their parish still need examination. Major information will come from the notaries' protocols and for Rome much still needs to be done.[30] The parish in which S Thomas's hospice was founded, S Caterina or de Caterinis, was large and the parish priest in 1362 had a mistress who lived opposite the church. S Chrysogonus' hospice was in S Chrysogonus' parish in Trastevere region. But the English lived in various parishes, not in one area. We may discover from wills whether they thought of their parish at death, which will be discussed below. We have no idea how they functioned within it during life. But a little about how the Romans did so appears from the notaries' protocols. In April 1365 Antonius Goioli recorded that certain men of the parish of S Tommaso de Yspanis in Arenula region (very near S Thomas's hospice) assembled in the usual way and on behalf of the parish chose an archpriest and appointed a proctor to present his election to the vicar-general.[31] Such an arrangement was unknown in England. Some of the men involved also appeared in the deeds of the new hospice.[32]

Although there were no distinct 'wealthy' quarters in the city there were certainly very distinct social circles. Interesting work has been done on the groups which gave evidence for the canonisation processes of S Francesca Romana, of the Bussa family, who had married into the de Ponzianis, and for S Bridget of Sweden.[33] This shows that the circles which knew the two were very different. Bridget was a great aristocrat and the evidence in her case is largely aristocratic. The de Ponzianis belonged to the *popolo*, the misleading name given to the political grouping which included rich cattle-owning citizens, below the noble aristocracy. S Francesca's support came from family, kin and neighbours of her own class.

In 1362, of course, the papal curia was in Avignon. One of the factors

---

[29] *m.* 132: *iam sunt xii anni proxime post idcirca ab urbe recessit et ivit vacabundus per mundum et non reperitur et est verum, probatum et manifestum et publica vox et fama in urbe maxime in regione Sancti Angeli, Arenule et Parionis inter notos ipsi Johanni.*

[30] See Passigli, 'Geografia', esp. pp. 62, 69–71, 77; Petrucci, 'Pievi e parrochie' also.

[31] Goioli, no. 40. pp. 62–63; mentioned by Passigli,'Geografia', p. 71.

[32] For instance, *m.* 71.

[33] A. Esch, 'Die Zeugenaussagen im Heiligensprechungsverfahren für S Francesca Romana als Quelle zur Sozialgeschichte Roms im frühen Quattrocentro', *QFAIB* 53 (1973). pp. 93–151.

which in the past had encouraged development of the city of Rome was thus absent. Since members of the western church needed to apply to the pope regularly for grants and favours, as well as to show loyalty by visits, much traffic produced by the papacy now went to Avignon, which benefited commercially and culturally. Rome suffered in consequence. It also suffered from intermittent warfare in Italy.[34] After 1313 the papacy's attempt to control the Papal States from afar meant that popes relied on outside assistance, with the leading nobles pursuing their personal vendettas under the pretext of serving a lord.[35] The history of the city itself is not clear, with the rebellion of Cola di Rienzo in 1347 being a more well-documented moment in a period otherwise very obscure.[36] Under pope Innocent VI (1352–62) the papacy strove to regain control of the Papal States, relying particularly on Cardinal Gil Albornoz, who struggled with various local tyrants, at vast expense to the papacy but with the ultimate effect that by 1367 Rome was thought safe enough for Urban V (1362–70) to re-enter. Briefly Rome benefited from the repairs made for his arrival.[37] War began again, however, and in September 1370 Urban returned to Avignon. His successor, Gregory XI, elected on 30 December 1370, was determined to take the papacy home. Again at vast expense and although facing a serious quarrel with the Florentines, the pope returned to Rome in January 1377.

The first English hospital, however, was founded while the papacy was still absent. During that period the most important people in Rome were the dominant noble families who held land both within and outside the walls and often protected themselves from within towers. Though their political power had been seriously eroded since the rising by Cola di Rienzo in 1347, some still retained considerable strength with formidable potential to make trouble if they wished.[38] The leading families had strongholds outside the city; during the episode of Cola di Rienzo their ability to cut off food supplies to the city had been made

---

[34] The best account that I know of Rome in this period is R. Brentano, *Rome Before Avignon, A Social History of Thirteenth Century Rome*, New York 1974, despite the title. See also Krautheimer, *Rome Profile*. The political history is excellently described in P. Partner, *The Lands of St Peter*, especially chapter 10.

[35] Partner, *Lands of St Peter*, p. 309 onwards.

[36] On Cola see especially G. Porta, ed., 'Anonimo', *Cronica*; see also D. Nicholas, *The Later Medieval City, 1300–1500*, London and New York, 1997, p. 126 and references.

[37] See Partner, *Lands of St Peter*, p. 356.

[38] S. Carocci, 'Baroni in città. Considerazioni sull'insediamento e i diritti urbani della grande nobilità' in E. Hubert, *Rome aux XIIIe e XIVe siècles*, pp. 139–73; and Carocci, *Baroni di Roma. Dominazioni signorili e lignaggi aristocratici nel duecento e nel primo trecento* (= Collection de l'école française de Rome 181, or Istituto storico italiano per il medioevo. Nuovi studi storici 23), Rome 1993.

very clear. From their stronghold in Marino in 1347 the Orsini had pillaged the local countryside; one reason why Cola fell was that roads were blocked so that grain could not enter.[39] Afterwards the commune organised itself and produced statutes very hostile to the nobility, including a citizen militia to keep order.[40] Theoretically therefore the nobility were much less powerful after 1362 but nevertheless they still had important capability to cause disorder. When the curia returned from Avignon in 1378 the French cardinals and papal courtiers soon gained very unfavourable impressions of the Romans, including their propensity to go armed and their undeferential behaviour towards great prelates.[41] Thomas Petra, in summer 1380 referred to the Romans as:[42]

armed according to the manner of the country in which even boys carry arms and no-one prohibits it, in my opinion because of the lack of general lordship.

Cardinal Bertrand Lagier compared the behaviour of the rude lower orders unfavourably with their like in Avignon. He added that he would love to live in Rome for the sake of the bodies of the saints, if the people were, 'I do not say good and devout but even human'![43]

In the Arenula district where the English hospice of S Thomas was founded, the leading noble family was the Orsini of Campo dei Fiori.[44] The head of that branch of the family in 1362 was Latino with his wife Golitia. Facing into the present Piazza Farnese, near the site where the English group bought their first house, was the palace of a family of Orsini allies, the de Papazurris.

Essentially the English encountered these families as their ground landlords. We meet the Orsini of Campo dei Fiori in the hospice deeds in this guise, represented by proctors, for example for the hospice house in Arenula called Scottis Torre.[45] The earliest reference in the deeds to such transactions is in 1333 where the seller of this house was Ceccus Capo da Ferro, whose family were powerful allies of the Orsini in the area.[46] When in 1364 the house was sold to William de Scotia, Paulus Gorcii Capo da Ferro still held property next door, which he had still in

[39] G. Porta, 'Anonimo', pp. 192–3. The Orsini are discussed in Carocci, *Baroni*, section 10, pp. 387–400.

[40] G. Fasoli, 'Richerche sulla legislazione antimagnatiza nei communi dell'alta e media Italia', *Rivista di storia del diritto italiano*, 12 (1939), pp. 86–133, 240–309.

[41] M. Seidlmayer, *Die Anfänge des grossen abendländischen Schismas*, (= Spanische Forschungen aus der Görresgesellschaft, Series 2/5), Münster 1940, p. 262; L. Gayet, *Le grand schisme d'occident*, 2 vols. Florence and Berlin 1889, II, pièces justificatives, p. 141: cardinal de Vernhio said he would not believe that this could happen where he came from!

[42] Seidlmayer, *Anfänge*, p. 262.   [43] Ibid., p. 329.

[44] A. Chastel and G. Vallet, eds., *Le palais Farnese* (= École française de Rome), 2 vols., one in two, Rome 1980–1, *Texte* I/1, esp. pp. 57–9.

[45] *mm.* 7, 39, 91.   [46] *m.* 7; Chastel and Vallet, *Le palais Farnese*, I/1, p. 86.

1377 when William died.[47] He was an important man. In 1378 Latinus Orsini named him proctor of the Romans and the city chamber (*camera urbis*). He died in 1393 and was buried in S Maria sopra Minerva where his tomb can still be seen. His sons continued to be important in the local government.[48]

One of the properties (called a *casalenum*, meaning perhaps a building plot or perhaps a building)[49] which the English member of the papal curia John Fraunceys bought in 1404 had as ground landlord (was *in proprietate* of) the other branch of the Orsini. We first encounter it in 1365 rented by Raynaldo Orsini to Edificato Tucii de Malpileis,[50] a well-connected tenant. Jacobus Edificatii de Malpileis was a canon of St Peter's in 1371.[51] Another member of the family was podestà of Sutri in 1399.[52] In 1382 *magnificus et potens* Jordanus de Ursinis was selling the *casalenum* to the proctor for Paulus Jacobelli, Colutia Brunco, a resident of Marino, the Orsini stronghold. The business was done in Marino.[53]

The de Pappazuris family were also allies of the Orsini, and an area in present Piazza Farnese was so much de Pappazuris territory in 1428 that an arbitration award for the English hospital was described as given 'in a certain podium in the portico or loggia called de Pappazuris' (*in quodam podio sito in porticali seu lovio quod dicitur de Pappazuris*).[54] The family appears at intervals in the hospice deeds. Domina Francisca de Pappazuris was noted as holding property on two sides of a house bought by the Englishman William Mantel in 1367.[55] It was left to S Thomas's hospice in 1383.[56] In 1360 Perna, widow of Jacobucius Homodei sold a palace in the Parione region which had been her dower[57] to Johannes Cardelli.[58] Among the witnesses was Johannes Petri Cole (de) Pappazuris. Jacobus de Pappazuris (canon of S Lorenzo in Damaso since at least 1365),[59] acted as a witness for domina Mathea, widow of Georgius, butcher (*macellarius*) and Johanna her daughter, widow of Bucius de

---

[47] *mm.* 39, 91.

[48] Staglia, L., *Il protocollo notarile di Lorenzo Staglia (1372)*, ed. I. L. Sanfilippo (= Codice diplomatico di Roma e della regione romana 3), Rome 1986, pp. 14–15 and notes (hereafter called Staglia); P. Supino, ed., *La 'Margarita cornetana'. Regesto dei documenti*, Rome 1969, no. 498, pp. 369–7; he was proctor of the *camera urbis* and marshal of Latino Orsini.

[49] E. Hubert, *Espace urbain*, pp. 128–31, for the word, pp. 309–13 for census payments and 267–70 for ground landlords.

[50] *m.* 41 and dorse.

[51] R. Montel, 'Les chanoines de la basilique de Saint-Pierre de Rome des statuts capitulaires de 1277–1279 à la fin de la papauté d'Avignon. Étude prosopographique', *Rivista di storia della chiesa in Italia*, 43 (1989), pp. 1–49, esp p. 46 note 4; see also *m.* 138 for another family member, a notary.

[52] Esch, *Bonifaz IX*, p. 637.   [53] *m.* 111.   [54] *m.* 195.

[55] *m.* 49 and see *mm.* 82, 83.   [56] *m.* 115.   [57] *m.* 9.   [58] *m.* 33.

[59] Goioli, p. 111, 158.

Bachariis, all of Parione, when selling a house to the English priest, Hugo de Hutyon, in 1379 and again when he sold it in 1380.[60]

The noble family de Saracenis were similarly ground landlords of some importance to the hospice. The family had a palace and other property in the Arenula region. A document of 1418 refers to property there towards the main palace (*versus palatium majus*) of Johannes de Sarcenis.[61] All the evidence suggests that the family needed money. In 1366 Johannes de Saracenis rented, to Raulinus son of John, an Englishman, a house said to be roofless (*discoperta*), for eighteen years on condition that within five it was made fit for habitation.[62] This was a standard method of dealing with properties which the proprietors could not afford to improve.[63] This house, 'once roofless now roofed' (*olim discoperta nunc coperta*) and called a *turris* with a *casella*, was sold by de Saracenis and his wife Cecilia in 1382 to the Englishman John Palmer.[64] The witnesses included the noble Matthucius, natural son of the late Benedictus Orsini of Campo dei Fiori. It came to the hospice of S Thomas in 1383.[65] The house owned by the English woman Sibilla Teste which she sold in 1391 to William, son of Richard, *paternostrarius* of Parione was also *in proprietate* of Johannes de Saracenis.[66] We can see it changing hands in 1365 when Johannes Cole de Saracenis, acting for his grandmother, Margarita, and his wife, Francesca, accepted a change of owner and received his census or payment for allowing it.[67] The property can then be traced until Sibilla sold it.[68]

By 1418 Johannes and Francesca were short of money. In March they sold one house in Arenula to the Englishman Philip Newton.[69] The guarantor for Johannes was Petrus Johannis Ley, or de Leis of Arenula who later caused such a problem with his waste water. In June that year, with Philip Newton as proctor for the deal, and with the consent of their son Anthonius, the de Saracenis sold the house next to their own palace to a German.[70] In December Johannes was having to acknowledge that he had been borrowing money from Johannes Cecchi de Leis by fictitious selling of a house used as a pledge.[71]

The families of Orsini, de Pappazuris and de Saracenis had in common that they had known S Bridget of Sweden when she had lived in Rome, first in S Lorenzo in Damaso and then with Francesca de Pappazuris. In 1383 Francesca had given her house for the new order which Bridget founded; it is still a Bridgettine convent in modern Piazza Farnese. A famous English pilgrim, Margery Kemp, in 1414 was

---

[60] *mm.* 96, 102.   [61] *m.* 190; see Staglia, p. 127 for a further mention.
[62] *m.* 45.   [63] E. Hubert, *Espace urbain*, p. 318.   [64] *m.* 114.
[65] *m.* 115, Palmer's will.   [66] *mm.* 121, 128, and see *m.* 68.   [67] *m.* 42.
[68] *mm.* 48, 68, 121, 128.   [69] *m.* 189.   [70] *m.* 190.   [71] *m.* 192.

easily able to meet Bridget's former servants because the convent was literally round the corner from the English hospice.[72] Latinus and Golitia Orsini gave evidence for Bridget's canonisation process in 1379, remembering events of 1362 and earlier.[73] They said they were on easy terms (*conversacionem familiarem*) with her. It is probably the first wife of Johannes de Saracenis who in 1379 also gave evidence. She reckoned that her son Nicolas had been healed by relics of the dead woman.[74] Francesca de Pappazuris gave evidence also.[75]

Such families could have great influence for good or ill. For instance in an agreement to keep the peace drawn up in 1365 by Antonius Goioli, the parties accepted that the peace between them could be considered broken if one attacked the other with armed men. Latinus Orsini witnessed this agreement.[76] The parties selected arbitrators,[77] then their sentence was given. The quarrellers had been involved in an affray and so one side was to come to a specific place with eight colleagues and four supporters and the other was to join him there and ask pardon in stated language. The injured party then asked to have his enemy as a brother. After this the offending straw which had caused the problem was to be removed within a stated time.[78]

During Bridget's canonisation process Margareta, widow of Paulus Branche of Arenula, recorded that in July 1365 her husband was killed and a feud resulted. Margareta's sons found it impossible to arrange any agreement with the family of her husband's killer until, so as at least not to lose her sons as well as her husband, she asked Bridget to pray for her. The following morning 'the relatives of the said killer came . . . and made an excellent peace'.[79] The city of Rome could clearly be a very turbulent place and great nobles were naturally crucial in either causing or defusing trouble.

Within the walls also great religious houses held the freehold of much property and are found receiving ground rent. In the second half of the fourteenth century many religious houses, like many of the older nobility, were in fact suffering from lack of funds and having to realise their assets by letting their properties on long leases or even sometimes selling them outright.[80] The beneficiaries were usually individuals who

---

[72] M. Kemp, *The Book of Margery Kemp*, ed. S. B. Meech and H. E. Allen *EETS* 217 (1940), chapter 39, p. 95, line 11 and 14.

[73] I. Collijn, ed., *Acta et processus canonizacionis Beate Birgitte* (= Samlingar utgivna av svenska Fornskrift-sällskapet, series 2, Latinska Skrifter 1), Uppsala 1924–31, pp. 352–63, 448–59.

[74] Collijn, *Acta*, p.432–3.   [75] Ibid., pp. 436–47.   [76] Goioli, p. 180.

[77] Ibid., nos. 90, 91, 92.   [78] Ibid., no. 105.   [79] Collijn, *Acta*, p. 564.

[80] J. C. Maire-Vigueur, 'Les casali des églises de Rome à la fin du moyen âge (1348–1428)', *Mélanges de l'école française de Rome, moyen âge/ temps moderne*, 86 (1974), pp. 63–136 for details, esp. pp. 72–83.

in England might have been called gentry, who had built houses on the land, though they often did not own the *proprietas*. A class of wealthy cattle owners and merchants and also notaries, was increasingly obtaining political power in Rome after 1360.[81]

The English were among buyers and renters, encountering the religious houses very often as ground landlords. The hospice of S Thomas owed ground rent to several convents by 1418, the most important being the abbey of S Biagio *in Canto Secuto* (della Pagnotta), still in via Giulia. Some Englishmen felt that such houses merited their support, for instance Walter Taylor evidently regarded S Biagio as to some extent 'his' church, since he left it 2 ducats for his soul.[82] The two senior Possewichs requested burial in their parish church of S Biagio.[83] Acknowledgement of the need for ready cash was given by S Biagio in 1374 when the Abbot and monks, 'pressed by necessity', let to John Champneys part of a garden, in return for which John paid six florins for the repair of their chapel called S Lucia Nova in Parione region.[84] This was a hospital in the present via Banchi Vecchi which had been in existence since about 1352.[85] In 1397 an Irish monk of S Biagio, John Oneachayn, referred in a petition to his monastery as 'poor'.[86] In 1405 S Biagio had a cardinal-abbot who held the monastery with his other benefices (*in commendam*) and must have been trying to recover full possession of properties previously leased. The abbot queried the terms on which the former Taylor house was held by S Thomas's and the matter went for arbitration before Hermann Dwerg, a famous German auditor and protonotary. He decreed that the hospice merely owed 6d per year to the abbot with one florin every time the house changed hands.[87] The abbot was Henry Minutoli, cardinal of Naples, who as well as being ground landlord of the Possewich family home was patron of the young John Possewich.[88]

Many Romans owned property just outside the walls, vineyards in particular, typically described as outside such and such a gate, in the place called so and so 'Outside Porta Castelli in the place called Varannecta';[89] 'outside Porta Portuensis, in the place called

---

[81] C. Gennaro, 'Mercanti e bovattieri nella Roma della seconda metà del trecento (da una ricerca su registri notarili)', *Bulletino dell'istituto storico italiano per il medio evo e archivio muratoriano*, 78 (1967), pp. 155–203, for the classic study.

[82] *m.* 163; 79, 80; for the community F. Caraffa, *Monasticon Italiae*, I, Roma e Lazio, Cesena 1981, p. 46.

[83] *mm.* 123, 158.   [84] *m.* 76.

[85] C. Huelsen, *Le chiese di Roma nel medio evo. Cataloghi ed appunti*, Rome 1927, pp. 302–3.

[86] *CPL*, V, p. 18.

[87] *m.* 171; for Dwerg see Schuchard, *Die Deutschen* , pp. 302–5, 307, 310–11.

[88] Vatican Archives, Reg. Lat. 127, fols. 46–7.   [89] Goioli, p. 124.

Montorio'.[90] In the canonisation records for S Francesca Romana, wife of a man from a well-known family in the Trastevere district, we find mentioned in passing their vineyard outside Porta S Paolo.[91] Thus the English who founded the two hospices set about buying vineyards as well as houses. Very often they would not expect to exploit these themselves but would let them or hire someone to run them. The notaries' books are full of examples of such bargains,[92] some specifying carefully how the renter was to labour and how the proprietor would receive some of the results.[93] Those in Rome who did not themselves own vineyards would make regular arrangements with an owner in spring, paying in advance for wine to be delivered at vintage.[94]

One can now ask what drove Englishmen (and women) to come to live in Rome? A major impetus was probably trade, both that connected with pilgrimage and more generally the hope of establishing a commercial foothold in a foreign centre. Without a resident papacy, late medieval Rome might seem to us a poor and insignificant place, but it was a significant pilgrim centre, its raison d'etre amply illustrated in the Jubilee year of 1350 when there was a huge influx of people, including perhaps 'several hundred from England'.[95] Matteo Villani, the Florentine chronicler, painted a somewhat idealised picture of the Holy Year of 1350 but the large number of pilgrims was excellent for all inhabitants: 'all the Romans became innkeepers' and put up prices.[96] There was a Rome not dependent on the presence of the papacy, though much of it still depended on S Peter and other saints and martyrs. This may explain why, even before the papacy returned, there were significant groups of non-Romans in the city.

The English were neither the only group of immigrants in 1362 nor the most significant. Like many other North Italian cities, Rome was full of incomers, though most were from elsewhere in Italy.[97] Shepherd's house was bought by him in 1361 from Antonius Smerucii, a woolman, formerly of Camerino.[98] In the protocols for 1365 of Antonius Goioli there were people from Arezzo,[99] from Bologna,[100]

---

[90] Ibid., p. 98.
[91] P. L. Lugano, *I processi inediti per Francesca Bussa dei Ponziani (Santa Francesca Romana) 1440–1453*, Studi e testi 120 (1945), p. 236.
[92] Goioli, pp. 201–4 for instance.   [93] Ibid., pp. 208–9.
[94] Caputgallis, pp. 267–8 is a good example.
[95] W. E. Lunt, *Financial Relations of the Papacy with England 1327–1534*, II, Cambridge (Mass.) 1962, pp. 460–1 for some details from England.
[96] M Villani, *Cronaca*, in G., M., and F. Villani, *Chronache di Dino Compagni e di Giovanni, Matteo e Filippo Villani*, One vol. in two parts, Padua 1841, part II, p. 27.
[97] Goioli, p. xix.   [98] *Venerabile*, p. 37; *m.* 34.
[99] Goioli, p. 209.   [100] Ibid., p. 60.

lately from Sienna,[101] lately of Pisa,[102] from Milan,[103] from Ferrara,[104] from Benevento,[105] from Rieti,[106] many Sicilians,[107] with Nicholas of Naples and a Genoese merchant.[108] There were also Spaniards[109] and even Germans; Raynaldus de *Lamania*, colleague of Count Guido.[110] Even before the papacy's return there were already Florentines in Rome. In 1376 during Pope Gregory's quarrel with Florence, he imprisoned thirty-one Florentine merchants in the city, of whom nine or ten had Roman wives and about eight were citizens.[111] This pattern is also found in other Tuscan cities which replenished themselves after the Black Death by drawing both from the surrounding countryside and from much further afield.[112]

Rome thus was thoroughly cosmopolitan, as it had always been. On the other hand it cannot have been very prosperous. Everything suggests that it was still very ruinous. One way in which Bartolomeo Prignano, the future Urban VI, was said to have endeared himself to the Romans before 1378 was to express deep sorrow at the state of the city and to say that he would build a great palace if he had the power.[113] The contracts of rent in Antonius Goioli's protocols specify repairs.[114] For example the rent of a palace in SS Lorenzo and Damaso region stated that the roof of the adjacent *casellam discopertam* was to be made good.[115] Some hospice deeds referred to properties as *scoperte* or *discoperte* as already noticed.[116] The *turris* which John Fraunceys eventually bought was called *disruptam* in 1382.[117] In some cases the repairs would come out of the rent,[118] in others a condition was that the holder repaired the house, as agreed in 1366 for the house which John Ponfred finally gave to the hospice of S Thomas.[119] Described as a simple house called lo Cafaria, roofless with no upper storey (*discoperta absque solariis*), it was let, as we saw, for eighteen years to Raulinus the Englishman on condition that it is made habitable within five years (*quod sit bene acta ad habitandum hinc ad v annos*). By 1382 it was described as with two storeys, formerly roofless, now roofed (*solarata, olim discopcerta nunc coperta.*)[120] So someone had roofed it and added a second floor.

Without any major industry, and relying for prosperity on pilgrims with the hoped-for presence of the papal curia, the Romans knew

---

[101] Ibid., pp. 41, 105.   [102] Ibid., p. 119.   [103] Ibid., p. 40.   [104] Ibid., p. 210.
[105] Ibid., p. 211.   [106] Ibid., p. 258.   [107] Ibid., pp. 59, 62, 175, 199, 257.
[108] Ibid., p. 153.   [109] Ibid., p. 17–18.   [110] Ibid., p. 33.
[111] A. Esch, 'Florentiner in Rom um 1400. Namenverzeichnis der ersten Quattrocento-Generation', *QFIAB* 52 (1972), pp. 476–525, esp. 479, note 7.
[112] Herlihy, 'The Tuscan town', pp. 85, 88.
[113] Seidlmayer, *Die Anfänge*, pp. 311–12.
[114] Goioli, p. xx.   [115] Ibid., p. 112.   [116] Above, p. 19.
[117] *m*. 111.   [118] *m*. 75, of 1374.   [119] Above, p. 19; *m*. 45.   [120] *m*. 114.

perfectly well what would bring prosperity. There are many examples where it was agreed that rent would rise if the pope or emperor came to the city.[121] In 1367 a testator specified that if the pope came his executor was to have made two bells to the value of 15 gold florins to be placed in the church of S Anastasia de Marmorata for his soul.[122]

But before the pope returned the majority of those who lived in Rome were various kinds of artisan and of course those, like inn-keepers and sellers of holy pictures and rosary beads, who made their living from pilgrims. The English belonged for the most part to the artisan and merchant classes. Where an occupation was given, which was not by any means always, they were predominantly called *paternostrarius*, *sutor*, *cernitor* or just merchant. Before the curia returned (that is before 1376) very few were clerics. When members of the group who founded the hospice in 1362 were given occupations in the sources they were *paternostrarii* (John Shepherd himself, Simon, son of John Barber, William son of Richard), a goldsmith (John, son of William), two *cernitores*[123] (Robert de Pigna and Henry son of John) and one oblate (Robert, son of John).

Run-down though it was, Rome could attract those seeking opportunities because, despite appearances, the economy was expanding in the second half of the fourteenth century, though the improvement was only beginning.[124] It must have been economic prospects which attracted most immigrants. Many of them never became citizens, which required birth in Rome or the acquisition of a house, land and a level of wealth,[125] but, as we shall see, some English people made Rome so much their home that they did not mention any other place in their wills and seem to have settled firmly into local society.

The attraction of Rome for English migrants is difficult to assess because little is known about trade between England and Rome in the second half of the fourteenth century but a main ingredient must have been trade in wool and cloth. The organisation of the trade from the English end was largely in the hands of Florentines and other Italians but there were certainly native groups in many English towns who

---

[121] Goioli, p. 113.
[122] Biblioteca Apostolica Vaticana, Archivio della Chiesa di S Angelo in Pescharia, 1/3, fol. 102v; for the church Huelsen, *Le chiese*, p. 174.
[123] See below p. 27 for explanation.
[124] For some indications L. Palermo, *Il porto di Roma nel XIV e XV secolo. Strutture socio-economiche e statuti* (= Fonti e studi per la storia economica e sociale di Roma e dello stato pontificio nel tardo medioevo 2), Rome 1979, esp. p. 102 for after 1376.
[125] For citizenship in general see D. Quaglioni, 'The legal definition of citizenship in the late Middle Ages' in A. Mohlo, K. Raaflaub, and J. Emlen, eds., *City States in Classical Antiquity and Medieval Italy*, Stuttgart 1991, pp. 155–67.

were anxious to wrest it from them and control it. In the very few cases where the origins of the laymen in Rome are known they come from major cloth towns which were expanding in the 1360s and 1370s: York, London, Massingham (Norfolk), Salisbury, Colchester and perhaps Pontefract (Ponfred alias Palmer). Details about the trade in Rome are few. The Florentines began in the 1340s to export to Florence large quantities of English wool[126] and by 1355 the Del Bene company, making cloth in Florence, was exporting from England 98 per cent of the wool the company used. But this tells us nothing of Rome.

Rome certainly contained men trading in wool. Apart from Antonius Smerucci,[127] Antonius Goioli's protocols in 1365 refer both to selling sacks of sheeps' wool[128] and to men working the wool *in apotheca . . . in arte lane*, where a man from Cortina worked for a Roman in the Colonna district.[129] There were several *lanaroli* in Goioli's documents. Coluccia Pauli,[130] Gerardus Petri,[131] Venturinus Thomaxi,[132] Franciscus, and his bother Balthelus Munalli[133] were all woolmen of Arenula, of whom Coluccia was *caporione* or elected representative for a *rione* and Franciscus an elector.[134] Ventura Johannis ser Gualterii was from the area of SS Lorenzo and Damaso[135] and Petrus Meoli from Parione region.[136] In 1368 the notary Pietro di Nicola Astalli's notebooks mention Meulus Danielis, another woolman of Arenula.[137]

The protocols of Lorenzo Staglia give even more details of the trade in 1372, though mostly concerning local wool. Woolmen ordered this at any time between Autumn and Easter or bought fleeces,[138] specifying the type of wool and explaining that it must be delivered well-washed and combed.[139] The sellers were local sheep-owners.[140] There were weavers,[141] wool-dressers,[142] and, in the Ponte and Pigna regions, dyers.[143] There were fulling mills also.[144] In Goioli's protocols also there were also several *sutores* or *sartores*, which at this time meant tailor

---

[126] H. Hoshino, *L'arte della lana in Firenze nel basso medioevo. Il commercio della lana e il mercato dei panni fiorentini nei secoli XIII-XV* (= Biblioteca storica toscana 21), Florence 1980, p. 141.

[127] Above, p. 10.   [128] Goioli, p. 103.   [129] Ibid., p. 160.

[130] Ibid., pp. 19, 56, 114, 160, 222, 225.   [131] Ibid., p. 96.

[132] Ibid., p. 104.   [133] Ibid., p. 114, 160, 225.   [134] Ibid., p. 114.

[135] Ibid., p. 119.   [136] Ibid., pp. 262, 267.

[137] Astalli, P., *Il protocollo notarile di Pietro di Nicola Astalli* (= Codice diplomatico di Roma e della regione romana 6), ed. I. L. Sanfilippo, Rome 1989, pp. 59–62 (hereafter called Astalli).

[138] Staglia, pp. 5–6, 38–9, 63–4, 84–5, 148–9, 163–5.

[139] Ibid., pp. 5, 20, 38, 132, 133, 148, 164.

[140] Ibid., pp. xxiv–v, who says that these types of wool had to be bought without use of middlemen.

[141] Ibid., pp. 46,-9, 51 57, 59–60, 62, 81, 92, 99.

[142] Ibid., pp 20, 31, 80, 84, 86, 95, 132, 148, 165.

[143] Ibid., pp. 83, 165–6.   [144] Astalli, pp. 41–2.

in a very general sense,[145] and more are found in other protocols.[146] Trade in wool and cloth must therefore have been well established.

Already in 1362 there were groups in London and elsewhere trying to advance native English trade in cloth and wool at the expense of aliens and there were strong connections between merchants of London and English institutions in Rome before 1400.[147] From 1359 the wool Staple was at Bruges and from 1362, the year of the founding of S Thomas's hospital, at Calais. This favoured English wool exporters at the expense of aliens.[148] Outside London too there were merchants who desired to break into the export trade, and resented how much was in alien hands. Groups were trying to develop Southampton as a port and many English merchants attempted to circumvent the government's regular bans on denizen exports (the Italians provided credit to the crown) by using Italians as partners. The 1370s were the period of most fluctuation in English government policy towards the wool-trade and therefore also a period when English merchants seeking new markets might have thought of Rome.

To these factors was added the presence of the pope in Rome after 1376. From the beginning of the reign of Gregory XI (December 1370) it was becoming steadily more certain that this pope intended to return to Italy.[149] As is well known, the move was unpopular with the French, and some English and many cardinals did not want it either, but if the pope was ever to control his own territory he needed to be present.[150] Vacillations over his return were more concerned with the state of Italy than with the pope's own uncertainty about this plan; at latest by February 1375 it was clearly only a matter of months before he would indeed leave Avignon. This was certainly well known to governments by autumn[151] and must therefore have been known to leading merchant communities, including those in London. This may have encouraged some merchants to think further about the value of giving support to

145 Goioli, pp. xviii–xix, 5, 26, 29, 33, 48, 96, 104, 137, 152–7, 181, 194, 202, 207, 224, 230, 261.

146 Astalli, pp. 5 (a Jew), 19, 57, 58, 73, 82; Staglia, pp. 11, 22, 54, 45, 72.

147 P. Nightingale, *A Medieval Mercantile Community. The Grocers' Company and the Politics and Trade of London, 1000–1485*, New Haven and London 1995, pp. 213, 216 and see below, pp. 59–61; M. Bailey, 'Historiographical essay: the commercialisation of the English economy 1086–1500', *Journal of Medieval History*, 24 (1998), pp. 277–311, covers recent literature, esp. pp. 299–300.

148 T. H. Lloyd, *The English Wool Trade in the Middle Ages*, Cambridge 1977, pp. 208–9, Nightingale, *Medieval Mercantile Community*, pp. 215–16.

149 S. Weiss, 'Kredit europäischer Fürsten für Gregor XI. Zur Finanzierung der Rückkehr des Papsttum von Avignon nach Rom', *QFIAB* 77 (1997), pp. 176–205, esp. pp. 190–205.

150 Weiss, 'Kredit', p. 200.

151 Gregory XI, *Lettres secrètes.et curiales . . . intéressantes les pays autres que la France*, ed. G. Mollat (= Bibliothèque des écoles françaises d'Athènes et de Rome), Paris 1962, nos. 3005, 3399, 3474.

English institutions in Rome; it was becoming evident that there was soon to be a shift of trade and a flow of personnel to Italy away from Avignon. There would certainly be curial business to transact, with a significant exchange of money and a much increased need for import of goods into Rome. Hence no doubt Englishmen were present in Rome simply called 'merchant' and hence also the evidence of their increase in numbers from 1370.

The English were also said to be *cernitores*. This word connects with milling and probably meant men who worked in sieving or refining, certainly when connected with *farinas* as it was in the English cases.[152] The few references not in documents where the English were involved always juxtapose them with millers (*molendinarii*).[153] There were many water mills along the banks of the Tiber, with a majority near Tiber island,[154] but there were evidently mills elsewhere.[155] *Molendinarius* is a frequently mentioned trade; some would be fulling millers but some were flour-millers, though none of these were Englishmen.[156] Some indication of the trade occurs in the protocols of Francesco di Stephano de Caputgallis where there are several references to Jacobellus Cole Lemmi of Trevi region, a flour miller.[157] In 1382 his wife bought half a mill, with a tower house and half its iron winches (*medietatem . . . ferrorum argangnorum*) and stones and half a small piece of land, which owed a ground rent to the Lateran church of six *rubla* of pure milled grain per year.[158]

The pilgrim trade naturally generated its own services. The large numbers of inns increased after the 1350 Jubilee year, when, apparently, the existing supply proved very inadequate,[159] though I have found no English inn-keepers in Rome. Before the return of the papacy *paternostrarius* is the most frequently mentioned trade connecting pilgrimage and Englishmen. Oddly enough, this is not a trade often mentioned in the notaries' protocols except in connection with English names. It does not seem a very common occupation. In 1527 only seventeen were noted in the Roman census.[160]

---

152 Professor Mosti was most helpful in answering my questions on this point. I would also like to thank Dr John Langdon.
153 Caputgallis, pp. 288, 289, 321.   154 U. Gnoli, *Topografia*, p. 170.
155 See for instance Caputgallis, p. 438, outside Porta Latina; Astalli, p. 42, outside Porta Appia.
156 For fulling, above p. 25. See for flour especially Caputgallis, index, and pp. 89–90, 288, 289, 291, 292, 312, 490–1; Astalli, pp. 12, 21, 23 31, 77, 85, 97. For some helpful ideas, see B. M. S. Campbell et al., *A Medieval Capital and its Grain Supply. Agrarian Production and Distribution in the London Region c. 1300* (= Historical Geography Research Series 30), London 1993.
157 Caputgallis, index.   158 Caputgallis, pp. 438–40.
159 Villani, quoted Maas, *German Community*, p. 68.
160 E. Lee, *Descriptio urbis. The Roman Census of 1527* (= Biblioteca del cinquecento 32), Rome 1985, p. 343.

In the Middle Ages to be *paternostrarius* was a distinct craft. He was the maker and seller of paternosters or prayer beads.[161] The use of beads to count prayers was very old; the most common use in the thirteenth century was to count 'Our Fathers', hence the name, but in the later Middle Ages many combinations of *aves* and *paters* might be used in prayer until the later development of the modern rosary, which was certainly not fixed by 1420.[162]

Rosary beads could be made of all manner of materials. In Etienne Boileau's *Livre des Métiers*, describing Paris in 1285, bone, horn, shell, amber, jet and ivory are referred to.[163] In the Flemish/French conversation manual called *Le Livre des Mestiers*, Wotier le Paternostier or Wouter de Paternostermakere, depending on what language you wanted, had paternosters of crystal, amber, glass, horn and agate.[164] When a jeweller called Adam Ledyard gave an inventory of his shop after theft in London in 1381 he had lost paternosters of white amber, amber, jet, silver-gilt, mazer (mixed) and white bone said to be for children.[165] Among valuable jewels and other goods listed by a Roman widow in 1374 as returned to her when her husband died was a rosary of coral.[166] Thus at one end of the scale were very expensive rosaries, sometimes found in wills, and at the other very cheap sets.

We know nothing about the organisation of the *paternostrarii* of Rome and it seems very likely that, as in England, and unlike in France, there was very little. They were not included in the *artes* in the city statutes of the fourteenth century.[167] In Paris between the thirteenth and the sixteenth centuries the trade was divided according to the materials used.[168] In England rosaries of gold or silver would have had to be made by a specialist gold-smith; in 1382 we find a London

---

[161] A. Winston-Allen, *Stories of the Rose. The Making of the Rosary in the Middle Ages*, Pennsylvania 1997, esp. Introduction, and pp. 14–15, 111–16, and next note. Also J. Blair and N. Ramsay, eds., *English Medieval Industries. Craftsmen, Techniques, Products*, London and Rio Grande 1991, pp. 151, 377.

[162] H. Thurston, 'The rosary,' *The Month*, 96 (1900), pp. 403–18, 513–27; 'A history of the rosary in all countries,' *Journal of the Society of Arts*, 50 (1901), pp. 261–76; 'Genuflexions and Aves', *The Month*, 127 (1916), pp. 441–52, 546–59.

[163] E. Boileau, or Boyleau, *Le livre des métiers*, ed. R. de Lespinasse and F. Bonnardot (= *Histoire générale de Paris*), Paris 1879, pp. xxxviii–xl, 57–61, 81–3 or ed. G.-B. Depping, *Reglemens sur les arts et métiers de Paris . . . connus sous le nom du Livre des métiers d'Étienne Boileau* (= Documents inédits sur l'histoire de France, series 3/iv), Paris 1837, pp. 66–71, 97–9.

[164] J. Gessler, ed., *Le livre des mestiers de Bruges et ses derivés*, Bruges 1931, p. 45.

[165] H. T. Riley, *Memorials of London and London Life in the XIIIth and XIVth and XVth Centuries*, London 1878, p. 455; Blair and Ramsay, *English Medieval Industries*, pp. 138–9, 368–9.

[166] Caputgallis, p. 6.

[167] G. Gatti, ed., *Statuti dei mercanti di Roma*, Rome 1885.

[168] Boileau, *Livre*, p. 57–61 or ed. Depping, pp. 66–71; R. de Lespinasse, *Les métiers et corporations de la ville de Paris*, III (in three parts), Paris 1886–97, III/2, pp. 96–9.

goldsmith losing a *paternoster* of silver and pearls.[169] But less specialised materials needed less accomplished craftsmen, who might make other kinds of jewellery as well. One Parisian group also made jewellery of other kinds, buttons and rings for example.[170] The Paris statutes simply refer to polishing the beads and insist that they be properly strung and made of true materials. Despite the attempts to produce a specialism, therefore, the trade cannot have required very specialist skills. Thus those who made and sold rosaries of cheaper materials probably also made and sold other jewels: the London jeweller in 1381 also lost necklaces, silver-gilt rings and crucifixes.[171]

Paternosters were certainly part of the commerce of Rome at this time. They are mentioned in the customs accounts.[172] Some individuals probably valued a Roman rosary, perhaps because it would have been specially blessed. John Launce, friend of the English proctor William Swan, went to expense at the beginning of the fifteenth century to ask 'for a pair of beads otherwise called paternoster' (*pro uno pari bedis alias dicto paternost[rario]*).[173]

The rather sparse evidence suggests that in London they lived in Faringdon Within Ward, with their shops in Paternoster Row and S Michael le Quern as 'their' church.[174] In Rome not only was there no 'guild'; the English *paternostrarii* did not all live in the same district, although the majority (seven) lived in Parione, among the most expensive areas in the fourteenth century.[175] One place where they had booths was on the steps of S Peter's church 'the first door at the head of the steps, where *paternostralia* are sold'.[176]

There were, of course, many clerics in Rome and there must always have been foreign clergy on pilgrimage, but the clerical population was the most affected by the absence of the papacy. Clergy were naturally drawn to permanent residence in the curia in pursuit of a career and until 1376 foreigners would seek that in Avignon. There were only a few English clergy in Rome before that. The group founding the hospice of S Thomas was almost entirely lay, with only an oblate representing the clerical estate. Even in Avignon, however, the number of English was small. The most numerous group before 1376 was in the

---

[169] Riley, *Memorials*, p. 470.   [170] Boileau, *Livre*, pp. 81–3 or ed. Depping, pp. 97–9.

[171] Riley, *Memorials*, p. 455.

[172] M. L. Lombardo, *Camera urbis: Dohanna minuta urbis liber introitus, 1422*, Rome 1963, p. 79.

[173] Oxford, Bodleian Library, Arch. Seld. B 23 f. 34v; f. 39v–40. They are referred to as *preces bedes vulgariter nuncupatas*.

[174] Riley, *Memorials*, pp. 20, 30.

[175] E. Hubert, 'Économie de la proprieté immobilière: les établissements religieux et leurs patrimoines au XIVe siècle', in Hubert, *Rome aux XIIIe siècle*, pp. 177–230, esp. p. 224.

[176] Schiavo, *Diario*, p. 22.

household of cardinal Simon Langham, who died that year.[177] There were also a few Englishmen holding offices in the papal administration and some English proctors.[178] But all these functioned in Avignon, a French-dominated city, to reach which, if one were English, France had to be crossed. In Rome itself an oblate of S Maria in Julia, Robert son of John, among the founder members of the hospital, was also promised a legacy of two florins in 1363 by the English Rosa Casarola and was her executor then.[179] Amata, an English woman, widow of Henry Orlandi, making her will in S Thomas's hospital in 1365 left one florin to John the English priest and named as an executor John the English *romitus*, presumably 'the hermit'.[180] John the English priest was a member of the Order of S Augustine of the church of S Augustine of Rome (and may be the same John), doing business about horses in August 1365.[181] But Rome was not a place where many English clerics came by preference to make a career in the 1360s.

The situation changed with the return of the papacy in 1376 after which, correspondingly, opportunities for English lay people may have become less. In the period before the return of the curia, however, Rome was sufficiently attractive to entice English laymen to settle.

It was not surprising that such people decided to found 'English' institutions. Other groups, for instance the Florentines[182] and the Germans[183] did so too, ultimately on a much larger scale, since the numbers were much greater. The groupings cast interesting light on ideas of 'nationhood' in the later Middle Ages. The German hospital S Maria dell'Anima gathered most of the 'Germans', who on closer inspection turn out to come from the Empire, especially the Low Countries and also Sweden.[184] The 'English' group centred on S Thomas's included Irish and Welshmen (though they were accepted with reservations and were not from native Irish speakers, apparently) and there was a Gascon called 'English' in S Chrysogonus' confraternity.[185] The object was as much the welfare of the local group of foreigners as the care of pilgrims. As an alien group in a foreign land Englishmen, and also their widows, might find themselves in old age without kin to care for them and without anyone to pray for their soul. Judging by the way the earliest English hospice operated, at least at first, these considerations played an important part in the foundation.

[177] M. Harvey, 'The household of Simon Langham,' *JEH*, 47 (1996), pp. 18–44.
[178] P. N. R. Zutshi, 'Proctors acting for English petitioners in the chancery of the Avignon popes(1305–1378)', *JEH*, 35 (1984), pp. 15–29.
[179] S Angelo in Pescharia, I/1, f. 141r/v.   [180] Goioli, no. 158.
[181] Goioli, pp. 187–8, no. 110.   [182] For them see Esch, 'Die Florentiner'.
[183] For them see Maas, *German Community*.   [184] Maas, *German Community*, p. 8.
[185] See below, p. 83.

Chapter 2

THE SETTING II: ROME, 1376–1420

In January 1377 the pope returned to Rome, leaving Avignon, for ever as it turned out. The situation was very unsettled; since 1375 there had been revolt in the papal states against the regime set up by cardinal Albornoz for the return of Urban V and the Florentines, quarrelling with the pope on their own account, were trying to persuade the Romans to join their league.[1] With the area round Rome in turmoil the Romans were very concerned that Gregory might return to Avignon. There was no reason to suppose that relations would be harmonious between those already in Rome and those arriving with the papal court, whatever their nationality. Their interests were too different. The city to which the pope returned was turbulent and although the citizens wanted the papal court that did not imply cordiality. In theory Rome had self government, with elected representatives, and no longer depended either on rule by great territorial nobility or on papally imposed officials. Thus the *popolo* were likely to be uneasy about the return of the pope, if that meant replacement of local authority.

The rebellion in the papal states, which had already consumed vast sums of money, not only destroyed the system of government carefully built up by Albornoz; it was also a source of many bitter experiences, which reverberated down the years and did not help the reputation of the papal governors. Three weeks after Gregory entered Rome one of the worst atrocities of the rebellion was perpetrated, the massacre on 3 February 1377 of the inhabitants of Cesena by papal troops under cardinal Robert of Geneva, soon to become a rival to the Roman pope.[2] Gregory returned against the wishes of many of the curia. There was much evidence already under Urban V of resistance to the return

---

[1] See R. C. Trexler, 'Rome on the Eve of the Great Schism', *Speculum*, 42 (1967), pp. 489–509.
[2] Partner, *Lands of St Peter*, esp pp. 361–5.

31

from the cardinals, some of which filtered into English sources, for instance a letter by the cardinal of Pamplona, Langham's executor,[3] and there was more later when information was collected about the 1378 election of Gregory's successor.[4] But the pope had returned and he began to make peace with the rebels at once, though not with Florence. All might have been different had Gregory lived but he survived only until 27 March 1378. Already before his death some people wanted the curia to return to the much greater safety of Avignon. Not surprisingly these voices became much louder when the pope died. The result is well known: a turbulent conclave with Roman crowds insisting on a Roman pope who would keep the curia in the city, frightened cardinals pretending to have elected the old cardinal 'of Rome', Tebaldeschi, but in reality choosing, as Urban VI, Bartolomeo Prignano, an Italian but not a cardinal.[5]

In 1377 among the existing English community in Rome there was a core of laymen from the days before the return of the papacy. The *custos* of S Thomas's in 1376 was John Palmer alias Ponfred, probably a *paternostrarius*, who had been *custos* at intervals since 1365 and lived until 1387.[6] The leader of the group round the hospice of S Thomas may have been William son of Richard, *paternostrarius* of the Parione region. He went back to the early days.[7] He had bought a house in 1374, described as being behind the house of cardinal Franciscus de Tebaldeschis. This is the cardinal 'of S Peter', or 'of Rome' mentioned above.[8] Another *paternostrarius*, John Clerk, son of John, of Ponte region, was still alive, buying and selling houses and property in the 1370s and 80s.[9] The long-established English families also included Thomas son of Nicholas, *paternostrarius*, dead by 1387, Henry of Trastevere, *cernitor* who died in 1378, Simon Barber mentioned from 1350 to 1401, the Testes, a family of tailors, and Stefania, widow of Richard, son of Roger, with possibly John Champneys.[10] They were soon to be joined by new faces.

The departure of the papacy from France caused some seeking employment in the curia, and many who depended on it for their

---

[3] London, BL MS Cotton Cleop. E II, f. 126: *audivistis mutacionem curie satis inopinate et indeliberate factam que utinam utilis ecclesie de quo satis dubito, sed spero in deo quod si non fit ad locum unde translata est infra pauca tempora revertetur.* The date must be 1366. For the English background G. Holmes, *The Good Parliament*, Oxford 1975, passim and R.G. Davies, 'The Anglo-papal concordat of Bruges, 1375. A reconsideration', *AHP*, 19 (1981), pp. 97–146.

[4] See above, p. 17.

[5] Out of many possible accounts see O. Prerovský, *L'elezione di Urbano VI e l'insorgere dello scisma d'occidente* (= Miscellanea della società romana di storia patria 20), Rome 1960.

[6] See pp. 94–5.   [7] Above, p. 11.

[8] Prerovský, *L'elezione*, pp. 149–50. For the house *m.* 71.

[9] *mm.* 66, 70, 75, 93.   [10] See pp. 93, 95, 98, 100–101.

livelihood, to leave Avignon and come to Rome. When Urban V had first left for Rome he had obliged all *curiales* who wanted to stay behind to become Avignonese citizens, no longer able to claim privileges as members of the papal court (*cortisani*). The options then taken were checked again in 1371.[11] There were few English names, but it is clear that at least one member of the English group in Rome after that could claim citizenship in Avignon.[12] Other Englishmen, without Avignonese citizenship, followed the curia from Avignon either as *cortisani* or merely as hangers-on. By July 1379, when Richard Teste, resident in Rome since at least 1373,[13] made over to his wife Sibilla his house in the Parione region, for the first time he had an English notary, John de Hynkeley of Lincoln diocese, and all his witnesses were English: Reginald Walpole, clerk and notary public, Roger Paunton, priest, of Norwich diocese, Thomas Baty, subdeacon of Lincoln diocese, John Brygstok of York diocese and John Bron of Canterbury diocese, the last two laymen, with Thomas Taylour and John Sporier, who were Englishmen from Parione. Of these Walpole must have been starting a career in the curia; later he was called 'proctor in the Roman curia' when buying an expensive house in Rome in 1384,[14] and he acted as such in a case where John de Hynkeley was one of the English agents.[15] Roger Paunton had come from Avignon where he had been a *cortisanus*, a member of cardinal Simon Langham's household.[16]

In 1376/7 some officers of the curia remained in Avignon. This could prove very inconvenient, with clients having to do business in two places. The move affected the household of the now-dead Simon Langham. He had died on 22 July 1376 and left devoted servants to deal with his vast estate, the bulk, books, valuable vestments and hangings, with jewels and plate as well as debts owed to him, was intended to help pay for the fabric of Westminster Abbey.[17] In Avignon Thomas Southam, the cardinal's auditor or legal adviser, kept a house and offered lodging to monks of Westminster who came to parcel up the

---

[11] ASV, Reg. Av. 204, ff. 204–505; ASV Collectanea 358, f. 20r/v For this see R.C. Trexler, 'A medieval census: the *Liber Divisionis*', *Medievalia et Humanistica* 17 (1966), pp. 82–5.
[12] ASV, Reg. Av. 204, ff. 433v, 438, 458, 461, 462, 467, 478v, 482v, 495, 495v, 498, 498v, 505; for the one example see p. 144.
[13] *m.* 68.   [14] *m.* 116.
[15] P. N. R. Zutshi, ed., *Original Papal Letters in England 1305–1415* (= Index Actorum Romanorum Pontificum ab Innocento III ad Martinum V Electum 5). Vatican City 1990, p. 183, no. 357, and no. 379 also; J. E. Sayers, 'Proctors representing British interests at the papal court, 1198–1415', in S. Kuttner, ed., *Proceedings of the Third International Congress of Medieval Canon Law* (= Monumenta Iuris Canonici, series C, subsidia 4), Vatican City 1971, pp. 143–63 esp. p. 153.
[16] Harvey, 'Langham', p. 43.   [17] Harvey, 'Langham', pp.18 and 20.

goods.[18] The household itself disbanded, however. Very soon Adam Easton, formerly the cardinal's *socius* or companion/secretary, came to Rome, with a few other former members, presumably including Paunton. The executors of Langham's will included the cardinal of Pamplona, Pierre de Monteruc, and cardinal Guillaume Aigrefeuille. The latter also came to Rome and took part in the election of Urban VI in April 1378.[19] The former, who was vice-chancellor, stayed in Avignon.[20] Easton talked about his discussions with Aigrefeuille (one of the major supporters of the election of Urban at this point)[21] in the aftermath of Urban's election and mentioned that he himself had already bought and repaired a house in Anagni, probably before the election but certainly before the schism.[22] When William Colchester, the abbot of Westminster, came to the curia in 1377 on business for the abbey, he had to make several uncomfortable journeys between Rome and Avignon and talked of staying with Southam in Avignon, although he did not specify where he stayed in Rome.[23]

It is clear from Colchester's accounts and from evidence given to investigators of the disputed papal election, that there were several important English members of the curia already in Rome by the time Urban VI was elected. As well as Easton they included William Andrew, OP, bishop of Achonry and later of Meath, Master of the Sacred Palace (that is the papal court preacher and theologian) and Robert de Stratton, who was a Rota judge or auditor. In addition Laurence Child, OSB, of Battle abbey, another executor of Langham's will, appointed papal Minor Penitentiary in Avignon, also came to Rome. These will be discussed further later; here we simply need to notice that they had all travelled from Avignon.[24] When Colchester needed lawyers in Rome he found Englishmen already there in 1377. He employed John Mowbray and John Upton as advocates (lesser lawyers, able to plead in certain courts only).[25] None of these was attached to the English hospice as far as one can tell; their names do not appear in its early records.

Soon, however, a recognisable group of employees of the papal curia, *cursores*, joined those round the English hospice. These were official messengers who carried papal letters all over Christendom. In 1379 John

---

[18] Harvey, 'Langham', pp. 29–30; Harvey, *Solutions to the Schism*, pp. 20–1.
[19] See p. 196.   [20] For him see Prerovský, *L'elezione*, pp. 16, 18, 19, 43n, 44.
[21] Prerovský, *L'elezione*, pp. 130–2.
[22] L. Macfarlane, 'An English account of the election of Urban VI, 1378', *BIHR*, 26 (1953), pp. 79–85, esp. p. 85.
[23] Harvey, *Solutions to the Schism*, pp. 20–1.   [24] See below pp. 133, 154, 162.
[25] Harvey, *Solutions to the Schism*, p. 20.

Champneys of London, living and working in Rome since 1374[26] and *camerarius* of the hospice in 1375,[27] sold to an incoming man from Avignon who became a *cursor*, Richard son of William Possewich, and his wife Alice, his house in Rome. This is the beginning in Rome of a family with a long connection with S Thomas's hospice.[28] The Posse-wichs are the best documented example of a family, some with Avignonese citizenship, though the origins were Irish, moving with the curia and making careers in its service in the new location.

The return of the curia was accompanied, as outlined above, by a serious quarrel of the pope with the Florentines between 1375 and 1378, and temporarily at least they lost their ascendancy over papal finance.[29] A few Florentine families were already established in Rome as we saw and some came with the papal court, but by 1377 Gregory was enforcing his Interdict against them, as he did also in Avignon.[30] The same occurred in England, where anti-alien feeling coincided with the Interdict and some Florentines, including one who will be encoun-tered later, Jacobus Giacomini, were attacked in the Good Parliament in 1376.[31] Giacomini had in fact already failed and left London, as had another Florentine group, the Biancardi; the evidence suggests that they had been suffering from a down-turn in trade since 1370, with wool and cloth exports sinking to a record low level in 1376.[32]

Though the Florentines were the most dominant Italian traders in England before 1377 they were by no means alone. By then Luccans were also of great importance and when they became papal bankers to replace the Florentines their prosperity increased.[33] In 1377 the papal collector in England was transferring money to the curia through the Luccan firms of Guinigi and Interminelli.[34] Already in 1365–6 Fran-ciscus Vinceguerra of Lucca was exporting 116 sacks of wool from London, the smallest of the eight leading Italian firms but still impor-tant.[35] Vinceguerra had his contact (*socius*) in Rome from 1376 in the

---

[26] *mm.* 74, 76, 81, 84, 86.   [27] *m.* 81.   [28] See p. 144.

[29] R. C. Trexler, *The Spiritual Power. Republican Florence under Interdict* (= Studies in Medieval and Reformation Thought 9), Leiden 1974, esp. pp. 44–54 .

[30] Trexler, *Spiritual Power*, pp. 29–43, 44–54, 92–101.

[31] Ibid., pp. 59–66; Holmes, *Good Parliament*, pp. 118–26.

[32] Holmes, *Good Parliament*, pp. 124–5.

[33] Lloyd, *English Wool Trade* p. 214; G. Holmes, 'How the Medici became the pope's bankers', in *Florentine Studies*, ed. N. Rubenstein, London 1968, pp. 357–80, esp. pp. 357–60; L. Palermo, 'Banchi privati e finanze pubbliche nella Roma del primo rinascimento', in *Banchi pubblichi, banchi privati e monti di pietà nell' Europa pre-industriale*, 2 vols. (= Atti del convegno, Genoa 1991), *Atti della società ligure di storia patria*, new series 31 (105) (1991), pp. 435–59, esp. pp. 451–7; Hoshino, *Arte della lana*, pp. 179–82, for instance.

[34] W. E. Lunt and E. B. Graves eds., *Accounts Rendered by Papal Collectors in England 1317–1378*, Philadelphia 1968, pp. 534–5, 536; Holmes, *Good Parliament*, p. 126.

[35] Lloyd, *Wool Trade*, p. 255.

person of Petrus Ugolini, who also had a near relative, Tommaso Fortebracci in London.[36] Ugolini had his Roman *contor* in the present via Banco S Spirito and was soon doing business with Englishmen, especially English clerics connected with the curia.

In August 1377 for instance, one finds an English priest, a canon of Wells named Roger Dawe, making his will in the *librata* or lodging of the cardinal of Amiens, Jean de la Grange, in Anagni.[37] Present were Thomas Cullyng, Robert Sybbesdon and Thomas Fenton who were all legatees, and witnesses were John Charlton and Fenton, with the notary William Gavel of Taunton, all clerics, Fenton being a refugee from Langham's household.[38] A further legatee was John Upton a proctor in the curia, the advocate used by Colchester. Dawe left possessions to the hospital of S Thomas. On 10 September, in Rome in Ugolini's office, Upton dealt with the legacy left him by Dawe, using Ugolini and his partner to cash a letter of exchange from Dawe with Philipus Astarii, a very important Lucchese merchant in Avignon, with whom Dawe had been doing business there.[39] The notary William Gavel or Ganel may be William Gamull prosecuted in England from 1378 for proceeding with a case in the curia contrary to the law of England (probably *praemunire*) and eventually fined. In 1380 he described himself as living in Rome next to the English hospice of S Thomas.[40]

Ugolini again dealt in April 1381 with John Aspull, priest of Wyly, of Bangor diocese, probably another refugee from Langham's household,[41] and Richard May who held the parish church of Donnington, Berkshire, both notaries, at the end of a case in Rome involving the now-dead John Wigmore and John Freethorpe, rector of Didcot.[42] The letters of exchange involved had come from Vinceguerra and the witnesses in Rome included Adam de Fenrother, describing himself as canon of Beverley.[43]

In 1384 the proctor of cardinal Nicholas Misquinus or Carraciolo dealt with Ugolini to process a letter of exchange from John Warden, the farmer of his English prebend of Thame, when the letter was drawn

---

[36] A. Esch, 'Das Archiv eines lucchesischen Kaufmanns an der Kurie, 1376–87', *Zeitschrift für historische Forschung*, 2 (1975), pp. 129–71, esp. pp 141–7 for his career. For him see also Lunt, *Financial Relations*, pp. 727, 751.

[37] Esch, 'Das Archiv', p. 150, no 2.   [38] Harvey, 'Langham', p. 43.

[39] J. Favier, *Les finances pontificales*, p. 483; see also Oxford, Bodleian Library, MS Lat. Th. d. 10, f 1v, for mention of a case in Avignon in which he figured.

[40] Esch, 'Das Archiv', p. 153, no. 11; *CPR 1377–81*, pp. 303, 449, 498.

[41] Harvey, 'Langham', p. 43; see also Zutshi, *Original Letters*, no. 345, proctor May 1378.

[42] Esch, 'Das Archiv', pp. 154–5, no. 16; see also *m*. 109; *CCR 1392–6*, p. 519. For Aspull see also Esch, 'Das Archiv', pp. 160–1, no. 37.

[43] R. J. W. McDermid, *Beverley Minster Fasti*, Yorkshire Archaeological Society Record Series 149 (1993 for 1990), pp. 38, 73.

by Vinceguerra.[44] Ugolini also dealt with Angelus Christofori, another Luccan working from Lombard Street in the parish of St Mary, Woolchurch, London. In January 1383 William Street, the English king's butler, quitted Ugolini for an exchange for 500 florins bought in London from Angelus and dealt with in Rome via his named proctors. There still remained 2300 florins to pay. The transaction in Rome was done in the house of Anselm of Milan, one of the advocates employed by William Colchester in 1377.[45] We know from other sources that Cristofori's brother Johannes was a banker in Rome.[46]

So the England/Lucca/Rome connection was very strong during Urban VI's reign and must have been based principally on the monetary dealings between the Luccans, the curia and the Luccan bankers in London. But some wool was also traded via Vinceguerra.

Urban VI's turbulent election changed the situation in Rome yet again. He proved an intransigant reformer, intemperate in his criticism of the cardinals and foolish in his alienation of local magnates and cultivation of the *popolo*. By May 1378 the non-Italian cardinals had withdrawn to Anagni, the territory of Onoratus Caetani, whom Urban had deprived of his office as count of Campagna, and there, on 20 September, backed by Queen Joanna of Naples and her husband, they elected Cardinal Robert of Geneva as Pope Clement VII. By September 1378 most of Urban's cardinals had quarrelled with him and withdrawn, first to Anagni and by early 1379 to Avignon. The result was an anti-pope with a rival curia, with the powers of Europe lined up behind their chosen candidates and existing members of the papal curia forced to make choices, so that most Englishmen still in Avignon, including Southam,[47] soon left. But this also offered new career opportunities to nationals of countries which remained loyal to the Roman pope, among others the English.

After 1379 alongside the *cursores* there were clergy in much greater numbers who now became involved in the English group round S Thomas's hospice in Rome. Some of these have been mentioned; some were clearly very temporarily in Rome, but there begin to be some clerks more regularly in evidence, who often turn out to be proctors. The earliest of these, after Reginald Walpole, was Henry Buyton, canon of Hereford, who in 1382 witnessed a hospice

---

[44] Esch, 'Das Archiv', pp. 160–1, no. 37; see also Le Neve, *Lincoln*, p. 116 and for Warden: *CPR 1377–81*, pp. 582, 520, *1389–5*, p. 446.

[45] Harvey, *Solutions*, pp. 21–2.

[46] Favier, *Finances*, pp. 441, 512; Lunt, *Accounts Rendered*, p. 189; Esch, *Bonifaz IX*, p. 53.

[47] He was in England for the Blackfriars council, June 1382, D. Wilkins, *Concilia magnae Britanniae et Hiberniae*, 4 vols., London 1737, III, p. 164.

transaction.[48] He may have been in Rome negotiating his own business about his canonry.[49] He appeared acting with Richard Drayton, a proctor in the curia in Avignon from 1372 onwards, and then in Rome, where he finally died before Boniface IX succeeded in November 1389.[50] In the same business of 1382 where Buyton appeared, Master Richard May, notary, was a witness.[51] We have already met him dealing with Ugolini. He was of Exeter diocese and was certainly still in the curia in 1392.[52] He also acted with Master Richard Young,[53] who, as an auditor of the papal court in 1391, was executor for Richard Possewich, but had been in the curia from 1382.[54]

The schism did not ensure that the pope resided continually in Rome, in fact it embroiled the papacy more directly in Italian politics. Urban was determined to make himself master of the papal states but depended in Italy on the loyalty of Florence, Perugia, Bologna and Rome itself. Clement, his rival, hoped to exploit Naples, which was supported by the French. In order to ensure that he had Angevin support Clement promised part of the papal states to the duke of Anjou (17 April 1379), and thus Queen Joanna of Naples adopted Louis of Anjou as her heir in June 1380. The tragic result was that the kingdom of Naples became a battle ground where the schism was played out.[55] Urban began by making an at first uneasy peace with Florence, so that Florentines could begin to return to Rome, though their true return was not until 1388.[56] But he backed a rival candidate for Naples, Charles of Durazzo, grandson of Robert of Anjou, with a Hungarian army. By July 1381 Charles had defeated and captured Joanna and was in effect ruling Naples. Louis of Anjou was not prepared to accept this and in early 1382 set off to rescue Joanna, partly financed by Clement VII. He was extremely unsuccessful; almost the only result was the murder of Joanna. In September 1384 Louis died on campaign and his army disintegrated.

None of this helped Urban, however. In Rome itself the schism at first caused attacks on foreign members of the papal court, and the brothers of Cardinal Jacobus Orsini, backing the rival pope, preyed on

---

[48] *m.* 109.　　[49] *CPR 1374–7,* p. 440, 442; *1385–89,* p. 351; *CCR 1392–6,* p. 521.

[50] *CCR 1392–6,* p. 521, also pp. 524, 525; ASV, Coll. 465, fols. 21, 41v; D. Royce, ed., *Landboc sive registrum monasterii Beatae Mariae Virginis et Sancti Centelmi de Winchelcumba . . .* 2 vols., Exeter 1892, II, p. 48; BL Cotton Vitellius F II, f. 47v.

[51] *m.* 109.　　[52] *BRUO,* II, p. 1271 under Mey.　　[53] *CCR 1392–6,* p. 519.

[54] *m.* 123; *CCR 1392–6,* pp. 519, 543; *CPR 1388–92,* p. 429; *CPL* IV, p. 479.

[55] S. Fodale, *La politica napoletana di Urbano VI,* Rome 1973 for the whole story.

[56] Esch, 'Florentiner in Rom', pp. 479, 482; G. Holmes, 'Florence and the Great Schism', in G. Holmes, ed., *Art and Politics in Renaissance Italy. British Academy Lectures,* Oxford 1993, pp. 19–40, esp. p. 20, 24.

the city and blockaded Rome, making victualling difficult.[57] Even when these local problems were overcome, the localities continued to be dominated by magnates and mercenaries and Urban was unable to capitalise on Louis' failure. In fact he fell out with Charles of Durazzo. Charles was unwilling to reward Urban's nephew Francesco Prignano with a Neapolitan fief and Urban, when attempts at negotation failed, resolved to deal with Charles himself.

In June 1384 Urban arrived at Francesco's stronghold of Nocera. There six of the cardinals, disillusioned by the pope's capricious behaviour, plotted to place him under some kind of tutelage but, unfortunately for them, he got wind of the plot and on 11 January 1385 had them arrested instead.[58] Many details of the story filtered into England, especially into the writings of Thomas Walsingham of S Alban's,[59] because the arrested cardinals included Adam Easton, thus evidently causing the pope to suspect all the English *curiales*. According to Dietrich of Niem, a German curial who was present, all the arrested cardinals were tortured.[60] Walsingham asserted that after the arrest Urban ordered the curials and lay people from the town to come to the citadel and when they were inside, preached to them, blaming the plot on the king of Naples and his supporters and then solemnly excommunicated the cardinals, with all their supporters. The result was disturbances in Nocera, during which an English proctor called John Aleyn, messenger of a royal clerk, was killed and robbed. In consequence those following the curia quickly packed their bags and left, though they were robbed as they did so. Urban then summoned the remaining English and ordered them to stay or lose their benefices. But, according to Walsingham, very few did so, except for Henry Bowet (a camera auditor), the bishop of Bethlehem (William Bottlesham, OP) and about twelve others.[61] Gobelinus Persona, a camera clerk who fled and was in Benevento most of the time in the service of the papal camera, left a harrowing description of the suffering of members who escaped.[62] But the situation of those who stayed must have been equally frightening.

Urban, convinced that Charles had been privy to the plot, declared Naples interdicted. Charles beseiged him. The pope was able to escape to Benevento in July 1385 and from thence to Genoa on 23 September. In Genoa several of the plotting cardinals (not Easton) were executed.

[57] Niem, *De Scismate*, pp. 30–1.
[58] The plot is best discussed in Fodale, *La politica*, pp. 112–19; some further details about personel: L Tacchella, *Il pontificato di Urbano VI a Genova (1385–1386) e l'eccidio dei cardinali*, Genoa 1976.
[59] T. Walsingham, *Historia anglicana*, 2 vols., ed. H. T. Riley, RS 28 (1863), II, p. 122–4.
[60] Fodale, *La politica*, pp. 121–3 has lengthy quotations.
[61] Walsingham, *Historia anglicana*, II, p. 124.
[62] G. Persona, *Cosmidromius*, ed. M. Jansen, Münster in W 1900, p. 106.

About twelve Englishmen were certainly present in Genoa, including an English embassy including Nicholas Dagworth and John Bacon with (later) the bishop of Ossory, Richard Northalis, O. Carm., and Peter Stapleton.[63] The English *curiales* known to have stayed were Bowet, Bottlesham, Thomas Walkyngton and John Trefnant, both Rota auditors,[64] Henry Godbarn, a consistorial advocate,[65] Nicholas Gilby a scriptor of apostolic letters[66] and Richard Drayton, the proctor encountered already.[67] Urban went on to Lucca and re-entered Rome on 8 September 1388.[68]

As if this was not enough to deter English participation in papal affairs, the pope was also quarrelling with the king of England. The financial needs of the papacy during the schism both strengthened local resistance and increased papal demands.[69] By Urban's death (15 October 1389) Anglo-papal relations were very strained and the advent of Boniface IX (2 November 1389 to 1 October 1404) did not improve matters at first. By 3 May 1391 the situation was so difficult that the king ordered all English clerks in the curia to return home by 11 November.[70]

This did not leave the curia or Rome without any English residents, however, though some may have left from Nocera and some may have obeyed the order of 1391. After the return of the curia from Naples English artisans (as well as other Englishmen without specified occupations) continued to appear in the deeds of the Rome hospice. So we find a will in 1396,[71] where what appears to be the Italian widow of a Gascon leaves as her heir David son of John of Wales, *cernitor*, from Parione district, with William Conelle, English *sutor*, as one witness. Cloths were among the goods she left him, as well as her house. In 1400 he sold it to S Thomas's.[72] Wills of the 1390s show new clergy joining

---

[63] Tacchella, *Il pontificato*, pp. 112–13, 53, 53–4, 85–6; Perroy, *L'Angleterre et le grand schisme*, pp. 289, 292.

[64] Tacchella, *Il pontificato*, pp. 112, 85, 87; P.N.R. Zutshi, *Original Papal Letters in England, 1305–1415* (= Index Actorum Romanorum Pontificum ab Innocentio III ad Martinum V Electum 5), Vatican City 1990, no. 374 for Bottlesham's promotion to Llandaff, 16 October 1385.

[65] Tacchella, *Il pontificato*, pp. 112, 53, 85, 87. [66] Ibid., p. 89. [67] Ibid., p. 112.

[68] E. Delaruelle, E.-R. Labande and P. Ourliac, *L'église au temps du grand schisme et de la crise conciliaire, 1378–1449* (= A. Fliche and V. Martin, Histoire de l'église 14), 2 vols., Paris 1962, I, pp. 56–7; G. Persona, *Cosmidromius*, pp. 98–123.

[69] R. G. Davies, 'The episcopate and the political crisis in England 1386–88', *Speculum*, 51 (1976), pp. 659–93, esp. pp. 677–9 for the English angle, though he exaggerates Urban's bargaining position.

[70] Perroy, *L'Angleterre*, p. 320; T. Rymer, ed., *Foedera, Conventiones et Literae*, 3rd edn, 10 vols., The Hague 1739–45 (I quote the reprint of 1967, citing the earlier edition from its margins), VII, p. 698 (III/4, p. 68); *CCR 1389–92*, p. 341; Davies, 'Episcopate', pp. 677–8.

[71] *mm.* 138, 145. [72] *m.* 151.

the group connected with S Thomas's. Elena Clerk, in July 1390[73] left four silver collars to John, Bishop of Derry, probably John Dongan, who was certainly in Rome in June 1389 when he took part in the consecration as bishop of John Trefnant, Rota auditor.[74] Elena also left a legacy for masses for the soul of Robert son of Peter, the penitenciary of the pope, almost certainly Robert Tymelby who died at the curia in 1389.[75]

The will of Richard Possewich in July 1391 adds further names. Not only was Richard Young an executor but also John Teyr, treasurer of Dublin and a proctor.[76] The will was drawn in Possewich's own house in Rome, the notary was Peter Wye, a priest from the diocese of Wells and the witnesses who were not *cursores* were English. One of them was a person of some notoriety, Master Anthony de St Quintin, rector of Hornsey in the diocese of York, from a prominent gentry family in the East Riding, retainers of Archbishop Neville, at the centre of a notorious case concerning the prebend of S Martin in Beverley Minster, which had involved him battling in the curia against various royal candidates and against an attempt to extract from him the revenues of S Martin's whilst he had held it. By March 1390 St Quintin had lost in England to the royal candidate, Thomas de Feriby, but he was far from accepting this and fought on.[77] Possewich's will was proved not before the civil court in Rome but on 4 September before Henry Bowet, auditor of the papal camera.[78] Possewich was a *cortisanus* or member of the papal court rather than a citizen or layman and Bowet was still in the curia despite his experiences in Nocera.

The need to pursue the papal court as it travelled about is vividly described in a petition dated 25 October 1386 from Richard de Thoren, prebendary of Holme in York, probably involved in the famous York quarrel between Archbishop Neville and John Clifford,[79] explaining that when he heard that the curia had reached Naples and was travelling on

he put himself to sea with other *cortisani* from December and there near the port of Ostia he was captured by pirates and supporters of the duke of Anjou

---

[73] *m.* 119.

[74] E. B. Fryde, D. E. Greenway, S. Porter and I. Roy, *Handbook of British Chronology*, 3rd edn, London 1986, p. 346; E. Perroy (ed.), *The Diplomatic Correspondence of Richard II* Camden Society, 3rd series, 48 (1933), no. 97, note p. 211.

[75] ASV, Arm. 29/1, fol. 89v.   [76] *m.* 123; see below, p. 149.

[77] Perroy, *Correspondence*, notes to no. 75; McDermid, *Beverley Minster Fasti*, pp. 51–2; R. B. Dobson, 'Beverley in conflict. Alexander Neville and the minster clergy 1381–8', *Medieval Art and Architecture in the East Riding of Yorkshire*, ed. C. Wilson, *Proceedings of the British Archaeological Association Conference*, 9 (1983), pp. 149–64, esp. p. 158 and see below pp. 153, 176.

[78] *m.* 123 dorse.   [79] Cotton Vitellius F II, f. 106.

and other enemies of the church and led captive wretchedly by them and kept in captivity . . .

While he was away his enemies in York (Clifford and Nicholas Feriby were the chief) despoiled him, accusing him of non-residence. He begged, and was allowed, to have his case referred back to England (*ad partes*).

By the time Urban VI died he had announced a 'Jubilee' year for 1390. This should have meant that many pilgrims flocked to Rome to obtain the Jubilee indulgence. There is no way of discovering whether S Thomas's profited from this influx of visitors. Lunt found several hundred English licences to set out for Rome and certainly the licences to go over the sea were more numerous in 1390 than in other years.[80] But the effect on the English group in Rome remains unknown. The Jubilee may have persuaded Sir Robert Knolles, probably a benefactor of S Thomas's, to make the Jubilee pilgrimage.[81] and Andrew Alene a Welshman, with Nicholas Henrici a German, made the most of it to add to the privileges of their recently founded hospice for Germans,[82] but the absence of research information makes impossible any more detailed analysis. It could have been this Jubilee which persuaded John White, a London merchant, that there was enough traffic to support another hospice for English people and thus to found S Chrysogonus' hospice, but that is not clear.

It is unclear too how far the commerce of Rome, both secular and ecclesiastical, was affected by the schism or by 'the great bullion famine' of 1395 to 1415, when actual coin became very scarce. This last must have had its effect and probably goes far to explain the reputation for avarice of the curia of Boniface IX. Sheer shortage of cash may explain why the monastery of S Chrysogonus was willing to allow John White in 1396 to found his hospice, but similar shortage may also explain why he returned to London the next year to chase up debts.[83] Boniface's search for money explains also why he cheated the English chaplain of the new venture and another English priest out of the proceeds for saying masses for the soul of Statius Manerii when the latter died in Rome in 1398.[84] But it is not possible to discover what wider effects, if any, Boniface's policies had on English enterprises.

In Rome the simmering unrest which disguised itself as a struggle of *nobiles* against *populares* but was in reality more often a cover for the rivalries of the Orsini and Colonna families and their allies, came to a head in the late 1390s. Paulus Orsini tried to restore a member of the

---

[80] Lunt, *Financial Relations*, p. 462.   [81] Below, p. 60.   [82] Below, pp. 86–7.
[83] See pp. 77, 79.   [84] *CPL*, V, p. 214.

popolo to power in the commune government and the rival Colonnas called on Boniface IX's assistance. The net result was the fall of the commune, which was replaced by direct papal rule in 1398.[85] This did not wholly solve the problem of local tensions but for the moment an uneasy peace prevailed and despite the difficulties, economic and otherwise, Rome in the late 1390s may have seemed a favourable location for a new enterprise.

Certainly for some men the papal curia must have seemed a safer haven than the England of the last part of Richard II's reign. A significant number of English political dissidents found their way there, including Alexander Neville in early 1390 and Thomas Arundel in 1398.[86] Though these two did not stay long, their presence and the situation in England probably faced existing *curiales* with dilemmas of loyalty. We may note that in January 1399 William London, monk of Canterbury, was pardoned because he came to the curia without his prior's licence in the household of Arundel, whose chaplain he was,[87] and Richard II accused William Brut, a Benedictine who had been long in the curia negotiating Edward II's canonisation, of forging royal signet letters for Arundel.[88]

Furthermore the English in Rome had to come to terms with a change of regime at home in 1399. The first senior member of the curia with a close connection with the group running the hospice of S Thomas was probably John Fraunceys, a papal abbreviator. Richard Young was certainly executor to Richard Possewich but Possewich was himself a *curialis*. Fraunceys was rather different. He first appeared in Rome in 1388 as a proctor.[89] By 1390 he had become an abbreviator.[90] In 1399 he was doing sufficiently well to buy a palace,[91] with one of the witnesses Simon, son of John, *paternostrarius*, an Englishman.[92] In 1400 he was buying vineyards and land[93] and by 1401 was sufficiently involved with the rest of the English community to witness the gift of a house to S Thomas's.[94] One of the other witnesses was Simon, son of

---

[85] Esch, *Bonifaz IX*, chapter 4, pp. 209–76; 'La fine', pp. 235–77.
[86] For Neville see R. G. Davies, 'Alexander Neville, archbishop of York, 1374–1388,' *Yorkshire Archaeological Journal*, 47 (1975), pp. 87–101, esp. p. 100; G. S. Haslop, 'Two entries from the register of John de Shirburn, abbot of Selby, 1369–1408,' *Yorkshire Archaeological Journal*, 41 (1963–6), pp. 287–96, esp. pp. 288, 291 and Dobson, 'Beverley in conflict', passim.
[87] Arundel: *CPL*, V, p. 202; see J. Greatrex, *Biographical Register of the English Cathedral Priories of the Province of Canterbury, c. 1066–1540*, Oxford 1997, p. 225 (under William London II) and J. B. Sheppard ed. *Literae Cantuarienses*, 3 vols., RS 85 (1887–89), no. 969.
[88] A. L. Brown, 'The Latin letters in MS All Souls 182,' *EHR*, 87 (1972), pp. 565–73, esp. p. 571.
[89] *CCR 1392–96*, p. 525; Zutshi, *Original Papal Letters*, no. 394, 397, 414, 431, pp. 199, 199–200, 210, 218.
[90] *CCR 1389–92*, p. 573.   [91] *m. 151.*   [92] See *m. 156.*
[93] *m. 153.*   [94] *m. 156.*

John, *paternostrarius*. The investment in Roman property and the involvement with the hospice suggest an intention to stay in Rome, which is also plausible in view of Fraunceys' known support from Richard II and hostility to him later from important supporters of Henry IV.[95]

From 1404, when Boniface IX died, the curia again faced disruption and this time so did the city. After 1406 the curia was never stable for long and the city was sucked into the politics of the schism. English people trying to make a living either in the curia or in the city were inevitably involved in these changes and upheavals. Only in 1420 did the curia come to rest again in Rome and by then many of the people with whom these pages are concerned had either died or left.

The disruption of Rome arose partly because Boniface IX had backed Ladislas of Durazzo, Charles' son, against the Angevin claim to Naples (supported by Clement VII).[96] When Boniface IX died there was at once trouble in the city and the Colonnas turned to Ladislas, who was actually on his way to Rome during the conclave. A few days after Innocent VII had become pope, on 21 October 1404, Ladislas entered Rome; in effect he was in charge of the Campidoglio area.[97] When, on 6 August 1405, the pope's nephew, Ludovico Migliorati, had some leaders of the popular movement murdered, there were serious city riots, led by the Colonnas. Innocent fled and was not in Rome between late 1405 and March 1406. In his absence the Colonnas controlled Rome. There are vivid contemporary descriptions of how courtiers also escaped and fled outside the city.[98] Innocent therefore found himself having to deal with both Ladislas and the unruly nobility in a three-cornered negotiation, and after many vicissitudes he returned to Rome and made peace with the king.

However, Innocent died in November 1406. His successor Gregory XII was not committed to Ladislas and the latter very much feared that the pope would make peace in the Schism with his French enemies. Any solution to the schism was likely to mean that Ladislas lost Naples. Hence he was very hostile to attempts at compromise. Gregory took the papal throne committed to working for re-union of the church even including resignation, which he had sworn before his election. He was thus bound to find himself at odds with Ladislas.

[95] See p. 175. [96] Esch, *Bonifaz IX*, pp. 40–2.
[97] A. Cutolo, *Re Ladislao d'Angio-Durazzo*, 2 vols., Milan 1936–44, vol. I for the whole story; with now R. Ninci, 'Ladislao e la conquista di Roma del 1408: ragioni e contraddizioni della diplomazia fiorentina', *Archivio della società romana di storia patria*, 111 (1988), pp. 161–224.
[98] L. Bruni, *Leonardi Bruni Arretini epistolarum libri VIII*, ed. L. Mehus, 2 vols., Florence 1741, I, pp 8–11.

Behind the scenes Ladislas and the Colonnas were trying to persuade the pope to favour their policies and when a Colonna army entered the city in an attempt to continue aristocratic feuding, Gregory finally fled, ostensibly to pursue his oath to end the schism. He left the city on 9 August 1407 to meet the rival pope. Ladislas decided to try to control the situation and marched on Rome, attempting a coup d'état relying on the Colonnas. Immediately this was foiled by their rivals the Orsini, but in September Ladislas was at the gates. He spent the next few months capturing territory in the vicinity and by March 1408 the Orsini had deserted Gregory and began negotiations with Ladislas' enemies, the French. Rumour circulated that Gregory was colluding with the anti-pope, to avoid ending the schism by resignation. On 22 April 1408 Ladislas took Rome and came to an agreement with the Orsini. He presented himself as anti-French, calling on Gregory not to abdicate. Contemporaries were sure that this situation, the background to the council of Pisa which was called in 1408 to end the schism, was the result of secret collaboration between the rivals.

Many English *curiales*, of course, followed the pope as he trekked round Italy in increasingly unconvincing attempts to meet for discussions with his rival. But not all the English were *curiales* and some business still had to be done in Rome.[99] Furthermore, the tortuous negotiations disillusioned some former supporters of Gregory, who left to join the council of Pisa, which began to meet early in 1409.[100]

The history of Rome is under-researched for this period and sources are scarce. To discover what happened to the English there are hospice deeds and the letters of William Swan, an English proctor, which can be supplemented by contemporary Roman chronicles. In 1406 the hospice of S Thomas compiled a rental.[101] The *custos* was John Thomasson alias Palmer. It may have been the unstable situation which left him in office for many years after 1406[102] but the *camerarius* in 1406 and 1407 was William Lovell,[103] followed for 1408 by Philip Newton, both clerks;[104] Newton was *camerarius* again in 1415[105] and 1418.[106] The English holders of houses from the hospice in 1406 were Robert Donne, Master John Estcourt, who held the house called Lo Confesse, John Haget, holding the house 'of the Lion', Richard Goldsmith, Stefania, widow of Richard son of Roger, and the son-in law of Perrinus Baker, partner of

---

[99] Niem, *Nemus unionis*, pp. 389–94, esp. p. 394 for Niem's fears in June 1408.

[100] For the Italian background here A. Landi, *Il papa deposto (Pisa 1409). L'idea conciliare nel grande scisma*, Turin 1985, esp. pp. 68–112.

[101] *m.* 172.   [102] *Venerabile*, p. 265.

[103] *m.* 175; 179 he is said to be absent, February 1407.

[104] *m.* 183.   [105] *m.* 120.   [106] *m.* 191.

John White in founding the second hospice. Walter Taylor's heir, Jacobus de Ferraria, still held his house.

Thomasson first appears in the deeds in 1406; he could have been a layman, but at this period the status *laicus* is usually mentioned specifically. Estcourt, a cleric, had been in Rome since at least 1403[107] when he witnessed Taylor's will, as a tenant of Taylor's house in Parione. In 1405, called Bachelor of Laws, he was a witness when S Thomas's sought arbitration from Hermann Dwerg concerning the rights of the monastery of S Biagio over Taylour's house.[108] He was to have a career in the curia later, acting for the archbishop of Canterbury, Henry Chichele.[109] In 1407 Swan did business with him before leaving Rome to follow the pope, to ensure that various goods of someone who had already left were safe.[110] Estcourt himself then also followed the curia and was in Lucca in March 1408.[111] John Haget became a papal abbreviator in 1406.[112] He too was already in Rome in 1403, when he rented bedding from Walter Taylor.[113] He was *camerarius* of S Thomas's in 1404 and 1405.[114] In 1406 he rented bedding from the hospice.[115] Swan's letters show him as executor of a will.[116] In 1408 he also was thought to be with the curia.[117] Donne seems to have been a layman.[118]

The hospice deeds do not exhaust the list of Englishmen in Rome, of course, and in fact do not give an accurate picture of the relative importance of the members of the English group. The most senior *curialis* may have been John Fraunceys, an abbreviator, but the most notable Englishman was probably Robert Hallum, soon to be a famous bishop of Salisbury, certainly living in the city in 1406. He was renting bedding and household utensils from S Thomas's for his house in Parione[119] when in May he was unsuccessfully promoted to be archbishop of York.[120] He had come seeking promotion after a career in the court of Canterbury and was strongly supported by archbishop Arundel.[121] Swan reported to a client some of Hallum's activities, describing visits to Oda of Colonna, the future Martin V. In September 1406 Hallum was said to have spoken to the pope about the situation of one of Swan's clients.[122] His promotion did not survive the politics of

---

[107] *m.* 163.   [108] *m.* 171.   [109] *m.* 163.
[110] Arch. Seld. B 23, ff. 38v, 129r/v.   [111] Arch. Seld. B 23, f 49v.
[112] *BRUO*, II, 848.   [113] *m.* 163.   [114] *mm.* 156, 171.   [115] *m.* 172.
[116] Arch. Seld. B 23, f. 37v.   [117] Arch. Seld. B 23, f. 23.
[118] *m.* 171 for him as a witness.   [119] *m.* 172.   [120] Arch. Seld. B 23, ff. 125v; 25r/v.
[121] Harvey, *Solutions*, p. 162.
[122] Arch. Seld. B 23, ff. 28v–29. The client was Macclesfield, see note 127 below.

the curia and of the English court.[123] King Henry or Henry Bowet persuaded the pope, against the wishes of many cardinals (Dietrich of Niem and others said that money passed)[124] into promoting Bowet and Hallum was demoted to the see of Salisbury. By 1 December 1406 at the latest he was back in England; that day his temporalities were restored for Salisbury.[125] Niem, who was exceedingly well placed to know, thought this betrayal of the pope's promise of York to Hallum was produced by the desperate need of the curia for money in the current political situation.[126] Much of Hallum's known activity in Rome looks like lobbying.

John Fytton whom Swan also knew in Rome in 1406, was certainly in Hallum's group and may already have been a member of his household as he certainly was later.[127] He can be seen in Rome before the curia left, also accompanying Swan to talk to cardinals Colonna and Jordanus Orsini.[128] Saying that he had visited both, Swan noted that the Orsini: 'are without doubt greater in the curia these days' (*Isti infallabiliores satis maiores in curia hiis diebus*).[129] Swan also had many dealings at this time with his most faithful friend (*amicus fidelissimus*),[130] Master Thomas Hendeman, who was in the circle of Hallum and Fitton,[131] living in Colonna region, near S Maria sopra Minerva.[132] He was probably in Rome at this point to obtain a papal provision;[133] by 1407 he had obtained a prebend of Exeter and papal reservation of a rectory,[134] but by August he too had left Rome.[135] Thus what might have become a new English group centred on Hallum broke up under strain from English politics and the schism.

There is evidence about the commercial relations between England and Rome in the period after 1404, some from Swan's letter book. When the English members of the curia wanted to provide a group in London to investigate Robert Newton, the English proctor of

---

[123] Arch. Seld. B 23, ff. 25r/v; R. G. Davies, 'After the execution of Archbishop Scrope. Henry IV, the papacy and the English episcopate 1405–8, *BJRL*, 59 (1976–7), pp. 40–74, esp. pp. 52, 59–63, 69; Niem, *De scismate*, p. 245.

[124] J. S. Davies, ed., *An English Chronicle of the Reigns of Richard II, Henry IV, Henry V and Henry VI*, Camden Society, original series, 64 (1856), p. 34.

[125] R. Hallum, *The Register of Robert Hallum, Bishop of Salisbury 1407–1417*, ed. J. M. Horn, CYS, 72 (1982), pp. x–xi for details.

[126] *De scismate*, p. 245.

[127] D. K. Maxfield, 'A fifteenth-century lawsuit: The case of St Anthony's Hospital', *JEH*, 44 (1993), pp. 199–223, esp. p. 201; Harvey, *Solutions*, p. 163.

[128] Arch. Seld. B 23, ff. 28v–29; 30v–31. See also Maxfield, 'Lawsuit', esp. pp. 202 and 223 for the dating of some of this material.

[129] Arch. Seld. B 23, ff. 30v–31.   [130] Arch. Seld. B 23, f. 27r/v.

[131] Arch. Seld. B 23, ff. 27r/v, 28–29.   [132] Arch. Seld. B 23, f. 125.

[133] *BRUO*, II, pp. 907–8.   [134] Provision: Arch. Seld. B 23, f. 27r/v.

[135] Arch. Seld. B 23, f. 39v.

S Thomas's, they called on William Waldern a leading London mercer and Thomas Knolles, a grocer.[136] Swan's letter-book reveals interrelationships between the London business world and the curia. John Launce, the parish priest of Southfleet, was litigating in the curia in 1405–6 about his prebend of Penffoes in St David's and went to Rome in person.[137] An unknown correspondent wrote to him or to Swan there, probably in 1407, saying that the writer had sent a letter of exchange via the Alberti merchants for the prebend but that Launce's money (probably for the crossing) had gone to Middelburgh (Myldelburgh) and returned again. However, if he came that way Henry Frowick, attorney of William Waldern and another attorney of John Tynbelden, grocer of London, would provide him with his expenses.[138] Launce did return via Bruges. Waldern will be met again and Frowick was no doubt a member of an extremely prolific London merchant family.[139]

The difficulties which the bullion shortage of these years caused Englishmen in Rome are also revealed here. Probably some time in 1406 John Launce told Swan that Robert Newton had not the money to pay Swan's debts in England, adding 'money in England is dearer now'.[140] Swan's situation was worsened by a travelling curia, but we find desperate letters from him complaining that his brother had sent no money for a year.[141] Not surprisingly therefore the English group thought Robert Newton had cheated them of collections in England for S Thomas's.[142]

Swan did business for many of the merchant class; as a proctor he was not solely engaged on clerical business, though many of his clients were clerics. Clergy of course had merchant relatives. Robert Chichele, brother of Henry, was a grocer and an alderman from 1402–26; William Chichele, another grocer was alderman from 1407–20.[143] Swan did business for such people, for instance for Dame Margery Barentine, wife of Drew Barentine, an extremely wealthy goldsmith and alderman, probably in 1408. She wanted a plenary indulgence at the hour of death.[144] She was the widow of Sir Nicholas Twyford, who died about 1391, whose relative John Twyford, was regarded as a founder of the hospice of S Thomas.

The whole situation in Rome changed for the worse when Gregory XII left on 9 August 1407, followed by the virtual absence of the papacy

---

[136] Below, p. 62.   [137] Le Neve, *Welsh*, p. 72 for the prebend.
[138] Arch. Seld. B 23, f. 35.
[139] S. Thrupp, *The Merchant Class of Medieval London*, London 1948, pp. 342–4.
[140] Arch. Seld. B 23, f. 51v: *pecunie in Anglia sunt modo cariores.*   [141] Arch. Seld. B 23, f. 49.
[142] See p. 62.   [143] Thrupp, *Merchant Class*, pp. 330–1.   [144] Arch. Seld. B 23, f. 23.

for some years.[145] The leading English members of the curia gradually followed, as we have seen. The blockade and then occupation of Rome by the Neapolitans produced hardship. In March 1408 there was talk in Roman sources of 'great hunger, lack of bread'.[146] The council of Pisa in 1409 which deposed the two popes and elected a third split the church even further. There were now three popes, each with his faction. The recognition of Ladislas' rival Louis of Anjou by the council simply produced a very harsh regime in Rome itself and this worsened as Baldassare Cossa, on behalf of the council, set out with Louis to retake the city.[147] Ladislas, who had returned to Naples, advanced to meet him and the entry of Louis, Cossa and the Orsini into the city, to occupy the Vatican area on 1 October 1409, was followed by Ladislas' sack of the Borgo. In Rome the citizens were terrorised by both parties. Street-fighting ensued, with the Colonna and Orsini factions shouting 'Viva the church and the Colonnas' or 'Viva the church and the Orsini.' Food was short, houses were looted and floods did not help, but by 15 February 1410 Paulus Orsini had driven out the Neapolitans. Although Louis of Anjou had no success against Ladislas in Naples, in Rome itself the Colonna were defeated. Under Cossa, who from May 1410 was Pope John XXIII, they submitted to the pope, allowing Louis to enter the city in triumph on 20 September 1410.

The rest is a tale of the treachery of Paulus Orsini and the uselessness as a general of Louis, who could not defeat Ladislas. In the complicated Italian politics of the period John XXIII was driven to make peace with Ladislas in June 1412, on condition that Ladislas ceased to support Gregory XII and John XXIII did not allow the Emperor Sigismund to enter Rome. Sigismund was pressurising the pope to hold another council to put a definitive end to the schism. In June 1413 Ladislas turned on the pope and John was forced to call for Sigismund's help. It could only be obtained by agreeing to a general council, which John summoned on 9 December 1413 to meet next year. Ladislas set out for Rome, saying that he would 'protect' it while the pope was absent. He entered on 6/7 June 1413, with the exit roads packed by crowds of fleeing refugees and proceeded to sack and burn. Ladislas' own departure for Naples in July still left the city occupied and all who had followed the pope were threatened with loss of property. He returned in March 1414 and further shortages were reported.[148] When he finally

---

[145] M. Harvey, 'England and the Council of Pisa: some new information', *Annuarium Historiae Conciliorum*, 2 (1970), pp. 263–83.

[146] Ninci, 'Ladislao', p. 196, note 121; Schiavo, *Il diario romano*, p. 25; Prodi, *Il papa deposto*, p. 97.

[147] Cutolo, *Re Ladislao*, I, pp. 315–75, for the next two paragraphs.

[148] Schiavo, *Il diario*, p. 87

died returning to Naples in August 1414 the pope would have wanted to re-enter Rome but was forced to stay for the council at Constance. The wretched Romans were not yet free of sufferings, because local feuds then took over,[149] but by 19 October 1414, Cardinal Antonius Correr was able to enter the city as the official papal legate.[150]

The Roman diarist Antonio di Pietro Schiavo recounted in vivid detail the destruction and hardship of these years. On 18 October 1409, he was harvesting his vines when armed men arrived and he fled.[151] In December the destruction round S Peter's was terrible.[152] On 31 December people in the Arenula and Parione areas rose in revolt.[153] Of the sack of 1413 he says that in June many members of the papal court were robbed as they fled.[154] On 9 September 1414 he recorded fighting in the Ghetto area (*platea Judeorum* where S Thomas's owned property). Even when the papal government was officially restored its weakness was such that on 28 November 1414 Paulus Orsini entered the city and behaved like a brigand.[155]

The destruction must have been severe. The deeds of S Angelo in Pescharia for 1408 show the church selling properties to pay taxes because of the wars (*propter guerras*).[156] Properties belonging to S Peter's remained ruinous in 1416, half its 300 houses were in ruins, with one list of twenty-one houses said to be 'all in ruins' (*omnes sunt positi ad ruynam*).[157] In 1406 one of the houses belonging to S Thomas's, in the Borgo S Pietro, near the Vatican, was already described as: 'destroyed by wars and men at arms' (*destructa est per guerras et gentes armorum*), probably because of particularly fierce fighting in the Borgo and S Angelo areas during the revolt of 1405.[158] By 16 September 1410, the vineyards left by John White for S Chrysogonus' hospice, outside the Porta Populi, were deemed unworkable because of 'shortages and wars'.[159] Almost certainly a reference to houses in S. Angelo badly in need of repair in June 1418 referred to property damaged in war.[160]

Both hospices must have lost money, but we do not know how much. In 1449 one of S Edmund's vineyards was still unproductive.[161] Those who followed the curia could not themselves pay their bills in Rome. A letter written in Rimini, presumably from Swan who went there with Gregory XII, refers to Henry Faber, presumably also with the pope (he is mentioned in the 1406 as renting a S Thomas's house

---

[149] Ibid., p. 92.   [150] Ibid., p. 95.   [151] Ibid., p. 47.   [152] Ibid., p. 51.
[153] Ibid., p. 54.   [154] Ibid., p. 79.   [155] Ibid., p. 102.
[156] Vatican Library, Archivio S Angelo, 1/24 passim.
[157] Vatican Library, Archivio Capitolare di S Pietro, Censuali, 4, f. 8v; Hubert, 'Economie de la proprieté immobilière', p. 225.
[158] Cutolo, *Re Ladislao*, p. 296.   [159] *m.* 185, see below, p. 79.
[160] See below, p. 72; *m.* 191.   [161] *Venerabile*, p. 88.

for 8 ducats),[162] asking S Thomas's for patience; Faber's wife could not pay the rent since he had not been paid by the pope.[163]

Swan's letters also give a few glimpses of the vicissitudes of the English community, to add to the very little otherwise known. Swan had to try to keep in touch with Rome, since he both left behind property and had rented a house. One of his correspondents was John Lincoln or Blyton, a clerk living in S Thomas's in 1407, who acted as Swan's Roman agent.[164] Swan fell ill at Viterbo and was nursed to health by Alice Tudor, whose proctor he was.[165] In late August 1407 Alice reached Rome. She had been travelling with three friends. Of these, one was sick in Venice, probably dying. Of the others, one died the week he reached Rome and was buried in the week of 18 September. The survivor offered money to cover the rest of Alice's expenses. Alice did manage to arrange some religious services for herself, but S Thomas's was not well placed to help her financially; it had no money 'while the curia is vacant' (*vacante curia*).[166] Swan helped her a little but complained of the expense to himself of following the curia.[167] The whole correspondence shows the hazards of travel and the dependence of the English on the presence of the curia.

Swan was also worried about his own house, probably rented from the hospice of S Thomas.[168] He had left a schedule with the *custos*, making it plain that he had paid 34 ducats. He thought that whilst he was away a friend could live in it until the rental period expired and he wanted the recipient of his letter to consult about future payments. Meanwhile he told the bearer of the letter (written from Viterbo, 13 August 1407) 'that he could place his kirtle at your table' (*quod poneret curtellam ad tabulam vestram*) and, since Swan had left clothes and papers with the *custos* of S Thomas's, asking the recipient to have a care, 'lest they are destroyed' (*ne destruantur*).

The bundle was indeed in the care of Lincoln and Thomasson, who told him, with their plea for money for Alice Tudor, that a friar preacher had come asking for papers belonging to John Launce. They had therefore opened it and found things about Launce but not what the friar wanted, so they put them safely away again.[169] Clearly Swan was in fairly regular contact with Rome; messengers came and went.[170]

[162] *m*. 172.

[163] Arch. Seld. B 23, f. 46v. See also Schuchard, *Die Deutschen*, p. 105; *RG* I, no. 1715.

[164] *m*. 179.

[165] Harvey, 'England and the Council of Pisa', p. 269; Arch. Seld. B 23, ff. 33v–34.

[166] Arch. Seld. B 23, ff. 34, 39, 39v.   [167] Arch. Seld. B 23, ff. 48v–49.

[168] Arch. Seld. B 23, f. 39v.   [169] Arch. Seld. B 23, f. 41.

[170] Arch. Seld. B 23, f. 49v, to John Ingram, priest in the English hospital in Rome, 6 March 1408, from Lucca.

Alas, all was not safe. By January 1410, when the Council of Pisa was over, Swan was still with Gregory XII. By then his proctor in Rome was Master Robert Ely who had been with Gregory's curia at Lucca in 1408[171] but must by then have left him. Swan was also thinking of giving up but he contemplated returning to England, so asked Ely to send his books to Florence and, if possible, sell the rest of his goods, including bedding, and entrust the proceeds to Master John Bremor, at this time a proctor.[172] Swan thought that his most useful book, his register of letters, might be with William Godfader who might be in Rome.[173] By late 1410 an agent of Swan's in Bologna was writing to London where Swan briefly was, acknowledging receipt of books and some clothes.[174] But some of Swan's possessions stayed in Rome; he asked about them when he had finally gone to the Council of Constance, between 1416 and 1418.[175] This time Philip Newton as *camerarius* told him on 24 February that he had informed John (Thomasson) the *custos*, 'in the presence of John Irlond your servant and others' about Swan's books and possessions and according to the list Swan had sent him:

there do not remain according to your estimate more than six ducats worth. In the time of king Ladislas in the disturbances they went to the home of the devil in Naples. Master Roger Basset has nothing left except for one leather sack and likewise Master John Bremor has very little and it is the same with others of our English gentlemen. John the *custos* says that none of your books are left. I don't know; I was not a *curtisanus* then and anyway on the day that there were disturbances I left the city with my lord Master Thomas Polton for Viterbo and stayed there six days and returned to Rome again. I had great troubles in my return . . . The English, praise to the most high, came safe, well, and secure to the city and were well received. Few remained after the first night, however, but went off to their hospices.

This looks like a reference to 1413. We can trace the careers of all those mentioned. Newton himself was a notary, for example for the document concerning execution in England of John White's will in 1405.[176] A cleric of S David's, who did not accompany the curia,[177] he was *camerarius* of the hospice in June 1408.[178] John Launce made him his proctor when he left Rome.[179] He was camerarius again in 1415 and

---

171 Arch. Seld. B 23, f. 49v.   172 See p. 53.
173 E. F. Jacob, 'To and from the court of Rome in the early fifteenth century', in Jacob, *Essays in Later Medieval History*, Manchester 1968, pp. 58–78, esp. pp 62–3, 73–4; Arch. Seld. B 23, f. 60r/v.
174 Arch. Seld. B 23, f. 124r/v.
175 Arch. Seld. B 23, f. 124v; Jacob, 'To and from', pp. 63–4.
176 London, Guildhall, Commissary Court of London, Register of Wills 9171/2, f. 65v.
177 Arch. Seld. B 23, f. 48r/v.   178 *m.* 183.   179 Arch. Seld. B 23, f. 40r/v.

1418 but after that he vanished.[180] Bremor, a proctor in the curia since at least 1397, had become secretary to Pope John XXIII by 1411 and must have gone to the council of Constance.[181] Basset was another friend of Hallum's, perhaps in Rome since 1406 and had been at the Council of Pisa representing Archbishop Arundel.[182] From 1411 he was in John XXIII's curia as a protonotary.[183] Polton had been resident in the curia from time to time from 1394 and by 1401 was an abbreviator.[184] Thereafter he was at intervals with the curia again, including attendance at the Council of Pisa. In 1414 he was appointed royal proctor in the curia, but then would have been largely at the Council of Constance until his return to Rome in 1420.

In summing up the experience of Rome and travel to it in the period one might well conclude that it was dangerous and unhealthy. References to death are frequent in English letters both among those following the curia and otherwise. Swan nearly died in 1407 on his way to Sienna in the wake of the pope. Writing to Launce in London he noted that there had been an outbreak of *fluxus sanguinis* (?dysentery) and among others Master Henry Hamerton was dead.[185] Two of Alice Tudor's male companions died on the way to Rome that year.[186] It was common to make one's will before setting out; as White explained in 1397 'because of the long journey and the dangers of the roads and cases of death' it could be a long time before return.[187] Some people simply vanished.[188] The dangers were very real. Colchester described losses from theft or the need to ransom himself or his goods and he did not dare enter the port of Rome in 1379 but disembarked at Ostia.[189] He was just one of a long line of suffering travellers.

Yet, of course, people continued to come and to stay. It is notable, however, that after 1404 the group round the English hospices became more and more clerical. William, son of Richard, *paternostrarius*, died in about 1407.[190] He was the only layman left from the founders of S Thomas's. Lay numbers thinned notably in the early fifteenth century; John Thomasson *custos* of S Thomas's from 1406 probably to 1425, may have been a layman, but few others are in evidence. Perrinus Baker vanished after 1410.[191] The main lay additions to the group were

---

[180] *mm.* 120, 189, 191.   [181] *BRUC*, pp. 90–1; *CPL*, VI, p. 333.
[182] Harvey, *Solutions*, p. 163.   [183] *CPL*, VI, pp. 302, 309, 329, 332, 335, 339.
[184] M. Harvey, *England, Rome and the Papacy, 1417–1464. The Study of a Relationship*, Manchester 1993, pp. 10–12, and below, p. 149.
[185] Arch. Seld. B 23, ff. 33v–34.   [186] Above, p. 51.
[187] *m.* 142: *ex longe itinere et viarum discriminibus et casibus mortis.*
[188] See p. 15.   [189] See p. 34.   [190] *m.* 179.   [191] *m.* 186.

John Gillyot, in S Chrysogonus' from 1406 to 1408,[192] and John Cross, last heard of in 1418.[193]

The inevitable conclusion is that Rome ceased to be an attractive place for English merchants in this period and that as the older generation died or went home few took their place. It is notable how very few of the houses owned by S Thomas's in the 1435 rental were held by English lay people not connected to the curia.[194] Perhaps the only ones left were John Barber and his wife Catherine, John Taylor, and Maria Powlet. Florentine merchants were by far the most important laymen in the dealings between England and Rome by then and even the number of English clerics was far less than it had been in the 1390s.

[192] See p. 83.
[193] Nagl, *Anima in Rom*, nos. 217, 233, 299; *mm.* 156, 171, 191, 197 and see below p. 99.
[194] *m.* 197.

Chapter 3

S THOMAS'S HOSPICE

At the centre of English activity in Rome in the late fourteenth and fifteenth centuries was the hospital of the Holy Trinity and S Thomas the Martyr, which survived the Reformation to become the present English College. Its origins are obscure, not helped by the loss of some of the basic information about its founders which would help us to uncover their social level. Even their aims are not as clear as they might seem.

In 1362 John Shepherd sold to the English group or guild (*universitas Anglorum*) in Rome the house which was to be the basis of the hospice of S Thomas. William Chandler who received the house did so

on behalf and in the name of the community and guild of English of the city and of the poor, sick, destitute and wretched persons coming from England in the city.[1]

Neither the name of the guild nor of the new hospital is certain. The earliest names are simply descriptive: for example in July 1363 Rosa Casarola left property 'to the poor of the hospital of the English newly built in the region of Arenula'.[2] In 1368 testators were leaving bequests 'to the society of the hospital of the English'.[3] But by 1371 it was called 'the society of the fraternity of the English of the hospital of the most holy Trinity of the city' (*societas fraternitatis Anglicorum ospitalis sanctissime Trinitatis de urbe*),[4] though the gift was made in honour of Our Lady, the Trinity and blessed Thomas of Canterbury, the martyr, when the givers Robert of Pigna and William the *paternostrarius* made it plain that the money used to purchase the property had come from the goods of

---

[1] m. 36; *Venerabile*, p. 38: *vice et nomine communitatis et universitatis anglicorum urbis et in urbe concurrentium pauperum infirmorum egenorum et miserabilium personarum de Anglia.*
[2] S Angelo in Pescharia, I/1 f 141r/v: *pauperibus hospitalis Anglicorum noviter edificati de regione Arenula.*
[3] m. 53: *societati ospitalis Anglicorum.*   [4] m. 60.

the society. In 1373 the officials were said to act on behalf 'of the society of the fraternity of the English of the hospital of S Thomas' (*societatis fraternitatis Anglicorum hospitalis Sancti Thomaxii*).[5] The name was not always used; in 1374 the group was referred to still as 'the society of the guild of Englishmen living in the city' (*societas universitatis et hominum Anglicorum existentium in urbe*).[6] But by then its officials had the alternate name of officials of 'the community and guild of poor English and wretched pilgrims coming from England of the house of the Holy Trinity and S Thomas the Martyr in the city next the church of SS Maria and Caterina' (*communitatis et universitatis pauperum Anglicorum et miserablium peregrinorum de Anglia venentium, domus sancte Trinitatis Sancti Thome Martiris in urbe iuxta ecclesiam Sanctae Marie et Caterine*).[7] The scribe copied *Sancte Trinitatis* as *Sancte Eternitatis* presumably because he was unfamiliar with it. This is probably why its location was also given as near the nearest known church. In 1375 it was still sometimes called the hospital of the Holy Trinity.[8]

The earliest name for the fraternity and perhaps of the hospital it built was therefore probably 'of the Holy Trinity'. By 1373, however, the name of S Thomas Becket had also become attached to the foundation and by 1377 his December feast was celebrated 'every year with honour' by the English in Rome.[9] The celebration may also have been held in Avignon[10] but the adoption in Rome first of the Trinity and then of S Thomas may reflect that some of those who fostered the hospital were mercers. The early mercers' guild in York was known as the guild of Our Lady and its hospital was of the Holy Trinity.[11] Some of the early members in Rome came from York, Chandler for instance, and they may have been trying to establish another organisation just like theirs in England, which dates to at least 1356. S Thomas Becket, however, whose father was a mercer, was patron of S Thomas of Acon, where the mercers of London met from at least 1390 and perhaps much earlier. In course of time Thomas became the most usual patron for 'Adventurers', English merchants of whatever kind who travelled abroad, especially in the Low Countries.[12] If, as I suspect, the London connection soon became very important to the Roman guild, this may explain the added dedication, specifically its addition in the 1370s. A

---

[5] *m.* 67.　　[6] *m.* 72.　　[7] *m.* 77.　　[8] *m.* 83; and see discussion *Venerabile*, p. 49.

[9] London, Westminster Abbey, Muniments, 9256B, William Colchester, in Rome in 1377 gives 2 florins: *procuratoribus sancti Thome martiris pro solemnitate eius sancti cuius festum colitur ab Anglicis ibidem omni anno honorifice.*

[10] M. Harvey, 'Preaching in the Curia: some sermons by Thomas Brinton', *AHP*, 33 (1995), pp. 299–301, esp. p. 300.

[11] M. Sellers, *The York Mercers and Merchant Venturers, 1356–1917*, SS 129 (1918), pp. x–xi, 26.

[12] E. M. Carus Wilson, *The Medieval Merchant Venturers*, 2nd edn, Oxford 1967, p. 150.

merchant connection with Avignon could explain the celebration of Becket's feast there also.

Whatever its official name the hospice was founded and administered by the confraternity of the English living in Rome, which constituted the corporate body which acted for it and received its revenues. 'English' included Scots, Welsh and Irish and the institution received some help from Italians, though it is not clear if they were members of the confraternity.[13] We do not know how long the fraternity had been in existence. In a deed of 1333 Henry the Englishman, servant of the monastery of S Silvestro *in capite* sold a *stirps* in Pigna region to Richard the Englishman of Arenula, *cernitor*.[14] Among the witnesses, all English, was Simon 'agent of the court of the English of the city' (*mandatarius curie Anglorum urbis*), which suggests that there was already a corporate body. In foreign parts alien groups often appointed a spokesman to act as their intermediary with authority; the English in Rome may have done so too.[15] In a list of the books about the hospital which the English College used to have was one dated 1358 (hence before Shepherd's purchase): 'Book of the foundation of the hospital or register of brethren and sisters' (*Liber fundationis hospitalis sive registrum confratrum et consororum*).[16] This could be a confraternity list, but assuming that someone had to collect for the first house it may also be the earliest subscription list.

The foundation was evidently conceived as a hospice for poor people and pilgrims. It is worth stressing that both are stated in the earliest deeds, which suggests both self-help for those already in Rome and a centre for pilgrims. That was in fact how the hospital functioned. Already in 1365 Amata, widow of Henry Orlandi, lately of England, ill in the hospital, left a will which, though it had entirely English witnesses, had almost entirely Roman references, including a legacy to the rector of S Maria in Campitello.[17] Most probably the testator was not a pilgrim but the widow of an Englishman living in Rome. But the organisation had other functions. It lent money. In the 1406 rental one house is held as a pledge[18] and when Alice Tudor, a pilgrim, found herself in Rome without funds she turned to the warden (*custos*) for help.[19] It also oversaw the property of older members[20] and served as a poste restante. William Swan, the English proctor, received letters

---

[13] See pp. 91–2.
[14] *m.* 8; for the monastery Huelsen, *Le chiese*, pp. 465–7 and Caraffa, *Monasticon Italiae*, I, pp. 78–9.
[15] A. A. Ruddock, *Italian Merchants and Shipping in Southampton, 1270–1600* (= Southampton Record Series I), Southampton 1951, pp. 133–8, for Italian consuls in England.
[16] Rome, Venerabile Collegio Inglese, *Liber* 23, f. 34v, quoted *Venerabile*, p. 28.
[17] Goioli, *Topografia*, pp. 248–9, no. 148; for the church, Huelsen, *Le chiese*, pp. 318–19.
[18] *m.* 172.   [19] See p. 128.   [20] See p. 70.

there; and when from 1406 the curia travelled round Italy several English members used the house for storage.[21]

The early organisation of S Thomas's hospital is lost to us, although the evidence of its deeds shows that from an early date it had a warden (*custos*) and one or two treasurers (*camerarii*).[22] At the foundation the *communitas et universitas* had a *camerarius* and officials[23] and Shepherd was called *custos* of the house of the community by the time he made his will in 1365.[24] He was the servant of the group, not the master of the institution.[25] The group was legally constituted to receive gifts at least by 1376. In that year Gilbert Newman wanted to give two houses to the fraternity and they assembled to receive these:

There were assembled and called together the brethren of the fraternity and guild of the English in the chapel of the said hospital at the sound of the bell as is the custom.[26]

Exactly the same would have been said of a monastic chapter. The names of the *confratres* then followed: John Toli, and John Pickering (Pickarinck in the deed), English priests, John Champneys (*Ciampenez*), Thomas de Ponte, William Mantel, William son of Richard, *paternostrarius*, and John Ponfred the *custos*, who acted on behalf of the fraternity. The witnesses here were Italian, both notaries.[27]

Everything that is known about the early organisation suggests strongly that John Shepherd did not sell his house to the group by a straightforward transaction. The house had been part of Antonius Smerrucci's wife's dower which he had acquired in 1359.[28] The Shepherds had bought it only in 1361,[29] which suggests that they did so in order to sell it next year to the English group. Behind this may lie a transaction organised not by them as individuals but by the group.

Included in a grant of indulgence by Bishop Edmund Stafford of Ely in 1398 was the group's own account, for collecting purposes, of the value of the hospice and the duties of membership of the confraternity. The value was that before it existed needy and sick English people in Rome were even devoured by wolves![30] The duties were outlined in

---

21 See p. 52.   22 List, as far as they are known from the deeds., in *Venerabile*, pp. 264–71.

23 *m*. 37; *Venerabile*, p. 40.

24 *Venerabile*, p. 42; Goioli, pp 189–90 and see also pp. 242, 249.

25 *Venerabile*, pp. 34–5 for the evidence.

26 *m*. 86: *coadinatis et convocatis confratribus fraternitatis et universitatis . . . in capella dicti hospitalis ad sonum campanelle ut moris est.*

27 Paulus Amistatis, of Arenula (no doubt a relative of the notary who drew up the deed, Johannes Bucii Amistatis), and Jacobellus Vannotti, of S Angelo.

28 *m*. 32.   29 *m*. 34.

30 E. Stafford, *The Register of Edmund Stafford (AD 1395–1419): an Index and Abstract of its Contents*, ed. F. C. Hingeston Randolph, London and Exeter 1886, pp. 308–9.

the statutes of the hospital which decreed that every priest staying in the house had to sing a mass weekly for the brethren and sisters, living and dead. Others who were literate had to say the psalter weekly. Illiterate laity had to do a *circulum*, perhaps a round of the 'stations' (certain Roman churches) weekly for the same intention: 'no one except God himself can count the great indulgences and remissions of these circuits' (*cuius circuli magnas indulgencias et remissiones nemo novit dinumerare nec potest nisi solus deus*). Masses were said in the hospice for benefactors who shared all masses, pilgrimages and other spiritual good. This account also added correctly that Pope Gregory XI had confirmed the building and its endowment. Since April 1373 the brethren and those staying in the house had had the right to receive the sacraments of penance, eucharist and extreme unction from a suitable priest serving in it. At the same time the pope confirmed the hospital with its endowments and chapel.[31]

According to Stafford's document, however (which must rely on the hospice's own account), even in 1398 the house was still not yet fully built (*et construccione indigeat non modicum sumptuosa*) and, as it was receiving many poor people who relied on it for alms, Boniface IX had given (the date is unknown) seven years and seven quarantines of indulgence to all its benefactors. In 1405 and 1412 the brethren had plenary remission once at the hour of death from their chosen confessor.[32] The house had a burial ground of its own by 1411 when Andrew Alene asked to be buried before S Maria et Caterina 'in the place where are buried the dead who are buried in the English hospital' (*in loco ubi sepeliuntur mortui qui in dicto hospitali Anglicorum sepeliuntur*).[33]

Publicity of the kind above must explain why John Stow in the early seventeenth century preserved a founders' list including Robert Braybrooke, bishop of London, Thomas Brampton (= Brinton), bishop of Rochester, Sir John Philpot and Jane his wife, Sir Robert Knowleys, Sir Hugh Calverley, Sir John Hawkwood, Sir John Thornam, John Twiford, John and Alice Shepherd, Robert Cristal and his wife Agnes, Robert Windleront, Walter Withers, Robert at Pine, Adam Steple, Henry Line Draper and other citizens of London in 1380.[34] Of these, as already shown, the Shepherds, and Robert at Pine were indeed in Rome at the foundation. More to the point, perhaps, they had left property before 1380.[35] Sir John Philpot and Jane his first wife were

---

[31] M. Harvey, 'Some documents on the early history of the English hospice', *Venerabile*, 30 (1994) pp. 39–43, for details.

[32] *CPL*, VI, pp. 13 (simply plenary remission), 332.

[33] Archives of S Maria dell'Anima, Instr. Litt B, tom. 1, f. 102.

[34] John Stow, *Annales*, p 335; see also *Venerabile*, p. 28.   [35] Above pp. 10, 55.

certainly benefactors. The very expensive Vivianus palace, bought in 1375 for 332 florins, and another house, were paid for with money given by them for their souls and the souls of all their relatives, as the deeds specify.[36] Philpot was a leading London stapler, a political figure of great importance, and the sum is very large.[37] Thomas Brinton, a contemporary of Cardinal Adam Easton as a monk of Norwich, had been papal Penitentiary for the English in Avignon and remained in post until he became bishop of Rochester in 1373. He had accompanied the papal curia from Avignon to Rome in 1368 so he had first-hand knowledge of the early hospice.[38] When he died in 1389 he left it a legacy.[39] The others are not among the known benefactors but Stow's names suggest that he had a list of those for whom the members were praying in 1380. Many of those named are perfectly credible as benefactors, especially if one assumes that in the earliest stage the hospice was particularly being publicised in London, presumably by a network of merchants. Knolles and Calveley (the preferred modern spelling) were wealthy and prominent soldiers, who had made significant fortunes in France and elsewhere, in the Hundred Years War and also as members of the Companies as mercenaries.[40] Both were well-known philanthropists.[41] It is possible that Sir Robert actually came to Rome for the Jubilee of 1390. He made his will in 1389[42] and had permission to set out for the Roman court, for the discharge of his conscience and the salvation of his soul, in fulfilment of a vow.[43] He appears to have been genuinely conscientious in religious matters; in 1366 he sought pardon from the papal Penitentiary for excesses committed by himself and his military followers in the diocese of

---

[36] *m.* 84.

[37] For him especially Thrupp, *Merchant Class*, Appendix; Nightingale, *Mercantile Community*, pp. 184, 221, 229–30, 253–61, 267–9, 278 and Index, p. 630; see also M. Darby, John Philipot. A 14th Century London Merchant, MSc for the University of London, 1976. I thank the author for allowing me to see this thesis.

[38] *BRUO*, I, pp. 268–9; proof that he did go to Rome is now in C. Burns, 'Sources of British and Irish history in the *Instrumenta Miscellanea* of the Vatican Archives', *AHP*, 9 (1971), pp. 7–141, esp 75, no. 219. See also Harvey, 'Preaching in the curia', pp. 299–301.

[39] T. Brinton, *The Sermons*, ed. M. Devlin, 2 vols., Camden Society, 3rd series, 85, 86 (1954), II, p. 503, from his will.

[40] J. C. Bridge, 'Two Cheshire soldiers of fortune of the XIVth century: Sir Hugh Calveley and Sir Robert Knolles', *Journal of the Chester Archaeological Society*, 14 (1909), pp. 111–231. I owe this reference to Professor Richard Britnell.

[41] For Sir Robert: Bridge, 'Two Cheshire soldiers', pp. 211–14, 217–23; R. H. Britnell, 'The new bridge', in *Traffic and Politics. The Construction and Management of Rochester Bridge, AD 43–1993*, eds. N. Yates and J. M. Gibson, Woodbridge 1994, pp. 43–59, esp. pp. 45–7. For Sir Hugh: Bridge, pp. 155–6. T. Walsingham, *Historia anglicana*. 2 vols., ed. H. T. Riley, RS 28 (1863), II, p. 277; *The St Alban's Chronicle*, ed. V. H. Galbraith, Oxford 1937, p. 22.

[42] Bridge, 'Two Cheshire soldiers', p. 221.

[43] *CPR 1388–92*, p. 94, 1389, 18 August, with twelve servants and horses, for as long as necessary.

Angers and Le Mans.[44] But he also had close associations with the Grocers of London and seems to have sympathised with their aims.[45] The hospice turned in 1406 to a relative of his, Thomas Knolles, one of his executors who was a London merchant, when looking for trustworthy persons to investigate complaints against its London agent.[46] Sir John Hawkwood is the well-known English *condottiere* in Italy in the period, sometimes in the pay of the papacy.[47] He was in Rome in 1382 and 1387, but there is no record of a legacy to the English institutions there.[48] John Twiford would either be a kinsman of Sir Nicholas Twyford, London goldsmith, an alderman between 1375 and 1391, or a cutler or wool packer of that name in the relevant period.[49] Adam Steple is probably Adam Staple or Stable, London mercer, an alderman 1372–7, 1378–9 and 1380–1. He had died by 1384.[50] Henry Line Draper was probably Henry Lynedraper, travelling abroad from Dover in January 1368.[51]

Stow's list thus reminds one of connections between the house and London trade. Its early encouragement by Philpot recalls attempts by English merchants to break into the Italian market, particularly for wool and cloth. But many merchants were interested in exports in general and would not have limited themselves to a particular commodity. The 1360s to 1380s are precisely that period when anti-alien agitation in England was at its height; some of the 'founders' were part of this: including Philpot, Stable and Knolles as an associate of the Grocers of London.

The hospice survived the various traumas of schism, civil strife and invasion of Rome from 1404 onwards, though it was looted and lost property.[52] A more or less continuous list of officers can be traced from the beginnings to 1420. In 1418 the *custos* may have been still lay as had been originally the case but already by then several clerics had been *camerarii*.[53] The earliest clerical officer was probably John Doneys *camerarius* in March 1401.[54] He was a canon lawyer, a canon of Chichester who also tried to become a canon of London and worked as

---

[44] *CPL*, IV, p. 55.

[45] Nightingale, *Mercantile Community*, pp. 241, 267, 285, 296, 321.

[46] Below p. 62.   [47] Partner, *Lands of St Peter*, pp. 360, 365, 366.

[48] G. Temple-Leader and G. Marcotti, *Giovanni Acuto (Sir John Hawkwood). Storia d'un condottiere*, Florence 1889, pp. 140, 178, 238; *Venerabile*, p. 28 is mistaken to think he was in Rome in 1364.

[49] Thrupp, *Merchant Class*, pp. 370–1.

[50] Ibid., p. 374; *Calendar of Letter Books Preserved Among the Archives of the Corporation of the City of London at the Guildhall, 1275–1498, Books A-L*, ed. R. R. Sharpe, London 1889–1912, *Letter Book G*, p. 383 and *H*, p. 515 (index).

[51] *CPR 1367–70*, p. 74.   [52] See p. 52.   [53] List in *Venerabile*, pp. 264–5.

[54] *m.* 156; not Newton in 1391, *Venerabile*, p. 264; this is an error, the document from which it comes was transcribed at Newton's request in 1415 from a 1391 document.

a proctor in the curia.[55] We find him acting for Guy Mone bishop of S David's, whose *familiaris* he was, clearly his patron, between 1397 and 1400. By 25 August 1401 he had died in Rome where he was litigating over the canonry of Lampeter in Abergwili, given by Mone.[56] The next *camerarius* certainly a cleric was John Haget, another canonist, in 1404, who began as a proctor in the curia. He acted for bishop Mascall in 1406[57] and also with William Swan, finally becoming an abbreviator.[58] From then until 1420 the *camerarius* was either Philip Newton, another proctor,[59] or William Lovell, already an abbreviator,[60] both clerics, with sometimes John Cross, a layman.[61]

The extent to which by 1407 the hospice was already heavily influenced by members of the papal entourage can be seen in a letter, probably from William Swan to Robert Newton, whom he calls his most special friend, written from Rome on 12 July.[62] Newton had written from London to Swan in April saying that he no longer wished to be hospice proctor in England. Swan replied that many members of the papal curia (*curtisani*) were in any case labouring to have him removed. Masters Robert Appleton and John Ixworth were saying that Newton had had hospital goods worth more than fifty marks and were working tirelessly on the ambassadors (Sir John Cheyne and Dr Henry Chichele[63]) and prelates of the English nation in the curia for Newton's removal and calling to account. There were meetings and disputes. They were unable to have Newton's appointment revoked, however, and many were prepared to testify to his faithfulness. Henry Chichele was saying many commendatory things. None the less it had been decided with the consent of the brethren that Newton should render account and they had appointed John Nottingham, chancellor of the exchequer, Thomas Thirsk, remembrancer, with Masters Walter Cook, Dionysius Lopham, Thomas Knolles and William Waldern, and were sending all his accounts and letters. They were particularly complaining about the local collection (*firma*) of the dioceses and the collection from the brethren and sisters (in England, understood). There was very little from these. So Swan warned Newton to look into this carefully.

Thus by about 1407 the group had a formal network in England, with English brethren and sisters, and could command the services of

---

[55] Le Neve, *Chichester*, p. 41; *St Paul's* pp. 15, 23.

[56] *CPL*, V, pp. 412–13; 283, 312–13, and see index; Lunt, *Financial Relations*, pp. 750, 751; G. Mone, *The Episcopal Registers of the Diocese of St David's, 1397–1518*, ed. R. F. Isaacson and A. Roberts, 3 vols. (= Cymmrodorion Record Series 6), I, *The Register of Guy Mone, Bishop of S David's 1397–1407*, London 1917–20, pp. 90, 122, 158.

[57] *BRUO*, II, p. 848 under Haket.   [58] See p. 149.   [59] See p. 82.   [60] See p. 149.

[61] See above p. 99.   [62] Arch. Seld. B 23, ff. 33r/v.

[63] For their mission to Rome see M. Harvey 'England and the Council of Pisa': pp. 264, 269.

very important royal clerks and London merchants. John Nottingham had been chancellor of the exchequer since 1390, was reappointed under Henry IV and held the office until 1410. He died in 1418 as treasurer of York and canon of London.[64] Thomas Thirsk was king's remembrancer between 1398 and 1419. He died in 1420. He was a canon of St Stephen's, Westminster, and vicar of St Michael's Coventry.[65] Walter Cook had been for many years a proctor in the curia and was now back in England[66] and Dionysius (or Denis) Lopham was a well-known London notary public, who had been functioning since at least 1380. His most notable role was as one of the two notaries who took the deposition of Richard II in 1399, but in 1386 he was attorney for Richard Drayton, a proctor in the curia.[67] Thomas Knolles and William Waldern were leading London merchants, Knolles a grocer who was an alderman between 1393 and 1435. He was in some way related to Sir Robert Knolles who appointed him an executor.[68] Waldern, a mercer, was an alderman between 1395 and 1424.[69] Robert Newton, clerk, was one of the executors of Waldern's will in 1424.[70] A further significant detail is that Waldern was one of the leaders of a group of London merchants who in 1412–13 were trying to break into the Italian market by trading directly there, so causing a major diplomatic incident when their ship was seized by the Genoese.[71] Thus the hospice of S Thomas continued to be fostered by merchants with a vested interest in entering the Italian market.

It looks as if Newton was not removed and did not resign. In 1410 he was given permission to export from London one hundred marks via Richard Victor (a Florentine merchant) for the use of S Thomas's

[64] T. F. Tout, *Chapters in the Administrative History of Medieval England*, 6 vols., London 1920–33, III, p. 357, note 1 and IV, p. 195, note 6; R. L. Storey, 'Gentlemen-bureaucrats', in C. H. Clough ed., *Profession, Vocation and Culture in Late Medieval England. Essays Dedicated to the Memory of A.R. Myers*, Liverpool 1982, pp. 90–117, esp. p. 113.

[65] Storey, 'Gentlemen-bureaucrats', pp. 113–14.

[66] *BRUC*, by 1390 chancellor of S Pauls. For career as proctor Zutshi, *Original Papal Letters*, nos. 382, 411, 412, 424, 425–6; and see J. Sayers, 'Proctors representing British interests', pp. 143–63, esp. p. 150.

[67] *CPL*, V, p. 224; *Calendar of Select Pleas and Memoranda of the City of London preserved among the Archives of the Corporation of the City of London 1323–1482*, 6 vols., ed. A. H. Thomas (1–4) and P. E. Jones (5–6), Cambridge 1926–61, *1364–81*, p. 266; *1381–1412*, p. 120; S. B. Chrimes and A. L. Brown, *Select Documents of English Constitutional History*, London 1961, p. 185.

[68] Thrupp, *Merchant Class*, pp. 351–2; J. S. Roskell, L. Clark and C. Rawcliffe, eds., *History of Parliament. The House of Commons 1386–1421* , 4 vols., Stroud 1992, III, pp. 531–3.

[69] Thrupp, *Merchant Class*, p. 372; Roskell, *History of Parliament, The Commons 1386–1421*, IV, pp. 745–7.

[70] H. Chichele, The *Register of Henry Chichele, Archbishop of Canterbury, 1414–1443,* , ed. E. F. Jacob, 4 vols., CYS, 42, 45–7 (1938–47), II, p. 278.

[71] Ruddock, *Italian Merchants*, pp. 58–9; see also Roskell, *History of Parliament, The Commons 1386–1421*, IV, pp. 745–7.

hospice in Rome, provided that gold and silver were not exported and the money offset by goods bought in England.[72]

The hospice of S Thomas presents an excellent example of a corporate body which kept itself in existence largely by dealing in real property in Rome, renting or sometimes selling or exchanging. The growth of its possessions from 1362 to 1420 can be traced in its deeds, and English sources give some insight into the other ways it gathered money.

Its early neighbours can be reconstructed to reveal how the group who ran it gradually bought or were given the nearby houses, so that by 1420 the English must have been one of the most powerful groups in the area. In 1361 the street on which John Shepherd bought his house consisted of the de Pappazuris property in what is now the Bridgittine convent in Piazza Farnese, next to which, moving into via Monserrato, was the property of Petrus Thomaxi and his wife Margarita,[73] next to whom were the *casalenas* of Cecchus Simonelli.[74] Along the same side was the house of Machiotius Velli, then Antonius Smerrucii's house which became Shepherd's, and next to it the house of Fina, concubine of the Archpriest of the church of S Maria and Caterina.[75] Next were Andreotti houses, the first of which was held in 1392 as her dower by Vannotia, widow of Nicola Francescoli Andreotti de Andreocctis[76] These last houses were given or sold in 1406 to S Chrysogonus' hospice.[77] Opposite these, apart from the church of S Maria and Caterina, was a house belonging to that church, next to which there was in 1397 a house belonging to the widow of Bucius Nannoli, daughter of Paulucius della Torre, *murator*. Beside was the *turris* of the heirs of John de Bulgariis, underneath which was one of the chambers of the house next door.[78]

Once the Smerucci house was bought in 1362 it was not until 1374 that Fina's house was bought by William of Richard.[79] Of the houses further towards the present Piazza Farnese Petrus Thomaxi's was acquired by John Ponfret and left by will to S Thomas's in 1383,[80] and the *casalenas* formerly owned by Cecchus Simonelli were acquired in 1406.[81] The houses mentioned as opposite the hospice of S Thomas belonged to John White and Perrinus Baker and came in the end to S Chrysogonus' (S Edmund's), the other English hospice which they founded.[82] By 1420 therefore the area round the hospice of S Thomas must have become very English.

It is not always possible to trace the origins of the properties which

---

[72] *CCR Henry IV, 1409–1413*, p. 449.   [73] *m.* 49.   [74] *m.* 175.   [75] *m.* 34.
[76] *m.* 126.   [77] Below pp. 82–3.   [78] *mm.* 141, 142.   [79] *mm.* 71, 75.
[80] *m.* 49 dorse.   [81] *mm.* 175, 178.   [82] *mm.* 141, 142.

the hospice came to own, but there is a rental for 1406, listing all the houses with their rents and tenants that year.[83] By then it owned twenty houses (though some were then vacant, no doubt because of the political situation) and two separate shops. *Stirpes* or cleared pieces of land and vineyards are not mentioned in the rental but from other documents we know that some were owned by 1420.

Tracing the origins of the property is made difficult because the modern chronological arrangement of the deeds of the English College masks the fact that once they were sewn together in groups concerning each individual house, vineyard or property.[84] Cross references are given in the college MS 1598 but it is not very detailed and so some matters remain obscure. The routes by which the hospice obtained its properties were varied and it did not own all its freeholds, though in the fourteenth century that did not usually matter.[85]

Twelve properties were purchased between 1362 and 1420. The earliest transaction involved three houses: one two-storeyed house with *griptae* in its courtyard and one behind it, implying ancient remains and one further house, *cum turitella*, with a dome *cum griptis*, a well and a garden, in Parione region, apparently given but really purchased in 1371 with hospice proceeds, by Robert of Pigna and William the *paternos-trarius*[86] The price was not of course specified but in 1356 these had sold for fifty florins[87] and seem to have been pledged or rented to the hospice since 1369.[88]

In 1374 another house was purchased for sixty florins,[89] and in 1375 a further one for sixty.[90] In 1391 two halves of a house were bought for thirty-five florins each.[91] In 1393 a further purchase cost ten ducats (twenty florins).[92] In 1395 another was added for fifty-five florins.[93] Davit of Wales sold his house to the hospice in 1400 for thirty-two ducats (sixty-four florins).[94] The final purchase was in 1406 of what are described as two properties (*casaleni*) in Arenula region, one next to the hospice, bought for ninety florins.[95]

Between 1362 and 1406 therefore the hospice spent at least 800 florins buying property. Its out-goings would also include the very small yearly sums spent on *census* or ground rent payments for some of these. Half the 1391 property for instance was *in proprietate* of Cephus Latini,[96]

[83] *m.* 172.

[84] See for instance *m.* 4 dorse *empcio cuiusdam domus seu pal.[acii]* . . . *unde habentur ista v instrumenta simul consuta.*

[85] See p. 20.   [86] *m.* 60; *Venerabile*, p. 49; AC Sez. I, tom. 649/11, ff. 20–5.

[87] *m.* 27.   [88] *mm.* 54 and 55.   [89] *m.* 77 and see *m.* 61.   [90] *m.* 81.

[91] *m.* 120; the whole is a copy made in 1415.   [92] *m.* 127.

[93] *m.* 136, 137. There were four daughters.   [94] *mm.* 152, 154.   [95] *m.* 175.

[96] *m.* 120.

and the 1393 house owed four *libri* per year as ground rent to Angela wife of Cecchus de Spuchicha,[97] Davit's house owed two *bolognini* per year to the hospital of S Antonius.[98]

Some of these were relatively near the hospital. The 1374 purchase was said to be in *contrata caccabariorum*[99] and two were in the Pizzomerle area, the area now near the present Sforza-Cesarini Palace.[100] Another, *in contrata de piscionibus* is described also as next to the largest of all the houses which the hospice came to own, *in sacco lupo*, that is near the church of S Lorenzo in Damaso.[101] A further house, however, was in Trastevere region in the parish of S Salvatore della Corte (*de curtibus*), next to the church.[102]

The properties varied very much in size and complexity. Those bought in 1371, with their ancient remains, can be matched by the description of the Trastevere purchase, which was two-storeyed with marble steps, a garden and a barbican (*quadam barbarca*).

Bought properties were by no means the only ones acquired. From the beginning house property was left to S Thomas's by will, about ten houses in all by 1420. The donors included Simon, son of Simon, in 1369,[103] and in 1381 Beatrice, widow of William son of Partriche formerly of Scotland.[104] John Ponfret, alias Palmer, left three in 1383,[105] and probably Sibilla Teste left one before 1406.[106] In 1401 in a rare example of an Italian leaving property to S Thomas's, Raynaldus Petri of Arenula, shoemaker (*calcolarius*), left his house in Arenula to his wife Vannotia, leaving his sister Jacobella the right to live there if she was in poverty, with reversion to S Thomas's after Vannotia's death.[107] On the dorse the deed says that the house, next to the church of S Giovanni in Ayno, near the present via Monserrato, came as a result of this will.[108] Walter Taylor, a papal *cursor* who was probably also a real tailor, left his house in the Parione region, *in proprietate* of S Biagio *in canto secuto*, to the hospice in 1403, with his partner Jacobus Guilelmi of Ferrara having the right to the shop (*apotheca*) in it with the use of the porch (*cum statio*

---

[97] *m.* 127.
[98] *mm.* 152, 154. For *bolognini* see P. Spufford, *Handbook of Medieval Exchange* (= Royal Historical Society, Guides and Handbooks 13), London 1986, p. 72.
[99] *m.* 77; for the place Staglia, p. 140, note; Hubert, *Espace urbain*, p. 367.
[100] *mm.* 127, 152.
[101] *m.* 81 dorse for location; *m.* 172 for the large house; for the place, Hubert, *Espace urbain*, p. 192 and Gnoli, *Topografia*, pp. 306–7, between present via della Pace and della Cancelleria.
[102] *m.* 136, 137; for the church, Huelsen, *Le chiese*, p. 438.
[103] *m.* 50, dorse for will.   [104] *m.* 7 dorse and *m.* 91.   [105] *m.* 49 dorse and *m.* 115.
[106] *m.* 172 for the house (see also *m.* 98) and see *mm.* 121, 128.
[107] *m.* 155, an extract from a will.
[108] M. Armellini, *Le chiese di Roma*, 2 vols., Rome 1942, under S Giovanni in Ayno; Huelsen, *Le chiese*, pp. 269–70.

et commoditate dicti porticalis) for a year rent free.[109] In 1406 Jacob held it, although this may refer to the *apotheca* only, paying S Thomas's 20 florins a year.[110]

Several deeds record on their dorse that the property concerned belonged to master John Fraunceys who died in 1413 so it may have been left by him.[111] One was a palace with a garden and two houses adjoining it in Parione, for which the price in 1399 was 309 gold florins.[112] In 1404 Fraunceys bought also a *turris* with some houses.[113] These were described as a *turris* with *casellae* in the Parione region *in contrata tribii parentum* (part of present Piazza del Fico, behind the Chiesa Nuova),[114] *in proprietate* of the Orsini of Campo dei Fiori.[115] John Fraunceys was a senior member of the curia for many years, considered later.[116] The hospice certainly owned these properties in mid-century.[117]

Wills could prove very contentious. Complications arose from that made in 1368 by Robert de Pigna, one of the 'founders'.[118] He left his wife Margaret his house in the Pigna region, in the *contrata* of S Stefano de Pigna (now del Cacco)[119] described in 1364 as two-storeyed, with rooms and chambers, with a *statio*, garden and wells. He also left her his *stirps* in the city for life. When she died the hospice of S Thomas was to get these for the remission of his sins.[120] Margaret apparently died first, since some of the transactions about the house contain what was said to refer to a codicil, a copy of which is in the deeds of the English College.[121] This stated that Robert left half the house for her life to Alice his servant, ordering the other half to be sold for his soul. The executors, Henry the Englishman of Trastevere and William the *paternostrarius*, had duly in 1377 sold half the house to Thomas of Nicolas, *paternostrarius*, another Englishman,[122] with Alice retaining the right to live in her half, carefully divided between herself and Thomas.[123] By 1387 the executors were agreeing that for the sake of Robert's soul they must sell the *proprietas* of Alice's half of the house to Simon of John (Barber) *paternostrarius*, whilst the other half remained to the heirs of the earlier buyer, Thomas.[124] The sum was 50 florins. Apparently the second half, belonging to the heirs of Thomas, came by 1395 to Statius Manerii, who gave it too in 1395 to Simon of John

---

[109] *m.* 163. [110] *m.* 172. [111] Below pp. 175–6. [112] *m.* 151.
[113] *m.* 167; the text is faded but Rome, Venerabile Collegio Inglese, *Liber* 1598, f. 76 says the cost was 70 fl. and I read it so. See also *m.* 111.
[114] Gnoli, *Topografia*, pp. 206–7. [115] *m.* 41. [116] See below pp. 175–83, 186–7.
[117] See them being let to John Lax, Rome, Venerabile Collegio Inglese, *Liber* 1598, f. 89.
[118] *m.* 53; copy also AC Sez I, 649/9, f. 27. [119] Huelsen, *Le chiese*, p. 481.
[120] *m.* 38; copy also AC Sez I, 649/7, ff. 39v–42. [121] AC Sez I 650, ff. 20–3.
[122] *m.* 88. [123] AC Sez. I 649/13, ff. 15–18. [124] *m.* 118.

(Barber), suggesting that the transactions were from the first arrangements by the hospice management.[125]

Contentions also resulted from the will of Richard of Roger, who in
June 1369 left four *stirpes* and his house in the parish of S Angelo in
Pescheria (*in foro piscium*) to his wife Stefania, his son John and daughter
Mabiliota with a possible posthumous child, since Stefania was preg-
nant.[126] The house was two-storeyed, with a columned portico in
front. In December 1369 he bought a house called Lo Confesse, also in
S Angelo, likewise with a portico but also with a *discoperta* behind.[127]
The executors were John of Robert, and William the *paternostrarius*,
both Englishmen. By 1373 Richard was dead.[128] In April 1395 the
surviving executor William brought a case before the city court (*camera
urbis*). He explained that the son John had now vanished and Mabiliota
had died while still a child (*in pupilari etate*) and William wanted to
execute the will. So knowing that Richard had revered the hospice of
S Thomas he gave to its guardian the house called Lo Confesse with the
stirps also.[129] In March and April 1395 the legal status of Lo Confesse
was being contested by Johannes Pucii Berte, shoemaker (*calcolarius*)
formerly of Velletri and now of S Angelo region, who was occupying
it. It was adjudged to William.[130] William then handed the house to the
hospice of S Thomas and Stefania continued to live in it as she was
doing at the time.[131]

The following year, however, Johannes Pucii Berte brought another
suit. His grounds were that he was married to Vannotia, daughter of
Stefania (was she the posthumous child?), and Vannotia had as her
dower all the rights in the goods which Stefania had, especially usufruct
in the house reserved to Stefania for her life.[132] The resulting compromise was that the hospital had to pay Johannes 40 florins to go away.
This, however, was not the end of the matter. Stefania remarried and
her first husband's will had only allowed her to live in the house as long
as she remained 'chaste', so in 1399 she was renting Lo Confesse and the
stirps from the hospital.[133] In 1408 when Stefania was dead,[134] Putius
Damiani formerly of Castrum Lariani and now of Castrum Molaris,
who was Stefania's nephew, next of kin of John her son (*frater soprinus*)
claimed Lo Confesse and the *stirps*. In this case a compromise was
reached by which he was paid sixteen florins.[135] The house can hardly
have seemed worth it and in 1418 the hospice agreed with Nicola
Bondi, a doctor of law, who lived next door, to exchange it with him

---

[125] *mm.* 130, 135.   [126] *m.* 56; for church Huelsen, *Le chiese*, p. 196.   [127] *m.* 57.
[128] *m.* 67.   [129] *mm.* 129, 130.   [130] *m.* 132.   [131] *m.* 133.
[132] *m.* 140.   [133] *mm.* 149, 150.   [134] *m.* 191.   [135] *m.*183.

for two houses which he had, also in S Angelo, *in plateo judeorum*, the ghetto.[136]

Likewise in 1390 Elena Clerk left the hospice one house in Pizzomerle which had been given to her and her late husband, reserving the house for the use of Agnes Taylour for her life.[137] There was a little house next to this in the Ponte region, *in proprietate* of the Orsini of Campo dei Fiori, which was to be sold and the money given for the souls of herself, John and their relatives.[138] The hospice had an option to buy this if it wished, and of course the executors were all closely associated with the institution. In 1391 however, when they found that they could not pay the legacies without selling the Pizzomerle house first, they did so for 150 florins.[139] The buyer was Eustatius or Statius Manerii, the English Florentine whom we have met before and who may have been acting for the community; one assumes that the money then went to S Thomas's for Elena's soul.[140]

Several of these houses also owed ground rent. The house which Simon son of Simon gave,[141] and Walter Taylor's house (at 6d per year), paid the abbey of S Biagio.[142] The house called Scotte Torre which came from Beatrice the widow, owed 12d yearly to the Orsini of Campo dei Fiori.[143] John Frounceys' *turris*[144] and Elena Clerk's house[145] which was to be sold in 1390, owed them ground rent also. Elena's other house, in which Agnes Taylour was allowed to remain, was *in proprietate* of the church of S Benedict *Sconci*.[146] John Saracenus de Saracenis was owed a ground rent for Sibilla Teste's house.[147]

The houses were inevitably somewhat scattered. One of three which Ponfret left by will in 1383[148] was situated towards the present Piazza Farnese. The second was also in Arenula. Robert of Pigna's house was near S Stefano de Pigna (del Cacco),[149] and Simon of Simon's was also in the parish of S Lorenzo in Damaso, now on corso Vittorio Emmanuele.[150] Scotte Torre was in Arenula in the parish of S Salvatore *in campo (domini campi)*.[151]

Some of the houses came with conditions. John Ponfret allowed William Mantel and his wife Alys to continue for life in the house he bought from them in 1375[152] for a yearly payment of 12d 'for the many pleasing services and benefits which he confesses he has received from

---

[136] *m.* 191. [137] *m.* 119. [138] *m.* 119.

[139] *m.* 122 an exemplification made at the request of John Thomasson *custos* of the hospice in 1408.

[140] See further for him pp. 67, 92. [141] *m.* 50. [142] *m.* 163.

[143] *m.* 7 and 5s for a sale. [144] *m.* 41. [145] *m.* 119.

[146] *m.* 119; for church Huelsen, *Le chiese*, pp. 211–12, subordinate to S Lorenzo in Damaso.

[147] *m.* 68. [148] *m.* 49 dorse; see *m.* 115.

[149] *m.* 53; for the church Huelsen, *Le chiese*, p. 481 and Caraffa, *Monasticon*, I, p. 80.

[150] *m.* 50. [151] Huelsen, *Le chiese*, p. 434. [152] *mm.* 82, 83.

them and hopes in future to receive better if the lord allows',[153] a
formula often disguising a pledge for a loan. It is notable that Mantel
apparently made a loss; he had bought the house in 1367 for fifty-two
florins and sold it to Ponfret for forty.[154] Ponfret also allowed Richard
paternostrarius with his wife Alys and their daughter Palotia to continue
for their lives in another of his houses, for a yearly payment of eight *libri*
to the hospice, and it was then to belong to the hospice.[155]

Various houses came to the hospice not as legacies but as gifts *inter
vivos*, sometimes saving the right of the donor to live in the house for
his life or that of his wife. This may have been a useful method of
ensuring care in old age. Examples include two houses from Gilbert
Newman, a priest, one in Arenula and one in Parione,[156] though since
Newman was an officer of the hospice on occasion, these may have
been purchases for it.[157] In 1401 John White, founder of S Chrysogonus' hospice, gave to S Thomas's a house in the Pigna district, with a
stirps called the *stirps* of S Stefano della Pigna, saving the use of both for
John's life.[158] The deed records taking possession on John's death in
1404. In 1402 William, son of Richard, the *paternostrarius* who had
served the institution for many years, gave it his house in Parione,
reserving use for his life and that of his wife Eloyse[159] In 1407, when his
wife was dead, he gave the house again, reserving usufruct for his own
life.[160] The house next this, belonging to William Holdernesse, another
one-time *custos* of the hospice, was given by Holderness on the same
day in 1402 that William of Richard gave his, reserving usufruct to
himself and his wife Margaret.[161] She was recorded there in 1407 in the
deed which William made out,[162] though by then Holdernesse was
dead and she was married to Raulinus, another Englishman.

Real estate was not the only type of gift. Some houses were sold and
the money must have come to the hospital. It also received some
outright gifts of money. Money from the Philpots in 1375 was invested
in houses:[163]

The buyers assert and say that the house was given to them by John *Philpocti*
and lady Jane his wife of England for their souls and those of their kin

The amount involved was 60 florins for one house and 332 florins for
the palace. Simon Langham, in Avignon, left 100 florins in 1376 to the
fabric of the hospital and the poor in it.[164]

---

[153] *m.* 83: *propter multa grata servicia et beneficia que ab ipsis confessus est habuisse et hinc inde speratus melius in futuro domino concedente . . .*
[154] *mm.* 49 and 82, 83.   [155] *m.* 115.   [156] *mm.* 86; 85; see also *m.* 51.
[157] *m.* 67, he acts for it in 1373.   [158] *m.* 156.   [159] *m.* 159.   [160] *m.* 179.
[161] *m.* 160.   [162] *m.* 179.   [163] *mm.* 81, 84.
[164] R. Widmore, *An History of the Church of St Peter, Westminster*, London 1751, p. 187.

Income was re-invested. A deed of 1371, recording the apparent gift of two houses, reveals that the money came from the goods of the society.[165] It also received household goods, some of which it must have sold. There are references to 'movable' goods in the will of John Ponfret in 1383,[166] Elena Clerk left towels in 1390,[167] and in 1394 the Italian notary Johannes Pauli Alisii of Arenula left the hospice a bed, a pair of sheets and three florins to buy a quilt or one of his best quilts and one litter.[168] Evidently therefore local Italians were involved in the charity, though nothing like the numbers involved in S Chrysogonus' hospital. Johannes Pauli Alisii had acted as notary for John Salmon in 1382.[169] One can see from the remaining deeds that the hospice rented out household goods to tenants and perhaps other residents.[170]

Andrew Alene, Welsh priest and co-founder of quite another establishment, nevertheless decided to die in S Thomas's and wished to be buried among its dead.[171] To ensure that this happened he left it his breviary (worth two ducats) and 'a book called a psalter' (*unum librum qui vocatur psalterium*) worth one gold ducat:

so that the officials of the said hospital of the English are bound and ought to cause my body to be buried (*ut officiales hospitalis predicti Anglicorum teneantur et debeant corpus meum faceri sepeliri*).

He also listed his debts and left them to S Thomas's and the other English hospice to collect. The prior of S Eusebius of rione Monti owed him fifteen florins 'which I lent him' and two *congitellas* of oil also'; the officials of the German hospice of S Maria dell'Anima owed him for the pension of a house he had let to them. Alene's gift may have resulted from quarrels within his own hospice, which was not successful.[172] He certainly died in S Thomas's; his will was signed 'in a certain chamber in a certain palace within the aforesaid hospital, which hospital is in Arenula' (*in quadam camera posita in quodam palacio posito intus hospitale predictum quod hospitale positum est in regione Arenula*) and the witnesses were English, several known from S Thomas's.[173]

A major source of revenue must have been the rent, collected by the warden and chamberlains specifying in the case of Stefania, for instance, that remarriage rendered her liable to pay.[174] Agreements sometimes specified that the rent would hold good unless the emperor or the pope

---

165 *m.* 60.   166 *m.* 115.   167 m 119.   168 AS 270, ff. 123–4.

169 *m.* 109.   170 *m.* 172.

171 Rome, Archives of S Maria dell'Anima, Instr. Litt. B, tom. 1, f. 102.

172 See below p. 88.

173 Witnesses were Thomas Fleming, John Possewych, John Thomasson, Stephen Newton (Nuton) John Selby, John God Uby (?Godby), William Lessrovill (?Lovell). See also p. 88.

174 Above p. 68 and *mm.* 149, 150.

was in the city, in which case the tenant would pay: 'as other English (?) tenants of other houses in the quarter where the house is' (*prout et sicut alii inglini pensionarii aliarum domarum positarum in contrada ubi dicta domus posita*).[175] This was a standard stipulation during the period.[176]

Given the Roman laws about inheritance, beneficiaries of wills might face claims from donors' kin, as they did in Stefania's case, unless care was taken to get their agreement.[177] Any alterations to property also needed to be legitimised by a notarised document. With the Holdernesse house came also a statement that in 1398 he had made an arbitration agreement about a common wall with his neighbour Jacobellus Petri Spechi.[178]

In the 1360s Rome was ruinous.[179] Repairs might come out of rent,[180] or the holder might repair the house as in 1366 Raulinus did for Lo Cafaria.[181] The hospice cared for its houses. In 1404 William Holdernesse obtained permission from the masters of the streets to rebuild a hospice house in Ponte region.[182] He wanted to remake the house, described as with a small hall (*salarello*) in front of it, 'completely from top to bottom with a second storey and other necessities' (*de novo de fundamento in altum cum solariis et aliis necessariis*). In 1406 the group had bought two *casalenas* next to the hospital.[183] and now set about building a wall between the houses and a conduit of piping (*de peperingino*) to take the water from the neighbouring roof.[184] The hospital also obtained permission in 1407 to raise the wall dividing the well between one of its houses and a neighbour's.[185] By 1418 Lo Confesse in the S Angelo region 'which is in great need of repair' (*qui eget magna reparacione*) was exchanged for two others, as noticed above.[186]

Deeds were not always what they seem. An apparent gift from an individual could mask a purchase with corporate money.[187] Equally an

---

[175] *m.* 75.

[176] Other examples, not English, Goioli, p. 113, concerning a palace in SS Lorenzo in Damaso region in 1365: *si contingat dominum nostrum papam vel imperatorem veniret ad urbem..teneantur..respondere prout respondebunt alii pensionarii in Urbe.* See also Maas, *German Community*, p. 79 and note.

[177] E. Re, *Statuti della città di Roma*, Rome 1880 p. 62, daughters of a woman or nephews from a son or daughter already dead could only seek what was in a will or given *inter vivos*.

[178] *m.* 147, which is very faded and hard to read; this was sewn to two other deeds originally as the dorse explains.

[179] Above p. 23.   [180] *m.* 75, of 1374.   [181] Above p. 23; *m.* 45.

[182] *m.* 166; see H. Broise, 'Les maisons d'habitation à Rome aux XVe e XVIe siècles: les leçons de la documentation graphique', in J. C. Maire-Vigueur, ed., *D'une ville à l'autre. Structures matérielles et organisation de l'espace dans les villes européenes (XIIIe–XVIe siècles)*. (= Collection de l'école française de Rome 122), Rome 1989, pp. 609–29, esp. p. 614.

[183] *m.* 175.   [184] *m.* 178.   [185] Above p. 13.   [186] *m.* 191; see above pp. 68–9.

[187] Above p. 55.

apparent purchase could mask a pledge. In 1406 the hospice held one house as a pledge, let for 28 florins yearly.[188] The system had serious hazards since the receiver might claim that the property had actually been sold and, because the deal was essentially designed to hide lending of money at interest, the truth might be hard to establish. It is thus of considerable interest to find one example where the true nature of the transaction is revealed. The deed is a copy, of 1423, from the protocols of the dead Laurentius Anthonii Lancetti Impona. According to this, Johannes Saracenus de Saracenis, with the agreement of his wife Francesca, sold a house to Johannes Cecchi de Leis for a loan of 30 gold florins. In the deed,[189] however, originally made in December 1418:

Johannes de Leis recognises in truth that the said instrument of sale was a fiction and pretence and made and conceived fictitiously and in pretence and valueless but only for the care and caution of thirty florins lent by John de Leis to the said Johannes Sarecenus (*in veritate recognovit dominus Johannes de Leys dictum instrumentum venditionis fuisse fictum et simulatum et ficte et simulate factum et conceptum et ad non valere, sed tantum pro cura et cautela xxx flor' . . . ad dictum rationem prefato Johanni Saraceno per ipsum Johannem de Leyis mutuatis*).

The house was probably one which Saracenus in fact sold to Philip Newton, *camerarius* of S Thomas, in March 1418 perhaps as a private buy and it was no doubt Newton who got Leis to recognise that he had never in reality bought the house.[190]

A further sign of careful management is that several hospice deeds are copies made later. Sometimes this was merely because a court case required them, but it was perhaps no coincidence that the hospice had trouble with neighbours precisely when the city itself was in trouble (1407 and 1408) nor that in 1408 confirmation of the sale of Elena Clerk's house to Statius Manerii and of Sibilla Teste's house, had to be obtained by John Thomasson, the *custos*,[191] nor that in 1415 Philip Newton had to get confirmation from the papal vicar-general of a sale in 1391 to John Cross as *camerarius* of S Thomas's.[192] This suggests either loss of documents or disputes about titles at the time when the city was in turmoil.

The hospice acquired vineyards and *stirpes*. As well as his house Robert de Pigna left *stirpes* among the properties of which his servant Alice had half.[193] There were four properties. One was in Pigna, called

---

[188] *m.* 172: *in pede montis Jordanis.* (at the foot of Monte Giordano) It was lived in by Petrus de Galfredinio (of Verona) secretary to the pope, for whom see W. von Hofmann, *Forschungen zur Geschichte der kurialen Behörden vom Schisma bis zur Reformation*, 2 vols. (= Bibliothek des kgl Preussichen historischen Instituts in Rom 12, 13), Rome 1914, II, p. 107.

[189] *m.* 192.   [190] *m.* 189.   [191] *mm.* 121, 122.   [192] *m.* 120.

[193] *m.* 53 for his will and see above p. 67 for Alice.

probably *stirps Sancti Stephani*.[194] One was called *stirpa de S Marco*, in the S Marco district.[195] The third was in the Monti region[196] and the fourth, called vacant when he bought it in 1353, was in Colonna.[197] Robert was a *cernitor* and these were described as *ad cernendum farinas*. With Lo Confesse went also *stirpes* described in 1373 as the *stirps* of *contrata mercati*, of *turris speculorum*, of *platea Judeorum* and of S Caterina in Ripa district.[198] They also were *ad cernendum*. These presumably also came to the hospice. Henry of John from Trastevere left two *stirpes* in Trastevere which seem to have gone with his house.[199] Certainly in 1406 the house in Trastevere had a *stirps* attached.[200] The house in Pizzomerle which Davit of Wales sold to the hospice had a *stirps* attached in 1406.[201]

In 1371 the hospice bought for 40 florins from domina Rita, daughter of the late Bartholomeus de Campania of Biberatica district, now of Monti, vineyards in the place called *undarias*.[202] In 1371 it was also letting out for planting (*ad ponendum*) vineyards beyond the Apian gate 'in the place called "Lord, where are you going?"' (*in loco qui dicitur domine quo vadis*). The hospice was to get half the must (new, incompletely fermented wine).[203] An inventory of 1630 says that these had been bought in 1370.[204] The arrangements were unsatisfactory and the next year another agreement was reached about the same vineyards.[205] One of those renting these vines in 1372 was William Mantel, whose house was eventually owned by John Ponfret.[206] Vineyards must have been left by John FrS Frauncys, who in 1400 had bought eleven pieces of land beyond Ponte Molle *in loco qui dicitur Falcone* for 50 ducats (100 florins) *in proprietate* of S Eustachius, for a census of one *salma* of must at vintage.[207]

From a very early date S Thomas's hospice raised money from England and Avignon. Though later there was a collector in England, the full operation of its fund-raising system was not evident at first. The earliest example of the publicity for it comes in the notice already discussed from the register of Bishop Edmund Stafford in 1398, which described the advantages both spiritual and practical to contributors. Stafford licensed questors and gave forty days indulgence to contributors.[208] He said that other bishops had done the same, listing the archbishops of Canterbury, Simon Sudbury, William Courtenay, and

---

[194] *m.* 172 and see also *m.* 12.   [195] *m.* 16.   [196] *m.* 17.   [197] *m.* 21.
[198] *m.* 67; for the places, Gnoli, *Topografia*, pp. 162–5.   [199] *m.* 93.   [200] *m.* 172.
[201] *m.* 172.   [202] AC Sez I, 649/11, ff. 18–19.
[203] AC Sez I 649/11, ff. 19v–20; ff. 50v–51.
[204] Rome, Venerabile Collegio Inglese, *Liber* 277 p. 67.
[205] AC Sez. I 649/12, fols 57r/v, 85–86v.   [206] *mm.* 49, 82.   [207] *m.* 153.
[208] Stafford, *Register*, pp. 308–9.

S Thomas's hospice

Roger Walden, as well as Alexander Neville of York, William Courtenay when bishop of London, William of Wykeham of Winchester, Thomas Brantingham of Exeter, Thomas Hatfield of Durham, Thomas Arundel of Ely, John Buckingham of Lincoln, John Harewell (probably) of Bath and Wells, William Reade of Chichester, Henry Despenser of Norwich, Thomas Trillek or more probably Brinton of Rochester, Ralph Ergham of Salisbury, and Henry Wakefield of Worcester.

Other grants of indulgence by local bishops can be traced. In 1388 bishop John Waltham of Salisbury licensed hospice collectors with forty days indulgence for subscribers.[209] Trefnant and later Mascall in Hereford did the same in 1390 and 1404 and 1405,[210] as did Scrope for York in 1400,[211] Wykeham for Winchester in 1399,[212] Bishop Bottlesham of Rochester, revealing that the collector locally was Thomas Russell,[213] and Bubwith for Bath and Wells in 1421.[214]

By 1402 Robert Newton was the proctor general in London, collecting from the dioceses and from the local members of the confraternity.[215] William Swan's letter complained that 'they especially complain of the dioceses at farm left by you from which almost nothing (has come?) and likewise nothing from the collections from the brethren and sisters . . .'[216] The system went back to at least 1398 when the proctor general was John Malpas. Much later the 'firma' or English revenue was a steady source of income.[217] There were even collectors in (English) Ireland by 1406.[218]

A few citizens of London are recorded as having remembered S Thomas's hospice in their wills. John Rous, a fishmonger, left a legacy in 1381 and William Kelleseye or Clophill in 1400 ordered his

---

[209] J. Waltham, The *Register of John Waltham, Bishop of Salisbury 1388–1395*, ed T. C. B. Timmins, CYS, 80 (1994), no. 156, p. 39.

[210] J. Trefnant, *Registrum Johannis Trefnant, Episcopi Herefordensis 1389–1404*, ed. W. W. Capes, CYS, 20 (1916), p. 193; R. Mascall, *Registrum Roberti Mascall, Episcopi Herefordensis, 1404–1416*, ed. J. H. Parry, CYS, 21 (1917), p. 190.

[211] R. Scrope, *A Calendar of the Register of Richard Scrope, Archbishop of York 1398–1405*, 2 parts (= Borthwick Texts and Calendars. Records of the Northern Province 8, 11), ed. R. Swanson, York 1981–5, II, p. 8.

[212] W. Wykeham, *Wykeham's Register*, ed. T. F. Kirby, 2 vols., Hampshire Record Society (1896, 1899) II, no. 316a, p. 492.

[213] Kent Archive Office, Maidstone, DRb/Art./6, f. 11v. There is a photo-copy of this in the English college archives: Scritture 117 (2) but my reference is the modern one.

[214] N. Bubwith, *The Register of Nicholas Bubwith, Bishop of Bath and Wells, 1407–1424*, ed. T. S. Holmes, 2 vols., Somerset Record Society, 29, 30 (1913, 1914), p. 412.

[215] *CPR 1401–4*, p. 79, with Henry Halum as his receiver.

[216] Arch. Seld. B 23, f. 33v: *maxime conqueruntur de diocesibus ad firmam per vos dimissis de quibus quasi non (sunt?) neque eciam de collectis ex fratribus et sororibus . . .*

[217] *Venerabile*, p. 54; *CPR 1396–9*, p. 324.

[218] N. Fleming, 'A Calendar of the Register of Archbishop Fleming', ed. H. J. Lawlor, *Proceedings of the Royal Irish Academy* 30 C, no. 5 (1912), pp. 94–190, esp. no. 7, p. 103.

executors to pay 2s a year for twenty years.[219] Perhaps he was a relative of Katherine Kelsey, of London diocese, who was an anchoress in Rome in 1399?[220] Though it was much more common in wills to specify that someone was to go to Rome on pilgrimage, to spend a certain time and to have masses at *scala celi*,[221] the holy stair at S John Lateran, supposed to come from Pilate's house, with its chapel, the *Sancta Sanctorum*, there is evidence that the English hospice of S Thomas was a recognised good cause among the merchant class in London from 1362 onwards.

By 1420, as we have seen, this largely lay enterprise had become much more clerical. It had gone through hard times but had not gone under; its revenues may have been diminished but it still had its buildings and its deeds, with a substantial amount of real estate to sustain itself. In this it was probably luckier than many institutions and seems to have been better placed than the few other English enterprises in the city, which are the subject of the next chapter.

[219] *A Calendar of Wills Proved and Enrolled in the Court of Hustings, London*, II, *1358–1688*, ed. Sharpe, R. R., London 1890, pp. 224, 405–6.

[220] See p. 127.

[221] Sharpe, *Calendar of Wills*, pp. 189, 234, 243, 250–1, 310, 333, 335.

Chapter 4

S CHRYSOGONUS' HOSPICE AND OTHER ENTERPRISES

The second English hospital which opened in Rome in the late fourteenth century was a product of the reign of Boniface IX and may even have been an aftermath of the 1390 Jubilee. It was largely the work of John White, a London merchant living in Rome, with his Gascon business partner Peter or Perrinus Baker and an Italian notary called Paolo dello Schocho but there seem to have been other local supporters in the Trastevere region where it was founded. The evidence suggests that this was a separate group, who knew the founders of S Thomas's but wanted their own work of charity.

The origins have been traced in the Sexcentenary edition of the house journal of the English College, in which the 'foundation' document was partially printed.[1] According to this, in 1396 the canons of S Chrysogonus' church in Trastevere assembled and heard White say that for forty years they had had a two-storeyed house in Trastevere, in the parish of S Chrysogonus, called the hospital of S Chrysogonus, and next to it a house which Nicola Nelli Johannis Cinthii of Trastevere had caused to be re-roofed also for the use of the poor, with John's house next to that. These houses were threatened with ruin and John wanted to repair them and build a new storey and re-roof them, to make them bigger, as a hospital for the poor, for his soul and that of his relatives, so he asked the canons for permission. The chapter then let the houses, for the peppercorn rent of twelve *denarii provisini* a year, to him and his heirs. John promised to put up a sign naming the hospital after S Chrysogonus and never to sell nor pledge the property without the consent of the canons and to appoint a proctor to run it. The canons promised not to reclaim the property for one hundred years, even were the rent not paid.

This as it stands is a work of piety prompted by a single person.

---

[1] *Venerabile*, pp. 92–4, from *m.* 139.

White was a merchant of London, probably a mercer, whose will shows that he was involved in banking operations in Rome via the Alberti merchants.[2] The witnesses were citizens of the Empire,[3] or Italians.[4]

An important question is why the canons were prepared to delegate the power over their hospital to an English benefactor.[5] The most likely reason was economic problems caused by the Great Schism. Maire-Vigueur has discussed how church property was being secularised in the second half of the fourteenth century. About one-third of the church's domain went in this period, caused by a combination of bad management and hardship from the heavy taxation consequent on the schism. Both Urban VI and Boniface IX taxed the churches of Rome, which can be seen selling or letting property to pay.[6] S Chrysogonus was in fact held in commendam by Cardinal Guy of Boulogne, as well as his titular church of S Cecilia, from 1351–73.[7] This was often a recipe for neglect. After that it was not immediately assigned to a cardinal. According to the 'founding' deed, in 1396 S Chrysogonus was 'governed' by Johannes Panella, archbishop of Durazzo.[8] He was chamberlain of Boniface IX and in 1393 had been put in charge of all cardinals' titles not assigned, to collect their revenues for the papal Camera.[9] Thus the church would have experienced exploitation by the papacy rather than an attempt to rectify its finances. The canons assembled to hear John White, with whom the plans must have been discussed and agreed beforehand, were Cecchus Malgionis, vicar general for Panella,[10] Franciscus Francisci de Campello de Setia, Franciscus Turii Andreotii, Franciscus Turii Velli Versi and Laurentius Johannis Laurentii Johannis Canis. It is worth emphasising that in this period the Roman nobility were also suffering both financially and politically and were therefore unlikely to come to the rescue of an institution in difficulties.[11]

The witnesses for White's deed included Nicolaus Herrici from Kulm, chaplain of S Lorenzo in Panisperna in Rome, whose presence here must be significant since he had founded a hospital of his own,

---

[2] White as mercer *CPR 1396–9*, p. 306. For his will see below pp. 79–80.

[3] See next note and p. 87.

[4] Magister Guilelmus Wuf STP canon of *Ortesecen'* (Ortesei?), the priest Peter son of the late Hermand of *Septemcastris* (Transylvania) in Hungary, now rector of the church of S Cecilia de Monte in Ripa region, Jacobellus Colecte, Petrus Lelli etc.

[5] For the community Caraffa, *Monasticon Italiae*, I, p. 51.

[6] J.-C. Maire-Vigueur, 'Les casali', pp. 102–5, passim.

[7] C. Eubel, *Hierarchia catholica medii aevi* , Munster 1913, I, pp. 18, 40.

[8] *m.* 139; Eubel, *Hierarchia*, I, pp. 232, 246; the deed gives no see, but he was transferred to Durazzo in 1395.

[9] Favier, *Les finances pontificales*, p. 336.

[10] Astalli, p. 85. In 1368 there was a notary in Ripa region called Georgius Malgionis.

[11] See above p. 17.

beginning in 1372.[12] This became known as S Andreas because of its connection from 1385 with Andrew Alene, a Welshman from S David's diocese.[13] Their hospice was exclusively for Germans, but it was a enterprise independent of other German efforts and as such may have interested White. Its buildings were near the Curia Pompeii, not far from Campo dei Fiori, thus near S Thomas's where Andrew was later buried. The notary for White's transaction was Paulus Johannis Damasi, a Trastevere man whose deeds can be found from 1368, probably White's preferred notary.[14]

The next we know is that White, of Arenula, was in April 1397 setting off for England on business with his partner Perrinus and, fearing the perils of the way, gave to the hospital of S Chrysogonus half a house, the other half to be lived in by Perrinus' wife for her lifetime, in the Arenula district. The executors, if John did not return, were Perrinus if he was there, or, in his absence the notary Paulinus dello Scocho of Trastevere.[15] This introduces the group of White's close associates who were as concerned as he in the early history of his hospital.

The remaining deeds reveal John White buying property. The 'founding' deed talks of a house of his next to the hospital of S Chrysogonus given to John by the lords of Monterano. He also shared a house in Arenula with Perrinus. In 1401 he gave to the hospice of S Thomas, reserving the right of use for his life, his house in the Pigna district, next to S Stefano's church, with also one *stirps* called 'of S Stefano'.[16] In 1404 White, said to be living in Arenula, bought a house in Trastevere and part of a garden from the notary Mathiotius Paulleli Johannis Jacobi with consent of his wife Paula. One of the witnesses was Perrinus (*Guilelmi dictus alias Perrinus Englese*) and the notary was Paulus Johannis Damasi.[17] In addition White bought land; in 1403 from the noble Johannes Antonius, son of the late Cole Scangiale-mosine of Parione, six pieces of vineyard outside the Porta Populi in the place called Morigenato[18] The proctor was Perrinus, who was also a witness; the notaries were Johannes Pauli Antonii Goioli (Anthony's son) and Damasi again.

Then in 1404 White died. His elaborate will was largely designed for the maintenance of his hospital. By then he was living in it. His executors and heirs were Perrinus, of Arenula, Paulus dello Scocho, and the *custos* of the hospital, Johannes son of Petrus, *Theotonicus*, one

---

[12] Maas, *German Community*, pp. 68–9 and see also pp. 86–7.
[13] Maas, *German Community*, p. 69 and see also AC Sez I, no. 785/2, f. 70r/v.
[14] Astalli, p. 45, n. 4. Deeds for White, *mm.* 164, 139, 165.
[15] *m.* 142.   [16] *m.* 156.   [17] *m.* 165.   [18] *m.* 164; see also *m.* 148.

supposes from the Empire. All White's movable and immovable goods in Rome and London were left to his heirs, who were to run his hospital and appoint their successors, with the exception of certain debts. He left to Perrinus for his life the newly bought vineyards just referred to, to come to S Chrysogonus after Perrinus' death. The half house in Arenula was left to the new hospice, with the little house in Trastevere bought in 1404, which as he says 'I have begun to fit out and repair for a chapel' (*incepi reparari et aptari pro capella.*) When the chapel was finished and decorated he wanted mass celebrated there 'by the authority of the sovereign pontiff or of someone else who has the power' (*auctoritate summi pontificis vel alterius potestatem habentis*). He made his heirs responsible for repairs and enlargements as needed. Thus by then the hospital chapel was in process of being built and evidently White wanted it given papal privileges, for instance the right to have mass said in its chapel.

The defenders of this testament were important people: Antonius de Caetanis, cardinal priest of S Cecilia in Trastevere, the Lords of Monterano, Franciscus, Gentile, Arturellus and Pensosus, Nicola de Bondis, doctor of Laws, Valerianus de Frangipanis, Laurencius de Macaranis, *iurisperitus*, Johannes Jacomini (or Jacobini) Cecchi de Acula, Cecchus de Romalis, Cola Nicoli and Andreas de Ponzianis. The notary was Alexius Cecchi Malgionis who was the final defender.[19]

This glittering array includes some of the most important people in the Trastevere district or even in Rome itself. Antonius Caetani was not only cardinal of the title of S Cecilia in Trastevere, but also belonged to one of the most important Roman families, related by marriage to Boniface IX and with strong Neapolitan links. He had been made cardinal in February 1402 and was a neighbour of the hospice of S Thomas, living in an Orsini house in Campo Fiore. His family dominated Tiber Island and part of the S Angelo region.[20] The Lords of Monterano, who seem to have favoured John White by giving him (?as a pledge) one of the houses later incorporated into his hospital, were a very important Trastevere family, the most dominant in the area of the new hospital, which was called the quarter of the lords of Monterano (*contrata dominorum de Monterano*).[21] The leading member, Gentile, mentioned in White's will, was a condottiere for Boniface IX and was to play an important part in the politics of Rome in the years

[19] *m.* 169. There are copies at *mm.* 168, 170 (a copy for the cardinal?).
[20] *DBI*, 16, Rome 1973, article by D Girgensohn, pp. 115–18; also Girgensohn, 'Kardinal Antonio Caetani und Gregor XII in der Jahren 1406–1408: vom Papstmacher zum Papstgegner', *QFIAB*, 64 (1984), pp. 116–226, esp. 118–19.
[21] *m.* 165.

immediately following this document.[22] The Frangipani were similar, a Trastevere family with a very illustrious past. Valerianus probably lived next to S Cecilia's church in Trastevere.[23] He played a prominent, and for him fatal, part in the upheavals of Rome in the period which followed White's death.[24]

Dr Nicola de Bondis belonged to a family prominent in local politics. He had been a *judex palatinus* in 1392, one of those whose legal skills were used to decide disputes in the commune[25] and his father Martinus a *speciarius*, was *consiliarius* for the S Angelo region in 1393. By 1408 they lived in the Torre de Bulgaminis in S Angelo next to the house called Lo Confesse which caused the hospice of St Thomas such problems.[26] De Bondis was one of the arbitrators used to settle a dispute about Lo Confesse in 1408.[27] In 1418 S Thomas's exchanged it with De Bondis for two houses of his *in platea Judeorum* near the Tiber in the fishmarket area.[28] The beginning of the connection with S Thomas's may have been the link with John White. Nicola's son lived in Trastevere in the 1430s and gave evidence for his and his family's knowledge of the family of S Francesca Romana.[29]

Laurentius de Macaranis of Trastevere also played an important part in the city upheavals of 1405 onwards.[30] Andreas de Ponzianis must have been a member of the family into which S Francesca Romana married, a wealthy upper-class clan, long established in Trastevere in a large house, owning many cattle, also very much involved in local politics.[31] De Bondis had connections with them.[32] The others were probably people who had played some part in the setting up of the hospital. Ceccho de Romalis was a notary from Trastevere, whose name is also found later witnessing the sale to S Chrysogonus' hospice of the Andreotti houses in Arenula.[33]

White's will was dated 23 October 1404 and he was certainly dead and buried (although the place of burial is not known) by 1 November, when S Thomas's took possession of its house.[34] On 28 December 1404 in Perrinus' house in Arenula, Perrinus and Paulus dello Scoccho

---

[22] Esch, *Bonifaz IX*, pp. 278, 333. [23] Gnoli, *Topografia*, p. 116.
[24] See below p. 86.
[25] A. Esch, 'Die Zeugenaussagen', p. 144; Esch, *Bonifaz IX*, p. 216.
[26] Ibid., p. 618; with in addition *m.* 183. For the Torre de Bulgaminis see A. Katermaa-Ottela, *Le casetorri medievali in Roma* (= Commentationes Humanarum Litterarum 67), Helsinki 1981, p. 58 no. 241, near S Maria in Candelabra al Fiume.
[27] *m.* 183. [28] *m.* 191.
[29] Gnoli, *Topografia*, p. 36; Esch, 'Die Zeugenaussagen', p. 144. [30] See below pp. 85–6.
[31] Esch, *Bonifaz*, p. 422; Esch, 'Die Zeugenaussagen', passim.
[32] Esch, 'Die Zeugenaussagen', p. 144; Lugano, *I Processi*, p. xxxvi; see Bartolomeo another relative, *Processi* pp. xix, 23–5, 28, 31–2, 35, 48, 64–9.
[33] *mm.* 173, 174 (called Franceschо). [34] *m.* 156 dorse.

constituted Robert Newton, perpetual chaplain of the church of S Sith, London, proctor and general *gubernator* of the hospice of S Thomas, the executor of this testament in England. The witnesses were Nicholas Claypool, priest of Lincoln diocese and Adam Vicford, priest of Salisbury diocese, with Philip Newton, clerk of S David's diocese as notary. Philip Newton figures later as *camerarius* of S Thomas's.[35] Claypool was mentioned as a creditor in White's will. Robert Newton was William Swan's representative in London, as well as the hospice of S Thomas's general proctor in England.

The two hospitals were thus not wholly separate. Evidently they were using the same agent in England. This was not the only link. By 1396 already S Thomas's had a house in Trastevere, sold to them in 1395 by Anthonia, widow of Collectus Marcelli, a miller of the region, for whom Valerianus de Frangipanibus acted as one guarantor. This house was in the parish of S Salvatore della Corte, beside the house of Nicola Nicoli, another of White's defenders.[36] In the course of business therefore the two hospitals would meet each other's supporters.

Robert Newton returned to London and presented White's will to the official of London diocese on 20 May 1405, when he was given White's English goods.[37] There was nothing to say what they were but by 1406 the new hospice was expanding. Perrinus with two new members of the group, John Giliocti and William son of Walter, Englishmen, called administrators of S Chrysogonus' hospital, with Paulus dello Scocho, their colleague, bought from Agnes, widow of the noble Franciscus de Andreottis, some houses in Arenula, in the same block as a house of Agnes' already given conditionally to the hospice, which itself was along the road from S Thomas's, on the right-hand side leaving the present Piazza Farnese. The price was the large sum of 700 ducats.[38] Agnes' donations were detailed in another document drawn the same day. They were a house with several storeys, a house with a stable and another house roofless (*discoperta*), next to the house she had just sold, all in Arenula, with four pieces of vineyard outside the Portese gate (*extra portam Pertusi*), in the place called *logiaddo*. These were given by Agnes because of her devotion to God and Our Lady and 'because of her devotion to the said hospital' (*propter devotionem quem habet in dictum hospitale*). The condition was that the hospital would remember the anniversary of Agnes and her husband, that Agnes had the use of the properties for life and that the hospital gave her 100 ducats within three years. In other words she was raising money on her 'gift'.[39] In

---

[35] *m.* 183 for instance.   [36] *mm.* 136, 137.
[37] London, Guildhall, Commissary Court of London, Register of Wills, MS 9171/2, ff. 64v–65v.
[38] *m.* 173.   [39] *m.* 174.

December 1408 the money was paid by Roger Chanyht (Knight), priest, *camerarius* on behalf of the hospital and fraternity.[40] Agnes was now remarried, to Petruccius Jubilei of Pigna.

In September 1406 dello Scocho and Perrinus, administrators of S Chrysogonus' hospital, acting on behalf of Giliocti and William of Walter, their colleagues, bought three houses in Trastevere in the parish of S Salvatore from Stephanus son of the late Johannes Jacobi Guarnerii for 100 florins.[41] The boundaries described show that these were in the same block as the new hospice. They represented some of Stephanus' part of the Guarnerii inheritance, which he had shared with his nephew in 1397.[42] In 1408 Johannes de Suecia and his wife Sabella sold to Roger Knight, dello Scoccho and Perrinus, administrators of the hospice, another house next to the hospital for 20 florins.[43]

Thus by 1408 the hospital of S Chrysogonus had officers and a confraternity, had spent a great deal of money and had acquired a block of property in Arenula with another in the same block as its original buildings. Of the earliest members Paulus dello Scoccho is known simply as a Trastevere notary who rented some vineyards outside Porta Portese.[44] Its early supporters among the non-Italian group are fairly obscure too. Perrinus Baker is the most well documented. In 1402 and 1403 he was involved in arguments with his neighbours in Arenula about a newly built wall to his house[45] and everything suggests a properous man. In 1403 he was a witness (Perrinus de Francia) when some Italians of Parione were making a agreement to sell wine in a tavern in Rome.[46] He had a wife Maria by 1397[47] and in White's will his daughter Ricciarda was left thirty florins for her marriage.[48] According to the list of founders now in the English College archives Maria was a Roman and Ricciarda married John Ely, a papal sergeant-at-arms, who was prominent later in the affairs of the English community. John and Ricciarda were benefactors of both English hospices[49] and the half house in Arenula which had been Maria Baker's was left by Ricciarda to S Chrysogonus' hospice, by then also called S Edmund's, in 1445.[50]

John Gilioti or Geylot, merchant, is only known from these deeds, unless he was John, son of John Gilgli, English *sutor*, of Arenula buying wine from a grower outside porta del Popolo (*porta Populi*) in 1412.[51] A John Gilliot, mercer, was a freeman of York in 1397.[52]

---

[40] *m.* 184. [41] *m.* 176. [42] *m.* 143. [43] *m.* 182.
[44] Astalli, p. 44, note 2, called Stoccho. [45] *mm.* 161, 162.
[46] Vat. Lat. 2664, f. 237. [47] *m.* 142. [48] *m.* 169.
[49] Rome, Venerabile Collegio Inglese, *Liber* 272, f. 1 and Harvey, *England, Rome*, p. 54; *m.* 201.
[50] *mm.* 201, 202. [51] AS Collegio Notarile Capitolini 848, ff. 184, 186v–187.
[52] *Register of Freemen of the City of York, I 1272–1558*, ed. F. Collins, SS 96 (1897), p. 101.

The other Italians in the early deeds are worth considering. The man who sold John White the roofless house and the garden with fruit trees which went to make the site of the future chapel was Mathiotius Paulelli (or Pauli) Johannis Jacobi a notary found in Trastevere from 1368 to 1404.[53] He had a wife Paula and a brother Nucius, also a notary.[54] The Scangialemosini family which held the vineyards which White bought were established as notaries in Campo Marzio area in 1360.[55] Cola Dominici who owned the land can be traced there from 1372.[56] When White bought the properties, for 400 florins, Johannes Anthonius, Cola's son, was living in the Parione region and was able to command some very important backers. His guarantors were Franciscus Andreotti de Ilperinis, one of the well-known Ilperini family of S Eustachio, whose rise dated from about 1342.[57] They were allies of the Orsini. Another was Sabbas Cole Galgioffi, also called Sabbas della Fragna, of S Angelo region, whose father Cola (of the river bank (*Ripa Fluminis*)) called Fragna also, was one of a family of millers from the S Angelo and Ripa areas found from the 1360s.[58]

The Andreotti houses in Arenula described in 1392 as next to the new English hospital reveal more about the circle of sellers. In 1392 Vannotia, widow of Nicola Francescoli Andreotti de Andreotiis sold a house and a *caselenus discopertus* which was a pledge for her dower, to Agnes, wife of the noble Johannes Francisci Andreotti de Andreottiis.[59] In 1401 Johannes Francisci left all his goods to his wife Agnes.[60] In 1406 when she did the various transactions leaving them or selling them to the hospice of S Chrysogonus the nature of the family was revealed by the guarantors and witnesses. For the houses sold the guarantors for Agnes were the noble Petrus de Andreottis, Johannes Ley, a neighbour, Johannes Nardi Pichi of Campo Marzio, probably a relative of Angelellus Nardi Picchi of Arenula, a *calsularius* in 1368.[61] The witnesses to this sale and for the gift included Laurentius de Macaranis, a backer for White.

When in 1408 the hospice of S Edmund bought the little house from Lucas Johannis and his wife Sabella, their guarantor was Stephanus Johannis Guarnerii, a neighbour.[62] When Stephanus sold his three houses to the hospice the witnesses included Anthonius Appoliti, described elsewhere as painter (*pictor*),[63] and Petrus Nucii Odarelli who both appear also for Lucas and Sabella. Another witness was Alexius Cecchi Malgionis, the notary who drew White's will and was another defender. Thus a group of neighbours cooperated to allow the sales.

---

[53] *m.* 165; Astalli, p. 45.   [54] Astalli, p. 37.   [55] Johannes Nicoli Pauli, p. 149.
[56] Staglia, p. 52.   [57] Ibid., p. 7.   [58] Astalli, p. 85 and note.   [59] *m.* 126.
[60] *m.* 157.   [61] Astalli, pp. 44, 59.   [62] *mm.* 182, 176.   [63] *m.* 176.

Not all this prosperity lasted. In 1410 Perrinus and Roger Knight leased their vineyards outside Porta del Popolo in perpetuity for must at the vintage and a small rent, because the land was not being properly worked, partly 'because of shortages and wars' (*propter caristias et guerras*).[64] By this time the two hospices were evidently much more closely identified, since this transaction was done in S Thomas's hospice, with witnesses including Paulus the archpriest of S Maria and Caterina, the church opposite S Thomas's, and Philip Wynty, called canon of the hospital of the English of Arenula.

This enterprise never flourished as did S Thomas's; it turned out that John White did not use the best backers. Many of the conservators became fatally involved in the civil wars in Rome. White made his will on 23 October and had died by 1 November 1404. Boniface IX died on 1 October and it must already have been clear that the city was in for trouble. Ladislas of Durazzo, backed by the Colonna, was on his way to Rome during the conclave begun on 12 October, which elected Innocent VII on 17 October and he entered the city two days later to face a city sharply divided as we saw between Colonna and Orsini parties.[65] Cardinal Caetani was on reasonably good terms with Ladislas but had other things to think about than the wills of obscure English founders of small hospitals. He sided with the other cardinals in the quarrel with Gregory XII over a general council and went to Pisa in May 1408. He was very much involved in the negotiations about the schism and in any case suffered from serious ill-health from 1408 onwards. He died in January 1412.[66]

Other backers fared even less well. Gentile of Monterano sided with the Colonnas and was excommunicated in June 1406. He came to Rome with Ladislas in April 1408 as one of his staunchest supporters and was one of the defenders left when the latter returned to Naples in July. By May 1411 Gentile had changed sides again and was supporting Louis of Anjou. On 15 April 1413 he was in prison in Castel S Angelo by order of Pope John XXIII.[67] In 1440 Arturellus, *ex dominis Castri Monterani* left S Chrysogonus' hospice a house in Trastevere near the Piazza S Chrysogonus.[68] He was the second of the lords of Monterano mentioned in White's will, so in the end Monterano patronage helped, but it was not achieved without trouble. Laurencius de Macaranis, who

[64] *m.* 185.   [65] Esch, *Bonifaz*, pp. 440–8; R. Ninci, 'Ladislao'.
[66] DBI, as note 20 above.
[67] Schiavo, *Diario*, pp. 13, 28, 29, 34, 67, 77; N. della Tuccia, *Cronaca di Viterbo*, ed. I Ciampi (= Documenti di storia italiana 5) Florence 1872, pp. 48–9; Infessura, *Diario* pp. 12, 13; Cutolo, *Ladislao*, I, pp. 287, 355, 376, 399.
[68] *m.* 198.

might have been an important ally, was one of the 'governors of the liberties of the city' in 1405, went to negotiate in Tivoli in August 1415 as *dominus per populum Romanum* (in other words podestà) and was murdered according to rumour by order of Jacopo de Colonna. He was buried in the church of S Chrysogonus.[69] In 1446 his two sons, Stephanus and Franciscus agreed that S Chrysogonus' hospital had the right to the house in Trastevere given by Arturellus de Monterano.[70] The hospital agreed that they in turn could rent it, repair it and then hand it back after thirty-nine years in return for a rent of one *libra* of prepared wax per year. It would appear therefore that they had been in some way trying to block Arturellus' gift and may have been finding life difficult as the sons of a politically suspect father.

Valerianus de Frangipanibus was one of the conservators of the city treasury in 1408 and in 1414 was one of the leaders chosen by the *nobiles* to resist popular unrest. As such he was sent to negotiate with the papal Legate in 1414 but was wounded and died. He was buried in S Cecilia in Trastevere on 24 November 1415.[71] The Ponziani also suffered very badly during the unrest because of their hostility to Ladislas. S Francesca's husband was seriously wounded in the fighting, his brother was exiled, their son Baptista was taken hostage, the house in Trastevere sacked and goods were confiscated. The worst of their suffering was in 1413 when Trastevere was the centre for the troops of Ladislas.[72]

Thus John White's enterprise was starting at the worst possible time for a Roman institution and many of its backers were in no position to help after its early stages. Despite the fact, therefore, that at first it had a much more illustrious set of supporters than the hospice of S Thomas and also that White's wealth was greater than the original money put into S Thomas's, the hospice of S Chrysogonus never became very large nor as quickly prosperous as the other.[73] In 1464 it was finally amalgamated into the other house.[74]

There was another hospital in which an Englishman was involved, though it was intended solely for Germans and was less successful even than S Chrysogonus'. Nicolaus Henrici, the German founder, was from Kulm but was chaplain in S Lorenzo in Panisperna in 1372 when he

[69] Schiavo, *Diario*, pp. 8, 99; A. Salimei, *Senatori e statuti di Roma nel medioevo*, I, *Senatori (1144–1447)* (= Bibioteca storica di fonti e documenti 2), Rome 1935, p. 158, *DBI*, 27, pp. 318–20, esp. p. 319, article by P. Partner on Jacopo (Giacomo) Colonna.

[70] *m.* 204.

[71] Schiavo, *Diario*, pp. 23, 94, 101; P. Egidi, *Necrologi e libri affini della provincia romana*, 2 vols. (= Fonti per la storia d'Italia 44, 45), Rome 1908, 1914, I, p. 340.

[72] Esch, 'Die Zeugenaussagen'; Lugano, *Processi*, pp. viii, 28, 45, 46, 170.

[73] *Venerabile*, pp. 87–9 for the history up to 1464.   [74] *Venerabile*, pp. 89–90.

made the first purchases for his hospital for Germans.[75] In the next seven years he added further properties.[76] By 1388 Nicolaus had met and agreed with Andrew Alene a priest of S David's diocese, as a private arrangement, that Andrew could live rent-free in a house between two already owned by Nicolaus, free of charge for life, in return for repairs.[77] The arrangement was said to be for the love Nicolaus had for Andrew and was probably a return for other, unspecified services. By May that year Andrew gave to Nicolaus, called founder and builder of the hospital now called of S Andrew, for the chapel of S Andrew built by Andrew in it, four pieces of vineyards with a house and garden which he had bought in Tivoli, reserving the usufruct for his life,[78] and in 1391 Andrew bought further houses in Tivoli.[79] These Tivoli houses were bought from the Celestine monastery of S Maria Magdalene and were said to be 'so damaged as to be almost ruined' (*taliter deguastata quod quasi in ruynam adducta*), the brothers compelled to sell because the abbot was so pressed for money for repair of the monastery of S Eusebius in Rome which was also ruined (*dominus abbas ad presens habet maximam necessitatem habendi pecunias pro reparatione monasterii Sancti Eusebii de urbe videlicet in partibus anterioribus dicti monasterii in loco qui dicitur locampidnolgio qui locus est de presenti ruynaturus nisi reparetur*), another indication of the state of religious houses. These vines and houses were sold in 1393 by Nicolaus and Andrew to buy further property in Rome for S Andrew's.[80] The document by the vicar general allowing the sale explained that bringing the produce of the vineyards to Rome from Tivoli was too difficult: 'the fruit of these vineyards cannot be brought to the city without great difficulty, labour, customs and other expenses and often not without great danger' (*quarum vinearum fructus non sine magnis difficultatibus, labore gabellis et aliis expensis sepiusque non sine periculis ad urbem possit deferri*). They were given licence to buy others 'in the Roman territory' (*in territorio Romano*). There is no evidence beyond this for what Andrew was doing in Rome, though he appears to have had money; his will showed him lending it. There is no evidence either as to why Nicolaus was a witness when John White made his agreement with S Chrysogonus to found a hospice in 1396.[81] But the various groups of nationals must have encountered one another in ways now lost to us.[82]

---

[75] Maas, *German Community*, p. 68; Nagl, *Anima in Rom*, no. 209.

[76] Maas, *German Community*, pp. 68–9; Nagl, *Anima in Rom*, nos. 210, 211.

[77] AC Sez. I, 785/2 f. lxxr/v; Nagl, *Anima in Rom*, no. 212; Archives of S Maria dell'Anima, Instr. Litt. B, tom. I, f. 15r/v .

[78] Nagl, *Anima in Rom*, no. 213; Archives of S Maria dell'Anima, Instr. Litt. B tom. I, ff 22–4.

[79] Nagl, *Anima in Rom*, no. 216; Archives of S Maria dell'Anima, Instr. Litt. B tom. I ff. 26–28.

[80] Nagl, *Anima in Rom*, no. 219. [81] See p. 78. [82] See p. 117.

Nicolaus resigned in 1410 and died in 1412, leaving his property to his hospital.[83] Andrew Alene made his will in September 1411 and left to the chapel of S Andrew in the hospital 'newly built and walled' (*noviter fabricati et murati*), vines outside the city walls in the place called Testaccio.[84] He was by then living in S Thomas's hospice and left it some books and the collection of some debts. He chose to be buried, not in the graveyard of S Andrew's but before SS Maria and Caterina, that is S Caterina della Ruota, opposite S Thomas's hospital, which may indicate that already there were problems in S Andrew's.

The year 1411 was a most unfavourable time for an institution in Rome to be left without proper leadership and S Andrew's fell on hard times at once, from which it never really recovered. It had always been intended for Germans only, despite Alene's support, and never seems to have attracted many other backers. First it fell prey to an embezzler appointed in 1411 by John XXIII, though a German auditor rescued it, and then there were quarrels. By 1431 it had been amalgamated into the much more successful hospice of S Maria dell'Anima.[85] The history of S Chrysogonus was not so different although there was no embezzlement.

There was considerable interaction between the English and the German communities in Rome, particularly but not solely among *curiales* who belonged to their national hospices. The 1406 rental of S Thomas's hospice showed several German tenants: Henry Faber rented one house for eight ducats a year; Johannes a German rented first one shop at the side of a house opposite Sibilla Teste's former home, selling different mercery, and then later (1407) another alongside, selling purses and gloves, held in 1406 by two further Germans.[86] Other documents reveal that a goldsmith who held a shop in 1406 was also German.[87] Sibilla Teste's former house was rented in 1406 by Dietrich of Niem for twelve ducats a year.[88]

Henry Faber was a member of the papal curia who occurs in Swan's letters, probably a friend of Swan's, unable to pay his rent when he followed Gregory XII.[89] Dietrich was a long-standing *curialis*, having begun his career in Avignon about 1370 as a Rota notary.[90] Urban VI promoted him to scriptor and by April 1380 he had become an

---

[83] Maas, *German Community*, p. 69.
[84] Nagl, *Anima in Rom*, no. 228; Archives of S Maria dell'Anima, Instr. Litt. B, tom. 1 ff. 102–3v.
[85] Maas, *German Community*, pp. 69–70.   [86] *m.* 172.
[87] Venerabile Collegio Inglese, *Liber* 232, f.7v.
[88] See also *m.* 50 dorse for mention of house of Dietrich.   [89] Arch. Seld. B 23, f. 46v.
[90] What follows is based on H. Heimpel, *Dietrich von Niem (c. 1340–1418)*, Münster 1932; and E. F. Jacob, 'Dietrich of Niem', *Essays in the Conciliar Epoch*, 2nd edn, Manchester 1953, pp. 24–43.

abbreviator also. He belonged to the upper echelons in the papal chancery and his *De scismate* shows that he had ready access to the pope.[91] He remained a leading person in the chancery under Boniface IX, by which time he was becoming very disillusioned (the pope's simony appalled him). After a spell in Germany he returned to the curia in 1403 and served Innocent VII. In 1406 William Swan described him as president of the chancery (*cancellarie presidens.*)[92] This must have been the period when he hired his house from S Thomas's since later he certainly owned a house in Campo dei Fiori.[93] He was one of those who followed the curia to Lucca with Gregory XII. He did not go to the Council of Pisa, however, but rejoined Alexander V and took an important part in the Council of Constance.

Dietrich was not only an important member of the curia but also one of the most important German residents in Rome, a notable donor to and supporter of the German hospice S Maria dell' Anima.[94] In both these capacities he encountered English people. When Swan was writing in 1406 to John Macclesfield in the course of the latter's litigation about S Anthony's hospital in England he also suggested writing to Dietrich, 'to whom we are much obliged'.[95] When in 1414 Swan's agent in Florence was trying to ship his goods, he consulted Niem about a safe way to do so.[96]

Niem had made gifts to the Anima hospital in 1406, intending to retain the use of his property for his life but after Ladislas captured the city in 1413 the king confiscated the goods of all who followed John XXIII and his lieutenant tried to confiscate Dietrich's goods also, including his gifts. In the end Ladislas took the German hospital under his protection. and the gifts were saved, though Niem lost the use of them.[97] Among Dietrich's properties was a vineyard and small house by the Tiber, near S Spirito in Sassia, sold to him in July 1407 by John Swayne, an Irish abbreviator who later became papal secretary.[98] Selling this property may have been Swayne's way of trying to avoid losing it altogether when he followed the curia and he may have given it to Niem in trust rather than in actuality.[99] In 1414 Niem talked of keeping back from his gifts to the Anima only one property, which was a house newly built at Niem's own expense, intended for a hospice for poor

[91] Ed. G Erler, Leipzig 1890.   [92] Arch. Seld. B 23, f. 31.   [93] Heimpel, *Niem*, p. 40.
[94] Maas, *German Community*, pp. 35, 72–4.   [95] See above p. 47 note 127.
[96] Arch. Seld. B 23, ff. 103v–4.   [97] Maas, *German Community*, pp. 73–4.
[98] Nagl, *Anima in Rom*, no 13; Archives of S Maria dell'Anima, Instr. Litt. B, tom. 1, ff. 73v–75; K. Walsh, 'The Roman career of John Swayne, Archbishop of Armagh 1418–1439. Plans for an Irish hospital in Rome', *Seanchas Ardmacha*, 11/1 (1983), pp. 1–31, esp. pp. 9–10.
[99] Walsh, 'Roman career', pp. 15–16.

Irish priests.[100] Possibly this represents Swayne's aspirations for his former property. If so nothing came of it.

Clearly the idea of founding hospitals occurred to several people in Rome at this point but to be successful was not easy. If one asks why S Thomas's succeeded when S Chrysogonus' was less successful and Alene's and Swayne's efforts came almost to nothing, timing may be the main explanation. S Thomas's was well established by 1404, with most of its property held with unassailable credentials and run still by a largely lay group who could not be accused of following the curia.[101] S Chrysogonus' lost its main backer in 1404 and its Italian supporters were far too involved in the troubles of the city to be able to help it. S Andrew's simply did not have backing and Swayne's may never have been more than a unrealised dream. It is also likely that there were not enough English people resident in Rome to support more than one successful institution; by 1464 at least that was what the English had decided.

---

[100] G. Erler, *Dietrich von Nieheim (Theodoricus de Nyem). Sein Leben und seine Schriften*, Leipzig 1887, appendix, no. 10, produces the document from the Anima archives.

[101] Dr Walsh is of course in error (p. 17) to think that none of the Anglo-Irish clerics 'closely identified with the English administration' were associated with S Thomas's, as is shown above.

Chapter 5

THE LAITY IN ROME

In seeking for English lay people in Rome I have concentrated on those who spent some time there, rather than merely coming for pilgrimage or briefly for diplomacy. The search produced about forty lay men between about 1360 and 1420 who probably carried on a trade of some kind. These are all men whose presence cannot be explained simply by the return of the Roman curia (which I shall discuss separately). The number of lay men whose presence in Rome can be attested is much larger, although some of these were probably there only fleetingly.

Some of the tradesmen had a known place of origin in England. Thus John son of William Champneys, who was active from at least 1374 to 1381[1] and John White who founded the second English hospice of S Chrysogonus (S Edmund),[2] both merchants, were described as from London, White in fact always being called citizen of London. Another merchant, William Chandler, was from York.[3] His name appears in 1362, acting for the hospice of S Thomas at its foundation, but not again until 1376.[4] John, son of William, a goldsmith also involved in the foundation of the hospice, was from *Maxigam*, probably Massingham in Norfolk.[5] Two brothers, Simon and John, with Simon's wife Cecilia, were recorded as being from Colchester (*de Conchesteri de Encleterr*) when buying a house in 1367 which Simon left to S Thomas in 1369.[6] John Salmon of Salisbury with his wife Elena can be traced between 1375 and 1382.[7] John Palmer alias Ponfret, active from 1365 until 1387, was perhaps from Pontefract in Yorkshire.[8]

However, Scots, Welsh, Irish, English and even Gascons were liable to be called English: William son of Patrick, late of Scotland, who seems to have been called Scossa, in 1364 bought a house from an Italian

---

[1] *mm.* 74,76, 81, 84, 86, 100, 107, 108.   [2] See below pp. 101–2.   [3] *mm.* 36, 37.
[4] *m.* 86.   [5] *m.* 37; *Venerabile*, p. 40.
[6] *m.* 50, with information about the bequest dorse.   [7] *mm.* 79, 110.
[8] Goioli, nos. 145, 148; in *m.* 118 of 1387 he is *dudum* dead.

woman using an Englishman as her proctor.[9] Davit, son of John, of Wales, in 1396 became the heir of a Gascon woman, Johanna, daughter of Peter de la Morte de *Gascognia*, widow of an Italian, Guilelmus de Civita Vecchia.[10] The terms on which Davit was given her house were that he must leave it for the good of her soul if he died without heirs. In 1400 he sold it to the English hospice.[11] Peter or Perrinus Baker, a Gascon, who played an important part in the beginnings of S Edmunds, with a Roman wife Maria[12] and a daughter Ricciarda,[13] occurs from 1397[14] to at least 1408[15] and was called either English[16] or *de Francia*.[17] Most intriguing of all is Statius Manerii, whose origin was given in 1395 as 'lately of Florence' but who, according to the papal registers, was also an Englishman (*natione anglicus*).[18] He was also called Eustatius Maneys, son of John. He certainly lived in the hospice of S Thomas for a time and had dealings with English people, so either he was a naturalised Englishman or an Englishman with trade connections in Florence and Rome.

Not all the laity were assigned occupations in the records but where we know what they were doing the following stand out: *paternostrarii*, *cernitores*, *sutores*, mercers and merchants. Certainly, where origins are known, connections with trade and possibly with cloth, seem very likely. At the end of the fourteenth century apart from London, Colchester, Salisbury and York would be towns very likely to produce merchants prepared to travel abroad for trade.[19]

An important group were the *paternostrarii*. It is not surprising of course to find them in a pilgrim centre like Rome. Between 1360 and 1420 eleven were named in hospice deeds or notaries' protocols. It is, however, rather striking that in other sources the trade is rarely mentioned and also that even in 1527 only seventeen (one a woman and none English) were noted in the Roman census.[20] Thus perhaps a disproportionate number of English people plied this calling in Rome at this early stage. The Englishmen were Simon, son of John Barber, of Parione region, mentioned from 1350 to 1401;[21] John, son of Peter Shepherd, of Arenula; John Ponfret or Palmer, of Parione and of

[9] *m.* 39; AC Sez. I 649/7, ff. 50–52v.   [10] *m.* 138.   [11] *m.* 152.
[12] AS 848, f. 181v.   [13] *m.* 169.   [14] *m.* 142.   [15] *m.* 184.
[16] *m.* 165: *Petrus Guilelmi alias Perrinus Englese.*   [17] *m.* 174: *Perrinus de Francia.*
[18] *m.* 130; *CPL*, V, p. 214.
[19] See tables in E. M. Carus-Wilson and O. Coleman, *England's Export Trade*, Oxford 1963, pp.138, 140 (London), 146 (Hull), 148 (Southampton); for Colchester: R.H. Britnell, *Growth and Decline in Colchester 1300–1525*, Cambridge 1986, esp. pp. 53–5, 65–8. Professor Britnell reckons that Colchester men did not participate in cloth export directly and the Barber family in Rome were *paternostrarii*.
[20] Lee, *Descriptio urbis*, p. 343.   [21] *mm.* 18, 153.

Arenula, active between 1365 and 1383, dead by 1387;[22] William, son of Richard, first of Parione and later of Arenula, mentioned between 1362 and 1407;[23] John Alnit mentioned only in 1367;[24] Raulinus, son of John, of Parione, found between 1365 and 1373;[25] John, son of John Clerk, of Ponte region, first recorded in 1373[26] and dead by 1390;[27] Thomas, son of Nicholas, of Colonna region, found from 1371 until 1376,[28] certainly dead by 1387;[29] and Richard, of Parione but then of Arenula, who may be the son of Thomas of Nicholas,[30] found perhaps in 1377 but certainly in 1383[31] To these we can add John, son of William, goldsmith (*aurifex*), formerly of Massingham but living in 1362 in Parione in the contrada called via Pape,[32] and Richard, another *aurifex*, living in Parione in 1397.[33]

Of these we know little about John Shepherd, credited with founding the English hospice by buying the house from Smerucci. The sum he gave for his house was not enormous, 27 florins and the house must have been very basic: the description *quandam domum terreneam* denotes a one-storey, simple house.[34] It is very likely that what looks like a simple purchase and sale actually masked another transaction involving Smerucci and already Shepherd, representing the group of Englishmen.[35]

Shepherd and his wife Alice were probably childless; little was specified in his will of 1365 because he was leaving all his goods to the hospice. Alice had her dower described in John's will as fifteen gold florins in one hand or ten shillings in the other, not the dowry of a wealthy woman.[36] She also had a bed with bedding and three gold florins from an earlier legacy, but as the *Universitas Anglicorum* was probably going to house her she may have been less poor than this suggests.

All these transactions involved a group of *paternostrarii*: Shepherd's purchase from Anthony, as well as his will, involved Simon of John (Barber), *paternostrarius*, John of William *aurifex*, and William of Richard, *paternostrarius*, all of Parione, and the will added Raulinus of John *paternostrarius* also.

Simon of John Barberii (?Barbour), *paternostrarius*, executor for Shepherd, frequently witnessed transactions involving English people in Rome between 1350 and 1401.[37] In the earliest, of 1350, he was described as of S Lorenzo in Damaso region,[38] and was witness with another Englishman, John *Parvus* (Little?) and an Italian, Guilelmus

---

[22] Goioli, nos. 145, 148; *m.* 115 (will).   [23] *Venerabile*, p. 37; *m.* 179.   [24] *m.* 52.

[25] *mm.* 45, 52, 68; Goioli, no. 111.   [26] *m.* 66.   [27] *m.* 119.   [28] *mm.* 60, 88.

[29] AC Sez. I, 650/1, ff. 20–3.   [30] AC Sez. I, 649/13, ff. 37r/v.   [31] *m.* 115.

[32] *m.* 37.   [33] *m.* 144.   [34] Hubert, *Espace urbain*, p. 172.   [35] See p. 10.

[36] Goioli, no. 111, pp. 189–90.

[37] *mm.* 51, 52 ,66, 82 ,83, 95 ,97; AC Sez I, 650/1, ff, 20–3.   [38] *m.* 18.

Johannis Ferarii, in the selling of four *stirpes* to Robert of the Ghetto (*de platea judeorum*) an Englishman. In the later documents Simon's residence was given as Parione. In 1387 however he bought from the executors of the will of Robert de Pigna half of Robert's house in Pigna district which was being lived in for her life by Robert's servant Alice, the problems of which were discussed above.[39] By 1395 when Statius Manerii gave the other half, Simon must have been very old but there was a last mention of him, now of Pigna, in March 1401, witnessing John White's gift of a house to the hospice of S Thomas.[40] Raulinus first appeared witnessing Shepherd's will,[41] but thereafter in 1366 was renting a house in Arenula at a lowered rent in return for doing repairs.[42] The last mention of him was in 1373 where he was said to be of Parione.[43]

William son of Richard, with (at least from 1390) a wife called Alice,[44] was an important member of the group for many years. As well as participating in the transactions involving the Shepherds,[45] he was frequently an executor of the wills of people connected with the hospice of S Thomas: a woman called Amata, widow of an Englishman called Henry Orlandi, in 1365,[46] the first will of Robert de Pigna in 1368,[47] the will of Richard, son of Roger, in 1369,[48] and of Henry of Trastevere both in 1373 and in 1377,[49] and in 1390 for Elena wife of John Clerk, another *paternostrarius*.[50] In 1374 he was *camerarius* of the hospice;[51] at other times he was one of a group receiving property for it,[52] or as a witness of transactions concerning it.[53] He was *custos* in 1391, 1393, 1395, 1397, 1399, 1400 and 1402.[54] He was certainly a man of some means. In 1374 he bought a house which he rented out,[55] and another in 1381.[56] By 1384 he was living in Arenula and in 1407, no doubt very old, he donated the 1381 house to the hospice.[57] Probably he died soon afterwards; his name appears no more.

John, son of Robert Palmer, alias Ponfret of the Parione region, probably a *paternostrarius* also,[58] was *custos* of S Thomas in 1365[59] and

---

[39] AC Sez. I, 650/1, ff. 20–3; *m.* 118.   [40] *m.* 156.   [41] Goioli, p. 189.

[42] *m.* 45.   [43] *m.* 68.   [44] *m.* 119   [45] Above p. 11.

[46] Goioli, no. 148, pp. 248–9.   [47] *m.* 53.   [48] *m.* 56.   [49] *mm.* 69, 93.

[50] *mm.* 119, 122.   [51] *mm.* 71, 72.   [52] *mm.* 86, 87.

[53] *mm.* 85 (1375); 91 (1377); 100 (1379).

[54] Archives of S Maria dell'Anima, Instr. Litt. B, tom.1, ff. 118–120v; *mm.* 127,130, 135, 136, 144, 149, 152, 160.

[55] *m.* 71, for purchase; *m.* 75, renting.   [56] *m.* 106.   [57] *m.* 179.

[58] He was an executor of the will of Robert son of Robert, described in AC Sez. I, 649/13, ff. 15–18 as John of Robert, *paternostrarius*. In AC Sez. I, 650/1, ff. 20–3, he is called Johannes Palmerucii.

[59] Goioli, nos. 145, 148. The alias is revealed in comparing *m.* 49, dorse where the house is said to be given by the will of John Ponfred, with the will of *m.* 115, of John Palmer. The house was *m.* 82.

again in 1374 and 1376.[60] He often witnessed actions concerning English people.[61] In his will, in 1383 when he was ill, he left legacies to the hospice of S Thomas.[62] By 1387 he was dead.[63]

As well as these *paternostrarii*, active in the early days of the hospice of S Thomas, there were others involved in its business before the papacy returned from Avignon. One was John son of John Clerk of the Ponte region, who can be seen from 1373 buying or renting pieces of land *(stirpes)*.[64] In 1376 he and his wife Elena bought a house in the region[65] and in 1378 a piece of garden.[66] He also owned land *ad cernendum* and was probably a *cernitor* also.[67] On occasion John witnessed business concerning the hospice[68] and was co-executor with William, son of Richard, of the will of Henry of Trastevere, one of its original founders.[69] The house which William bought in 1381 from Elena Clerk may have been for the purpose of donating it.[70] The Clerks thus appear to be fairly substantial people. Elena's will, in 1390 when John was already dead, gives an incomparable snapshot of the network of relationships in which she was then living but since this was also the world of the restored papal curia, I will deal with it elsewhere.[71]

The final *paternostrarius* found frequently in the early deeds was Thomas, son of Nicholas of the Colonna region. In May 1371 he was *camerarius* of the hospice.[72] and he witnessed a renting in 1374 by William, son of Richard.[73] In 1376 he bought half of Robert de Pigna's house from Robert's executors and half Robert's property[74] and also came to an agreement with Alice, Robert's servant, about the exact meaning of 'half' when sharing: because 'sharing is often wont to cause scandal' *(quod communio sepe solet scandalum generare)*.[75] In 1387 Thomas was dead; Alice's half, with Alice still in it, was then sold to Simon, son of John, *paternostrarius*, in other words Simon Barber.[76]

Much less can be found about the other *paternostrarii*. John Alnit appears only once in 1367.[77] Richard and Richard of Thomas, originally of the Parione region, but living in Arenula in 1383, may be the same.[78] If so he had a wife Aloysia and a daughter Palotia and they were tenants in Arenula of John Ponfret. Of the two goldsmiths nothing more is known.

In the remaining documents there are a number of Englishman called *cernitor* and some examples of persons with property *ad cernendum* or to

---

[60] *mm.* 77, 82, 83, 84, 86.   [61] *mm.* 75 91,100.   [62] *m.* 115.   [63] *m.* 118.

[64] *mm.* 66, 70, 101.   [65] *mm.* 90, 92.   [66] *m.* 94 and see *m.* 103.

[67] See below p. 96.   [68] *m.* 100.   [69] *m.* 93.   [70] *mm.* 104, 105, 106.

[71] *m.* 119.   [72] *m.* 60.   [73] *m.* 75.   [74] *m.* 88.

[75] AC Sez I, 649/13, ff. 15–18; 37r/v.

[76] Astalli, p. xxvii, but the details there and at p. 81 are inaccurate.

[77] *m.* 52.   [78] *m.* 115; AC Sez. I, 649/13, ff. 37r/v.

which is attached the right to do so (*ius cernendi*). The English names associated with this trade are John, Mabel and Michael de Girlandia, Stephen the Englishman (Mabel's late husband), Henry *servitor* of the church of S Silvestro *de capite*,[79] Richard the Englishman of Arenula, Robert of Pigna, Robert Odoguardi of Ripa, Robert *de calcalario* of S Eustachio, Robert of Platea Judeorum (the Ghetto area), Rosa Casarola and her two English servants John Bramante (whom she married) and John the Englishman, with also Jacobus of Robert, Henry of Trastevere, Davit of Wales and John Clerk, who was also a *paternostrarius* and John Cross.[80]

It is not easy to decide what the occupation was. In the Roman examples it looks most like some sort of milling and the best explanation seems to be sieving, though machines were involved.[81] The task (or tasks) has various descriptions in our sources, by no means easy to decipher and translate. The earliest (1333) describes a *stirps* in the Pigna region, in *contrada* S Stephano,

with all the things and the gear in the house in which Henry the seller now keeps or has kept *cernitores* for the sake of ? in it (*cum omnibus et singulis rebus et massaratiis in domo in qua ipse Henricus venditor nunc tenet et pro temporibus retinuit cernitores causa [sicoli conizandi] in ipsa*)

together with another vacant *stirps* in *contrada Sancti Marci*

with each and every right of those *stirpes* according to the use and custom of the English and the *cernitores* of the city (*cum omnibus et singulis indictionibus ipsarum stirparum secundum usum et consuetudinem Anglicorum et cernitorum urbis.*)[82]

The seller in 1333 was Henry the Englishman, *servitor* of the monastery of St Silvester *de capite*, selling to Richard, another Englishman, of Arenula. What was probably the same property was sold again by Henry's widow in 1347,[83] with the same description of its use. The buyer was also English, Robert *Odoguardi* of the Ripa region. None of these persons is called *cernitor*, whereas in 1353 Robert the Englishman of Pigna was called *cernitor* when he bought a vacant *stirps* in Colonna district, for use *secundum morem et consuetudinem anglicorum et cernitorum urbis.*[84] Thus there seems to have been something peculiarly English at least about some of this activity. It would appear that there was a group of Englishmen engaged in it at this early period, and this may explain

---

[79] Huelsen, *Le chiese*, pp. 465–7, a female convent.   [80] See p. 120 also.
[81] I would like to thank Dr John Langdon for his considerable help with this problem. Professor Mosti also was of considerable assistance.
[82] *m.* 8.   [83] *m.* 12.   [84] *m.* 21.

why the earliest of our documents includes Symon *mandatarius curie Anglicorum urbis* as a witness.[85]

The 1333 document however, although it looks like a sale, was probably in fact a pledge (since Henry's widow later re-sold the property), which may explain why all those concerned were English. The witnesses, apart from Simon the *mandatarius*, were Philip and Raulinus, Englishmen, both of Arenula and the transaction took place in the home of the buyer, Richard, the Englishman of Arenula. The notary in 1347 was, as he had been in 1333, Johannes Porfili but the witnesses included several Italians as well as Richard the Englishman of Trevi district and John de Girlandia, of *contrada SS Apostoli*.[86]

The last man belonged to a family of English people called de Girlandia from S Marco, near present Piazza de Venezia or SS Apostoli, the Colonna palace area. There were several people of this name all connected with *stirpes ad cernendum*. The earliest reference was 1347 when Johanna, widow of William and Michael de Garlandia, both English and of S Marco, sold to fulfil William's will, of which they were executors, the *stirps* of S Marco to Robert de Pigna. for nine *libri*.[87] The witnesses included John de Garlandia Englishman of S Marco. The final de Girlandia is Mabilia de Girlandia, widow of Stephen the Englishman of Campitelli district, who in 1354 gave her consent to the sale of a *stirps* in Trastevere called the *stirps* of S Chrysognonus, to Henry the Englishman of Trastevere. Robert of Pigna was again a witness.[88] Robert was a *cernitor* and all his other *stirpes* were *ad cernendum*.[89]

There seems usually to have been flour-milling involved; another *stirps* which Robert (of Pigna) the Englishman bought in the Monti region was said to be *ad cernendum farinas*.[90] In 1363 Rosa Casarola, probably the Italian wife of an Englishman, left in her will the right to remain (*sedium*) in two houses to her servant (and later second husband) John Bramante, an Englishman, with use for his life 'of the winches for *cernendum* with my area' (*totius argangii pro cernendo cum convinio meo*).[91] A later version of her will called this 'the quarter of Rose for *cernendum* flour' (*contrada ipsius Rose pro cernendo farinas*)[92] and further described it as 'with all the winches and standing pools for *cernendum* flour in the said houses' (*cum omnibus argangiis et stanungiis pro cernendo farinas in dictis*

---

85 *m.* 8.   86 Huelsen, *Le chiese*, pp. 201–2.   87 *m.* 16.   88 *m.* 25.
89 *mm.* 12, 17, 21.   90 *m.* 17.
91 Vatican Library, S Angelo in Pescharia, I/1, ff. 141r/v. I take *argangium* to mean winch (= Italian *argano*), see Caputgallis, p. 438.
92 S Angelo, I/1, f. 17.

domibus). Much the same was repeated in another later version.[93] All this suggests that machinery and water were involved and, since Rosa employed John and another servant, that there was a regular business.

In 1373 likewise a *stirps* was let to John Clerk, *paternostrarius*, for use *ad cernere faciendum*.[94] In 1379 probably the same piece was let again but this time described as to be used:

ad cicoli conizandum seu cernendum cicoli conicati cernere faciendum per se et alium eius nomine et famulos suos toto tempore titulo et inscripto hominibus et personis dicte stirpe farinam cernere volentibus et exigentibus.[95]

The man letting the *stirps* said that he or his men could

sell, grant or concede flour in the houses and through the houses of those living in the said areas wishing to sieve flour or to ? it, and to accuse or cause to be accused others sieving flour in the areas of the *stirps* (*vendere, cedere et concedere farinam in domis et per domos habitantium in dictis contradis farinam cernere et cicoli conizare cernere et cicoli conizare facere et alias personas cernentes farinam per dictas contradas dicte stirpe accusare et accusari facere*)

All this involved considerable business, though in John Clerk's case we must assume that, as with Rosa Casarola, it was done for him and this must have continued to be so when these *stirpes* belonged to the hospice.

The *cernitores* included Henry of Trastevere, so-called first in 1354,[96] who in 1373 in his will left to Jacobus of Robert, an Englishman, all his *stirpa pro cernendo* for two years to pay his debts.[97] He witnessed one of the founding documents for S Thomas's,[98] and one of Rosa Casarola's several wills in 1363,[99] and was involved in other transactions for English people.[100] His first will in 1373 revealed a wife Margaret and a son Richard;[101] his second in 1378 showed that by then he had a second son.[102]

Probably more important than Henry in the early life of the first English hospice was Robert de Pigna. We have already seen him in 1350 buying a *stirps* in the S Marco region,[103] and another in 1353 for use *ad cernendum*.[104] He witnessed Henry of John's purchase in 1354,[105] and was a proctor in the 1362 transactions about S Thomas's.[106] In 1364 he bought half a house from Nicholas de Astallis, rector of the church of S Nicola in Pescharia, of a famous family including one well-known notary.[107] It was Robert's will, made in 1368 but later added to, which

---

[93] S Angelo, 1/3, f. 9: *contrada pro cernendo farinas existens in dictis domibus.*   [94] *m.* 66.
[95] *m.* 101.   [96] *m.* 24.   [97] *m.* 69.   [98] *Venerabile*, p. 41.
[99] S Angelo, 1/1, f. 141r/v.   [100] *m.* 53, AC Sez I, 649/8, f. 131.   [101] *m.* 69.
[102] *m.* 93.   [103] *m.* 16.   [104] *m.* 21, above p. 96.   [105] *m.* 24, 25.
[106] *Venerabile*, pp. 38–9.   [107] *m.* 38.

caused such a problem because he left the half house to his servant Alice.[108] In 1368 he had a wife Margaret and his executors were Henry of Trastevere and William the *paternostrarius*. He did not die then, however, because he was *custos* of the hospice in 1372 and *camerarius* in 1374,[109] as well as frequently acting for it, often with William the *paternostrarius*, in the years 1371 to 1374.[110] By May 1376, however, he was dead and so evidently was his wife, leaving the complicated task of executing his will with its codicils to the surviving executors, Henry of Trastevere and John Ponfret/Palmer.[111]

Davit of Wales of the Parione region, who sold a house to S Thomas's, was also called *cernitor* in 1396,[112] but we know nothing more. John Cross is the final English *cernitor*. He was in Rome living in Colonna from at least 1391 and probably before, because that year he married an Italian woman, Angillela, orphan but not poor daughter of Paulus Macarii of Parione, whose widowed mother Francesca gave her a dower of one hundred gold ducats.[113] He was already associated with S Thomas's then, because the dower was to go to it if the pair died without heirs; William *paternostrarius* the *custos* witnessed this. Cross had perhaps a relative in Rome. In October 1402 John Appollinaris, alias Janni Croce of Pontis, was guarantor for Perna, widow of Andreas Mannus of Parione, Janni's mother-in-law, husband of her daughter Anna, whose consent was also necessary, when John Cross senior was buying two expensive houses from Perna.[114] The price was 194 florins. John Cross also bought a vineyard beyond Porta del Popolo for 25 florins in October 1411 and in 1417, when he was called *cernitor*.[115] Cross was *camerarius* of S Thomas's in 1401,[116] 1404,[117] 1405,[118] and in 1418,[119] which suggests that he stayed in Rome throughout its troubles. But that is all we know.

A further trade represented among the English was *sartor* or *sutor*, both meaning tailor in fourteenth-century Italy.[120] Few of these can be identified beyond one reference: Thomas, son of John, of Parione in 1381, a witness,[121] William, son of William, of the Parione region, a witness in 1391,[122] or William Conelle of Ponte, in 1396, again a

---

[108] *m.* 53.   [109] AC Sez. I, 649/12, f. 57r/v; *m.* 77.
[110] *m.* 75; AC Sez. I, 649/11, ff. 19v–20, 20v–25, 50v–51.
[111] *m.* 88.   [112] *m.* 138.
[113] S Maria dell'Anima, Instr. Litt. B, tom I, f. 118–120v; Nagl, *Anima in Rom,* nos. 217, 223, 229, 231.
[114] S Maria dell'Anima, Instr. Litt. B, tom. I, ff. 120v–123v; for Andreas see Goioli, pp. 86, 194.
[115] S Maria dell'Anima, Instr. Litt. B, tom. I, ff. 125–127v; f. 151, Nagl, *Anima in Rom,* no. 231, called *cernitor*.
[116] *m.* 156.   [117] *m.* 156, recording taking over the property.   [118] *m.* 171.
[119] *m.* 191.   [120] Goioli, pp. xviii–xix.   [121] *m.* 104.   [122] *m.* 121.

witness.[123] Helen, the daughter of William *sutor*, who received a legacy from the widow of John Clerk in 1390, may have been the daughter of either.[124] In 1404 William *sartor* of Arenula district was mentioned in the will of the London merchant John White as owing four ducats for a loan, for which White had a pledge of two books and two tunics brightly coloured (*colore clarioli*).[125] A little can be known about one other, called John, son of John Gilgli (? son of William) of Arenula. His name occurs between 1410 and 1412. In 1410 he was acting with Perrinus Baker, the former partner of John White, founder of the hospice of S Chrysogonus,[126] with whom he owned a house. In 1412 he can be seen buying wine[127] but also, more interestingly perhaps, as a witness when John Lougham, an Englishman, did the same.[128] Lougham was an associate of John Frainceys, a leading English cleric at the curia.[129]

More can be discovered about Richard Teste (Head?) *sutor* of Parione and his wife Sibilla Knight. In 1373 he had bought an expensive house (90 florins) in Parione.[130] One of his witnesses was Raulinus of John, the English *paternostrarius*. In 1379 he made it over to his wife, Sibilla, reserving usufruct to himself for life.[131] Since the curia had now returned to Rome several witnesses were English clerics or laymen who were perhaps only temporarily in Rome. The notary was an English cleric. The same day, with the same witnesses and notary, sound of mind: 'although he lies in bed afflicted with a certain illness' (*quamvis ex quadam egritudine in lecto iacet afflictus*), he made over to Sibilla all his goods including two gold cups and three gold spoons, all his beds, and 'linen and woollen garments and all other cloths' (*vestimenta linea et lanea et omnes alios pannos*).[132] Sibilla was also mentioned in 1390 in the will of Elena Clerk, widow of John *paternostrarius*, as receiving some clothes.[133] In 1391 she sold the house for 100 ducats to William of Richard, *paternostrarius*, with as one witness the *sutor* William, son of William.[134]

The only other *sartor* about whom one can discover much is Walter, son of Simon, of Parione. He was also a papal courier (*cursor*), so will have to be looked at in another context. But he was also probably a genuine tailor. In 1382 he bought a house from John Salmon from Salisbury.[135] He had a wife Christine and was described as 'Walter the Englishman tailor courier of our lord the pope' *Gualterus Anglicus sutor cursor domini nostri pape*. This could be merely a latinising of Taylor and he certainly witnessed for other English *cursores*. But in his will in 1403,

[123] *m.* 138.   [124] *m.* 119.   [125] *m.* 169.   [126] *m.* 186.
[127] AS 848, ff. 184, 186v–187.   [128] AS 848, f. 234v.   [129] *CCR 1392–96*, p. 525.
[130] *m.* 68.   [131] *m.* 98.   [132] *m.* 99.   [133] *m.* 119.   [134] *mm.* 121, 128.
[135] *m.* 109.

he had an associate called Jacobus de Ferraria, *sutor*, to whom because he was indebted, he left his shop (*apotheca*) in his house in Parione for a year rent-free.[136] Jacobus was an executor and was still renting the house from S Thomas's in 1406.[137] Walter's wife must have been already dead. Some of his trade appeared in this will. Robert the Englishman owed him 4 ducats, 'as the testator says appears in his account book' (*prout in libro rationis eiusdem testatoris dixit apparere*). John Sauler owed him 20 ducats for which he thought John should be excommunicated. He left the task of collection to S Thomas's. He had evidently lent beds and bedding to Master John Ixworth, and Master John Haget and household goods to Master Adam Usk. These were all important members of the papal curia.[138]

Since by definition mercers dealt in many goods and travelled widely, it is not surprising to find an English mercer, Geoffrey (*Galfridus*) present at the drawing up of the statutes of the Roman guild of mercers in 1375, though we know nothing further about him and he was not among the early group round the hospice.[139] John White, citizen of London, the founder of the second English hospice in Trastevere in 1396, was probably also a mercer. In April 1397 he was about to leave Rome for England[140] and in June the next year John White, citizen and mercer of London, had been pursuing a large debt in England.[141] He first appeared in the Roman records in 1396. He was a man of considerable property. Since he left this to both S Chrysogonus' and S Thomas's hospices the remaining archives contain details of the houses,[142] vineyards[143] and gardens he owned in Rome. But his will also revealed that he acted as a banker for a wide circle of people and that he had property in London too.[144] This will, dated 23 October 1404,[145] was proved both in London and Rome.[146]

At death John White had on deposit in the Alberti bank in the Ponte region in Rome 80 ducats, for which 'I have a private pledge written in their own hand' (*habeo quamdam apodissam privatam scriptam eorum manu propria*). He owed Nicholas Claypool 12 ducats, which he had in that bank. He had in the bank of Marcus Marchese in the same region 8 ducats and he owed 20 ducats to the English priest Roger Burstede (a canon lawyer, rector of S Nicholas Olave, London, who had been

---

[136] *m.* 163.   [137] *m.* 172.   [138] See below pp. 133, 149, 159.
[139] E. Stevenson, *Statuti dell'arte dei merciai e della lana di Roma*, Rome 1893, pp. 8, 20.
[140] *m.* 142.   [141] *CPR 1396–99*, p. 306.   [142] *mm.* 142, 153, 165.
[143] *m.* 148, 164.   [144] *m.* 169.
[145] *m.* 169, with several other copies in the archives of the college.
[146] Guildhall, London, Commissary Court of London, Register of Wills, MS 9171/2, ff. 64v–65v, spelled Wight.

doing business in the curia[147]), also in that bank. He had lent the hospice of S Thomas fifty ducats with as pledge a mitre. He was owed sixty ducats by Perrinus Baker, his partner and heir,[148] and eighty ducats by John of Peter, a German, another heir, *custos* of the hospice of S Chrysogonus. He had left at Perrinus' house twenty-three measures (*caballatas*) of must from his vineyards, which Perrinus had been cultivating. He had entrusted to Perrinus six pieces of vineyards for life.

Apart from detailing real property left in Rome White also noted that John Kirkeby, a monk, owed him rent for a house, William *sartor* owed him four ducats for which he held a pledge, and the English Peniten-tiary[149] owed him two ducats for a loan. He had *in commendam* from Guilelmus *de Porticchie* fifty-three florins which must be repaid. In other words this was a man thoroughly ensconced in the world of Rome, including the Roman curia and Roman banking, even if we cannot be quite sure what the merchandise was. It is significant that his dealings in Rome were partly with the Alberti who between 1396 and 1436 were the most prominent firm of Florentines dealing with England.[150] As well as Baker and the German he named as his heir Paulus son of John dello Scocho, a notary of the Trastevere district. He was able to obtain support for his new hospice from some of the most notable residents of Trastevere.[151]

The small group of *sutores* leads one to look also at a further group of merchants, who certainly dealt in cloth, though probably also in other goods. The earliest recorded example of cloth dealing is an agreement between Sir Thomas Chandos and his wife Lucy, living in Arenula in 1365.[152] Thomas was the son of Sir Roger Chandos of Snodhill, Wellington and Townhope in Herefordshire,[153] in Italy perhaps on business. They made their proctor Cinpus ser Francisci of Florence, of SS Lorenzo and Damaso in Rome, to receive for them from Leonardus Justi a Florentine living in Venice, the three hundred pounds sterling which Leonardus owed them. The bill was in the hand of Jacobus Giacomini of Florence, living in London. Cinpus was also to receive for them 615 gold florins which were owed to Thomas by Michael Vannis ser Locti of Florence, by a bill in the hand of Leonardus. If Cinpus got the money Thomas and his wife agreed to make a partnership (*societas*) with him for five years, Cinpus to invest the money in new cloth and

---

[147] *CPL*, V, pp. 90, 613; died at curia by December 1404, *CPL*, VI, p. 38; and see below p. 173.
[148] See below p. 104.   [149] See below p. 154 for the person.
[150] G. Holmes, 'Florentine merchants in England, 1346–1436', *Economic History Review*, 2nd series 13 (1960), pp. 193–208.
[151] See p. 80.   [152] Goioli, no. 50.
[153] G. E. Cokayne, *The Complete Peerage*, various eds, 2nd edn, 13 vols., London 1910–1940, III, pp. 148–9; Roskell, *History of Parliament*, II, p. 515.

other merchandise (*in pannis novis et aliis mercantiis*) to be brought to Rome by Cinpus, and Chandos and his wife to contribute 2,000 gold florins. The proceeds were to be shared equally, half to Cinpus, half to the couple, with arrangements about predecease. If Edward III recalled Chandos, Cinpus would repay within six months.

Cinpus occurs in 1365 in the protocols of Antonius Goioli as a banker.[154] He was factor for Donatus Pauli Ramalgicinus of Florence[155] and dealt with Michael Vannis on other occasions.[156] In Goioli's protocols Cinpus, Vannis, Donatus and his brother acted together in exchanging money from England.[157] Michael Vannis was usually based in Avignon, and was a banker for the pope in June 1369 when the curia was briefly in Rome.[158] Giacomini, a Florentine living in London, occurs frequently in English records as a banker and wool trader.[159] As noticed above he was the main Italian named as a defaulting debtor in the Good Parliament[160] and probably fled from London in 1375 at the beginning of the Florentine war with the pope, with its Interdict.[161] Probably Chandos' arrangement with Cinpus did not last long. In December 1366 Robert of Pigna and Henry of John of Trastevere, the two *cernitores*, were his proctors to collect money owed him by Donatus, from Gregorius Henrici, representing Donatus, another Florentine.[162]

Others among the English group given no specific trade were clearly merchants also. Some evidence of trade by Englishmen between Avignon and Rome before and after the outbreak of the schism (1377–9) is seen in the accounts of William Colchester who travelled to Avignon and then to Rome during those years. He noted that on his first visit to Rome from Avignon in 1377/8 he was entrusted by Thomas Southam in Avignon with eight florins to pay in Rome to creditors of John Draper.[163] Draper travelled regularly from Avignon to London and later to Rome. He was entrusted by Westminster Abbey with shipping Cardinal Simon Langham's possessions from Bruges in 1377.[164] On William's second stay in Avignon in 1378 Draper brought a document from London to Avignon for him. On Colchester's return

[154] Goioli, nos. 26, 56, 57.   [155] Goioli, no. 26, 56.
[156] Goioli, no. 26.   [157] Goioli, no. 20.
[158] Y. Renouard, *Les relations des papes d'Avignon et des compagnies commerciales et bancaires de 1316 à 1378* (= Bibliothèque des écoles françaises d'Athènes et de Rome 151), Paris 1941, p. 292.
[159] *CPR 1361–4*, p. 466; Holmes, 'Florentine merchants', pp. 201 n. 4, 212 n. 2.
[160] Holmes, 'Florentine merchants', p. 203.
[161] Ibid., p. 203; *Rot. Parl.* II, p. 332; *Calendar of Letter Books. Letter Book G*, p. 302, 314; *Calendar of Select Pleas 1364–81*, p. 233.
[162] AC Sez I, 649/ 8, f. 131.   [163] WAM, 9256B.   [164] WAM, 9233.

to Rome via Marseilles and Ostia, Draper came too at Westminster's expense.

A reasonable amount can be discovered about Perrinus Baker. The records call him either *de Anglia* or *de Francia*. The S Edmund's list of founders called him a Gascon and noted that he was a citizen of Rome.[165] That implies ownership of both a house and land in the city.[166] The earliest information is from 1397 when his *socius, investititus* and *amicus* John White was returning to England with Perrinus and 'both because of the long journey and the dangers of the roads and cases of death etc.' (*et tam ex longe intinere et viarum discriminibus et casibus mortis etc.*) thought he might not be able to return to the city for a long time. Hence White gave to the hospice of S Chrysogonus half a house, with one of the proctors Paulus dello Scocho and Perrinus if he was in the city.[167] Perrinus' wife Maria lived in the other half.[168] From 1402 onwards Perrinus litigated about his house in Arenula which he was repairing and rebuilding,[169] and was a witness for John White when John was buying property in 1403 and 1404.[170] His mercantile activities may have included wine, since White's vineyards were entrusted to him[171] and in 1403 he witnessed the setting-up of a wine shop.[172] Perrinus continued to discharge duties for S Chrysogonus' until at least 1408.[173] White's will shows that Perrinus had a daughter Ricciarda.[174] The 1406 rental of S Thomas's hospice shows a house lived in by the 'son of Peter Baker', probably Ricciarda's husband, since a deed records that the son-in-law (*gener*) of Peter Baker held a former Ponfret house.[175] Ricciarda did marry, a papal sergeant-at-arms called John Ely, who had a career as a diplomatic courier between the papacy and England, as well as being a distinguished member of the hospice of S Edmund.[176]

The only other merchant about whose status one can be sure is John Giliot or Geylot, who was an administrator of S Chrysogonus' hospice between 1406 and 1408.[177] S Edmund's founders' list calls him simply *mercator*.[178]

Statius or Eustatius Manerii or Maneys must have been a merchant also. He is first encountered in 1391, buying a house left by Elena Clerk, whose executors had not money to fulfil her will unless they sold it.[179] The cost was the large sum of 150 florins. Statius was next in 1395

---

[165] *Venerabile*, p. 94; from *Liber* 272, f. 1. [166] See p. 24. [167] *m.* 142.
[168] See also AS 848, f. 181v. [169] *mm.* 161, 162. [170] *mm.* 164, 165.
[171] Above p. 80. [172] Vatican Library, MS V, 2664, f. 237: *Perrinus de Francia*.
[173] *m.* 185. [174] *m.* 169. See also p. 125. [175] *mm.* 172, 49 dorse.
[176] Harvey, *Engand, Rome and the Papacy*, pp. 33–4.
[177] *mm.* 173, 174, 176, 184. [178] *Venerabile* p. 94, from *Liber* 272 f. 1. [179] *m.* 122.

living in the hospice of S Thomas, where a gift from him to Simon Barber, Englishman and *paternostrarius*, of the half a house in Pigna region which later caused such problems,[180] 'on account of the love and affection which he has for the said Simon and for the pleasing and honest services which he confesses he has had from Simon', was witnessed in S Thomas's hospice, in Statius' room (*in camera dicti Statii*).[181] When Statius died (before December 1398) he had constituted Julianus Johannes Lipi Alberti, citizen and merchant of Florence, his executor and sole heir.[182] The use of an Alberti was probably significant. Julianus hired two English priests, Roger Knight, of Salisbury diocese, almost certainly in 1408 and 1410 one of the administrators for S Chrysogonus' hospice,[183] and Thomas de Truria, OP, STM, to say masses stipulated in the will.[184]

The persons discussed so far had fairly clear roles in Rome, but there were others who, at present at least, cannot be given an occupation, yet spent a considerable time in the city. There were other Barbers, though they may not have been English. In June 1372 Simon son of the late Cecchus Nardi de Pupo, butcher (*macallarius*), of Parione sold his house in the district to Johannes . . . (the document is very damaged) Barberii de *Sagoia* for 50 florins. This was sold in 1378 by Johannes, described as son of the late Johanetta Barberii de *Saoya*, with a wife Leone and a son Peter, to William Roberti, an Englishman, with, as guarantors for Johannes, Jacobus Johannis de *Saoya* workman (*laborator*), Petrus Johannis de *Saoya*, one supposes the son, staying in (*morans in*) Arenula. A witness and proctor for William is Simon *paternostrarius* of Parione, in other words the Simon Barber whom we know to be English. But there is nothing to say the others were. John Barber is not to be identified with a man living in Trastevere in 1397 and still in 1406.[185]

On the other hand there was another Simon the Englishman not identified with Simon of John the *paternostrarius* This was Simon, son of Simon, with a wife Cecilia and a brother John, from Colchester. According to the deeds, in 1367 the three bought a house in Parione, which was *in proprietate* of S Biagio *in canto secuto*. A witness was Simon Barber.[186] The dorse of the deed records that this house (said in 1406 to be opposite that given by Sibilla Teste[187]) was given in 1369 by Simon's will and was the house which Henry Faber was holding (in 1406). Simon purchased more than this, however. Later in 1367 he bought the house next door, again with Simon Barber as one witness, from Lellus domini Johannis *cabalerii* de Saracenis,[188] only to sell it again that day to

---

[180] See below pp. 67–8.   [181] *m.* 130 (3 April 1395); *m.* 135 (29 July).
[182] *CPL*,V, p. 214.   [183] *mm.* 182, 184, 185.   [184] For Thomas see also *CPL*,V, p. 153.
[185] *mm.* 143, 176.   [186] *m.* 50.   [187] *m.* 172; see above p. 66.   [188] *m.* 51.

John son of John, another Englishman (?Clerk) for half what he had just paid, which must represent a hidden bargain now obscure.[189] The witnesses for the last transaction were one Italian, Nicola de Judicis, with a benefice in S Peter's, and then three English *paternostrarii*: John Alnit (or ?Alene), Simon Barber and Raulinus of John.

There is also an intriguing group of Doneys. John was a well-attested cleric, discussed above, but there was also a lay Robert Dune, Downe or Donne, who held a hospice house in Pizzomerle in 1406 and witnessed a deed in 1405,[190] and William Doneis, Englishman also called *Guilelmus dello ospitale* of Arenula who witnessed for John Cross buying a house in 1402.[191]

The group of English lay men whom we have discussed were in Rome doing largely lay business, though it is true that after 1377 the presence of the curia made a difference. Only Walter Taylor, the *cursor*, however, had employment from the papacy and even he did not call himself *cursor* at the time of his death.

Most of the evidence about the group comes from notarial documents drawn by Italian notaries. Only in 1379 for the first time was a document (Richard Teste's will) drawn up by an English notary and entirely witnessed by English people,[192] and this practice remained rare. Most documents have at least some Italian witnesses. This was obviously sensible, since the transaction had to be valid and provable in Rome. John White's will is the only one I know which was proved also in England.

Although the English dealt frequently with one another, they also made business partnerships with Italians, as in the case of Perrinus Baker, John White with Paulus dello Scocho, and Walter Taylor with Jacobus de Ferraria. The wool dealings and borrowings depended on Italian connections, in particular on a Florentine/Rome axis which must have been part of the beginning of the Florentine involvement in the English wool trade. Professor Holmes has detailed the Florentine merchants in England between 1346 and 1436.[193] There were distinct phases. In the first the Alberti merchants became the leading bankers for papal business between 1363 and 1375.[194] Between 1350 and 1376 at least sixty Florentine merchants worked in England, some very active in exporting wool, including Jacobus Giacomini, with whom Chandos dealt in 1365.[195] After 1376 and the papal interdict, the Florentines abruptly left Rome and also London.[196] The Alberti lost their leading

---

[189] *m.* 52. [190] *mm.* 171, 172.
[191] Archives of S Maria dell'Anima, Instr. Litt. B, tom. I, ff. 120v–123.
[192] *m.* 98. [193] Above p. 102. [194] Holmes, 'Florentine merchants', p. 193.
[195] Ibid., pp. 201, 202, 203. [196] Ibid., pp. 202–3.

position to the Guinigi of Lucca who, with other Luccans, became very important in the exchange system with England as we saw.[197]

The presence of an English group in Rome can at least partly be explained by the state of trade in England. The most lucrative commodity which the English had to export was wool, either raw or as cloth. The government therefore used taxes on wool and interference with its trade to raise revenue, since cloth manufactures in both Flanders and Italy needed English wool. In return for privileges, particularly the right to export English wool, Italians, particularly Florentines but also Genoese, were prepared to lend to the crown. English merchants might have wished to participate in this export but were frequently unable to do so, because they could not provide the shipping or the capital or because they were legally debarred from doing so.

From 1353 to 1357 in theory exports of English wool were a monopoly in the hands of aliens, to facilitate taxation. Then in 1359 a Staple where all exported wool had to be traded (and therefore taxed and checked) was fixed at Bruges and finally from 1363–69 in Calais.[198] Between 1363 and 1375 the English, especially the wool merchants, were trying to break into the alien trade and despite the ban on denizen exports some English merchants certainly colluded with foreigners.[199] Between 1375 and 1396 English merchants flourished in the export trade.[200] This may explain why the names associated by Stow with the founding of the hospice of S Thomas included those leading London merchants who were involved in exports precisely in the 1370s and 1390s.[201] In the 1360s when English merchants were again able to export wool via Calais, one of the leading exporters was already John Philpot.[202] From 1365 onwards the anti-alien movement in London was gathering pace because Edward III began to allow Italians to export wool directly to Italy. The Grocers of London in particular tried to contest this but several other groups also protested. But Edward III did not favour privileges for English trade and in 1368 again withdrew the Staple from Calais, forbidding the export of wool by denizens though allowing evasion for a fee.[203] This thoroughly annoyed many London wool exporters who began to organise themselves politically to have the staple restored and to remove aliens. Philpot was involved, not least by marriage. From 1370 Adam Stable also became prominent. Philpot was

---

[197] Ibid., p. 193.   [198] Lloyd, *Wool-Trade*, p. 206–10, 217.
[199] Ibid., p. 214–15.   [200] Holmes, 'Florentine merchants,' p. 203.
[201] See p. 59.
[202] Nightingale, *Mercantile Community*, pp. 217–47 for much of what follows in the next two paragraphs.
[203] Lloyd, *Wool Trade*, pp. 217–20.

one of those merchants elected to the Commons in 1371 who presented anti-alien petitions to the king, aiming, among other things, to keep the Genoese out of Southampton.

Unrest among London's merchants was made worse by losses in the Hundred Years War renewed from 1372, which diverted wool from Calais and allowed the trade to be taken over by Italians. Again Philpot was one of those involved in anti-alien politics in London. Interestingly, in the newly organised Grocer's Company in 1373 at least one-third of the membership was involved in the wool trade, bonded against alien competition and to counteract the effects of war on trade. In 1375 they had a majority in the court of aldermen, including Philpot, their ally. This was the alliance which launched the attacks on aliens in the Good Parliament in 1376, although in fact the results benefited only the staplers and not the rest.[204] The alliance held afterwards, however, and in September 1375 Adam Stable's election as mayor of London can be seen as part of the strategy. Anti-alien policy was in the ascendant in 1377. Some English merchants in this period are known to have taken to exporting wool direct to the Mediterranean, 'to beat the aliens at their own game'. In the early 1370s there was already a sizeable English mercantile colony in Lisbon, for instance, exporting wool and importing wine.

The native attempts to seize the export trade did not succeed. This was partly because the wool trade declined in any case in the face of civil war in Flanders and unrest in Florence, one of our other outlets, in 1379. In 1377 of course a new king took power and at first the crown favoured the London staplers, who, including Philpot, were prepared to lend large sums. Philpot even provided ships at his own expense. But Richard II quarrelled with the Londoners in the 1390s and the government moved the Staple from place to place and changed its policy in order to raise instant revenue. Meanwhile the export of wool actually fell and the evidence suggests that few English were sending wool to Italy even when they could do so in the early 1390s, though some did so from Southampton.[205]

As is well known, as the English wool trade declined, cloth exports increased, but cloths sent to the Mediterranean were usually in the hands of the Italians. Nonetheless some Englishmen did export cloth to Italy on their own account.

From 1396 onwards, moreover, the Florentines returned to London and Rome, having patched up their quarrel with the pope.[206] The

---

[204] Holmes, *Good Parliament*, pp. 79–90, 118–126.
[205] Lloyd, *Wool Trade*, p. 233. [206] Holmes, 'Florentine merchants', p. 203.

Alberti reappeared in London, where their firms became the leading Italian banking houses, particularly important between 1400 and 1433 in controlling the exchange system between England and the curia.[207] From the late 1390s there was also an increasing shortage of bullion, worse after 1400, and only those (largely Florentine) with the ability to acquire it were able to succeed in the foreign markets. In 1400 again about 60 Florentine families were living in the Ponte region in Rome, in the area around S Angelo bridge.[208] This explains John White's dealing with the Alberti bank and also no doubt Statius Manerii and his Alberti executor.

It was not only financially that the English interacted with Italians, of course. They naturally had to conform to local customs. A most telling example is in 1365, when Anthonius Goioli recorded an agreement between two Englishmen, Roger, son of the late Nicholas, now living in Velletri and John son of the late William son of Thomas, now living in Arenula. John was the nearest relative, cousin and heir of the late Thomas son of Thomas an English clerk, who had been killed by Roger. The two agreed to seal with a kiss of peace an agreement not to pursue any injuries which might exist between them, especially concerning this killing, and to be bound for one hundred *libri provisini* to keep the city statutes. John, as the injured party, agreed that he accepted 'for reverence of almighty God, his most glorious mother blessed Mary, for the remission of the sins of Thomas himself, on whom may God, who is the Father of all, have mercy' (*ob reverentiam omnipotentis Dei et gloriossisme matris beate Marie et ob remissionem peccatorum ipsius Thomaxii cui Deus qui Pater omnium valeat miserari*).[209] The agreement was made in the hospice of S Thomas with two Englishmen among the witnesses, William Daras of Parione and the *custos* John Palmer, the rest being Italians. The English, like their Italian neighbours, naturally also took arguments over buildings before the street magistrates (*magistri stratarum*), for instance Perrinus Baker in 1402 and 1403,[210] arguing with his Italian neighbour Jacobus Rubei about a wall.

Conformity to local custom included making a local will. Up to 1420 there are thirteen lay wills by English people, preserved because they made gifts to one or other of the hospices. There was nothing at all unusual in these; they were typical Italian wills and since they were drawn up by notaries they tell little about the attitudes of the testators. Apart from John White, who owned property in London, though he

---

[207] Ibid., pp. 195–6. [208] Esch, 'Florentiner', p. 486. [209] Goioli, no. 145.
[210] *mm.* 161, 162.

made no bequests there, and the Possewich family, which came from Avignon,[211] the testators referred only to Roman bequests.

Some were very simple indeed, leaving one house.[212] Others were slightly more elaborate: Robert of Pigna, the *cernitor*, made his will with the notary Paulus de Serromanis in 1368.[213] As was customary he first named three poor men as his heirs, to receive a tiny sum to pray for him. In 1390 Elena Clerk, widow of the *paternostrarius* John Clerk of the Ponte region, left 12 pence to three poor men, but also added that thirteen poor people were to have five *bologni* 'for a meal together' (*ad comedendum*) on the day of her death.[214]

Some testators specified the desired place of burial, sometimes their local parish church. Robert of Pigna wanted to be buried in S Stefano de Pigna, for which he left one florin. He left its rector Nicholas and Laurentius de Serromanis, a canon there, half a florin each. Elena Clerk asked to be buried in the church of S Cecilia de Turre Campi, to which she gave wax for candles. Richard Teste, Sybil's husband, in 1379, after commending his soul to his creator and to the blessed Virgin 'and to the whole court above' (*et toti curie supernorum*), asked for burial in the church of S Stefano in Parione and left eighteen florins for his funeral, of which twelve were to go to priests for mass and burial.[215] Walter Taylor, in 1403, asked to be buried in the church of S Gregorio,[216] and Alice Possewich or Irland, who died in 1401, asked to be buried in her parish church of S Biagio, to whose abbot she left three ducats.[217]

Alice's is one of the few of these wills (her husband's is another) which makes more complicated (and expensive) stipulations about burial. She left six ducats for wax on the vigil and day of her funeral, for six torches and great candles. After her death two of these were to go to S Biagio, two to the hospital of S Thomas and two to her executors. She wanted three trentals, one at the altar of S Gregorio in S Peter's church, one in S Biagio and a third in the hospital; her husband had asked for one at the altar of S Gregorio in S Peter's and two at the hospital.[218] This is probably an example of a devotion very popular in the fifteenth century in England, whereby thirty masses were said throughout the year, three in each octave, using the masses of the Nativity, Epiphany, Purification, Annunciation, Easter, Ascension, Pentecost, Trinity, the Assumption of the Virgin and her Nativity, with

---

[211] See below p. 144.   [212] *m.* 91.   [213] *m.* 53; AC Sez. I, 649/ 9, f. 27.
[214] Armellini, *Chiese di Roma*, p. 183; Huelsen, *Le chiese*, pp. 224–5. For choice of burial place E. Hubert, 'Élection de sépulture et fondation de chapelle funeraire à Rome au XIVe siècle, donation et concession de l'espace sacré', in A. Paravicini-Bagliani and V. Pasche, *La parrochia nel medio evo. Economia, scambi, solidarità* (= Italia sacra. Studi e documenti di storia ecclesiastica 53), Rome 1995, pp. 209–27, esp. pp. 217–21, for canon law.
[215] *m.* 99.   [216] *m.* 163.   [217] *m.* 158.   [218] *m.* 123.

the daily recitation of *Placebo* and *Dirige*.[219] In 1396 the Gascon Johanna, of Parione, left her house to Davit of Wales, with all her movable goods on condition, among other things, that he caused to be celebrated masses called masses of S Gregory (*que dicuntur le messe de sancto Gregorio*).[220]

While executors were usually English, including English widows, witnesses nearly always included Italians. Robert of Pigna's executors were Henry of Trastevere and William the *paternostrarius*, both Englishmen, with no English witnesses. Elena's were William the *paternostrarius*, William Holdernesse and Sybilla Teste. Holdernesse was to play a considerable part in the affairs of St Thomas's hospice up to 1404.[221]

A feature of some of these wills is a series of small payments to a variety of Roman churches. In Elena Clerk's one florin each went to S Peter's, S Paul outside the Walls, the monastery of S Anastasia outside the city, the monastery of S Sebastian near the city,[222] S Lorenzo outside the walls, the Lateran, S Croce, S Mary Major, S Marcellus, S Maria Ara Celi, S Maria Sopra Minerva and S Maria Nova. It is not clear why someone like Elena would wish to donate to the particular churches mentioned but this kind of statement is not unusual; some Roman churches were soliciting funds for expenses during the schism.[223] Richard Teste left one florin each to S Stefano's, S Peter's, S Paul outside the walls, the Lateran and S Mary Major and Walter Taylor left two ducats to S Biagio, two to S Paul outside the walls, and one to S Peter's and the Lateran. Alice Possewich left one *carlino* to the fabric of S Peter's.

The wills were preserved because they contained legacies to the hospital and it is clear that the testators were expecting to be prayed for by the beneficiaries. As well as leaving S Thomas's the reversion of his house, Richard Teste left one florin for the poor sick in the hospital. The poor of the English hospital (S Thomas) received Elena Clerk's three best beds, three quilts, three pairs of sheets, one great copper kettle and one house in the area called Pizzomerle, given to her and her husband John by the noble Rodolphus of lord Theobald, an English knight from *Vectoren'* 'that is from England' (*scilicet de Anglia*), who was perhaps a mercenary. She reserved a place in the house for Agnes Taylour, an English women for her life and, if Agnes agreed, also a place for Cecilia Howden, also English. A long series of bequests of

---

[219] R. W. Pfaff, 'The English devotion of St Gregory's Trental', *Speculum*, 49 (1974) pp. 75–90.
[220] *m.* 138. [221] See p. 70.
[222] Probably *in catacumbas*, Caraffa, *Monasticon*, I, p. 97.
[223] A-M. Corbo, 'I legati 'pro anima' e il restauro delle chiese a Roma tra la seconda metà del XIV secolo e la prima metà del XV', *Commentari* 18 (1967), pp. 225–230.

cloths and utensils followed, to English people and Italians. Her executors were to sell one house for the souls of her husband and their relatives. If the hospice wished to buy this house it was to be sold to them.

None of this reveals much except that these people were very well integrated into their areas and appear to have had little attachment to the places from which they had come. They responded to local conditions, and used local laws and customs. They also, as we shall see, usually used local notaries.

In the last ten years Italian scholars have begun systematically to publish and study the notebooks of the fourteenth-century Roman notaries. Whereas protocols reveal a notary at work over a whole community, a collection of deeds such as that of the English College allows one to study individuals and institutions using notaries. The English College deeds for the period contain the names of about 58 notaries who drew up the documents. But many were responsible for only one, whereas some acted regularly. The most common names were Antonius Goioli Petri Scopte, responsible for 18 deeds between 1359 and April 1397 with his son Johannes Paulus adding four more (one a copy from his father's books and one from those of Laurentius Anthonii Lancetti Impona[224]) dated 1408 to 1418; Johannes Hugolini Bartholomei Johannis Gentilis, responsible for 18 deeds between 1361 and 1381; Paulus de Serromanis responsible for 9 between 1364 and 1404; Petrus Nannoli Johannis Andree, responsible for 13 between 1393 and 1418; and Johannes Bucii Amistatis, an Arenula notary sometimes also found in the notebook of Goioli, responsible for 8 between 1367 and 1376.[225]

Antonius Goioli has been described as 'the confidential solicitor of the English in Rome',[226] but this is far from the truth, though there are more references to him among the archives than to any other notary.[227] His protocol book for 1365 exists and has been printed and his life is fairly well documented. He lived and mainly functioned in Arenula district.[228] He was a capitoline and a papal notary, able to work for both the commune and the papal administration. He vanished after 1397 when he probably died. His son Johannes Paulus whose sign is on four of the S Thomas deeds,[229] was an Arenula notary from 1392, very active between 1407 and 1425. In 1414 he was *caporione*, elected representative, for Arenula.[230] In 1403 he acted with Paulus Johannis

---

[224] *mm.* 121, 192.   [225] For Amistatis: *mm.* 51, 58,82, 83, 86, 87; Goioli, index.
[226] *Venerabile*, p. 31.
[227] *mm.* 32,34, 49, 71, 75, 77, 81, 84, 91, 114, 115, 116, 119, 122, 128, 141.
[228] Goioli, pp. xv–xvi.   [229] *mm.* 121, 192, 164.   [230] Goioli, pp. xvi–xvii.

Laity in Rome

Damasi in a sale of vineyards by Johannes Antonius son of Cole Scangialemosine of Parione to John White.[231] Another son, Goiolus, was a grocer (*speciarius*). In Antonius' 1365 protocol book several English clients occur, including some also represented in the college archives, like John Shepherd.[232]

Goioli, however, was not a notary for the English in particular, though it is probably significant that whilst Elena Clerk, for instance, was not resident in his area but in Ponte and more often used a different man for her personal affairs, she none-the-less made her will with Goioli in 1390, when using executors resident in Arenula, closely associated with the hospice.[233] Antonius was also used for the subsequent administration by the executors.[234] When the *universitas* of the English was involved corporately, Goioli was used on five occasions[235] but more often (twelve times)[236] the name of Petrus Nannoli Johannis Andree of Campo dei Fiori occurs for these between 1393 and 1418.[237]

Some people did have a preferred notary, however. John White may have preferred Paulus Damasi; he used him in 1403,[238] when setting up S Chrysogonus' hospice[239] and when buying a house and garden in Trastevere from the notary Machtiotius Paulleli Johannis Jacobi and his wife Paula in 1404.[240] The Clerks often used Johannes Hugolini Batholomei Johannis Gentilis, probably from Ponte, who had died by 1383.[241] He was one of the proctors for Nicola Orsini in 1372,[242] and in December 1376 when Lellus Cappa sold a house to Clerk he was not only the notary but also acted for an Orsini neighbour, with his son Jotius as a witness.[243]

Robert of Pigna probably preferred Paulus de Serromanis, whose protocols exist in great numbers and will be edited by Dr Renzo Mosti.[244] There are comparatively few hospice deeds witnessed by him. He was the notary when Nicola de Astallis, rector of S Nicholas de Pescharia, son of the notary Paulus who had been heir of Johannes de Astallis, sold to Robert of Pigna half a house in Pigna in 1364.[245] Nicola was a member of a well-known family.[246] In the same year Bona, widow of Bucius Nucii sold to William son of Partrich of Scotland a

---

[231] *m.* 164 (and see *m.* 120). [232] Goioli, nos. 49, 50, 110, 111, 145, 148.
[233] *m.* 119. [234] *m.* 122. [235] *mm.* 32, 34, 77, 81, 84.
[236] *mm.* 127, 129, 131, 133, 140, 130, 135, 136, 137, 144, 175, 178.
[237] Goioli, p. 198. The date 1418 was for a private transaction by Philip Newton, *m.* 189.
[238] See p. 79. [239] *m.* 139. [240] *m.* 165.
[241] As Johannes Ugolini or Hugolini in Goioli, pp. 7, 132, 186; Staglia, p. 139; Astalli, p. 49 and note. For the Clerk transactions: *mm.* 66, 101, 70, 90, 92, 94, 103, 104, 105, 106; *m.* 41, a copy from his notebooks, made in 1383 when he was already dead.
[242] Staglia, p. 139. [243] *mm.* 90, 92.
[244] Note about him in Staglia, p. 144 and note, where he is acting with others for Niccolo Orsini.
[245] *m.* 38 and AC Sez I, 649/7, fol 39v. [246] Astalli, p. xiv.

house in Arenula with Robert of Pigna as her proctor and de Serromanis as notary.[247] He was notary for Pigna's will in 1368,[248] and the complicated problems it raised.[249] When Pigna and William the *paternostrarius* gave to the hospice in 1371 a house bought by them with hospice money, Serromanis was again the notary.[250] In de Serromanis protocols there are transactions involving English clients, not in hospice deeds. For instance there is an agreement of 1366 where Robert of Pigna and Henry of John of Trastevere acted as proctors for Sir Thomas Chandos,[251] and a sale, in 1371, to the hospice represented by Robert of Pigna among others, of vineyards by Rita daughter of the late Bartholomeus de Campania,[252] or a letting of vineyards by hospice officials including Robert of Pigna in 1371 and 1372.[253]

Robert left a legacy to Nicola, rector and to Laurencius de Serromanis, canon, of S Stefano de Pigna, his parish church, as we saw.[254] In the transaction when Robert and William gave the houses to the hospice in 1371 Nicola the rector of S Stefano de Pigna and Laurencius de Serromanis were among the witnesses.[255] It would appear therefore that they were friends of Robert.

It is of considerable interest to look not only at the English persons involved in the making of these deeds but also at those who were selling, to find out what kind of market the English were working in. The archive allows one to trace several of the properties quite far back but three examples must suffice here.

The oldest deed which the English college possesses is dated 1280; it is a dower instrument for the notary Vivianus (*Bibianus*) whose son Mattheus was marrying Theodora, niece of Johannes Gregorii, she being the orphan daughter of Johannes Romani de Rubeis. The dower of 100 *libri* was invested in a palace in the region of S Lorenzo in Damaso.[256] In 1300 the son Mattheus, likewise a notary, gave his brother Petrus half the palace, which was carefully divided between them, and also one house. This was clearly a division of their inheritance. The heirs of Johannes Rubei lived next door, so the son had married a neighbour.[257] In 1312 Vivianus, son of Mattheus, another notary, received 110 florins for the dower of his fiancée Angela, niece of Jacobus Magaleoti of Portica S Petri (the present Borgo district), orphan daughter of Angelus Brunelli de Brunellis, for which Mattheus gave his

---

[247] *m.* 39.   [248] *m.* 53 and see AC Sez. I, 649/9, f. 27.

[249] *m.* 88 and see AC Sez. I, 649/13, ff. 15, 37; 650, f. 23.   [250] *m.* 60.

[251] Ac Sez. I, 649/8, f. 131.   [252] AC Sez. I, 649/11, ff. 18–19.

[253] Ac Sez. I, 649/11, ff. 19v–20, 50v–51; 12, ff. 57r/v, 85–86v.   [254] *m.* 53.

[255] *m.* 60.   [256] *m.* 1, with some notes in E. Hubert, *Espace urbain*, pp. 254–6.

[257] *m.* 2; for family groupings see also H. Broise, 'Les maisons d'habitation', pp. 614–16.

half of the palace.[258] Petrus Vivianus and Mattheus his brother still lived on the boundaries of the property. This is a typical example of an extended family living in the same complex of houses. In 1361 Tuciarellus (or Cucciarellus) magistri Johannis Viviani of Ponte sold to Cola (Nicola) domini Viviani, *speciarius*, half the palace for 58 florins. Perna, daughter of Petrus Vivianus agreed (Tuciarellus was her nephew and she presumably lived in the other half).[259]

All these are well attested in other documents. In 1367 Nicholas domini Viviani, *speciarius* of Parione was guarantor (*fideiussor*) for the seller of the house that Simon of Simon of Colchester bought,[260] and for his widow when she sold a house to John Salmon in 1375.[261] Petrus son of Cola (Nicola) Viviani of Parione, swearing he was independent of his father, acted, as we shall, see, as *fideiussor* in 1375 in a sale to the hospice of S Thomas.[262]

In 1375 Tuciallerus Vivianus, acting for Nicola Viviani and for Petrus his son, sold the whole Vivianus palace, with three adjoining houses, to the hospice of S Thomas, which was investing Philpot money.[263] Among those who agreed to the sale, were Andrea, wife of Nicola Viviani and Paula daughter of Jordanus de Cappis, notary of Monti region, wife of Petrus, Nicola's son. Tuciarellus' backers included the kind of solid citizens that one might expect: Bartholomeus de Tostis, found in the protocols of Antonius Goioli Petri Scopte living in the area of Ponte region called *Scortheclariorum*,[264] north of Piazza Navona, near the church of S Apollinare, where he owned property, a *speciarius* called Lanciarius Jannectolus Pauli Celibis also known as Lomnencho, Laurentius Johannis Galerie, farrier (*ferurius*) of Ponte and Petrus son of the late Nucius Petri Pangrotte also called Sclavi of Colonna. This last was another neighbour. His mother Francesca, with his consent, in May 1375 sold to the hospice her house in Ponte beside the house of Cola i.e. Nicola, Vivianus.[265] Among the *fideiussores* was Petrus Viviani, and the witnesses included Laurentius Johannis Galerie. Tuciarellus Viviani, who conducted the sale of the palace, occurs in Antonius Goioli Petri Scopte's protocols in 1365, as a proctor.[266] We also find other Viviani notaries in other deeds. Martinus domini Viviani was notary for the sale of a *stirps* in Monti region to Robert of Pigna in 1350[267] and for one sold by Robert de Calcalario to Robert of Platea Judeorum, both Englishmen, in the same year.[268]

---

[258] *m. 4.* [259] *m. 35.* [260] *m. 50.* [261] *mm. 80, 89.* [262] *m. 81.*
[263] *m. 84.*
[264] Goioli, pp. 5–8; for the place: Krautheimer, *Rome*, p. 253; Gnoli, *Topografia*, pp. 294–6.
[265] *m. 81.* [266] Goioli, p. 8, as Cucciarellus Biniani. [267] *m. 17.*
[268] *m. 18.*

The people for whom the Viviani males acted as guarantors are interesting also. In 1375 for the Salmon house it was for Johanna, widow of John Assisi *calsolarius* and now wife of Cola della Gribossa of Ponte and *contrata pontis Sancti Petri*.[269] In the same year for the sale to the hospice of S Thomas for Francesca widow of Nucius Petri Pangrotta also called Sclavi, and her son Petrus, noted above, Petrus son of Nicola Viviani was *fideiussor*.[270] In other words there was a group of neighbours who acted for one another, as one would expect.

So this family of substantial non-noble Romans who seem to have produced notaries in every generation, finally sold their palace to an English institution after almost one hundred years of joint family occupancy. The family was large and acted for its members, intermarrying with neighbours and guarding its interests.

Interesting, though with a shorter history, was property belonging to master Angelus Johannis Andree Luce. In 1338 Ceccus Cappodaferro of Arenula sold to Andrea, widow of master Angelus, a *turris* which Angelus had once owned, whose ground landlord was the Orsini of Campo dei Fiori. This seems to have been the house called Scottis Torre.[271] The notary was Franciscus son of the late Stephanus Julianus de Porcariis. In 1364 Bona, master Angelus' daughter, widow of Bucius Nucii Gacchi, alias Liose, marble worker (*marmorarius*), of Pigna, her mother's heiress, sold this to William son of Partriche, formerly of Scotland.[272] Paulus Cappodaferro lived next door and the transaction was completed in the house of Nicola de Porcariis, a witness. The house in the end came to S Thomas's.[273] Nicola de Porcariis was a notary and a notable figure in the city and the Pigna district.[274]

Similarly a house in Parione which John Champneys bought in 1374, sold by him to the Possewichs whence it came to S Thomas's,[275] can be traced to 1359[276] when Andrea, a widow of Arenula bought it. Andrea the widow, may have been poor enough. She was able to buy the house because she had money

from her work in making bread for sale and from providing a home for her son Anthony (*ex sua industria ad faciendum panem ad vendendum et ad faciendum hospitium Anthonio filio suo.*)

Anthony was a notary.

Not all the properties of the two hospices can be traced in the same way, but the evidence suggests that men such as John Fraunceys and the

---

[269] *mm.* 79 and 80, 89.   [270] *m.* 81.   [271] *m.* 7.
[272] *m.* 39; also in AC Sez I, 649/7, fols. 50–2, from whence the *marmorarius*.
[273] *m.* 91 looks like the will of William's son.   [274] Staglia, p. 144.
[275] See below p. 144; *mm.* 74, 100.   [276] *mm.* 30. 62, 63, 74.

Possewichs habitually dealt with Roman families at the level below the great nobility; the well-established local notaries must have been at the same social level.

Much can also be learned about the circles in which the English moved by looking at the people whom they had to witness their deeds or guarantee their acts. Witnesses seem to have been chosen with care and were not simply plucked off the streets ad hoc. Even more important, if they exist, were *fideiussores* who backed a person selling a property or doing a deal, pledging that he or she would carry out the transaction as arranged.

The little group of transactions in which the hospice of S Thomas was established reveals how significant choice of witnesses could be. All the deeds had some Italian witnesses but some significantly more than others. The buying of the house by John Shepherd, for example had only one Italian, the rest being known members of the English Guild, for whom, it seems likely, Shepherd was buying.[277] The one Italian, Mathias Paccia is the sort of worthy citizen who often appeared as a witness.[278] He had a house in Arenula and on one occasion received with a colleague called Guilelminus de Massa, *conestabilis*, who was living there, a deposit of twenty florins from a Colonna resident called Lellus Baracta. When Chandler was invested with the future hospice, however, the Italian witnesses included three important local residents: Jacobellus Cafagi, *murator*, Paulus Alisii, notary, and Lellus *domini Johannis cavalerii*.[279]

Lellus was an Arenula resident, probably of considerable substance, holding at least three houses in Parione.[280] He was a member of the family de Saracenis, presumably one of the heirs of *dominus Johannis militis*, mentioned in 1348 holding a house next to the one which later belonged to the Testes.[281] The designation *miles* or *cabalerius* (*cavalerius*) indicates a person worth 2000 *libri provisini* which is probably the family's own perception of itself.[282] Lellus' standing is revealed when he is found as guarantor (*fideiussor*) for a payment of 170 florins in 1365 for instance.[283] In 1367 Lellus sold a house to Simon of Colchester next to another he owned.[284]

The second Italian witness, Paulus Alisii, was a local notary from at

---

[277] *m.* 34.
[278] Goioli, pp. 12, 19, 58, 129, 251 (pledge). For a Nicolas Baracta, guardian of the Society of the Image at Sancta Sanctorum in 1379 see Johannes Nicolai Pauli, pp. 269, 280.
[279] *m.* 36.   [280] *mm.* 50, 51, 52.   [281] *m.* 14.
[282] Gennaro, 'Mercanti', p. 159, a person with goods worth 2000 libri provisini.
[283] Goioli, p, 95; see ibid. p. 17 for him as a witness, but not, I think *cal[sularius]*, as there, read *cabalarius*.
[284] See above p. 105.

least 1354.[285] He had two sons, Nicola[286] and Johannes. Johannes, who left the hospice of S Thomas a legacy in 1394,[287] was a notary of Arenula from 1359,[288] a member of the Società del Salvatore, a city confraternity, buried in his parish church of S Giovanni in Ayno.[289] As a capitoline notary he registered the statutes of the wool guild or Arte della Lana in 1368.[290] Loysius Johannis Alisii, Johannes' son, was a witness in 1373 when Benedictus Guidicii sold his house in Parione to the Testes when the notary was Antonius Goioli, and he was a witness for his father elsewhere.[291]

Jacobellus Casagi or Cafagi, builder (*murator*), of Arenula belonged to another important local family, a person of substance, traceable from 1358 at least.[292] He and his brother Barthelutius alias Marcille, both *muratores*, sons of the dead Cafagi, lived with their wives Johanna and Angela in adjoining houses in Arenula *in proprietate* of Johannes de Saracenis, which in 1365 they divided between them.[293] In 1358 Jacobellus was a *fideiussor* for Bucius Thomaxii Valsarii who sold the house to Fina the concubine, and at other times in 1365 was a *fideiussor* or witness in Arenula.[294] He invested the hospice with the Vivianus house in 1375, and witnessed several hospice deeds to 1376.[295] Bartholucius was *fideiussor* with his brother.[296] Not surprisingly Bartholuccius Cofagi or Cafagi *murator* was *fideiussor* for Lellus *domini Johannis militis* when the latter sold his house in Parione to Simon of Simon, Englishman.[297] Other members of the family also figure in the deeds. The garden of Johannes Cafagi was mentioned as behind the houses that Agnes gave to S Chrysogonus in 1406.[298] Bartholucius' son Paulus, notary of Arenula, was a witness with Jacobellus in 1376 concerning the house of William of Richard.[299]

The study of this group of laymen reveals much more than their inter-relations with one another. They were very thoroughly embedded in the life of the city, even if not citizens and even if seldom encountered except when 'English' business was being done, though that is not wholly true, Perrinus Baker and the wine bar come to mind. They must by 1420 have been a very strong presence in Arenula and by then S Thomas's had become recognisably a centre catering for many

---

[285] Goioli, pp. 104, 186; see also Johannes Nicolai Pauli, p. 81.
[286] Astalli, p. 36 (1368).   [287] AS, 270, ff. 123–4 for will.
[288] Johannes Nicolai Pauli, pp. 112–13.
[289] Goioli, pp. 17, 118; Staglia, pp. 6, 7 and note, 76.
[290] Stevenson, *Statuti*, p. 68, from Staglia, p. 7 note.   [291] Staglia, p. 6 and *m*. 68.
[292] *m*. 29.   [293] Goioli, p. 244–8.
[294] Goioli, p. 233; witness p. 243. See also ibid. pp. 147–51.
[295] *mm*. 71 77, 84, 87.   [296] Goioli, pp. 147–51; see also p. 193.   [297] *m*. 51.
[298] *m*. 173.   [299] *m*. 87.

needs of the expatriate English in the city. It was not yet an 'official' centre but it was certainly treated as if its well-being was of importance to powerful people in London. But the strong lay presence of the period to about 1404 had waned by 1420; the curia had become much more important to the life of Rome by then. That must be considered after we first look at the experience of the women who also played their part in the history of English institutions in Rome.

Chapter 6

WOMEN

Over thirty English women can be identified who lived for some time between 1360 and 1420 in Rome. Since they could not do most things men did, act as travelling merchants nor of course become clergy, most English women who lived for any length of time in Rome were either wives or widows. There were very few unmarried daughters and few religious. Their experience must have been very different from their sisters in England. Some were probably pilgrims, perhaps pilgrims who stayed. Again the experience must have been different for a woman.

Whereas notaries' protocols usually contain a number of marriage contracts, I found none for English couples in Rome, and only one for an English man, John Cross,[1] (*Croce*) of Colonna in 1391, several times *camerarius* of S Thomas's beginning in 1401, whose dower arrangements when he was marrying Angillela, daughter of Francesca, widow of Paulus Macarii, are preserved,[2] though some of the other marriages must have taken place in Rome also. Marriage in Italy differed from England and indeed from city to city in the peninsula, though the exchange of 'words of present consent', essential for a canonical marriage, was always carefully recorded.[3] In the Roman protocols the actual marriage (*subarratio*) was before a notary and remembered in a document by which he recorded that the young couple before him were asked in turn if they wished the other to be their wife or husband, replying *volo*.[4] The man then put a ring on the ring finger of the girl, in token of matrimony by words of present consent. The notary then said 'What God has joined together let no man put asunder, in the name of

---

[1] Nagl, *Anima in Rom*, no. 217, S Maria dell'Anima, Instr. Litt. B tom.i, ff. 118–120v, for Johannes Croce or Cross, marrying an Italian in 1391.

[2] Nagl, *Anima in Rom*, no. 217.

[3] C. Klapisch-Zuber, *Women, Family and Ritual in Renaissance Italy* (trans), Chicago 1985, especially chapters 6, 9 and 10. Chapter 9 discusses the differences between Roman and Florentine customs.

[4] Goioli, pp. 4–5.

the Father and of the Son and of the Holy Ghost, Amen.' Names of witnesses were given. But the ring-giving and exchange of consent was merely the culmination of family bargaining. John Cross' dower document explained that the marriage had not yet been completed 'he has not yet taken her to his home' (*nondum ad eius domum transductam*).[5] Women had a dowry, varying in size naturally according to wealth.[6] Thus a few English wills contain gifts to young girls for their marriage. Walter Taylor, the English *cursor* turned tailor, making his will in 1403, left to Nonna the girl of his business partner (*puella sua*) all his household goods and other bedding, except what was in his shop, for her marriage.[7] John White, founder of S Chrysogonus' hospice, left to Ricciarda, the daughter of his partner Perrinus Baker, thirty ducats for her marriage.[8]

When a woman married she was given clothes and jewels by her husband, and a small *donatio propter nuptias*,[9] as John Cross' dowry deed explained, 'according to Roman custom'. Very often the dowry was invested in the house in which the couple would then live, or at least in real property.[10] If the woman was then widowed she had a right to her dower and half the *donatio propter nuptias*. If the money had been put into property the widow could live in it.[11] If the woman died first, the husband had her dower. Though many notaries' protocols contain written agreements, these were not necessary; the law in Rome said that where a ring had been given the gift was presumed. The only English example, John Cross', was that the dower of 100 gold ducats would go after both the deaths of both partners, subject to certain conditions, to S Thomas's.

If women wanted to sell property they needed their husband's consent.[12] There are examples of this in the hospital deeds, where an Italian woman sells the hospital a property for instance.[13] During his lifetime the husband administered the dowry,[14] but a widow had the

---

[5] See p. 120.
[6] Goioli, pp. 170–1, where Stefanello receives as the dowry for his future wife Andreotta from her mother the widow Lorenza half of 50 libri provisini, the rest to follow.
[7] *m.* 163.   [8] *m.* 169.
[9] Goioli, pp. 73–4 where Giovanni, of Ripa region receives as deposit from Petrucciolus 50 gold florins which are for ornaments for Altadonna, future wife of Petrucciolus, daughter of Giovanni.
[10] Caputgallis, pp. 209–10: Lorenzo son of Corrado or Renco de Sabella gets a dowry of 60 libri for his future wife Caterina and promises to invest it in property, in 1379.
[11] Re, *Statuti*, I/1, chapter 44, p. 31.
[12] Re, *Statuti*, I/1, pp. 51–2.
[13] *m.* 77: Paula wife of Nucius Sclavi sells a house to the hospice of S Thomas with permission of her husband.
[14] Klapisch-Zuber, *Women, Family*, p. 216 for instance.

right to claim it and, in theory, could remove herself from her first husband's family, with her dowry, and either return to her father or remarry.[15] This could prove very costly for her first husband's heirs and it was thus in the interests of the first husband's family that the widow remained unmarried; wills often stipulate that the wife's legacy will be greater if she does.[16] The English testators in Rome often followed the same ideas, as Richard son of Roger laid down for Stefania in 1369: she was to live in his house with her children in her widowhood with a quarter of the goods, but if she remarried she took only the goods with no rights in the house.[17] Henry of John in his second will left his wife a *stirps* if she did not remarry.[18] Hence although there are plenty of examples of these English widows remarrying: as did Rosa Casarola (mentioned below) and Stefania, others did not. Alice Possewich seems to have lived with her sons and Elena Clerk, who was apparently childless, must have lived alone and disposed of her own property.[19] Angillela remarried when Cross died. Her new husband was a German papal cursor and S Thomas's did not get her property. Her second husband became guardian of the German hospice, S Maria dell'Anima and it was eventually the recipient.[20]

Married women could make wills while their husbands were alive when the wife was not ill, though it was unusual. An interesting example, where the woman may be Italian, is Rosa Ubertini Casarola of the Biberatica region, near Trajan's forum, evidently with property of her own to protect and quarrelling with her husband. In July 1363,[21] as the wife of John the Englishman, she annulled the gift of a house to him because it was 'forced by the violence of her husband, because of the many wounds her husband continuously gave her and his threats'.[22] If Rosa herself was not English born she moved in a very English ambience. On 30 July the same year she made her will,[23] leaving her servant John Bramantis, an Englishman, the use (*sedium*) in two houses for his life, with the arrangements already discussed earlier. All of this was to go to the monastery of SS Andrew and Gregory for her soul after Bramantis' death.[24] She left to her parish, SS Apostoli, money for

---

[15] Ibid., esp. pp. 120–4.

[16] For instance, Caputgallis, no. 659.

[17] m 56.   [18] *m.* 93.   [19] *m.* 119.

[20] A. J. Schmidlin, *Geshichte der deutschen Nationalkirche in Rom, S Maria dell'Anima*, Freiburg im Br. 1906, p. 50.

[21] S Angelo, I/1, ff. 121v–122. Referred to briefly by Brentano, *Rome before Avignon*, pp. 283–4.

[22] *Vi cohacta ab ipso eius marito et propter multa vulnera que continue dictus eius maritus dicte Rose inferibat et minas quas continue faciebat et facit dicte Rose.*

[23] S. Angelo, I/1, f. 141r/v.

[24] Now S Gregorio al Celio, in via S Gregorio, Caraffa, *Monasticon*, I, p. 56.

masses, to the female convent of S Maria in Julia money for masses and to Robert the English oblate there, an executor, a small legacy.[25] The 'poor of the hospital of the English newly built in Arenula region' were given bedding. Robert de Pigna received a small legacy. Richard the Englishman of Trevi region, her godfather, was an executor. Simon, *paternostrarius* of Parione, was another. Henry the Englishman of Trastevere was a witness. Her husband was carefully excluded, on the same grounds as before. In October the same year she made another will, again annulling her gift to her husband.[26] This time she left parts of her houses to the monastery of S Andrew, another part to SS Apostoli, with *sedium* again to Bramantis and John the Englishman, her servants. She left another legacy for Margaret her English servant, and ten *libri* for Bocard her brother. Bramantis and Richard the Englishman of Trevi were executors. Yet another arrangement followed in 1367;[27] this time houses went to S Andrew's and SS Apostoli, with *sedium* for John Bramantis and a legacy for Bocard, with the cassation of the gift to her husband and Italian executors. Finally in 1369 Bramantis had become her husband, doubtless the best arrangement in her interests, and a house went to S Andrew's, with usufruct to the couple for their lives.[28] Thus in the end Rosa married the servant, but first ensured that her property would have good protectors.

Rosa's is the only will I have found by an Englishwoman whose husband was still alive. Four wills survive by English widows between 1360 and 1420. The earliest was of Amata, widow of Henry Orlandi, living in Arenula in 1365, and apparently actually resident in the hospice of S Thomas.[29] She was simply identified as Amata wife of the late Herrici. Her heir was a son Angelus who received six florins, a quilt and a pair of sheets. He was not an executor. Elena Clerk, who left an elaborate will in 1390, was described as her husband's widow. No children were mentioned and the executors, including one woman, were all English.[30] Johanna de la Morte de Gascognia, making her will in 1396, was described as Johanna, daughter of the late Peter de la Morte de Gascognia, wife of the late Guilelmus of Civita Vecchia, now living in Parione region.[31] They counted as English because Gascony was English territory; they certainly identified themselves as such. No children were mentioned and she left her house in Parione and goods to Davit son of John of Wales, *cernitor*. It is not clear what relation existed between the two.

Alice Possewich made her will in 1401. In it she was called Alice

[25] Caraffa, *Monasticon*, I, pp. 65–6.   [26] S Angelo, I/1, ff. 173v–174v.
[27] S Angelo, I/3, f. 9.   [28] S Angelo, I/5, ff. 51v–52.
[29] Goioli, p. 248–9, no. 148.   [30] *m.* 119.   [31] *m.* 138.

Irland, widow of the late Richard Irland, otherwise called Possewich, *cursor* of the pope.[32] When we first meet her in Rome in 1379 she was identified as Alice, daughter of the late William de Ricchal of a diocese which may be York, and the deed revealed that 150 florins of the 200 that bought their house in Parione was from Alice's father.[33] The Possewichs are discussed in detail elsewhere. Here it is enough to notice that Alice's husband Richard made her his heir and one of his executors in 1391 when their two sons John and Richard junior were still very young.[34] She must have spent ten years as a widow in Rome when she finally made her will but there was nothing in her husband's will which prevented her from remarrying; she was there made guardian of her two sons, the house in Rome and all his goods given her for herself, for Richard's soul and for their two sons.

The complications of the Roman inheritance laws and the implications of relationships can be illustrated in the case of the house called Lo Confesse already encountered.[35] The case illustrates better than many the widow allowed to live in the house with her children if she did not remarry. Stefania was very vulnerable and seems to have relied on the executors of her husband's will, who were also officials of S Thomas's, to protect her. They were, of course, also protecting their own future legacy. Although the gift to S Thomas's by William *paternostarius* was said to be for the highest religious motives 'so that God might pardon the soul of the testator and of his relatives' (*ut Deus indulgeat anime ipsius testatoris et parentum suorum*), the officials still asked Stefania for rent once she remarried. The institution offered protection but not great generosity.

Women could be executors of wills, though they were often associated with men, as Richard Possewich's will showed. In 1379 Richard Teste made his wife Sibilla his executor.[36] He had already left her a house, *inter vivos*, and in his will also left her all his goods. He named the *custos* of the hospice of S Thomas's, John Ponfret as her assistant (*adjutor*) if she wished. If she did not want the task of executor, then John would do it but only with Sibilla's consent. Sibilla in the event sold her house to William son of Richard *paternostrarius*.[37] Sibilla was also executor, along with William *paternostrarius* and William Holdernesse, of the will of Elena Clerk, widow of John Clerk, *paternostrarius* in 1390.[38] In the end this will caused problems, because Elena's legacies could not be met without first selling her house. So the three executors were recorded doing so.[39]

[32] *m.* 158.   [33] *m.* 100.   [34] *m.* 123.   [35] See above p. 68.
[36] *m.* 99.   [37] *m.* 121.   [38] *m.* 119.   [39] *m.* 122.

Women

There are very few cases where we can tell the national origin of the women. When a wife was called *Anglica*, like Rosa Casarola, it is not always clear whether she was English by origin or just by marriage, but some English men married Italian wives. Maria Baker, wife of Perrinus Baker, the Gascon merchant who joined with John White in establishing S Chrysogonus', was called *Romana*.[40] Perrinus' daughter Ricciarda who must have been born in Rome, later married the Englishman John Ely.[41] Evidently Vannotia the daughter of Stefania, wife of Richard son of Roger, an Englishman, married an Italian, though it is not clear if Stefania was herself Italian,[42] and as we have seen John Cross married the Italian Angillela.[43]

Where the women married again, as did Rosa Casarola, Stefania and Margaret, widow of William Holdernesse by 1407,[44] the second husband was often English. Henry of John of Trastevere, in his second will made in 1378, asked for prayers for the souls of his wives, one of whom, Margaret, was still alive.[45]

Like their husbands, of course, the women could not live in a wholly English ambience, but they nevertheless did associate with many English people, showing what a small society the English group in Rome actually was. The will of Elena Clerk in 1390 is particularly interesting for what it reveals about English women known to Elena. She had been married to John Clerk, *paternostrarius* since at least 1376[46] and lived from then onwards in Rome but was a widow by the time she made her will.[47] The house which she left to the English hospice in the Pizzomerle district was given on condition that Agnes Taylour, an Englishwoman, could stay in it for her life and with her, if Agnes agreed, Cecilia Howden, also English. Cecilia also received a ducat and a bed cover with a pair of sheets and one head scarf and Agnes a head scarf. In addition there were legacies to Elena, daughter of William the English tailor (two gold ducats and a bed), to Alice, wife of Simon Brugge the Englishman of Ponte region, two of the four ducats he owed Elena, to Agnes Sparcha, an English woman, one woollen gown (*juppolantem*) a hood, a cloak of cameline cloth and one ducat, to Alice, wife of William the *paternostrarius*, one head scarf, to Alice Possewich one linen sheet and a towel, and to Sibilla Teste who was an executor a cloak with a hood of 'mixed', a pair of stockings and a head scarf, with four gold ducats. Of these only Alice Possewich, Alice, wife of William, and Sibilla Teste can be traced otherwise. This suggests at least that

---

[40] *Venerabile*, p. 94. [41] *Venerabile*, p. 65.
[42] See for the story p. 68. [43] See p. 120.
[44] For Margaret *m*. 179, her husband was Raulinus, an Englishman.
[45] *m*. 93. [46] *m*. 90. [47] *m*. 119.

there were some single (widowed?) English women living in Rome. It seems unlikely that these were merely pilgrims passing through.

There were no English women running businesses, although there were female businesses in Rome: for example we hear of women fruiterers and the hospice of S Thomas in 1406 was renting a shop to Vetula who sold green stuff and apples (*herbas et poma*).[48] There was also the woman who made her living baking bread, noticed earlier.[49] It was probably much easier for a woman to run a business in England than anywhere in the Mediterranean countries and the businesses that Italian woman did run were often lowly.[50] In Florence for instance the types of jobs commonly done by women were domestic service, as uncloistered religious, weavers, spinners, sellers of dishes and of fruit. Rosa Casarola relied upon her servant, John Bramantis to run what she called in 1367 *contrada pro cernendo farinas* with everything for the task in her houses where she left him the right to live.[51] Henry of John of Trastevere had two *stirpes ad cernendum* in the Trastevere region which he had bought in 1354.[52] His widow Margaret was to have these unless she re-married, according to his will in 1378.[53] But there are no examples of Englishwomen taking over as *paternostraria* for instance, though in 1527 there was one woman *paternostraria* in Rome.[54] A few English woman were servants. Robert of Pigna left the use of half a house for life to Alice an English woman who had been his servant and she lived in it with her husband John.[55] Rosa Casarola had an English servant called Margaret in 1363.[56] When Margery Kemp came to Rome in 1414 and quarrelled with her travelling companions, her servant girl obtained temporary employment in S Thomas's hospice as keeper of the wine.[57] Thus there would be servants in most of the households encountered here, though we cannot now recover them, and one supposes that some brought female servants from England, as Margery did. The Agnes 'who is wont to carry the water', left a bed by Alice Possewich in 1401 was, however, probably Italian.[58]

An alternative career for women was in a religious order or as a 'penitent', for which several possibilities existed in the areas of Rome where English people lived.[59] No English names occur among the lists

[48] Goioli, p. 220: Margarita *pomarola*; *m.* 172.   [49] Above p. 116.
[50] D. Herlihy, *Opera Muliebria. Women and Work in Medieval Europe*, New York etc. 1990, pp. 159, 160.
[51] Above p. 126.   [52] m 24.   [53] *m.* 93.
[54] Lee, *Descriptio Urbis*, p. 343.   [55] m 88 and other refs, p. 67.
[56] S Angelo, I/1, ff. 173v–74v.   [57] Kemp, *The Book*, pp. 94–5.   [58] *m.* 151.
[59] L. Temperini, 'Fenomeni di vita communitaria tra i penitenti franciscani in Roma e dintori', in R. Pazzelli and L. Temperini, eds., *Prima manifestazioni di vita communitaria maschile e femminile nel movimento franciscano della penitenzia (1215–1447)* (= Commissione storica internazionale T.O.R), Rome 1982, pp. 603–53, esp. pp. 628–9.

of nuns in the protocols of notaries. In the papal letters there is only one religious, Katherine Kelsey, of the diocese of London, who in 1399 was living enclosed near S Peter's as what would in England have been called an anchoress[60]. She was given permission to visit relatives or go on pilgrimage.[61] Her father may have been a patron of S Thomas's; if so he was a London merchant.[62]

There are examples of extended families living together. In 1367 for instance Simon, son of Simon, his wife Cecilia and brother John bought a house jointly.[63] But more commonly our sources suggest English family units of husband, wife and children and even more commonly only of husband and wife. There are in fact remarkably few children, perhaps because several couples were very young and lived in Rome only briefly; but it is also noticeable that, out of fourteen wills for the period 1362 to 1420, few mention children. Amata Orlandi mentions one son,[64] Richard of Roger had a son, a daughter and probably a posthumous child, and there was no mention of grandchildren,[65] Henry of Trastevere probably, and the Possewichs certainly, had two sons[66] The other nine wills seem to be of childless people, though John Shepherd, Robert of Pigna,[67] William Scossa[68], Richard Teste,[69] Elena Clerk,[70], Walter Taylour,[71] and Joanna de la Morte[72] had all been married. Even so very wealthy a merchant as John White does not seem to have acquired a wife. This evidence perhaps conforms to the information about low birth-rates which others notice for Italian cities of the period.[73]

Membership of the confraternity of both hospices must have been open to women; both John Shepherd and his wife were to live in the hospice of S Thomas and share its care.[74] Much later Alice Possewich expected to have masses said for her soul within S Thomas's and talked of 'the brothers and sisters of the hospital', who were distinguished from the poor in general.[75] In 1412 the papal indult was granted to the brethren and sisters of the hospital of S Thomas, wherever they may be.[76] The case of S Chrysogonus was similar. The list of early *confratres*,

---

[60] For definition P. H. Cullum, 'Vowesses and female lay piety in the province of York, 1300–1530', *Northern History*, 32 (1996), pp. 21–41, esp. pp. 21, 25.
[61] *CPL*, v p. 249; mentioned in J. A. F. Thomson, 'The 'well of grace': Englishmen and Rome in the fifteenth Century', in R. B. Dobson, ed., *The Church, Politics and Patronage in the Fifteenth Century*, Gloucester 1984, pp. 99–114, esp. p. 107. For vowesses see also M. C. Erler, 'Three fifteenth-century vowesses', in: C. M. Barron and A. F. Sutton, eds., *Medieval London Widows*, London, 1994, pp. 165–183.
[62] Above pp. 75–6.   [63] *m.* 50.   [64] Goioli, p. 248.   [65] Above p. 68.
[66] *m.* 93; and see below p. 144.   [67] *m.* 53.   [68] *m.* 91.   [69] *m.* 99.
[70] *m.* 119.   [71] *m.* 109.   [72] *m.* 138.
[73] Herlihy, 'The Tuscan town in the Quattrocento', esp. p. 97, 103.
[74] *m.* 37.   [75] *m.* 158.   [76] *CPL*, VI, p. 332.

though mostly men, included Perrinus Baker's wife Maria.[77] By no means all Roman confraternities were mixed. The confraternity of S Salvatore ad Sancta Sanctorum, for instance, was a male association and thus hardly received legacies from women.[78]

Some of the lone women may have been pilgrims and for them the English hospice of S Thomas performed a vital function. In William Swan's letter book there is a series of letters about Alice Proude alias Tudor, who came in 1407 to do business whilst the curia was wandering and then made a pilgrimage to Rome. Alice travelled to Italy via Cologne with a party of at least three. At Cologne in July she met Swan's friend John Launce returning to London and told him how she had been cheated in an exchange of money in London or Bruges, having been given a traveller's letter (*literam traffatoriam*) on which she was likely to lose six marks. Launce gave her a letter of recommendation to Swan and took the details to Bruges and even to London to try to get her a remedy, but meanwhile Alice was short of money. She went first to do her business at the curia in Viterbo, where she met and nursed Swan who fell very ill there and reckoned he owed her his life. She then came to Rome, where Richard Brisby, who had been in her original group, promised to pay her expenses. Evidently she wanted to hire priests to do a circuit of churches and celebrate six masses at *scala celi*.[79] John Lincoln at the hospice of S Thomas told Swan that enquiries showed she could have this for one ducat. Swan had clearly undertaken to organise money for Alice but on 22 October John Thomasson and John Lincoln from the hospice wrote to Swan that she still had received only half a ducat and it was costing her that for her weekly board. They could not lend her any because, with the curia absent, they too were very short. By December Swan was writing that she had left to return home.[80] But her stay in Rome had been made at least possible, if not comfortable, by the kindness of others and particularly men.

The lengths to which Launce was prepared to go to try to remedy her wrongs were impressive. Once back in London he wrote to Swan about the result of his labours. He searched for Philip Glefarde who had cheated her but he was not to be found either in Bruges at the sign of the Keys where the widow would not even acknowledge that Alice had stayed there, nor at the sign of the Bear in London. He had spoken with merchants at Bruges whom Alice had also talked to. John Aurifaber, however, in the parish of S Bartholemew the Less in London said that

---

[77] Venerabile Collegio Inglese, *Liber* 272, f. 1.
[78] Hubert, 'Economie de la proprieté immobilière', pp. 198–213, 218–25.
[79] See above p. 76 for the place.
[80] Arch Seld. B 23, ff. 34v, 39, 40–40v, 41, 48r/v.

he would make arrangements (*ordinabit*) for her. In other words Launce made possible her financing.[81]

The story makes it easier to understand how Margery Kemp survived in Rome in 1414 even when she had quarrelled with her companions. Clearly a woman could not travel alone. Margery, with one maidservant whose tasks included preparing food and washing clothes,[82] travelled in a group and at first one of the company looked after her money, about twenty pounds.[83] The group of course went armed.[84] She always describes men doing the exchange of money, or helping her to do it.[85] In Rome itself she borrowed from Richard, a broken-backed Irishman, who was willing to wait for his money until they both got to Bristol, when she duly paid two years later.[86] From Constance onwards, when she had quarrelled with her earlier companions, Margery was obliged to travel with an unknown man. Both were very frightened, he of what others might do to him because she was so strange, Margery of rape.[87] Equally, when Richard the broken-backed man met her, he was reluctant to escort her alone, partly because the conventions would have found such a partnership unseemly. When Margery returned to Norwich rumour had gone before that she had conceived and borne a child while away.[88] As soon as possible in Rome therefore, Richard consigned her to a company which included another woman.[89] In Rome Margery never approached clergy directly herself but got Richard to do it for her.[90] Rome was full of supposedly celibate clerics and their female companions. One may notice here the casual way the location of S Thomas's hospice was given in the records for 1362: 'opposite is the church of SS Mary and Catherine, on one side Fina the concubine of the late Archpriest of the said church is the holder'.[91] Dietrich of Niem, the outstanding critic of curial corruption, had a concubine, casually mentioned living in one of his houses.[92] Thus a single woman could acquire a bad reputation in Rome very easily. This was no place for an unprotected woman.

Margery's description of living in poverty in Rome is very real and horrible. She had no bed clothes; the group had been carrying their own and presumably when she fell out with them they took the bedding. Washing must have been difficult for the poor; Margery

---

[81] Arch Seld. B 23, ff. 40r/v.   [82] *Book*, p. 66, lines 14–15.
[83] *Book*, chapter 26, p. 62, lines 3–5; p. 64, lines 15–18.
[84] *Book*, chapter 30, p. 77, lines 6–8.   [85] *Book*, chapter 27, p. 64, lines 20–21.
[86] *Book*, chapter 37, p. 92, line 17; chapter 44, p. 106, lines 21–31.
[87] *Book*, chapter 27, p. 65, lines 6–13; chapter 44, p. 106, line 11.
[88] *Book*, chapter 43, p. 103, lines 7–13.   [89] *Book*, chapter 30, p. 77, lines 4–24.
[90] *Book*, chapters 32 and 33, pp. 80–2.   [91] m. 32; *Venerabile* p. 29 note 60.
[92] Erler, *Dietrich*, Appendix, p. xxiii.

became covered with vermin.[93] But many were willing to give her alms.[94] One way corporate institutions like the hospice of S Thomas functioned was to provide protection for women alone in Rome. That must explain why Rosa Casarola's first scheme for preventing her husband from obtaining her property was to will it to a monastery.[95] Likewise in 1402 William Holdernesse gave a house to the hospice of S Thomas with *sedium* for his wife and any one future child for life.[96] In 1407 his widow was living in this, having married again.[97] William the *paternostrarius* did the same for himself and his wife Eloyse at the same time, 1402.[98] When Robert of Pigna died and left half his household goods for the use of his servant Alice for her life with reversion to S Thomas after her death, the hospice officials kept very careful eyes upon the property and by 1377 agreed with Alice that, since the goods were now worn out, Alice would promise to restore 8 florins worth to the hospice at her death; her husband guaranteed this.[99] Essentially, one assumes, this meant that if Alice died first, her husband, who had had a house free, would make good the loss. Very probably the single old of either sex who were benefactors moved into the hospice to die there, as Amata apparently did in 1365.[100] John Palmer clearly did the same in 1383,[101] and John White was ill and living in his own hospice of S Chrysogonus when he made his will in 1404.[102]

The levels of wealth of these women varied greatly. Alice Shepherd, wife of the 'founder' of S Thomas's hospice, had a dowry of fifteen gold florins in one hand and ten shilling in the other, as her husband's will put it, a small sum.[103] Alice Possewich on the other hand had at least 150 florins from her father.[104] Elena Clerk owned two houses at her death, one worth 150 florins.[105] Ricciarda, daughter of Perrinus Baker, who married John Ely, sergeant-at-arms to Martin V, eventually left her father's house in Arenula, to S Edmund's hospice in 1445. It must have been hers to leave.[106]

Few conclusions can be drawn about the life of English women in this expatriate group. They probably had a more restricted life than their contemporaries in England, where some of them might have conducted business, as Margery Kemp so famously did.[107] The hospices provided an artificial kin group for unprotected women, though it is evident that the men who ran their affairs were shrewdly able to exploit

---

[93] *Book*, chapter 34, p. 86, lines 1–5.   [94] *Book*, chapter 38, pp. 92–4.
[95] Above p. 24.   [96] *m.* 160.   [97] *m.* 179.   [98] *m.* 159.
[99] AC Sez. I, 649/ 13, ff. 18v–19.   [100] Goioli, p. 249.   [101] *m.* 115.   [102] *m.* 169.
[103] *Venerabile*, p. 42; Goioli, pp. 188–90.   [104] Above p. 124.   [105] *mm.* 119, 122.
[106] *mm.* 201, 203; for the house see above p. 83.
[107] See C. M. Barron and A. F. Sutton, eds., *Medieval London Widows*, London 1994, for discussion of the whole question.

the chance to add to the properties of the institutions. It certainly looks as if Stefania allowed the men running the hospice of S Thomas to acquire property which they should not have had, otherwise it is difficult to see why compensation was adjudged to Vannotia's husband. But in general a widow, left alone in a foreign country, must have been glad to have a corporate institution to rely on. It would have supported Sibilla Teste to have as her helper in executing her husband's will the *custos* of S Thomas's hospice, though her husband did not force her to accept him. If, by the time a husband died, the wife was too old to return home to England to her own family, the hospice could be expected to take some care, particularly if a legacy was involved!

Chapter 7

THE ENGLISH IN THE CURIA 1378–1420: I

The return of the curia to Rome in 1376, followed so soon thereafter by schism may have been a disaster for the Western Church but it was a boon for some non-Italian clergy. Many former members refused to leave Avignon or fled back there once the schism hardened. The vacuum, both among the cardinals and in the lower levels of administration, had to be filled and was largely supplied from nations remaining loyal to the Roman popes. Thus many Germans obtained curial posts, whereas the French, so numerous during the Avignon exile, become far fewer.[1] After the first few years English numbers in Rome also increased, though never so much as Germans, for reasons explored below. What follows discusses the careers and prospects of the most important English holders of curial posts.

The curia can be divided into the papal and cardinals' households proper and the administration of the wider church.[2] The administration was divided into the judiciary, departments which granted favours, which dealt with finance and which administered the results, particularly sending out bulls.[3] Between 1378 and 1420 much was changing and spheres were less clear than later; under stress of schism men became pluralists, but these rough distinctions still held.

The Rota was the central court of the curia where, in particular, benefice cases were decided. Its judges, *auditores sacri apostolici palacii*, were papal chaplains, enjoying the privileges and benefits of being papal *familiares*. Between 1378 and 1420 fifteen Englishmen were auditors, though in some cases very briefly. The individuals, with their periods of

[1] Schuchard, *Die Deutschen*, pp. 35–6.
[2] Summary descriptions of all offices now in Blouin, *Vatican Archives*.
[3] Useful diagram for fifteenth century: J. F. D'Amico, *Renaissance Humanism in Papal Rome. Humanists and Churchmen on the Eve of the Reformation*, Baltimore and London 1983, p. 22.

recorded activity, were Robert Stratton[4] (1362–80), Nicholas Bodi-sham[5] (1376 or 1377), John Mowbray[6] (1379–89), Richard Scrope[7] (1380–6), Thomas de Sudbury[8] (1380–93 or 96), John Trefnant[9] (1384–9), Thomas de Walkyngton[10] (1385–1405), Henry Godbarn[11] (1386–?1390), Andrew Barret[12] (1384–95), Ieuan Trefor[13] (1391–5), Richard Young[14] (*c.* 1391–9), Lewis Aber[15] (1398 and before), Nicholas Ryssheton[16] (1398–1401), John Prene[17] (1396 -1425), and Adam Usk[18] (1402–6).

4   *BRUC*, 1362: *CPP*, p. 395; resigned September 1380, died in the curia 20 October, Oxford, New College MS 214, f. 209; E. Cerchiari, *Capellani Papae et Apostolicae Sedis. Auditores Causarum Sacri Palacii Apostolici seu Sacra Romana Rota ab origine ad diem usque 20 Septembris 1870*, 4 vols., Rome 1919–21, II, p. 34.

5   *BRUC*, p. 80, under Botlesham. 1376: G. Hoborch, *Decisiones*, Mainz 1477 (= London, BL IB 214), no. ccccii. He had died before 22 July 1382, see Le Neve, *Lichfield*, p. 40, if this is he.

6   *BRUO*, II, p. 1326, 1379: Harvey, *Solutions*, p. 24; Zutshi, *Original Papal Letters*, no. 358. 1389: VCH, *Yorkshire*, III, p. 364; *CPL*, IV, p. 335.

7   *BRUO*, III, pp. 1659–60, 1380: Dietrich of Niem, *Liber Cancellariae Apostolicae vom Jahre 1380 und der Stilus Palatii Abbreviatus*, ed. G. Erler, Leipzig 1888, p. 208. 1386: became bishop of Coventry; consecrated in Genoa by Urban VI.

8   *BRUO*, III, Appendix, p. 2219, 1380: Oxford, New College, MS 214, f. 208v; Wells, *Calendar of the MSS of the Dean and Chapter of Wells*, 2 vols. (= Historical Manuscripts Commission), London 1907, 1914, I, p. 293; *CPL*, IV, pp. 452–3; 1396: he was dead by June that year, *BRUO*, annotated copy in the Bodleian Library; Cerchiari, *Capellani*, II, p. 31.

9   *BRUO*, III, pp. 1900–1, 1384: Niem, *Liber Cancellariae* p. 209, without year; Cerchiari, *Capellani*, II, p. 36; *CPL*, IV, p. xv, corrected from B. Schwarz, *Regesten der in Niedersachsen und Bremen überlieferten Papsturkunden, 1198–1503* (= Quellen und Untersuchungen zur Geschichte Niedersachsens im Mittelalter 15), Hannover 1993, no. 1093, 1389: in that year he became bishop of Hereford.

10 *BRUO*, III, pp. 1964–5, 1386: Cerchiari, *Capellani*, II, p. 35; Niem, *Liber Cancellariae*. p. 210, 1405: *BRUO*; M. Gastout, ed., *Suppliques et lettres d'Urbain VI (1379–1389) et de Boniface IX (cinq premières anneés, 1389–1394)*, (= *AVB*, 29: DRGS, 7), Brussels and Rome 1976, p. 131, note.

11 *BRUO*, II, pp. 776–7. 1385: ASV Arm. 31/36, f. 77. 1390: English will 1384 proved 12 December 1390; York, Borthwick Institute, Register Arundel, York Registers 14, ff. 22–22v; Gastout, *Suppliques*, p. 271, note; Cerchiari, *Capellani*, II, p. 36.

12 *BRUO*, p. 2150, 1384: Niem, *Liber Cancellariae*, p. 210; 1395: bishop of Llandaff that year, see Zutshi *Original Papal Letters*, no. 428 for bull; Cerchiari, *Capellani*, II, p. 35.

13 R. R. Davies, *The Revolt of Owen Glyn Dwr*, Oxford 1995, pp. 59, 213–14. 1391: *CPL*, IV, p. xv; 1395: bishop of St Asaph April 1395; Cerchiari, *Capellani*, II, p. 37.

14 For the fullest discussion to date of his career C. Allmand, 'A bishop of Bangor during the Glyn Dwr revolt, Richard Young', *Journal of the Historical Society of the Church in Wales*, 23 (1986), pp. 47–56, 1391: *m.* 123, executor of will, as auditor. 1398: appointed bishop of Bangor, certainly in England by 1400; Cerchiari, *Capellani*, II, p. 38.

15 *CPL*, V, pp. 99, 179.

16 *BRUO*, III, pp. 1618–19; add Harvey, *Solutions*, pp. 147–9, 163, 167–9, 171. 1398: *CPL*, V, p. 90; B. Schwarz, *Regesten*, no. 1240, 10 October 1399 in Rome. 1401: I. J. Churchill, *Canterbury Administration*, 2 vols., London 1933, I, p. 265, II, p. 243; Cerchiari, *Capellani*, II, p. 41.

17 *BRUO*, Appendix, III, p. 2207. 1396: *CPL*, V, p. xv; B. Schwarz, *Regesten*, nos. 1250, 1278, Rome 1400 and 1401; Walsh, 'Roman career', p. 2.

18 *BRUO*, III, p. 1937–8; A. Usk, *The Chronicle of Adam of Usk, 1377–1421*, ed. and trans. C. Given-Wilson (= Oxford Medieval Texts), Oxford 1997, pp. xiii–xxxviii. 1402: Niem, *Liber Cancellariae*. p. 214. 1406: *Chronicle*, p. 211; Cerchiari, *Capellani*, II, p. 39.

All were lawyers by training, several (Godbarn, Mowbray, Trefor, Young, Ryssheton, and Prene) doctors of both laws.[19] Bodisham was only a bachelor, Sudbury, Stratton, Trefnant, Barret and Usk were doctors of civil law and Aber may have been;[20] Walkyngton was doctor of canon law. The majority had probably obtained these degrees in England, though the university of Aber, Sudbury and Prene is unknown. At least two had degrees from Bologna. Barret took his civil law doctorate there in May 1382,[21] and Ryssheton, found in Rome from 1382,[22] read civil law in Bologna with his licence by 1396,[23] when, on grounds that he could not afford to keep his obligation to take his doctorate only in Bologna, he obtained a dispensation,[24] so his doctorate of both laws may be Roman.

How did one set about a career as auditor? Several of these English clerks were well-connected. Stratton may have been a relative of Bishop Robert Stretton of Coventry and Lichfield, whose proctor at the curia he became in 1364,[25] but his career in Rome began with Bishop Bateman, the founder of Trinity Hall, Cambridge, where Stratton had been master and studied his civil law. Bateman went to Avignon where by 1352 Stratton had joined his staff, being noted as one of the bishop's familiars left behind when Bateman died there in 1355.[26] He next joined the staff of Master Thomas Neville (brother of Alexander, later archbishop of York) who in 1361 died at Villeneuve-les-Avignon.[27] Next year Stratton became auditor. Bodisham or Bottlesham may have been related to the bishops of Rochester of that name.[28] Mowbray was the son of John Mowbray, a Yorkshire knight,[29] almost certainly Sir John Mowbray of Kirklington, justice of the King's bench, one of whose sons, William Mowbray of Colton, mentioned in his 1391 will his dead brother Master John Mowbray.[30] John seems to have gone to Rome first as an advocate (a lawyer with right to plead

---

19 References in *BRUO* or *BRUC* unless otherwise stated. Godebarn is called 'of both laws' in ASV Arm 31/36, f. 77, letters of protection 1388; he may be Henricus de Anglia, given DCL in Bologna in 1382, A. Sorbelli, ed. *Il Liber Secretus Juris Cesarei dell'università di Bologna*, I, *1378–1420* (= Universitatis Bononiensis Monumenta 2), Bologna 1938, p. 21.

20 *CPL*, IV, p. 192.

21 Sorbelli, *Liber Secretus*, pp. 19, 23; G. B. Parks, *The English Traveller to Italy*, I, *The Middle Ages to 1525*, Rome 1954, p. 625.

22 *CCR 1392–6*, p. 518.   23 Parks, *English Traveller*, p. 625.   24 *CPL*, V, p. 68.

25 R. de Stretton, *The Registers or Act Books of the Bishops of Coventry and Lichfield. Book 5: The Second Register of Bishop Robert de Stretton, AD 1360–1385*, ed. R. A. Wilson, William Salt Archaeological Society, new series 8 (1905), p. 105.

26 *CPP*, p. 276, as Sutton.   27 *BRUO*, II, p. 1351; *CPP*, p. 374–5.

28 William Bottlesham, bishop of Rochester, 1389–1400; John, 1400–4.

29 *CPL*, IV, p. 79.

30 *Testamenta Eboracensa*, I, SS 4 (1836), p. 159.

only in certain courts) just before the death of Gregory XI.[31] Probably the schism persuaded him to return home, since he participated in the 1379 condemnation in Oxford of Wyclif's views on the Eucharist, one of two lawyers taking part,[32] but in November 1380 he was back in papal service.[33] Scrope, the later archbishop of York, was the third son of Henry, first baron Scrope, of Masham, Yorkshire. His time as auditor looks like a shrewd career-move for a well-born young man, whose family connections and abilities would have marked him for promotion. His first post in 1375 (to 1379) was as official of Thomas Arundel, bishop of Ely[34] and he was also chancellor of Cambridge in 1378.[35] Scrope probably owed this start to his cousin Sir Richard Scrope, a friend and executor of Arundel's father.[36] Arundel became his close friend and probably helped his career in this early stage.

Sudbury was the brother of the archbishop of Canterbury which must have been of enormous help; it is recorded in a manuscript which also notes his arrival as auditor.[37] Trefnant was said to be closely related to nobles near to the king when Richard II wrote to the pope backing his promotion to the episcopate in early 1389.[38] It is unclear who actually wrote this letter, since the Appellants, though challenged by Richard, were still in power at least until the council held on 3 May 1389.[39] The 1389 promotions to the episcopate were in any case at least partly Urban VI's hostile reaction to the Appellant refusal of money.[40] Trefnant began his curial career as an advocate.[41]

Walkyngton had an early connection with Bishop Brantingham of Exeter. They were fellow northerners, born in almost adjacent parishes in the Durham franchise of Howden.[42] All Walkington's early preferment was in Brantingham's diocese.[43] His earliest appearance in the curia was in 1383 as proctor for Durham priory. The formal arrange-

---

[31] Harvey, *Solutions*, p. 20; see Vatican Library, MS, v, 6330, f. 284r/v, given the parish church of ?Bennocte Durham diocese by provision as priest and advocate.

[32] *Fasciculi zizaniorum magistri Johannis Wyclif cum Tritico*, ed. W. W. Shirley, RS, 5 (1858), p. 113.

[33] See below p. 139; Register Neville, York, Borthwick Institute, Register 12, ff. 9v, 12.

[34] BRUC, from Register Arundel, Ely.

[35] J. H. Wylie, *The History of England under Henry IV*, 4 vols., London 1884–96, II, pp. 200–1.

[36] M. Aston, *Thomas Arundel. A Study of Church Life in the Reign of Richard II*, Oxford 1967, pp. 305–6.

[37] Oxford, New College MS 214, f. 208v.   [38] Perroy, *Diplomatic Correspondence*, no. 97.

[39] A. Steel, *Richard II*, Cambridge 1941, pp. 174–6; Perroy, *L'Angleterre*, p. 307.

[40] Perroy, *L'Angleterre*, pp. 307–8; R. G. Davies, 'Richard II and the church in the years of "tyranny"', *Journal of Medieval History* 1 (1975), pp. 329–62, esp. pp. 332–3, for another view and Davies 'The episcopate and the political crisis', pp. 677–80.

[41] Vatican Library, MS v, 6330, f. 483r/v, in a supplication under Urban VI, no date: *ut asserit in dicto palacio advocatus existit*.

[42] McDermid, *Beverley Minster Fasti*, p. 27.   [43] BRUO.

ment made with him by Durham also talked of his membership when in England of the *familia* of the earl of Northumberland.[44]

Godbarn had travelled to the curia first in May 1378 on business for Alexander Neville, archbishop of York, about the treasurership of York and John de Clifford.[45] This was part of Neville's serious quarrel with his chapter (among others), the residentiary canons being led by Clifford.[46] From this visit Godbarn obtained an expectative in York which Neville honoured with the prebend of Dunnington in 1379.[47] By October 1386 he was an auditor.[48] Godbarn was thus in Rome before Neville, in flight from England, arrived in January 1390.[49] Godbarn had died by 12 December 1390.[50] For him the curia may have represented a haven from English politics. The same may be true for Andrew Barret. He was received as auditor on 17 March 1384.[51] But shortly thereafter he must have returned home and became involved in the Appellant crisis. In January 1387 he was released from prison in England on grounds that he had never behaved treasonably in the curia or anywhere else,[52] and he left for the curia in December 1389, 'to obtain benefices'.[53] From 1390 he was functioning as an auditor.[54] When in 1391 he was acting in a case involving John Waltham, bishop of Salisbury and his chapter, Gilbert Stone, Waltham's chancellor, had him bombarded with letters from the king and others to decide in Waltham's favour.[55] Stone suggested that the king must not 'so write as if he held the auditor suspect in any way, which God forbid' (*sic scribit tamquam in aliquo suspectum habens auditorem, quod absit.*)[56]

Trefor was a highly born member of a family in north-east Wales.[57] He undoubtedly owed his advance in the curia to Richard II. When he first came there, in March 1390, he had permission to seek papal confirmation for his appointment to S Asaph,[58] but when he reached

---

[44] Durham, Dean and Chapter Muniments, Register II, ff. 197, 213v (formal arrangement).
[45] *CCR 1377–81*, p. 528, passport.
[46] G. E. Aylmer and R. Cant, eds., *A History of York Minster*, Oxford 1977, pp. 100–1; J. Raine, ed. *Historians of York and its Archbishops*, 3 vols., RS 70 (1886), II, pp. 423–4.
[47] Neville Register, York, Borthwick Institute Register 12 , f. 7v; Le Neve, *Northern*, p. 46, royal rival.
[48] Date from ASV Arm. 31/36 f. 77; Niem, *Liber Cancellariae.* p. 213; Lunt, *Financial Relations*, pp. 730, 738.
[49] S. G. Haslop, 'Two entries' passim; Davies, 'Alexander Neville', esp. p. 94 note 26.
[50] Will in Arundel Register, York, Borthwick Institute, Register 14, f. 22r/v.
[51] Niem, *Liber Cancellariae*, p. 210.
[52] *CCR 1385–9*, p. 206.   [53] *CPR 1388–92*, p. 166.
[54] *CPL*, IV, p. xv; also ASV, Reg. Suppliche, 104A, ff. 15, 39v.
[55] Perroy, *Diplomatic Correspondence*, no. 182; Oxford, Bodleian Library, MS Bodley 859, ff. 18, 18r/v; 18v-19.
[56] Bodley 859, ff. 18v–19.   [57] Davies, *Glyn Dwr*, p. 59.
[58] *Rot Parl*, III, p. 274; *CCR 1392–6*, p. 529.

Rome he found the see already given to the king's confessor Alexander Bache, which must have been as a result of machinations in England.[59] At that point he also became auditor to Cardinal Adam Easton.[60] His activities as papal auditor can be traced in the registers.[61]

It is not possible to discover Richard Young's English patron. He was already at the curia in 1382[62] and was an auditor by 1391.[63] When he departed in 1397 he left one of his works with the cardinal of Naples,[64] probably Henricus Minutoli, who may have been his Roman patron. Ryssheton pursued an academic and church career abroad, with time spent in Rome and Bologna.[65] The most likely explanation for his long stay in Rome is that he was a Lancastrian who did not sympathise with Richard II. His will revealed his loyalties.[66] He also claimed kinship with Thomas Langley, keeper of the privy seal, later bishop of Durham.[67] In the curia he had support from cardinal Angelo Acciauoli of Florence[68] and his English career was entirely after 1400.

John Prene, an Irishman, has no known patrons. The last auditor, Adam Usk, owed his early career in England to the earl of March but was lucky enough, when he came to Rome first in 1402, under a cloud because of his Welshness in the face of the outbreak of the Glyn Dwr revolt in 1400, to find patronage from Cardinal Baldassare Cossa (later John XXIII).[69] Under the circumstances this very ambitious clerk had much more chance of promotion out of England.

Thus the curia acted both as a refuge and as a stepping stone for some Englishmen. A papal auditor could expect to be rewarded with a bishopric, though if English seldom a lucrative one; but, as several found, politics at home were as influential as papal wishes. Of those who achieved bishoprics Trefnant had royal backing for his appointment to Hereford but this may in fact indicate Appellant support. He had, however, stood by Urban at Nocera.[70] After consecration in Rome in June 1389 by Cosmato Gentilis, former English collector and

---

[59] *BRUO* and Appendix for Bache; Perroy, *L'Angleterre*, p. 316.   [60] See p. 209.
[61] ASV, Suppliche 104A, f. 15 as substitute for Walkyngton, ff. 118, 152v, 157, all 1394.
[62] Gastout, *Suppliques*, pp. 516, 576. For 1382: *CCR 1392–6*, p. 519.   [63] *m.* 123.
[64] Harvey, *Solutions*, p. 107, note 45.
[65] *CCR 1392–6*, pp. 518 (1382), 523, 525, 544, 546, 547 (1392).   [66] Below p. 139.
[67] Henry IV, *Royal and Historical Letters*, ed. F. C. Hingeston, 2 vols., *RS*, 18 (1860, 1965), I, p. 431: called John *vester consanguineus et clericus humillimus*. See R. L Storey, *Thomas Langley and the Bishopric of Durham*, London 1961, p. 92 for a Richard Rishton employed by Thomas Langley.
[68] See below p. 166; *CPL*, IV, p. 345.
[69] Usk, *Chronicle*, pp. xiv–xxxviii. This supersedes everything else written about him. See also: Davies, *Glyn Dwr*, p. 163–4; *BRUO*, III, p. 1938; Niem, *Liber Cancellariae*, p. 214.
[70] See cases by him in 1384 in Naples and in 1387 at Lucca, Schwarz, *Niedersachsen*, nos. 1093 and 1105.

later Pope Innocent VII, he returned to England and never thereafter took much part in politics.[71] Scrope was no doubt destined for high church office from the start but his promotion as bishop of Coventry and Lichfield in August 1386 was not the first attempt. He had been elected bishop of Chichester (where he was already dean) in 1385 but Richard II had insisted on the appointment of the royal confessor, Thomas Rushook, bishop of Llandaff, later impeached and transferred by the Appellants. Urban agreed, provided that William Bottlesham, OP, titular bishop of Bethlehem, a relative of Nicholas, another who stood by him in Nocera, was given Llandaff.[72] Scrope's appointment therefore came as much from his standing with the pope as from politics in England, though at this point it probably represented an appointment for someone who did not wholly enjoy royal favour.[73] He was consecrated in August in Genoa, where Urban's curia currently resided, and left to take up his see in England in November.

Barret eventually (in 1395) became bishop of Llandaff, replacing the royal physician Tydeman of Winchcombe.[74] Since Richard by this time seems to have been determined to have a complacent episcopate, one can assume that he trusted Barret. Gilbert Stone had been asserting since 1391 that Barret's conscience might be moved by a promise of richer benefices in Salisbury, so he was recognised as ambitious.[75] He only survived a year in his new post and was dead by 12 April 1396.[76]

Trefor was the only Welshman successfully appointed to a Welsh see at this period; his appointment, as well as satisfying the pope, looks like an attempt to supply the king with a bishop in Wales who would act as a link to the native Welsh. Though often dismissed as unimportant by historians of the English church, in terms of his own world he was a leader. His decision to support Henry IV was most important for that monarch in Wales and his subsequent defection to Glyn Dwr a major blow.[77]

Young on the other hand was rewarded with Bangor, partly to keep out a native Welshman. In 1398 Boniface IX provided to Bangor Lewis Aber, like Young a papal auditor and treasurer of S David's, but the English government must have resisted this and Aber probably never held the see in reality, though he left Rome and went to Bangor, and

---

[71] Eubel, *Hierarchia*, I, p. 274.
[72] Perroy, *L'Angleterre*, pp. 299–300; Steel, *Richard II*, 157–8, for the impeachment; Raine, *Historians*, II, pp. 428–9.
[73] Steel, *Richard II*, pp. 120–4 for alignments at this time.
[74] Zutshi, *Original Papal Letters*, no. 428 for bull.
[75] Bodley 859, ff. 18v–19.   [76] Fryde, *Handbook*, p. 293.
[77] Davies, *Glyn Dwr*, pp. 9–10, 59, 116, 213–14; G. Williams, *The Welsh Church from Conquest to Reformation*, Cardiff 1976, pp. 221–2.

subsequently litigated.[78] Young's provision was dated 2 December 1398, accepted by the crown on 19 May 1399. This was almost certainly both a change of mind by the pope and a reward for a man who had suffered a great deal, including imprisonment in Germany, for his loyalty to the Roman see.[79] In 1397 he had gone on a papal mission to the Reichstag and had suffered kidnap.[80] On appointment he returned home and at once sided with Henry IV.[81]

The others did not achieve bishoprics. Why not? Very likely Stratton simply had a highly successful career in the Rota where he ended his days as the senior judge.[82] Mowbray was employed as a papal diplomat in 1380 to negotiate about the schism in the Iberian peninsula[83] and could therefore have expected some reward, but because he was English and therefore represented an enemy, he fell foul of the Castilians, so that part of his mission was a failure.[84] In 1381 he was back in England assisting Alexander Neville in his visitation of Beverley Minster.[85] Perhaps this association was not conducive to advance in England! He evidently returned to the curia and there died by 1389; he may be the John Mowbray whom the king was trying to arrest in January 1389.[86] The association with Neville probably also told against Godebarn.

Ryssheton justifiably felt very disappointed that he did not obtain a bishopric. Arundel appointed him auditor of Canterbury by November 1400 and he returned to England to take the post by late September 1401.[87] Thereafter he had an English career as a diplomat.[88] But at the end he was unrewarded and bitter. His will complained against royal injustice. He explained that he merited reward because:

I sustained many labours for the king at the time of his exile and of his adversities . . . and likewise for his lord father the duke of Lancaster.[89]

but the king, although he had ratified all Ryssheton's benefices in England, took from him after his coronation the prebend and arch-

---

[78] *CPL*, V, pp. 99, 179; VI, pp. 502–3; Allmand, 'Richard Young', pp. 47–8.

[79] Allmand, 'Richard Young', pp. 47–8; R. G. Davies, 'After the execution', pp. 47–8.

[80] Harvey, *Solutions*, pp. 106–7, where by error he is called a camera auditor.

[81] Harvey, *Solutions*, p. 117. [82] See below p. 141.

[83] A. Segre, 'I dispacci di Cristoforo da Piacenza procuratore mantovano alla corte pontificia (1371–83)' *Archivio storico italiano*, 5th series, 44 (1909), pp. 253–326, esp. p. 302.

[84] Seidlmayer, *Die Anfänge*, p. 241.

[85] A. F. Leach, ed., *Memorials of Beverley Minster. The Chapter Act Book of the Collegiate Church of St John of Beverley, AD.1286–1347*, SS, 108 (1903), p. 232; Dobson, 'Beverley in conflict', pp. 153–4 for dispute.

[86] *VCH Yorkshire*, III, p. 364; *CPL*, IV, p. 335, *CPR 1388–92*, p. 53.

[87] Churchill, *Canterbury Administration*, I, p. 265; II, p. 243.

[88] Harvey, *Solutions*, pp. 147–9, 163, 167–9, 171.

[89] PRO Prob. 11/2A, ff. 205–207v: *sustinui multos labores pro dicto rege tempore exilii sui et in passagiis adversiis..ac eciam pro domino patre suo duci Lancastrie.*

deaconry of Buckingham in the church of Lincoln which he conferred on Thomas Tutbury (dead when Ryssheton's will was drawn), clerk and treasurer first of John of Gaunt's household and then of Henry's. Tutbury had been treasurer of Henry's household from the very beginning of his reign.[90] The disputed benefice had been claimed in 1399 as a provision by Walter Cook, a proctor in the curia, when the incumbent, a councillor of Richard II, retired into a monastery,[91] but Cook had given up by 25 November, saying that he had been despoiled by royal clerks with the connivance of the bishop.[92] Tutbury must have been the claimant supported by the king. He was given the benefice by royal grant on 10 March 1402, but was already claiming.[93] Ryssheton disputed it with a provision and with a pardon from Richard, but when Tutbury died the king appointed William Milton, Arundel's registrar,[94] and Ryssheton failed.[95] The will also revealed that Ryssheton thought that the king still owed him wages for many diplomatic journeys, including to the Council of Pisa.[96]

If Ryssheton had reason to feel aggrieved it is doubtful that Adam Usk was justified in the resentment he also certainly felt. He was a protégé of the earl of March, who was the lord of Usk and then of Thomas Arundel, archbishop of Canterbury, but in England by 1402 his Welshness was a stumbling block. He certainly tried for bishoprics, the turning point being in 1404 when he tried to gain Hereford, which went to Robert Mascall.[97] In the same year, when Robert Braybrooke, bishop of London died (28 August), he recorded that his fellow auditors suggested that Guy Mone, bishop of S David's should be translated to it and Usk be made bishop of S David's.[98] Usk asserted that on both these occasions 'the English' maligned him to the king, threatened the cardinals who supported him with loss of benefices in England and cheated him of his chance. It is true that at the curia the English group looked at him very askance, even though he had dealings with them. Writing in December 1404 to Walter Strickland, bishop of Carlisle, William Lovell, probably Strickland's proctor, told him it was unwise to have written to Usk because 'he is not uncontaminated by Owen

---

[90] J. L. Kirby, *Henry IV of England*, London 1970, pp. 72, 259; R.L .Storey, 'Clergy and common law in the reign of Henry IV', in R. F. Hunnisett and J. B. Post, eds., *Medieval Records Edited in Memory of C.A.F . Meekings*, London 1978, pp. 341–408, esp. pp. 404–7 for the case.

[91] *CPL*, V, pp. 102, 309; *BRUC*, pp. 157–8; Storey, 'Clergy and common law', pp. 404, 406; Le Neve, *Lincoln*, p. 15, no mention.

[92] Le Neve, *Lincoln*, pp. 15–16.   [93] *CPR 1401–5*, p. 49, appointment of Tutbury.

[94] *BRUO*, II, 1283–4; Storey, 'Clergy and common law', p. 405; *CPL*, IV, pp. 345–6; *CPR 1396–9*, p. 513.

[95] *CPL*, VI, p. 59.   [96] For this Harvey, *Solutions*, pp. 149, 161.

[97] *Chronicle*, pp. 174–6.   [98] Ibid., pp. 188–90.

Glendour and we do not commonly communicate with him in this nor in other matters' (*non multum purus de Ivone de Glendour et non in hac nec in alia quacumque materia ut communiter secum communicamus*).[99] Exactly who his enemies in Rome were, apart from Lovell, is difficult to ascertain. Roger Walden obtained the bishopric of London in the end, not before there was considerable scheming in England.[100] Nothing suggests that Usk was seriously considered in England for these sees. Mascall was the royal confessor and close to Henry IV. He had lost his household position in January 1404 at the request of the Commons and Henry may have felt that he owed Mascall this appreciation.[101] As for London, the chapter and the king wanted Langley, keeper of the privy seal, and Thomas Arundel at first supported Robert Hallum, his protégé, but the pope appointed the ex-archbishop of Canterbury, Roger Walden.[102]

The ordinary working lives of these men can be glimpsed in the papal registers, where they are recorded as hearing cases.[103] One can sometimes also find their advice being sought from clients in England; Mowbray for instance was thought a good person to give advice on the endowment of Durham College, Oxford, since he had a relative and friend in the community who was therefore sent to the curia.[104]

All these men were learned and several left writings and/or books to prove it. Stratton was responsible for ordering the collection of Rota conclusions by William Horboch which contained several of his own judgements.[105] By 1376 as senior Rota Auditor he was the 'memory' of the group, presumably becoming more important when others joined the anti-pope.[106] Trefnant's register containing many of his judgements, reveals a very learned man.[107] He also left a notable library of 66 volumes apart from his chapel books.[108] One contained his own

---

[99] Arch. Seld. B 23, ff. 60v–61; see him renting household goods from the English hospice of S Thomas, *m.* 163.

[100] Wylie, *Henry IV*, III, pp. 125–7. Davies, 'After the execution', pp. 49–50.

[101] C. Given-Wilson, The *Royal Household and the King's Affinity. Service, Politics and Finance in England 1360–1413*, New Haven (Conn.) and London 1986, p. 197.

[102] Storey, *Langley*, pp. 14–15; Henry IV, *Royal and Historical Letters*, I, pp. 415–6; Davies, 'After the execution', pp. 48–50.

[103] See also Schwarz, *Niedersachsen*, for several; Zutshi, *Original*, no. 358; Royce, *Landboc*, pp. 45–76 for Baret.

[104] Durham, Dean and Chapter Library, MS C IV 25, f. 57.

[105] Hoborch, *Decisiones*, numbers xcviii, cxvii, cxxii, ccvii, cclxxvii, cccliii, cccclxxxiii; Oxford, New College, MS 214, f. 128.

[106] Hoborch, *Decisiones*, no. ccclii a recollection of an opinion of the cardinal of S Angelo (Guillaume Noelletti); no. cccclxxxix a recollection of the now dead cardinal Guilelmus (?Sudre), *presente rev. do, P. tit. Eustachi* (Flandrin).

[107] Trefnant, *Registrum*, pp. 53–5, 73–90, 103–14, 131–5.

[108] B. D. Charles and H. D. Emanuel, 'The library of John Trefnant, Bishop of Hereford

judgements and possibly his Rota judgements, if it was not simply a general collection of Rota decisions, and another had writings about Urban VI's election and healing the schism.[109] At least one manuscript contains a civil law lecture of about 1376 by him.[110] Walkyngton left a *repertorium* and lectures from his Oxford days.[111] Godbarn died in the curia, so the camera had right of spoil and compiled a list of his books.[112] All were legal, except a lecture and a breviary; they included basic canon and civil law but also *Novella* of Joannes Andreas, a tract of Guillaume Mandagout on elections,[113] *Novella* on the second book of Decretals, *Lectura* of Butrigrarius on the Codex and Innocent IV on the Decretals. He left additional books to legatees in England, including Hostiensis' *Summa*, a *tabula* of Johannes Calderini on the *Decreta; Lectura* of John of Legnano on the *Clementines* and the *Margarita*.[114]

Trefor has been credited with authorship (of *Eulogium historiarum* for instance) of works unlikely to be his, but he certainly patronised Welsh poetry, in particular of Iolo Goch, Owen Glyn Dwr's bard.[115] Young and Ryshheton left writings from diplomatic missions for the curia and for England where their legal expertise can be readily seen.[116] In addition both left books. Ryssheton talked in his will of conveying his books from Paris to Rome. He left Arundel two books (unspecified), to Richard Young *Sermones Parisienses*, to others Hostiensis' *Summa*, a tract *De Virtutibus* and to his nephew Nicholas, whose career he was fostering, *Constitutiones Provinciales*.[117] Usk, of course, was the author of a famous chronicle in which he paraded his legal learning. He mentions also one snub in a legal case by Trefnant.[118]

Few of these great men had known dealings with the English hospices while in Rome. Young did so because he was an executor of the will of

---

1389–1404', *The Journal of the National Library of Wales*, 6 (1949–50), pp. 355–60; list in *BRUO*.

[109] Nos. 63 and 84 in the list in Charles and Emanuel, 'Library'.

[110] Oxford, New College, MS 179, art. 3; J. I. Catto and T. A. R. Evans, eds., *The History of the University of Oxford*, I, *The Early Oxford Schools*, Oxford 1984, p. 560.

[111] R. Sharpe, *A Handlist of the Latin Writers of Great Britian and Ireland Before 1540 (= Publications of the Journal of Medieval Latin 1)*, Turnhout 1997, pp. 687–8; Catto and Evans, *University of Oxford*, I, p. 560; The manuscript of the *repertorium* (not seen by me) is Canterbury Cathedral MS Lit. C 12; lecture as B Cn L in BL MS Royal 9 E VIII, ff. 122–5, ff. 130, 129r/v; further lecture in Royal 9 F II, ff. 206, ?207v, ?209.

[112] D. Williman, *Bibliothèques ecclésiastiques au temps de la papauté d'Avignon*, I, Paris 1980, pp. 268–70.

[113] J. F. von Schulte, *Geschichte der Quellen und Literatur des kanonischen Rechts*, 3 vols., Stuttgart 1875–89, II, p. 183, canonist of Bologna, d. 1321.

[114] Arundel, York, Register 14, f. 22 r/v.

[115] Davies, *Glyn Dwr*, p. 59 and note 25, 214.

[116] Most easily accessible via Harvey, *Solutions*, pp. 107–9, 118–20, 167–9, 170–1.

[117] Not Lyndewood, because the date is too early.   [118] *Chronicle*, p. 59.

Richard Possewich, a papal *cursor* and a notable benefactor of the institution.[119] Ryssheton left S Thomas's a legacy, but only from the residue (if any) of payment to the Italian merchants who had conveyed his books.[120] Usk rented household goods from S Thomas's in 1403, but as we have seen he was distrusted by the English group.[121]

The camera, under the chamberlain, was of course the papacy's main finance office.[122] It had a secretariat and its own legal section, as well as employing the couriers (*cursors*) who carried the major routine international correspondence. The camera auditors were judges in the legal section of the camera. In the later fourteenth and early fifteenth century they were often also Rota auditors. They were papal chaplains and *familiares* of the pope. I know of only one Englishman, Henry Bowet.[123] This may be another example of a man taking temporary refuge from English politics. He belonged to a well-born Lincolnshire family. After a Cambridge education (at King's Hall), and ordination by Arundel when bishop of Ely, he had joined the staff of Henry Despenser by February 1380. He actively promoted Despenser's schism crusade and was therefore lodged for a time in the Tower late in 1383.[124] The next year he was sent by the king to the curia where he was the king's advocate.[125] By 1385 he had become a papal chaplain and was noted for not deserting Urban VI at Nocera.[126] By 1386 he had acquired the doctorate in both laws. That year he was made a camera auditor.[127] He must have left the curia by 1397 when he became chief justice of Acquitaine. He was, or came to be, a servant of Henry Bolingbroke[128] and was declared a traitor with him, thus ensuring a renewal of career in England when Bolingbroke became Henry IV.

Thus for Bowet the curia was a stepping stone to a career as a court bishop. He was probably reasonably learned. His library, valued at £33 at his death in 1423, consisted of the basic texts of canon and civil law: the bible, a gloss, the Sentences, Gregory the Great's *Pastoralis*, Anselm's *Cur Deus homo*, Aquinas on the fourth book of the Sentences, Bromyard's *Distinctiones*, Guido de Baysio's *Rosarium*, a glossed Sext, Godfredus on the Decretals, Joannes Andreas' *Novella* on the Decretals, Hostiensis' *Lectura* on the Decretals, Rofredus with other tractates, and

---

[119] *m.* 123.   [120] Will above p. 139.   [121] *m.* 163.
[122] Blouin, *Vatican Archives*, pp. 106–7.   [123] *BRUO*, III, Appendix; *BRUC*, pp. 83–4.
[124] Aston, *Arundel*, pp. 306–7.
[125] *CPR 1381–5*, p. 224; Perroy, *L'Angleterre*, p. 203; Cotton Vitellius F II, ff 47v, 148v, for him as advocate; Zutshi, *Original Letters*, no. 127.
[126] Walsingham, *Historia Anglicana*, II, p. 124.
[127] ASV, Arm 29/1, ff. 107v–8. See also f. 211v; Zutshi, *Original*, nos. 386, 387, auditor in 1386.
[128] Kirby, *Henry IV*, pp. 49, 51–2.

works of Azo on civil law.[129] None of this is startling; it represented the working library (several of the volumes were old or worn out) of an ecclesiastical lawyer. Contact with his fellow English via the hospice is not evident. The only connection is that the will of Richard Possewich, a papal *cursor* and therefore a curial, was proved before him in 1391[130] but this was routine. Possewich's Englishness was immaterial. The document revealed, however, John Deek, clerk and priest of Bangor diocese as one witness, presumably employed by Bowet. The notary was from Teramo diocese and the other witness from Liège.

Papal *cursors* were messengers, forming the pope's own postal service, an elite group for carrying routine papal letters to all parts of Christendom. They could be clerks or laymen and held office for life. They were organised into a college, with a *magister*.[131] Little is known about them before 1420 but clearly there were a few English members.

In 1379 John Champneys,[132] sold to an incomer from Avignon, Richard, son of William Possewich, and his wife Alice, his house in Rome. William Possewich called Englicus or de Yrlandia, with his wife Christine, of Meath diocese, citizen of Avignon and probably Richard's father, was buying and selling property in Bourg Neuf in Avignon in the 1360s and owned a house in Bourg de St Veran in 1370–1.[133] In 1371 William Possewich, of Meath diocese, made an arbitration award with John Stanchon, prior of S Peter, Newtown Trim in Meath diocese;[134] and he and his wife Christine, citizens of Avignon, obtained confessional privileges in May 1371.[135] Richard Possewich of Meath diocese, described as innkeeper (*hostalarius*), bought a house in Burg Cabassole in Avignon in 1358 and sold it in 1374.[136] This was probably Richard Irland of the parish of S Peter, Avignon, of Meath diocese, described as a citizen in the list of those who opted for citizenship just before the papacy left for Rome, registered in Avignon Register 204.[137] His wife was described in the deed by which they bought their house in

---

129 Will: *Testamenta Eboracensa*, I, pp. 398–402; Inventory: III, pp. 69–85, with library 76–7.
130 *m.* 123, dorse.
131 E. Rodocanchi, 'Les couriers pontificaux du quatorzième au dixseptième siècle', *Revue d'histoire diplomatique*, 26 (1912), pp. 392–428.
132 *mm.* 74, 76, 81, 84, 86.
133 A.-M. Hayez, 'Les bourgs avignonnais du XIVe siècle', *Bulletin philologique et historique (jusqu'au 1610) du comité des travaux historiques et scientifiques*, Paris 1977 for 1975, pp. 77–102 esp. p. 97; ASV, Reg. Av. 180, f. 372; Archives de Vaucluse, H Ste Praxede d'Avignon 55, no. 73; 58 no. 39. I warmly thank Madame Hayez for all her help.
134 ASV, Reg. Av. 173, f. 466v. For the monastery, A. Gwynn and R. N. Hadcock, *Medieval Religious Houses, Ireland*, Bristol 1970, p. 190.
135 ASV, Reg. Av. 180, f. 372.
136 Hayez, 'Les Bourgs', p. 97; Achives de Vaucluse, 8 G 44 Ste Agricole.
137 ASV, Reg. Av. 204, f. 433v.

Rome as Alice daughter of William de Ricchal of *Albiens* diocese,[138] (perhaps *Eboracensis* garbled). Alice and their son John received legacies in 1390 from Elena Clerk.[139] In 1391 Richard made his will.[140] This showed that he had by then become a papal *cursor*. He left a ducat to his fellow *cursores*; the witnesses included Walter Taylor, alias Symund, Tyderic Stempel, Gracia Petri of Spain and Antonius Francisci, *cursores*. Walter Symonis, *cursor*, was also a witness to Alice's will in 1401.[141]

The Possewichs had two sons, Richard and John, to whom, with their mother, Richard senior left his house in Rome. Both must have been young. In 1397 Richard junior was twenty-one,[142] thus born in Avignon in 1376 and fifteen when his father made the will. He was joint heir to his father and mother with John.[143] Richard inherited the household goods and shared with John the house in Rome, which was only to be sold if both agreed. But in his own right his mother left him a house in Avignon. Like Richard junior, John Possewich the younger son took orders. Details of both careers will be further discussed under cardinals' households.

This may be a very well-connected family. Possewichs occur in Ireland, including Hugh Possewich, keeper of writs of the Common Bench, with property in Newlands, Co. Dublin.[144] John Possewich, who had Roman citizenship, claimed, when petitioning for a benefice in Armagh diocese, that his parents were of the English nation and that he spoke the local language, not Irish but English one assumes.[145]

The Possewichs are the best documented example of a family moving with the curia and then making careers in its service in the new location. Walter Taylor, alias Symund, a witness in the Possewich wills, may be another. He, described as *cursor*, with his wife Christine, first appears in 1382 buying a house in the parish of S Biagio in Parione, from John Salmon, another Englishman, with many English witnesses.[146] He appeared after this as a witness.[147] He became *custos* of S Thomas's in 1397 and twice after that was its official.[148] By the time he made his will in 1403, however, he was actually functioning as a tailor. There is mention of an *apotheca* or shop and of cloths in it.[149] By then he made no mention of being a *cursor*.[150]

---

[138] *mm.* 100, 107, 108.   [139] *m.* 119.   [140] *m.* 123.   [141] *m.* 158.

[142] ASV, Reg. Lat. 49, ff. 165r–66v.   [143] *m.* 158.

[144] *Rotulorum Patentium et Clausarum Cancellariae Hiberniae Calendarium*, vol I/I, London 1828, p. 93, 104; J. Alen, *A Calendar of Archbishop Alen's Register*, ed. C. McNeill, Dublin 1950, p. 236; *CPR 1370–4*, pp. 328, 378, 465; *CPR 1374–7*, p. 97; *CPR 1377–81*, p. 562. I thank Professor Robin Frame for all his help with this.

[145] ASV, Reg. Lat. 127, ff. 46–7.   [146] *m.* 109.

[147] *mm.* 116, 123, 158.   [148] *mm.* 149, 152.

[149] *m.* 163.   [150] *m.* 171, an arbitration about his property does call him *cursor*.

The papal chancery was the main 'writing office', responsible for much of the correspondence.[151] Its personnel included abbreviators, who drew up the documents, scriptors who wrote fair copies, registrars who registered them, an audience chamber for hearing those who questioned them (*audientia litterae contradictarum*) and a group of bullators. There was also an important group of protonotaries. There is more evidence of an English presence here than in the camera.

The role of protonotaries was changing rapidly in this period but essentially they served the vice-chancellor in the consistory, where the most important questions about major benefice were decided.[152] I have found five English protonotaries in this period: Richard Scrope, Thomas Polton, Roger Basset, John Catterick and Richard Derham. Polton, however, did not achieve the position until about 1414 and his main career in that office was after 1420; the part of most interest here was as an abbreviator. Scrope was made protonotary in April 1386, prior to his consecration as bishop and only shortly before his departure from the curia.[153]

Derham is considerably more interesting. He came to the curia in 1405 from his position as chancellor of Cambridge and warden of the King's Hall there from 1399 to 1413, as well as dean of S Martin le Grand in London, to represent the king in the curia as royal proctor.[154] He was master of theology of Cambridge and was probably made protonotary after a highly important role in the period before the council of Pisa and in giving evidence at the council itself.[155] He must have been at the curia from April or May 1405 until he returned in July 1408 to explain to the king and government the sins of Gregory XII. He participated in the council of Pisa and, in its aftermath in 1410 as he collected privileges, was named protonotary.[156] He may have functioned as such. In 1413 he was sent to England, presumably to announce new negotiations in the schism.[157] In 1415 he was again Warden of King's Hall until his death in 1416, but he spent 1415–16 at the council of Constance.

Roger Basset probably equally owed his promotion to the council of

---

[151] Blouin, *Vatican Archives*, p. 127.

[152] Convenient summary in Schuchard, *Die Deutschen*, pp. 93–4.

[153] Niem, *Liber Cancellariae*. p. 208; Cerchiari, *Capellani*, II, 35; Perroy, *Diplomatic Correspondence*, no. 90.

[154] *BRUC*, pp. 184–5; *Calendar of Signet Letters of Henry IV and Henry V (1399–1422)*, ed. J. L. Kirby, London 1978, nos. 270, 277; Henry IV, *Royal and Historical Letters*, II, p. 45; A. B. Cobban, *The King's Hall within the University of Cambridge in the Later Middle Ages* (= Cambridge Studies in Life and Thought, 3rd series 1), Cambridge 1969, pp. 283–4.

[155] Harvey, *Solutions*, pp. 137–8, 148, 154, 161.

[156] *CPL*, VI, pp. 208–10, 289, 312, 332, 335.

[157] *CPL*, VI, p. 168; Zutshi, *Original*, no. 506.

Pisa. He may be the Roger of England studying for a doctorate in Bologna in 1392, achieved in 1400 and lecturing there in 1395 to 1396;[158] but he probably first came to Rome representing Guy Mone bishop of S David's in 1399 and was living in Robert Hallum's house in Parione in 1406.[159] At the council of Pisa he was Arundel's proctor and by late 1411 was a protonotary with an array of privileges.[160] There is a brief glimpse of him in the Roman disturbances, when he lost property.[161]

Catterick was another clerk who owed his promotion to the end of the schism. He was at the curia in July 1413 as a protonotary (and referendary, a lawyer who referred bulls to the chancery) paying service taxes for Courtenay as bishop of Norwich.[162] His curial career went back earlier, however. He had been sent first in 1405, acting for the king, though essentially as an agent of his patron Beaufort, whose chancellor he was, with whom his connection probably went back to their time at Oxford, to excuse the execution of Archbishop Scrope and to promote Thomas Langley's appointment to replace him.[163] His task was to reward the most influential cardinals, Angelus Acciauoli and Henricus Minutoli, who were to be allowed to hold English benefices up to 300 marks (Angelus became archdeacon of Canterbury).[164] Catterick did not stay in the curia after 1406.[165] His appointment as protonotary came in 1409, in the aftermath of the council of Pisa, as a reward to Beaufort and Chichele no doubt, though he declared his intention then to make his career in the curia.[166] He returned in 1413 representing both Beaufort and the king and thereafter his story is bound up with the council of Constance rather than with the curia as such. There is no evidence that he played any part in the English group in Rome, where he must have spent time only in 1405–6. He was undoubtedly the chief agent used by Henry V to communicate with Pope Martin V from 1417 until his death in December 1419, though towards the end of his life Polton was probably becoming more

---

[158] Sorbelli, *Il Liber secretus*, pp. 76, 136; U. Dallari, ed., *I rotuli dei lettori, legisti e artisti dello studio bolognese dal 1381al 1799*, 4 vols. (= Deputazione di storia patria per le provincie di Romagna, 1. Dei monumenti istorici pertinenti alle provincie della Romagns, series 2), IV, Bologna 1924, p. 21.

[159] *BRUC*, p. 43; Arch. Seld. B 23, f. 125v; Mone, *Register*, p. 140.

[160] *CPL*,VI, pp. 302, 309, 329, 332, 335, 339.   [161] See p. 52.

[162] Lunt, *Financial Relations*, p. 783.

[163] Storey, *Langely*, p. 18; G.L. Harriss, *Cardinal Beaufort. A Study of Lancastrian Ascendancy and Decline*, Oxford 1988, pp. 25, 40–1; *Calendar of Signet*, ed. Kirby, p. 92, no. 389, p. 91, no. 382; Davies, 'After the execution', pp. 50–9.

[164] *Calendar of Signet*, p. 92, nos. 390, 391; *CPR 1405–8*, p. 260.

[165] Harriss, *Beaufort*, pp. 47, 65.   [166] *CPL*, VI, p. 155.

important (if only because younger and more active).[167] Catterick's activities, however, were essentially those of a diplomatic agent and his title of protonotary and referendary must mainly have given him access to the right channels for the promotion of royal appointments and policies. He also promoted Beaufort's plan to hold Winchester with the cardinal's hat in 1417.[168] It was perhaps fortunate that he died, because this would certainly have roused Henry V's wrath.

[167] Harvey, *England, Rome*, pp. 11, 130–3 for further information.

[168] K. B. McFarlane, 'Henry V, Bishop Beaufort and the Red Hat', in McFarlane, *England in the Fifteenth Century. Collected Essays*, ed. and intro. G. L. Harriss, London 1981, pp. 79–113, esp. pp. 84–5.

Chapter 8

THE ENGLISH IN THE CURIA 1378–1420: II

Abbreviators were responsible for drawing up and ensuring the legal correctness of draft letters.[1] Their role was evolving and in the course of the fifteenth century they became divided into upper and lower ranks. But the division was not so apparent for those described below. I have found nine English abbreviators during this period, here listed with their known period of office: John Fraunceys[2] (1380–1413), Richard Holme[3] (1386–?97), William Tart (1394),[4] John Swayne[5] (1404–11), William Lovell[6] (1401–10), John Teyr (1400–c. 1405),[7] Henry Gardiner[8] (1400), John Haget[9] (1406–12) and Thomas Polton[10] (1401–14). The careers of most are clear enough. They were probably all lawyers with degrees known for certain in some cases. Holme was bachelor of civil law by 1397 and doctor by 1406. His legacy of books to Cambridge was from a 'licentiate of both laws', so he must also have had canon law training.[11] Swayne was a doctor of both laws; by 1408 he was calling himself rector of the university of Sienna.[12] Haget was bachelor of canon law by 1405[13] and finally doctor of civil law. Polton was bachelor of canon law by 1388 and of both laws by 1402.[14] Lovell was bachelor of civil law by 1400.[15] The qualifications of Teyr and Gardiner are unknown.

Almost all can be traced first as proctors; this is true of Holme,

---

[1] B. Schwarz, '*Abbreviature officium est assistere vicecancellario in expeditione litterarum apostolicarum.* Zur Entwicklung des Abbreviatorenamtes vom grossen Schisma bis zur Grundung des Vakabilistenkollegs der Abbreviatoren durch Pius II'. in E. Gatz, ed., *Römische Kurie, kirchliche Finanzen vatikanisches Archiv. Studien zu Ehren von Hermann Hoberg*, II, Rome 1979, pp. 789–823.

[2] See below pp. 174–9, 186–7.   [3] *BRUC*, pp. 311–12.   [4] See below p. 196.

[5] *BRUO*, Appendix, pp. 2219–20; K. Walsh, 'The Roman career', pp. 1–21.

[6] *CPL*, V, pp. 462–3.   [7] Ibid., p. 366.   [8] *BRUO*, II, p. 742.   [9] Ibid., II, p. 848.

[10] *BRUO*, III, pp. 1494–5.

[11] *BRUC* and H. Bradshaw, *Collected Papers*, Cambridge, 1889, pp. 19, 20.

[12] *BRUO*, III, Appendix; *CPL*, VI, p. 143.   [13] *CPL*, VI, p. 16.

[14] *BRUO*, p. 772 from PRO; Rymer, *Foedera* VIII, p. 253 (IV/1, p. 26).

[15] *CPL*, V, pp. 297, 446–7.

Swayne, Lovell, Teyr, Gardiner and Haget. Richard Holme was undoubtedly supported by the king. His earliest benefices, in 1374 and 1375 were royal grants[16] and by 1383 he was 'royal clerk'.[17] By early 1386 he had gone to Rome where he was identified as an abbreviator 'from the diocese of York'.[18] He was proctor in a notorious case about Beverley Minster for John Ravenser, executor of Richard Ravenser, a royal clerk.[19] Ravenser, of a powerful Yorkshire family, one of the major groups of families in Yorkshire, was a leading royal clerk, a favourite of Edward III. He was master in the chancery from 1362–86[20] and became a leading opponent of Alexander Neville in the Beverley chapter in 'a vendetta' which lasted years.[21] When, in August 1381, Neville removed Richard from the prebend of S Martin's, Beverley, and put in Anthony de St Quintin, Ravenser immediately started a case in the curia, which was continued after his death in 1386 by Thomas de Feriby, the papal surrogate for Ravenser, and the royal appointee after Neville fell.[22]

Holme probably became a supporter of Arundel: he witnessed an archiepiscopal act at Weelhall in June 1396.[23] He was next in the service of the bishop of Durham, Walter Skirlaw, as chancellor perhaps in 1397, and his career in Rome was by then regarded as behind him.[24]

Swayne was from Kildare diocese, the son, he confessed, of two unmarried lay people.[25] In 1399, when beginning his career, he sought all necessary dispensations, to hold the highest office despite this. He probably owed his rise to his career in the curia which can be traced from 1404.[26] He probably began as a proctor for John Madock bishop of Kildare.[27] It is striking, however, that he was so successful and rose so high in the end, becoming archbishop of Armagh, a most unusual elevation for an illegitimate son, even from Ireland where clerical sons were not unusual.[28]

Lovell was from York diocese, son of a priest and an unmarried

---

16 *CPR 1374–7*, pp. 2, 132.   17 *CPR 1381–5*, p. 281.
18 ASV 29/1, ff. 47, 49, 52r/v, 62v; Zutshi, *Original Letters*, no. 412.
19 McDermid, *Beverley Minster Fasti*, pp. 49–52 for the people.
20 Ibid., p. 51.   21 Ibid., p. 51; Davies, 'Episcopate and crisis', p. 663.
22 McDermid, *Beverely Minster Fasti*, p. 51; Dobson, 'Beverley in conflict', pp. 156–8.
23 *CPL*, V, p. 67.
24 M. D. Legge, *Anglo-Norman Letters and Petitions from All Souls MS 182* (= Anglo-Norman Texts 3), Oxford 1941, no. 49, p. 96: *ad este de grand temps passe un grand officier du pape en la court de Rome et familierement conu de lui seint pere et de tous mes seigneurs les cardinaulx . . .*
25 *CPL*, V, p. 203; Walsh, 'Roman career', pp. 7–14 for career to 1413.
26 *CPL*, V, pp. 614, VI, pp. 143, 333, 334, 375.
27 *CPL*, VI, p. 6; Walsh, 'Roman career', pp. 8–9.
28 M. J. Haren, 'Social structures of the Irish church. A new source in papal penitentiary dispensations for illegitimacy', and C. Schuchard '*Defectus natalium* und Karriere am römische Hof. Das Beispiel der Deutschen an der päpstlichen Kurie (1378–1471)', both in L. Schmugge

woman.[29] Little can be gleaned about his supporters, though he seems to have changed his English political allegiance about 1406 and one wonders whether the fall of Scrope had anything to do with it.[30] He acted for Durham priory in 1408.[31] He was still an abbreviator at death in 1410, having followed Gregory XII's curia.[32] Teyr was apparently an Irishman, another who began as a proctor, first met as an executor of the will of Richard Possewich in 1391.[33] His principal was the bishop of Carlisle.[34] Henry Gardiner was also already at the curia, as proctor for Edmund Stafford, when he was appointed abbreviator in 1400.[35] Haget also began as a proctor, representing Robert Mascall, bishop of Hereford in 1406 when he was made abbreviator.[36] Of the others Fraunceys was described as a scriptor of apostolic letters in 1380 when he was made an abbreviator.[37] Thomas Polton became a papal chaplain in 1394 or 1395 and was called abbreviator by 1401.[38]

Some of these must have spent a very short career in papal service. Tart was only mentioned during 1394, as a member of a cardinal's household.[39] Gardiner, who was dead by 1419, served Bishop Guy Mone of S David's in England from 1402.[40]

Like their colleagues in other offices the English abbreviators often became embroiled in English politics. Fraunceys seems to have been close to Ralph Ergham, bishop of Bath and Wells, who called him 'my most dear colleague' (*socius meus dilectissimus*)[41] when thanking the cardinal of Bologna (probably Cosmato Gentilis) for not being transferred to an Irish see, which had evidently been tried probably in the late 1390s.[42] After 1393 William Courtenay was calling Fraunceys 'sincere friend' (*sincerus amicus*).[43] After 1388 he spent his time almost exclusively in the curia and we know a great deal about his activities.[44] His career merits a section on its own.

Swayne evidently followed Gregory XII from Rome in 1406, his

and B. Wiggenhauser *Illegitimät im Spätmittelalter* (= Schriften des historischen Kollegs, Kolloquien 29), Munich 1994, pp. 207–26, 149–70 respectively.
[29] *CPL*, VI, p. 28.   [30] See p. 181.
[31] Durham Dean and Chapter Muniments, Misc. Ch. 1357, at Lucca; see also V, 2664, ff. 228, 235v for him acting with the Alberti in 1403.
[32] *CPL*, VI, p. 197.   [33] *m.* 123.   [34] Arch. Seld. B 23, ff. 60v–61.
[35] Stafford, *Register*, p. 110; *CPL*, V, p. 306.
[36] Mascall, *Register*, p. 29; *CPL*, VI, pp. 16, 73.
[37] Niem, *Liber Cancellarie.* p. 207; *CPL*, IV, p. 269.   [38] *CPL*, IV, pp. 292, 331, 528.
[39] See below p. 196.   [40] *BRUO*, II, p. 742; Mone, *Register*, pp. 284, 306, 379.
[41] Bodley 859, f. 22v.
[42] Davies, 'Episcopate and crisis', pp. 687–8; Davies, ' After the execution', pp. 46–7.
[43] Edinburgh, University Library, Laing MS 351A (C. R. Borland, *A Descriptive Catalogue of the Western Manuscripts in Edinburgh University Library*, Edinburgh 1916, no. 183), ff. 31v–32. For date Perroy, *Diplomatic Correspondence*, no. 156, and notes.
[44] See pp. 174–5.

rectorship of Sienna in 1408, if genuine, came no doubt when he had gone there with the pope.[45] William Lovell was also absent from Rome in 1407 following the curia,[46] to Lucca in 1408.[47] He was a friend of Fraunceys and a bitter and outspoken enemy of the latter's opponents in England, thus in opposition to the king.[48] Haget had been in Rome from at least 1403[49] and was another who probably followed the curia in 1408.[50] Polton came and went to Rome in his early career. He was, for example, in England when appointed to attend the Council of Pisa in 1409.[51] He owed most of his later rise to his activities at the Council of Constance (not part of this story) but also to the patronage of Henry Beaufort.[52]

Unlike the auditors, several of these men had relations with the hospices. Fraunceys was the most notable; he must have ended a wealthy man and much of his property came to S Thomas's.[53] Haget was *camerarius* of S Thomas's in 1404 and 1405[54] and was living in a hospice house in 1406.[55] Lovell was *camerarius* in 1406 and 1407, though absent in the latter year.[56] He was proctor in the curia for John Bremore when the latter was in London in 1405.[57] Teyr's executorship for Possewich may perhaps be explained more by Irish links than by the hospice connection.[58] Polton was said to be a member of the confraternity of S Edmund but he may have joined it when he returned to the curia after the schism.[59] There is no evidence for his connection with either hospice before that.

For some of these men office in the curia was merely a temporary phase in their careers. Holme, who had always depended on the crown, returned first to serve Bishop Skirlaw and then the king.[60] He had a notable career as a member of the royal council from 1408, king's secretary by 1412 and a diplomat, before retiring as master of King's Hall, Cambridge, between 1417 and his death in 1424.[61] Gardiner probably had a short curial career also. But for some being an abbreviator was only a step in a curial career. We have seen that Polton became a protonotary (and royal proctor) and will see below that Swayne became papal secretary

The *audientia litterarum contradictarum* was the court where objections to papal bulls were heard. I have found only one Englishman working in it, Mowbray, who under the stress of the schism combined his job as

---

[45] *CPL*, VI, p. 143; Walsh thinks the title may be hearsay but it should reflect his petition.
[46] *m.* 179.   [47] Above p. 47.   [48] Arch. Seld. B 23, ff. 43v–44.   [49] *m.* 163.
[50] Arch. Seld. B 23, f. 20.   [51] Harvey, *Solutions*, p. 155.
[52] Harriss, *Beaufort*, p. 66.   [53] Below, pp. 175–6.   [54] *mm.* 136, 171.   [55] *m.* 172.
[56] *mm.* 175, 178, 179.   [57] See Burns 'Sources', no. 314, p. 105.   [58] *m.* 123.
[59] Rome, Venerabile Collegio Inglese, *Liber* 272, f. 1v.
[60] Legge, *Anglo-Norman*, no. 48; *BRUC*.   [61] Cobban, *King's Hall*, p. 284.

Rota auditor with that of auditor in this tribunal. He was also referred to as referendary.[62] This is not the only example of pluralism during the Schism.[63]

The position of secretary was less formal in this period than it became later but secretaries were already responsible for the pope's more private correspondence.[64] The disruptions of the curia after 1406 probably gave some Englishmen who would otherwise have had no chance the opportunity to fill this office. William Swan was one. After a career between 1404 and 1406 as a proctor, he followed Gregory XII's flight and became a papal secretary. He did not stay with the pope, however, but returned to join the Council of Constance, where he was acknowledged as secretary although completing his career as an abbreviator. His letter books contain some evidence of his work for Gregory. During Constance, his position was acknowledged in February 1417, described thus: 'granted to him by Lord Gregory, so-called in his obedience and in so far as it is held by virtue of the chapters agreed in the union of the two obediences' (*sibi per dominum Gregorium in sua obedientia nuncupatum concessum et hoc in quantum tenetur vigore capitulorum in unione duarum obedientiarum conclusarum*).[65]

Swayne was named papal secretary in 1411, thus working for the Pisan pope John XXIII.[66] He was at the Council of Constance, as his register as archbishop reveals.[67] Martin V must have made him archbishop of Armagh in 1418 as a reward for loyalty, though possibly Richard Clifford recommended him. There had been a dispute over the appointment, with the chapter wanting another candidate but Martin V set aside the local election and provided Swayne; he was consecrated at Constance.[68] Bremore similarly 'followed the curia' from 1398, hoping for some formal office but acting as a proctor supported by Richard Clifford before becoming a secretary in 1411 under John XXIII.[69] He had died by September 1418.[70]

The papal penitentiary was the characteristic 'pastoral' office which granted pardons for 'reserved' sins and breaches of canon law. It also

---

[62] *CPL*, IV, p. 418. [63] See p. 158.

[64] P. Partner, *The Pope's Men. The Papal Civil Service in the Renaissance*, Oxford 1990, pp. 42–4 .

[65] Arch. Seld. B 23, ff. 105v, 68, 57v, 58, 59v; Constance: ASV, Arm 29/3, f. 35. For the situation Partner, *The Pope's Men*, pp. 8–9.

[66] *CPL*, VI, pp. 333, 349, 374–5; Zutshi, *Original*, no. 500.

[67] ed. D. A. Chart, Belfast 1935, pp. 19–35; Walsh, 'Roman career', pp. 1–7, 18; A. Gwynn, 'Ireland and the English nation at the council of Constance' *Proceedings of the Royal Irish Academy* 45C (1940), pp. 183–233.

[68] Gwynn, 'Ireland and the English nation', pp. 225–30; Walsh, 'Roman career', pp. 19–20.

[69] *CPL*, VI, pp. 251, 290–91, 297, 300, 369, 333, 490, 454; Hofmann, *Forschungen*, II, p. 109; Zutshi, *Original*, no. 504, p. 259; MS Bodley 859, f. 36v; Edinburgh, Laing 351A, f. 46r/v.

[70] *BRUC*.

granted 'favours' such as permissions to have one's own confessor.[71] The boundaries between it and the chancery were not wholly clear and only one register (1) covers a few of the relevant years. Thus its workings are unclear in this period as are the names of many of the lesser personnel. The whole office was under a cardinal penitentiary beneath whom minor penitentiaries acted, roughly divided among the various language divisions of Christendom. Thus there was always at least one English penitentiary, holding a position below the cardinal in charge, able to speak the language of those who came in person. The English officers in this period were Lawrence Childe, OSB, Robert de Tymelby, John Preston OSB and Hugh Whathamstede, OSB.

Childe held the position when the curia was still in Avignon, appointed in August 1373.[72] He was a monk of Battle and had studied in Oxford, where, in 1365, he became a bachelor of canon law. He was thus contemporary with Adam Easton and this may explain why he was an executor of Simon Langham's will in 1376.[73] There is no evidence, however, that he was an active executor. He returned to Rome with the curia and no doubt the see of S Asaph in June 1382 was a reward for service to Urban VI. He was consecrated in Rome and must then have returned to England.[74]

Almost certainly Childe's successor was Brother Robert de Tymelby, recorded as a papal minor penitentiary dead at the curia in May 1388.[75] This was probably the late Robert, son of the late Peter, penitentiary of the pope, for whose soul Elena Clerk asked prayers in 1390.[76] He may thus have had a connection with the hospice of S Thomas. His successor was probably John Preston, OSB, monk of S Augustine's, Canterbury and DTh.[77] It is unclear when, if at all, he left England to take up the position, to which he was appointed by 1391.[78] He was a notable benefactor to the Abbey library. The final name we can ascertain is Hugh Whathamstede, monk of S Alban's, who had papal permission, as minor penitentiary, to hold a benefice in 1406.[79]

John Forster was a scriptor in the penitentiary in 1414[80] and John de Winthorpe, in May 1391 was proctor of letters there,[81] a specialist who

[71] Blouin, *Vatican Archives*, pp. 213–16.
[72] *BRUO*, I, p. 414; ASV, Collect. 357, f. 2; T. Majic, 'Die apostolische Pönitentiarie im 14 Jahrhundert', *Römische Quartalschrift*, 50 (1955), pp. 129–77, esp. p. 165.
[73] Widmore, *An History*, p. 187.   [74] Eubel, I, p. 112; Zutshi, *Original*, no. 366.
[75] ASV, Arm 29/1, f. 89v.   [76] *m*. 119.   [77] *BRUO*, III, p. 1518.
[78] Zutshi, *Original*, no. 411; *CPL*, IV, p. 404.   [79] *CPL*, VI, p. 79.
[80] *CPL*, VI, p. 414.
[81] *CPL*, IV, p. 414 and see also p. 404; for the task see L. Schmugge, P. Hersperger and B. Wiggenhauser, *Die Supplikenregister der päpstlichen Pönitentiarie aus der Zeit der Pius II (1458–1464)*, (= Bibliothek des deutschen historischen Instituts in Rom 84), Tübingen 1996, pp. 41–2.

could guide petitioners in the correct forms necessary for successful applications.

The consistory was the meeting of pope and cardinals where important cases were discussed and major appointments decided.[82] Its organisation also was still evolving. Consistorial advocates were lawyers who could plead in consistory. We have noticed a few already; Mowbray in 1378, before promotion to auditor,[83] and John Trevenham employed by Colchester in 1378.[84] John Shipdam may have functioned about the same time.[85] Called canon of Beverley in 1363 he can be found in Avignon acting with Stratton.[86] In Niem's *Liber Cancellariae* four English consistorial advocates appeared: William Dwirstede, probably entered in 1382,[87] Michael Cages, doctor of both laws, who became one in 1384,[88] John Lenne, in 1386,[89] and Simon de Anglia in 1404.[90] So far I can find nothing more about any of these.

Others known to have functioned included Richard Carleton, doctor of both laws, first named in 1390, when seeking provision to a canonry of London.[91] He was a product of the University of Bologna, since at least 1385, rector of the Ultramontane University in 1386.[92] He died in 1393 before 5 October near Monte Rotondo as he was following the curia from Perugia to Rome.[93] Michael Cergeaux (or Sergeaux, who may be Cages above) doctor of both laws was another advocate, named in 1390,[94] with training in Oxford, studying law there from 1373.[95] Having acted as advocate of the court of Canterbury in 1382, he must have gone to Rome, but was back as dean of Arches from 1393.[96]

Proctors smoothed the path of those trying to do business in the curia, acting on behalf of the absent, advising on procedure and selecting lawyers, if they were themselves not able to represent a client in a particular court. There was a large army of English proctors already in Avignon.[97] In Rome too there developed a semi-professional group

---

[82] Blouin, *Vatican Archives*, pp. 28–30.   [83] Harvey, *Solutions*, p. 24.
[84] Ibid., p. 24.
[85] T. Walsingham, *Chronicon Angliae*, ed. E. M.Thompson, *RS*, 64 (1874), pp. 244, 256.
[86] Lunt, *Financial relations*, p. 733; No mention in McDermid, *Beverley Fasti*.
[87] Niem, *Liber Cancellariae*, p. 209.   [88] Ibid., p. 209.   [89] Ibid., p. 112.
[90] Ibid., p. 112.
[91] *CPL*, IV, 375–6; BL Cotton Vitellius F II, ff. 79, 103. He never held his canonry, Le Neve, *London*, p. 40.
[92] *BRUO*, Appendix, pp. 2159–60; Sorbelli, *Il Liber Secretus*, I, pp. 32, 38 (called Tarliton); *CPR 1388–9*, pp. 429, 466, 474.
[93] *CPL*, IV, p. 444; for the curia leaving Perugia: Esch, *Bonifaz IX*, p. 119.
[94] *CPL*, IV, p. 376; for a reply by him as such to a legal *questio* , see BL Cotton Vitellius F II, f. 148v.
[95] *BRUO*, I, pp. 377–8, without reference to time in the curia; Roskell, *History of Parliament, The Commons 13886–1421*, II, pp. 506–7, for his brother Richard, related by marriage to Arundel.
[96] *CPR 1391–6*, p. 339; *CCR 1392–6*, pp. 231, 513.
[97] Zutshi, 'Proctors', pp. 15–16, 22 for the task.

as well as some sent ad hoc merely for one task. Some of these have already been named in passing.

There was as yet no formal royal proctor. Henry Bowet and Richard Derham were called royal advocate or proctor but seem to have been sent ad hoc.[98] John Catterick was more truly a royal representative in the sense later understood, appointed in 1413 to cover the political problems at the end of the schism.[99]

The best example of the task of an ordinary proctor is the work of William Swan, much of whose success in the curia came after 1420 but who began his long career about 1404 as a 'proctor-general in the court of Rome'.[100] From his letter books and the wills of his brothers and his widow Joan, the family can be placed in their setting in England as well as Rome.

The Swans came from Southfleet, near Rochester. William's brother, Richard, who died in 1429, said in his will that he was the son of Thomas Swan (by then dead) and married to Joan.[101] In the period with which we are dealing his mother was still alive.[102] He referred to the church of S Nicholas, Southfleet, and mentioned two brothers, John, married to Petronilla and William, the proctor, married to another Joan (as we know but she is not mentioned by Richard), with two daughters. He also referred to a sister Annette or Agnette. Richard mentioned his own three children Elena, Christine (Althon) and Thomas.

Richard was a skinner and a citizen of London (which means that he was a freeman of the Skinners' company)[103] with a house in London, 'in the street called Watlingstreet, next the church called Aldmary-church' (*in vico vocato Watlyngstret iuxta ecclesiam nuncupatam Aldirmary-cherche*).[104] If he died in London he wanted to be buried in St James, Garlichithe. This placed Richard among the very prosperous London traders who by the mid-fourteenth century dominated the luxury fur trade of England.[105] In Richard's house in Southfleet lived his mother, William's wife Joan when not with her husband, which seems often, and William's children, at least two daughters before 1420.[106] The parish priest was John Launce, who had been a proctor in the curia in

---

[98] Bowet: Raine, *Historians of York*, II, p. 433; *CPR 1381–5*, p. 224; *1388–92*, p. 466; *CCR 1389–92*, p. 189; Rymer, *Foedera*, VII, p. 569 (III/4, p. 18). Derham: *CCR 1405–9*, p. 33.

[99] See Harvey, *England Rome*, pp. 8–11; Rymer, *Foedera*, IX, p. 12 (IV/2, p. 31) for his proxy. See also Zutshi, 'Proctors', pp. 26–7.

[100] Jacob, 'To and from', p. 68 for a description of him about 1410.

[101] PRO, Prob 11/3, f. 90r/v.

[102] Arch. Seld. B 23, f. 137v, printed by Jacob, 'To and from', pp. 77–8.

[103] E. Veale, *The English Fur Trade in the Later Middle Ages*, Oxford 1966, p. 102.

[104] Arch. Seld. B 23, f. 102r/v. [105] Veale, pp. 52, 71.

[106] Joan Swan's letter to William of *c.* 1420 mentions *filiam vestram juniorem*. See Jacob, 'To and from', pp. 70–1 also.

the 1380s and later, among others, for the prior of Rochester, and thus, not surprisingly, was a correspondent of Swan's.[107] Letters from Swan in Rome came either to the Southfleet house or to the house in London. The other brother John may have been a pewterer,[108] but he lived in Southfleet and his will in 1441 revealed nothing of any London trade. His legacies were largely of farm animals and produce; his (second) wife Dionisia received sheep, cattle and pigs. He had one son, another William.

In the period of this study William Swan senior had at least two daughters, Joan and Elizabeth, mentioned in his brother John's will in 1441,[109] and in William's wife's will of 1453, where her son, another William with a wife Joan, was able to be Joan senior's executor.[110] Swan also took an interest, perhaps financial, in the schooling of his nephew Thomas, who was being educated by the well-known grammar master, John Seward, and went on to have a modest ecclesiastical career.[111]

William the proctor attended Oxford university, studying law (he was bachelor of civil law by 1406).[112] He must have reached the curia about 1404 and his letter books from then onwards detail his cases and contacts. After the Council of Pisa, very disillusioned by Gregory XII's court, he considered returning to Oxford, though he probably did not.[113] His letters give ample evidence of his grasp of legal as well as political niceties.[114] Swan used his brother or Robert Newton as his London agents.[115] Newton, proctor in England of S Thomas's hospice, was also perpetual chaplain of the London church of S Sith in Cheap.[116] Because of this benefice he must have been in contact with the skinners, whose centre was S John Walbrook, in East Cheap.[117] Skinners actually lived in S Sith's lane. We also find John Laurence another skinner and Richard Swan, writing to Richard Hollant on his way to Middleburgh, to communicate with Swan who was then in Bruges staying with

---

[107] *BRUO*, II, p. 1107–8. BL MS Cotton Faust C V, f. 58v for him as proctor of Rochester.; *CPL*, v, p. 5–6. Correspondence with Swan is found above, p. 128.

[108] Jacob, 'To and from', p. 71; *CCR*, 1422–9, p. 388, though his wife is Margaret, so perhaps not.

[109] Kent Archives Office, Town Hall, Maidstone, Rochester Consistory Court, I, f. 3a.

[110] Kent Archives Office, Town Hall, Maidstone, Rochester Consistory Court, II, f 4b.

[111] Jacob, 'To and from', p. 71; for him see *BRUO*, III, pp. 1674–75 and V. H. Galbraith, 'John Seward and his circle. Some London scholars of the early fifteenth century', *Medieval and Renaissance Studies*, I (1941–3) pp. 85–104.

[112] Jacob, 'To and from', p. 69.   [113] Ibid., p. 63.

[114] Jacob, 'To and from', gives plenty of examples.

[115] Arch. Seld. B 23, ff. 29–30 or ff. 35v–36v, where he is called *procurator vester*, for instance.

[116] Arch. Seld. B 23, f. 33r/v.

[117] Veale, pp. 44, 106, 86; for John White's will see above p. 82.

Lubricus Swetelers.[118] For the transfer of money Swan used the Florentine firm of Alberti and sometimes John Victor.[119]

Swan followed Gregory XII and had a brief career as papal secretary but deserted (in 1408 Henry Bowet appointed him *familiaris* and secretary)[120] and finally joined the Council of Constance, ending his career as abbreviator. His most successful time was after Constance; he stayed in the curia until probably 1435, though he did not finally resign until 1442, after which he probably lived in his *mansio* in Southfleet, until his death probably soon after 1445.[121] There is no extant will. Joan Swan senior made her will in 1453 and asked to be buried in the cemetery of the church of S Nicholas, Southfleet.[122]

Presumably the prosperity of Richard and William, senior, made the family fortune. The Swans of Hook Place in Southfleet continued to be buried in S Nicholas' church, where brasses are mentioned of William and his brothers and of Richard's grandchildren.[123]

Despite William's career abroad he continued to be interested in his property in Southfleet. Joan Swan wrote a famous letter about 1420, excusing herself for not joining her husband.[124] In it she also said that John Swan was himself going to plough the land which Joan had been cultivating in the last year.[125] We may presume, therefore, that much of Swan's earnings came back to England. It is worth noting that as a *clericus conjugatus* authorised to hold a benefice without cure he claimed a canonry and prebend of Chichester, the result of an expectative papal provision granted on 15 November 1404 but never securely held.[126]

To see what a religious institution expected of a proctor at the curia one might look at Durham priory's indenture with Thomas Walkyngton in 1383. Thomas was to give counsel and aid and would only absent himself from the priory with permission. In return he received five marks per annum until Durham promoted him to a benefice, with cloth for his *armiger*, food for Thomas, stabling and the room which his predecessor had, and firing.[127] Like many another Walkyngton had

---

[118] Arch. Seld. B 23, f. 11v.
[119] Arch. Seld. B 23, f. 86r/v; for these merchants see Holmes, 'Florentine merchants', p. 196.
[120] York, Borthwick Institute, Bowet Register 17, ff. 16v–17.
[121] Harvey, *England Rome*, p. 30; for the house, will of John Swan, above p. 157.
[122] For will above p. 157.
[123] E. Hasted, *The History and Topographical Survey of the County of Kent*, 12 vols., Canterbury 1797–1801, II, pp. 435–7.
[124] In full: Jacob, 'To and from', pp. 77–8.
[125] A. Brown, 'London and North West Kent in the later Middle Ages. The development of a land market', *Archaeologia Cantiana*, 92 (1976), pp. 145–55, esp. p. 150.
[126] Arch. Seld. B 23, ff. 29, 31r/v, 35r/v, 35v–36v, 51v, 57v, 63, 114v–115; *CPR 1405–8*, p. 244; Le Neve, *Chichester*, pp. 23–4.
[127] Durham, Dean and Chapter Muniments, Reg. II, f. 213v.

come to the curia seeking promotion. By 1394 as we saw above, he had become an auditor. Durham's pension then rose to fifteen marks as long as he was in the curia or in Houghton or with the earl of Northumberland in his *familia*, with less if he resided elsewhere, with robes also. This was repeated in 1404.[128] As the proctor became more influential his value increased.

In William Swan's letters John Ixworth figured frequently.[129] After the Council of Constance he became a papal referendary but seems to have been a proctor from before 1395,[130] acting for instance for Cambridge University in 1399 and for the bishop of Ely in 1406.[131] In Swan's letters he can be seen coming and going to the curia. and he evidently took an interest in the hospice of S Thomas,[132] as well as being credited with being a *confrater* of S Edmund's.[133] He rented bedding from Walter Taylor.[134] A correspondent sent letters to William Lovell, or Swan or Ixworth as an accepted group[135] and Ixworth's name was coupled, for greetings, with Thomas Hendeman and John Launce.[136] But he considered himself an old man, over sixty, by 1417,[137] and by then was not at Constance but in London.

Other clerks, some mentioned already, attached to the hospices sometimes turn out to be proctors.[138] Andrew Alan or Alene, the priest from S David's diocese who collaborated to found the second German hospice, was perhaps one though not so described.[139] A further proctor appearing in S Thomas's records was John Doneys, canon of Chichester, *camerarius* in 1401.[140] Almost certainly he came to the curia pursuing his own business but also as a proctor. Between 1397 and his death in 1401, described as a bachelor of canon law and a priest, he acted for Guy Mone, bishop of S David's,[141] into one of whose provisions he had been surrogated at the curia.[142] He tried, though unsuccessfully, to 'inherit' other benefices held by Mone before the latter's promotion as bishop.[143] He litigated at the curia with Walter Cook, another proctor[144] and was also litigating about another benefice there when he died by 25 August 1401, a benefice over which Bremore

---

[128] Durham, Dean and Chapter Muniments, Reg. II, f. 315; Loc. X: 42.

[129] *BRUC*, pp. 329–30. [130] *CPL*, IV, p. 500. [131] *BRUC* as note 129.

[132] Arch. Seld. B 23, f. 33v. [133] *Venerabile*, p. 95. [134] *m.* 163.

[135] Arch. Seld. B 23, f. 44v. [136] Arch Seld B 23, f. 51.

[137] Arch. Seld. B 23, f. 139v, if that is the date. It might be 1416.

[138] For some see above p. 41. [139] See above pp. 87–8. [140] *m.* 156.

[141] Lunt, *Financial Relations*, pp. 750, 751. [142] *CPL*, V, pp. 312–13.

[143] Le Neve, *London*, pp. 155, 23; *Chichester*, p. 41; *Index*, pp. 62, 63, 75.

[144] *CPL*, V, p. 283. For Cook, *BRUC*, pp. 157–8; and see Sayers, 'Proctors', p. 150 and Zutshi, *Original*, no 411, 412, 424, 425, 426; *CPL*, V, pp. 65, 73; Legge, *Anglo Norman*, no 185; *CCR*, 1392–6, p. 531.

and Hendeman were contending with him in Rome.[145] At the curia he acquired various privileges.[146] Apart from this we catch a brief glimpse of him in 1398, witnessing a transaction concerning the Roman church of S Angelo in Pescharia, conducted by Gerard Gulf, who was acting for Panella, the overseer of the cardinal's titles encountered in the foundation of S Chrysogonus' hospice.[147]

In Swan's letters occurred also John Morhay, Bowet's chaplain and proctor.[148] He appeared briefly but intriguingly because leaving the curia, probably in 1407, he entrusted some business to Swan. He was certainly not a 'proctor general' like Swan but what he wrote indicated how such men utilised their time at the curia. Explaining that he had come safely with the 'possessions and letters' which he had carried from the curia, and had finally left Rome in company,[149] he sent Swan an inventory of his goods left for merchants of Florence to bring to Rome, where he wanted Swan to look after them or sell them if he did not return. He sent in addition a list of names of those for whom Swan was to complete business, with commendations to John Fraunceys, Thomas Hendeman and John Estcourt. Fraunceys had acted with him for Bowet in 1406;[150] a pair of small knives were to be returned to him. Estcourt, who served Chichele, was described as 'following the curia' still in 1421, and witnessed S Thomas's deeds in 1403 and 1405, lodging in a hospice house.[151]

In June 1407, Swan and Estcourt divided the goods between them, the list giving an insight into Morhay's possessions.[152] Swan had a gold ring with a sapphire, three purses with cloth of gold, and one blue cloth (*blodei coloris*), one green gown (*toga*), alias bukhorn, with a hood of the same colour, lined, with sleeves edged with fur, one great set of three knives in one sheath with handles apparently of ivory, gilded and silvered with a gilded sheath, two pairs of knives 'de Lyskerd' with shears of latton (copper alloy) and black sheaths signed with the letter d., one ? of Menebeyr (?miniver) for a hood, two white night caps, three black lined caps of thick wool, two round caps for doctors, two other simple caps, pillows (*auricularia*), one old and used, and one cloak bag of leather.

---

[145] *CPL*, v, pp. 412–13.   [146] *CPL*, v, p. 114.

[147] S Angelo in Pescharia, I/19, f. 34; for Gulf see Schuchard, *Die Deutschen*, p. 264; and see also above p. 78.

[148] ASV, Arm 29/2, f. 4; Arch. Seld. B 23, f. 129, proctor (with Swan) for Bowet, as archbishop, 1407, 7 November. Arch. Seld. B 23, f. 40, proctor for Bowet as bishop of Bath, with Swan; see also Henry IV, *Royal and Historical Letters*, I, pp. 446–57; Bowet, York Register 17, f. 3, of Exeter diocese, rector of Yppelpene.

[149] Arch. Seld. B 23, f. 38v.   [150] Arch. Seld. B 23, ff. 127v–128.

[151] *mm.* 163, 171, 172; Harvey, *England, Rome*, p. 35.   [152] Arch. Seld. B 23, f. 129v.

Estcourt had one great black lined hood, one old pair of sleeves of 'scarlet' (a cloth), something in which the goods were wrapped, and two pairs of gloves, one bigger, lined with miniver. These are not the possessions of a poor man and it becomes more understandable that Morhay was also a donor to, and member of, the German fraternity of S Maria dell'Anima.[153]

Swan's letters also give considerable insight into his own possessions, including his books, as he tried to ship them to and fro. In January, probably 1410, when he was thinking of leaving altogether, he told Robert Ely, his proctor in the curia, what Ely was to keep for him. This included the *Decisions of the Rota* with *Belial* and other treatises, bound together,[154] the formulary for the *Audientia Litterae Contradictarum*, the Chancery rules in one quire, a sack containing other papers, muniments and letters, a quire of petitions and a quire of medical matters. In addition there were three painted cloths, viz. a bed-coverlet, a head-cloth, another of the same design and a fourth, which was a banker (bench-cover) well worked, which were to be sold if possible or sent to Florence. At that point Swan thought his great paper book with letters, which may be survive as Oxford, Bodleian Library MS Arch. Seld. B 23, was with William Godfader.[155]

An agent wrote from Bologna to him in London, explaining that Swan's servant, William Ywin, had left various of Swan's goods with him, asking what he wanted done. These included a green tunic (*joppa*) fur-lined with miniver, another tunic of the same colour lined with bocasine (a cotton fabric), two chests full of papers but the servant had taken the key, a rough cloth(? *valusea*), a *Sext* (part of the decretals), a great paper book, containing letters and other things, a *Belial*,[156] a pair of thigh boots (*par ocrearum*), two saddles, and one bridle.[157] Thus Swan travelled with a small but useful library, as well as his 'files', but also owned surplus clothes and bedding. It was a practice to hire some household utensils needed in Rome; the *custos* of the hospice hired items out. Equally, however, men bought others and sold them at the end of their stay. Swan's list, unlike Morhay's, was of those extras that he either wished to leave or did not mind about. In both cases, however, something of their standard of life is revealed.

Like other great men the pope had his own household, separate from his secretariat. It included however some persons not found in other households, such as his resident theologian, the master of the Sacred Palace.

---

[153] Egidi, *Necrologi*, II, p. 71.   [154] See Jacob, 'To and from', p. 62, note, for this.
[155] Jacob, 'To and from', pp. 62–3, for translation, original printed 73–4.
[156] Probably a prophetic work by James of Teramo.   [157] Arch. Seld. B 23, f. 124r/v.

The master was the leading theologian in the curia, who also preached before the pope.[158] Two Englishmen held this post in the period: William Andrew and Edmund Bramfield (Bramfield rather than Bromfield was his preferred spelling).

Andrew was a Dominican graduate of Oxford, prior of the Guildford convent and vicar of the English Dominican province in 1368. By 1374 he was in Avignon,[159] examining theologians to see if they were fit to teach. He followed the curia to Rome and had reached the position of master by 1378. His evidence in 1379 about his experience and views of Urban's election revealed him receiving letters from the cardinal penitentiary left in Avignon.[160] In May 1378 his sermon against simony provoked a very enthusiastic but intemperate reaction from the pope. He preached too about the canonisation of S Bridget, when the process was still continuing under Urban.[161] He was made bishop of Achonry in 1373 but was translated to Meath in 1380 and held it till his death in September 1385. He had left the curia by the time he died, since in April 1385 when he sent to Oxford a condemnation of the heretical views of Henry Crump, he had examined these in Ardbrachen, in his see of Meath.

Bramfield, alias Halesworth, was a Benedictine, from Bury S Edmund's, professed there about 1350.[162] He was a doctor of theology by 1373, almost certainly promoted thereto after examination by Simon Langham as legate, at Bramfield's own request to the pope.[163] This desire for advancement may have annoyed some of his fellow monks; certainly his monastery found him difficult and the abbot probably organised his sending in 1375 to the curia as general proctor for the order, with the usual prohibition against seeking his own advancement.[164] The first evidence that he would not observe the prohibition was his obtaining by papal provision the priory of Deerhurst, which the pope had reserved in October 1376, and which the curia considered vacant in May 1377 by the death of the previous holder John Bokenhull, lately coming to the Roman curia (*nuper ad Romanam curiam veniendo*).[165] These bland words cover much more than appears. Bokenhull, a Benedictine of Westminster and Langham's treasurer, was

---

[158] Schuchard, *Die Deutschen*, p. 145. [159] *CPL*, IV, p. 194, William, bishop of Achonry.

[160] Harvey, *Solutions*, pp. 17–19. [161] See p. 199.

[162] *BRUO*, I, pp. 275–6, under Bromfield; the most recent account (which says he was known as Bramfield) is R. L. Storey, 'Papal provisions to English monasteries', *Nottingham Medieval Studies*, 35 (1991), pp. 77–91.

[163] ASV, Reg. Av. 185, ff. 201v–202.

[164] W. A. Pantin, *Chapters of the English Black Monks. Documents Illutrating the Activities of the General and Provincial Chapter*, 3 vols., Camden Society 3rd series 45, 47, 54 (1931–7), III, p. 76.

[165] ASV, Reg. Av. 203, f. 448v.

granted Deerhurst by provision in 1376. He was an executor and beneficiary of Langham's will and died on the journey from Avignon.[166] The claimant for Deerhurst before him (in 1369) had also been in Langham's household.[167] The crown, however, insisted that Deerhurst was in the king's hands as an alien priory and no papal provisor in fact held it, but a group based on Langham's household had apparently been keeping an eye on the possibilities.[168] The executors of Bramfield's provision in 1377 were the bishops of London (Courtenay) and Rochester (Brinton) with the dean of Gap, of whom the first two would probably have been sympathetic to papal claims.

Bramfield did not obtain Deerhurst and was not content. In 1379, contrary certainly to the wishes of some of his brethren, he had himself provided to his own abbey of Bury, to replace John Brinkley, when the abbey (with royal consent) agreed on John Timworth. Bramfield had clearly colluded with some fellow monks, not least in having money sent from England to pay proctors.[169] Timworth, however, had the king's support; the Bury chronicle described the monks in the curia, sent to and fro, forced to pay cardinal Alençon for the provision of Timworth and the pope's reluctance to yield his prerogative.[170]

Back in Bury however, it was different. In August 1379 Bramfield returned with his provision. A royal order for his arrest as a violator of the statute against provisors rapidly followed. The local authorities did not act and they were certainly abetted by Bramfield's brother, Thomas Halesworth, a great man locally.[171] A local skirmish occurred; the royal justices arrested Bramfield with his supporters and he appeared before the royal council.[172] He was finally tried with his supporters at Bury and sent to the King's Bench where the case was heard from January 1380. Thomas Halesworth with others had to give bonds not to proceed against Timsworth.[173] Bramfield, who pleaded that he had merely been obeying the pope, and denied that he had solicited the provision, was found guilty and kept under arrest at Nottingham.

This was not all, however, since Urban still regarded Bramfield as abbot. Bramfield's advocate in consistory was Master John Schipdam, encountered already,[174] who apparently canvassed support and had Cardinal Agapito Colonna write to the king for Bramfield, some time

---

[166] Harvey, 'Langham', pp. 28–9.   [167] Ibid., pp. 23–4.
[168] Ibid., p. 39; Deerhurst was a priory of S Denys, VCH, *Gloucestershire*, II, p. 103.
[169] Storey, 'Papal provisions', p. 83, for information from King's Bench rolls.
[170] T. Arnold, ed., *Memorials of S Edmund's Abbey*, 3 vols., RS 96 (1896), III, p. 116.
[171] Storey,' Papal provisions', p. 84.   [172] Ibid., p. 85.
[173] Storey, 'Papal provisions' from Kings Bench rolls.
[174] Walsingham, *Historia Anglicana*, I, p. 415; wrongly called a Flemming; see Lunt, *Financial Relations*, p. 733, paying common services for Chichester, 1362, 1364, canon of Beverley.

before late 1380.[175] Archbishop Sudbury, however, wrote to convince the pope that the king was adamant.[176] Adam Easton almost certainly got involved also, according to the Bury chronicle to persuade the pope to allow a free election (which meant of Timworth).[177] In the end compromise was reached. Timworth was elected again, and the pope also provided him, to Walsingham's fury; and Bramfield was provided to the abbey of Sauve Majeure in Gascony. Shortly before Timworth's final 'election' (22 June 1385), Bramfield was released and allowed to leave England.[178]

He joined the curia, though we do not know when nor how he fared in the comings and goings of Urban VI in Naples, but by the end of Urban's reign he was master of the Sacred Palace and playing, with Easton, an important role in discussions about the institution of the feast of the Visitation.[179] Edmund's task was at first to put arguments against,[180] but on 8 April 1389 when the pope had decided to allow the feast, he preached before Urban on the reasons why it should be promulgated. In this he paid graceful tribute to John of Jenstein, archbishop of Prague, who had been one of its main promoters, and talked of its value for prayers to end the schism, as also did Easton in one of his hymns for the feast.[181]

This produced the reward of a bishopric, Llandaff, an appointment probably intended by Urban VI to send hostile signals to Richard II's government.[182] The exact date of Bramfield's consecration is uncertain. It was part of a group of papal appointments, rewarding those who had continued to support Urban at Nocera, as well as Bramfield. On 4 May 1389 Brinton of Rochester died and William Bottlesham, of Llandaff, was said to have been translated there on 27 August.[183] Already on 9 August, however, Bramfield as elect of Llandaff had undertaken to pay the service taxes of his predecessor William and the papal camera regarded Bottlesham as already provided by 18 August.[184] The continuation of the Polychronicon and the Westminster Chronicle compound the problem by asserting that Bramfield was consecrated in

---

[175] Walsingham, *Historia Anglicana*, I, pp. 428–9.   [176] Ibid., I, pp. 429–30.
[177] Arnold, *Memorials*, p. 135.
[178] Storey, 'Papal provisions', p. 88; Lunt, *Financial Relations*, pp. 812–13.
[179] See J. V. Polc, *De Origine Festi Visitationis B.V.M.* (= Corona Lateranensis 9A) Rome 1967, p. 78–9; Polc, 'La festa della Visitazione e il giubileo del 1390', *Rivista di storia della chiesa in Italia*, 29 (1975), pp. 149–72, esp. p. 154, printing some of Bramfield's sermon from Wroclaw, MS, I F 177, ff. 123–29.
[180] Wroclaw, I F 177, f. 123.
[181] Polc, *De origine*, pp. 78–9; for the hymn, Dreves, G. M., *Analecta Hymnica Medii Aevi*, 52, ed. C. Blume, Leipzig 1909, p. 49: *Lux pellens cuncta schismata*.
[182] Perroy, *L'Angleterre*, pp. 307–8.
[183] Lunt, *Financial Relations*, p. 742; from Courtenay Register.   [184] Ibid., pp. 741–2.

Rome on 14 June by the archbishop of Bologna, Cosmato Gentilis, former papal collector in England, later Innocent VII.[185] Cosmato certainly undertook the third of these transactions, the consecration of Trefnant as bishop of Hereford, on 20 June in the chapel of S Gregorio in S Peter's, in which task he was assisted by John (?Dongan) bishop of Derry and Angelo Correr, bishop of Castello, later Gregory XII.[186] He may therefore also have consecrated Bramfield. Surprisingly Bramfield was allowed by the English government to hold the see; he died in 1393 and was buried in Llandaff.

A very few Englishmen held positions in the pope's household, more strictly defined. For instance Thomas Grey of Helperby in York diocese, was made a papal sergeant-at-arms (usually employed as confidential messengers) in 1389.[187] He worked for the abbot of Nonatola when the latter was legate in England in 1398.[188] William Cheyne was acknowledged as master usher (*hostiarius camere domini pape*) from at least 1388[189] and still in 1394; this was a largely ceremonial position before the papal door.[190] Cheyne was said to be of noble birth from the diocese of Lincoln. There were probably others but the absence of records makes them difficult to trace.

There was only one resident English cardinal in this period, Adam Easton, whose career and household will be dealt with below.

All cardinals kept a household, some very lavish. Anyone who could gain appointment as *familiaris continuus commensalis*, that is continuously resident as a true member of the house, enjoyed, if his master had the privilege, the right to be non-resident in any benefices and could also be given priority in rolls of supplications by his master for benefices and privileges. So in petitions the *familiaris* might claim that his master was supporting his supplication.

There seem to have been very few Englishmen in the households of cardinals, though this may reflect the lack of Roman sources for the schism period rather than the true situation. When the curia left Avignon some of Langham's household stayed there; John de Tristro, perpetual chaplain of the chapel of *Bellovisii* (?Beauvoir) in Therouanne diocese, claimed in 1379 that he had served Langham for several years

[185] *Polychronicon Ranulphi Higden, Monachi Cestrense*, ed. J. R. Lumby, 9 vols., *RS*, 41 (1865–86), IX, pp. 211–12; *The Westminster Chronicle, 1381–1394*, eds. L. C. Hector and B. F. Harvey, Oxford 1982, p. 395.
[186] Trefnant, *Register*, pp. 2–3, letter from Cosmato.   [187] *CPL*, IV, p. 282.
[188] Perroy, *L'Angleterre*, p. 350 from BL, MS Cotton Cleop. E II, f. 235; for the post, Schuchard, *Die Deutschen*, p. 137–8.
[189] Perroy, *Diplomatic Correspondence*, nos. 192 and 193 and notes.
[190] *CPL*, IV, p. 488; for the post see Schuchard, *Die Deutschen*, pp. 136–7.

but was then serving Cardinal Corsini.[191] He joined Clement VII and in 1384 was serving Guillaume Noellet, cardinal of S Angelo.[192] Robert Ferghane had served Langham until he died, but, claiming the prebend of Combe in October 1377, said he was now a *familiaris continuus commensalis* of Jacobus Orsini, cardinal of S George in Velabro, so he must have come to Rome.[193] There is no evidence for what he did when Orsini died in 1379. As noticed already, other former (English) members came to Rome.[194]

A few other names can be found. Ralph Pelaton, a priest, was a continual familiar of Petrus de Vergne, cardinal of S Maria in Via Lata in October 1376.[195] The cardinal joined Clement VII. William Tart rector of Bukenhall in Lincoln diocese was abbreviator in the chancery and *familiaris* of the Cardinal of Bologna (Cosmato Gentilis) in September and October 1394.[196] Cosmato had been papal collector in England from 1379–88.[197] He employed at least two other Englishmen. John Arlam, of Durham diocese, was one for whom in 1400 we have what is very rare, an actual document making him a *familiaris*.[198] Arlam was received as a *familiaris continuus domesticus*, to enjoy all the privileges which others enjoyed. Cosmato asked that he be allowed to pass freely anywhere with three companions and three horses. The second was Richard Possewich the younger, who must have moved into Cosmato's household after Easton died. In 1402 as *familiaris* he was granted the church of S Ursula in Urbino.[199] He was then studying canon law in Perugia.

In 1389 Angelo Acciaiuolo, cardinal of S Lorenzo in Damaso, called of Florence, supported Nicholas de Ryssheton's petition for a canonry of Lincoln.[200] In 1406 John Possewych, Richard's brother, was supported as *familiaris* by Henricus Minutoli, cardinal of Tusculum, who as titular abbot of S Biagio *in canto secuto* had dealings with S Thomas's hospice. John was a Roman but, true to his Irish origins, this earliest grant to him was of the parish church of S Columba the Abbot in Armagh diocese. He may not have held this and in 1407 exchanged it for S Mary, Bentybrigg, Ossory diocese.[201] He may be the John Irlond mentioned as hospice chaplain in 1410.[202] The house in Rome which the brothers inherited was given to S Thomas's, mentioned as such in

---

[191] ASV, Reg. Supp. 49, f. 40; not noticed by me in 'Langham'.
[192] ASV, Reg. Supp, 49, f. 10; H. Nelis, ed., *Suppliques et lettres de Clément VII* (= *AVB* 13, *DRGS* 3), Rome 1934, no. 1071.
[193] ASV, Reg. Av. 202, ff. 290v–91.   [194] Above p. 36.
[195] ASV, Reg. Av. 200, f. 108v.   [196] ASV, Reg. Supp. 104A, ff. 113, 178v.
[197] Lunt, *Financial Relations*, p. 409.   [198] Henry IV, *Royal and Historical Letters*, I, p. 45.
[199] ASV, Reg. Lat. 110, ff. 235–37v: *pro tibi dilecto familiari suo.*   [200] *CPL*, IV, p. 345.
[201] ASV, Reg. Lat. 132, ff. 47v–48.   [202] Arch. Seld. B 23, f. 124v.

1445.[203] Minutoli also employed Patrick Foxe or Ragget, of Ossory, in 1407 called scholar of canon and civil law, who had studied at Oxford.[204] Alexander V tried to reward him with the see of Cork but an appointment by Gregory XII conflicted and in the end his activity at the Council of Constance achieved Ossory for him.[205]

Adam Usk first found his way in the curia under the auspices of Balthassare Cossa,[206] later John XXII, as did Thomas Prys, a friend and supporter of John Fraunceys, who was *capellanus commensalis* to Cossa as cardinal and in March 1411 was rewarded with the archdeaconry of Bangor.[207] Prys had a rival for his archdeaconry[208] but may have held it. He was still calling himself archdeacon in 1417 when at the Council of Constance he witnessed the probate of Robert Hallum's will in the camera of the council.[209]

Since the preceding pages have been a study of Englishmen in Rome one must ask whether these men felt any corporate unity. It may appear so. In 1385 Walsingham wrote as if there was a recognisable English group whom Urban VI could summon at Nocera and Richard II implied that he could recall them en masse in 1391, the second action assuming some method of contacting all.[210] In 1407 writing to Newton about his possible removal from the hospice of S Thomas, William Swan referred to John Ixworth and Robert Appleton who 'have laboured tirelessly both with the lord prelates of our nation and with the ambassadors and other courtiers for the revocation of your power' (*indefesse laborarent tamen penes dominos prelatos nostre nacionis quam eciam ambassiatores et ceteros quoscumque curtisanos pro revocacione potestatis vestre*), where the prelates would be the leading members (protonotaries were prelates) and the ambassadors, though not members of the court, clearly had considerable influence with the national group, not least because they could influence the king.[211] *Nacio* here may refer to the group rather than to the country as a geographical entity, as 'nations' existed in medieval universities.

By then also a group of *curtisani* had influence over the hospice of S Thomas and one might assume that membership of its confraternity

---

[203] Venerabile Collegio Inglese, *Liber* 232, f. 25.   [204] *CPL*, VI, pp. 114, 124.

[205] Gwynn, 'Ireland and the English Nation', pp. 214–16; *BRUO*, II, p. 715.

[206] Usk, *Chronicle*, p. 154.

[207] *CPL*, VI, p. 187; Zutshi, *Original Letters*, no. 436, for him as proctor in 1396 for a Durham monk.

[208] *CPL*, VI, p. 251.

[209] Chichele, *Register*, II, p. 129. He may be T. Prys who was a proctor in 1396, Zutshi, *Original Letters*, p. 220, no. 436.

[210] *CCR 1389–92*, p. 341.   [211] Arch. Seld. B 23, f. 33v.

would have given a certain cohesion, from the common worship implied, at the least. Yet this has left little trace. Of those mentioned in this one letter: Swan himself, Ixworth, Appleton, Launce and the ambassadors Chichele and Cheyne, only Swan and Ixworth left traces in the hospice archives to show that they were involved at all in its activities, though Launce apparently transferred money for it.

By no means all English people in Rome, much less Welsh and Irish, were members of the hospices of S Thomas or S Chrysogonus. The undoubtedly (Anglo-)Irish Possewichs were leading members, and Teyr was associated with them, but Swayne, Foxe, and Prene do not seem to have been involved in the institutions. Adam Usk's association with S Thomas's was uneasy and Trefor does not seem to have had one at all. By 1412 the hospice of S Thomas had put the royal arms over its door but this may have been partly to protect it against Roman factional riots, to show that it did not take sides, and by no means implied a royally managed institution, certainly not 'the' English institution.[212] Even in 1414 most English *curiales* had little to do with the running of S Thomas's and nothing to do with S Chrysogonus.

Members of the papal court identified with their offices rather than with their nation at this time. Various groups, such as auditors, abbreviators, scriptors and even *cursores*, already belonged to 'colleges' by 1420, worshipping together, bound by oaths and confraternities.[213] Rota auditors and protonotaries were resident in the papal household, worshipping with the pope and identified with his interests and probably with those of particular cardinals. Usk, who was fascinated by the ceremonial, also described how his fellow Rota auditors together petitioned the pope (*collegium auditorum unanimiter ad papam ascendit*) for his promotion to S David's.[214]

However, the balance was changing. Until 1406, despite the statutes against provisors (especially that of 1390), an Englishman resident in a leading position in the curia with the right influence and suitable patrons at both ends, could usually make good a papal provision; Rota auditors, for instance, did often obtain bishoprics even without the support of a faction in England, as we saw, and lesser benefices could be obtained with a royal licence.[215] From about 1406, however, the number of Englishmen in leading positions in the curia fell and never

---

[212] Illustrated *Venerabile*, p. 148 facing.
[213] See for instance B. Schwarz, *Die Organisation kurialer Schreiberkollegien von ihrer Enstehung bis zur Mitte des 15 Jahrhunderts* (= Bibliothek des deutschen historischen Instituts in Rom 37), Tübingen 1972.
[214] Usk, *Chronicle*, p. 188.
[215] For other provisions see Lunt, *Financial Relations*, esp. pp. 389–408.

afterwards recovered. There were several reasons. After 1406 provisions to lesser benefices had little hope of success. The popes were in no position to argue. Rome itself, with its political struggles, became more and more unpleasant to live in, yet leaving it to follow the papal court simply meant that members often went without pay. When the papacy finally returned to Rome in 1420 the pope was obliged to employ some members of the 'obediences' of the rivals in the schism and for a while there was little prospect for new recruits.[216] When they began to come they were more often Italians, so the favourable situation of the early schism did not return. By 1420, in contrast to 1376, an ambitious English clerk would not have thought a job in the papal curia a safe stepping-stone in a career.

All too often also English rivalries spilled over into the curia and poisoned relations, preventing much solidarity on a simply 'national' basis. Frauncys may have been a supporter of Richard II; certainly he had no cause to love Henry IV's supporters;[217] Polton certainly disliked Robert Hallum and thought the feeling reciprocated but was in turn regarded by William Swan as untrustworthy.[218] The curia was a hotbed of malicious gossip; letters are filled with anguished complaints about 'enemies' blackening one's reputation with the Holy Father and working in secret behind one's back, often all too true. Adam Usk was a great one for these.[219] Richard Clifford's letters also give many excellent examples. Sending the pope gifts of two cloths of scarlet and white, and of English work for use in winter, with money for buying furs, he referred to jealous persons who daily said things in the curia against his name and honour; 'these serpents some of whom I would have believed before to be my most true and constant friends'.[220]

In consequence friends and supporters in the curia were essential and correspondence was full of advice about the most influential people. One of the more surprising features of Urban VI's curia would have been its newness and the need for its members to remake their networks of alliances, since so many departed to serve the anti-pope. Colchester's experience in the lawsuit for his abbey, where he paid good money only to have several of his chosen lawyers desert, was shared by those like Easton who thought they had the support of cardinals (Aigrefeuille

---

[216] B. Schwarz, 'L'organizazzione curiale di Martino V ed i problemi derivanti dallo scisma', in M. Ciabo et al. eds., *Alle origini della nuova Roma. Martino V (1417–1431)*, (= Nuovi studi storici 20), Rome 1992, pp. 329–45, esp. pp. 333–8.

[217] Below p. 176.   [218] Harvey, *England, Rome*, p. 11; *Solutions*, p. 163 and note.

[219] Usk, *Chronicle*, p. xxvii, 174–6.

[220] Bodley 859, ff. 23v–24: *isti viri versipelles quorum aliquos antea fuisse credebam amicos meos verissimos et constantes.*

for instance) only to have them change sides.[221] In this situation, however, the English had good chances of advancement; their king was loyal to Urban and their money was needed. It is thus not surprising to find an English cardinal in this reign (1378–89), with seven English Rota auditors, one camera auditor, two abbreviators, a minor penitentiary, several consistorial advocates, both masters of the sacred palace and about two members of the pope's own household, as well as many proctors.

However Urban's unreliability and his sudden attacks on individuals cannot have helped those trying to make a solid career. We do not know which Englishmen also fell from influence with Easton, for example, but his servants and *familiares* must have suffered, and those whom Urban rewarded, Bramfield or Bottlesham for example, were not necessarily *persona grata* to the crown. Of Bottlesham the Westminster chronicler said that he did not know who was behind the promotion to the episcopate.[222]

Boniface IX's (1389–1404) curia, by contrast, though not plagued by the irrationality of the pope, was subject to simony and manipulation to a degree hitherto unprecedented.[223] Part of the difficulty was the need to increase resources when much revenue was lost to the Avignonese obedience. A further problem of course was the great bullion famine, at its worst precisely during this pontificate and the next. We get complaints about shortage of cash.[224] The curia was also by then thoroughly under the thumb of the Neapolitans, particularly a circle of Boniface's own relatives and their protégés.[225]

From the English standpoint the most favourable factor was that a former papal collector, in England between 1379 and 1388, Cosmato Gentilis de Miglioratis of Sulmona, was at once (18 December 1389) promoted cardinal (of S Croce, known as 'of Bologna' usually).[226] As collector he already considered Cardinal Tomacelli (Boniface) his special lord and acted as go-between for him and England.[227] As we saw Cosmato employed at least two Englishmen in his household as cardinal. But he was also recognised as a possible patron for English petitioners

[221] See pp. 34, 37, 197.   [222] *The Westminster Chronicle*, p. 144; Zutshi, *Original Letters*, no. 374.
[223] A. Esch, 'Simonie-Geschäft in Rom 1400, "Kein Papst wird das tun, was dieser tut"', *Vierteljahrschrift für Social- und Wirtschaftgeschichte*, 61 (1974), pp. 433–51.
[224] Esch 'Simonie', p. 440: *de denari zi e gran charestia*.
[225] A. Esch, 'Das Papstum unter der Herrschaft der Neapolitaner; die führende Gruppe neapolitaner Familien an der Kurie während des Schismas 1378–1415', *Festschrift für Hermann Heimpel zum 70 Gebürtstag*, ed. J.Fleckenstein et al., 3 vols. (= Veröffentlichungen des Max-Planck Instituts für Geschichte 36), Göttingen 1972, II, pp. 713–800.
[226] For his career J. N. D. Kelly, *Oxford History of the Popes*, Oxford 1986, under Innocent VII.
[227] Perroy, *Diplomatic Correspondence*, no 69.

and was said to have been very good to the English as a cardinal.[228] He was canvassed and given gifts during the quest for Winchester privileges,[229] and Edmund Stafford clearly thought he had been helpful over his promotion to Exeter.[230]

Under Boniface and Innocent VII (1404–6) the English recognised the important influence of papal relatives and Neapolitans. Four names stand out in petitions: Migliorati, of course, and then Acciaiuoli, Carbone and Minutoli. Three of these recruited English members of their households. Until 1402 the important names in Boniface's curia were undoubtedly these.[231] Boniface's sacred college was very small, he created only six cardinals of his own and restored four; he had only eleven cardinals until, in 1402, he promoted Cossa and Antonius Caetani.[232] Carbone was the pope's cousin, combining several important curial posts and living with numerous relatives of his own alongside the pope's own family in their quarters, in the hospital of S Sprito in Sassia on the Tiber near S Angelo castle.[233] Henricus Minutoli, perhaps also related to Boniface, became *camerarius* of the sacred college.[234] Angelo Acciauolo of Florence, a staunch adherent of Urban VI, belonged to a family of ardent supporters of Ladislas of Durazzo, important in Neapolitan finance and in the recovery of Naples.[235] He had been a possible candidate in the 1398 conclave and the pope owed him a debt for agreeing a compromise.[236] English perceptions that these were the most important, and that Easton was not,[237] were undoubtedly correct. Of the two who became cardinals in 1402, Caetani was a relative by marriage of Boniface also, but, just as important, belonged to an important Roman family.[238] Cossa, another Neapolitan who of course became pope John XXIII, was promoted for his soldierly gifts and perhaps also his money.[239]

A sign of better relations between the pope and the English crown was that under Innocent VII Henry IV granted more pardons to

---

[228] Laing 351A, ff. 46v–47, from Edmund Stafford thanking him for Exeter; ff. 70v–71, from Henry IV, congratulating him on becoming pope and thanking him for his services to the English hitherto.

[229] H. Chitty and E. F. Jacob, 'Some Winchester College muniments', *EHR*, 49 (1934), pp. 1–13, esp. p. 6.

[230] Laing 351A, f. 46.   [231] Esch, *Bonifaz IX*, p. 379.   [232] Eubel, *Hierarchia*, I, pp. 25–6.

[233] Esch, *Bonifaz IX*, p. 17 and notes; *DBI*, 19, by Esch, pp. 691–2, under Carbone.

[234] Esch, *Bonifaz IX*, p. 138; M. Souchon, *Die Pastwahlen in der Zeit des grossen Schismas. Entwicklung und Verfassungskämpfe des Kardinalates von 1378 bis 1417*, 2 vols., Brauschweig 1898–9, reprint 1970, I, p. 46 but see Esch, *Bonifaz*, p. 17, who does not say this.

[235] *DBI*, I, pp. 76–7; Souchon, *Die Papstwahlen*, I, p. 46.

[236] Esch, *Bonifaz IX*, p. 138.   [237] Though the *Westminster Chronicle* disagreed, p. 410.

[238] See p. 80.   [239] Kelly, *Oxford Dictionary of the Popes*, under John XXIII.

provisors.[240] In general this papacy was considered favourable. Henry IV, writing in 1406, just after the death of Innocent VII, to try to influence the cardinals to favour his ambassadors John Cheyne and Henry Chichele, with their various messages, commended them in the vacancy to Acciaiuoli, Minutoli and Carbone.[241] John White thought Caetani a suitable protector for a Roman hospital, as in 1404 he would have appeared to be.[242] John Cresset, litigating in the curia in 1403, came with a commendation to Acciaiuoli.[243]

In 1406, however, the situation changed again. Gregory XII was a Venetian and the influential people altered. Acciaiuoli announced the election of Gregory to Henry IV, presumably as bishop of Ostia, but Jordanus Orsini told the king of the election capitulation binding the pope to end the schism.[244] Early in Gregory's reign, before the pope set off on his travels, Swan perceived the truly important cardinals as Odda Colonna and Orsini.[245] This was doubtless correct, reflecting the importance of the politics of Rome. However once Gregory had left Rome the power of his own family became notorious. By late 1407 Swan was complaining that the pope was only interested in advancing his relatives.[246] He told Robert Newton that letters should be channelled though Antonius Correr, the pope's nephew and *camerarius*, and Paulus Correr, another nephew. *Omnia per ipsos facta sunt et sine ipsis factum est nichil etc.* (John 1:3) he added, gloomily.

Once the Council of Pisa had been called the politics of the curia became positively abnormal and it is of little value to try to follow them here. Many *curiales* probably returned home; certainly no one who did not have to would have joined it in 1408 for ambition. Dietrich of Niem left vivid descriptions from June that year of the problems of following the curia.[247] Normality began to return only in 1420; by then many of the English *curiales* mentioned here had either left or died.

The interactions of the English with the Germans and Italians remind one that the curia was a cosmopolitan world; it was equally a small one. A study of Langham's household in Avignon revealed that its members acted on each others behalf and 'inherited' each other's benefices, or at least each other's claims.[248] It is more difficult to conduct this kind of study during the schism but the same principles applied. For instance, Bramfield's claim to Deerhurst must have been based on information

[240] Lunt, *Financial Relations*, p. 403.
[241] Laing 351A, f. 36; see also Henry IV, *Royal and Historical Letters*, II, pp. 139–40.
[242] See p. 80.   [243] *CPL*, V, p. 553.
[244] Harvey, 'England and the council of Pisa', p. 266.
[245] See p. 47.   [246] Harvey, 'England and the council of Pisa', p. 272.
[247] *Nemus unionis*, pp. 334–6, 337–8.   [248] Harvey, 'Langham', pp. 38–9.

from the members of Langham's household, arriving in Rome. When Roger Dawe died in Anagni in 1377, surrounded by English clerics, including one former member of Langham's household, Robert Ferghane, another former *familiaris* of Langham's, now serving Jacobus Orsini, was granted his canonry of Wells, with Robert de Stratton an executor.[249] In 1405 Roger Burstede died in the curia, where he had been litigating and had run up a debt with John White; his benefice of S Nicholas Olave in London was promptly 'inherited' by Philip Newton, who obtained a provision and must have known about it because of his role in White's affairs.[250]

In conclusion one can assert that the curia had become in some ways a less desirable place for Englishmen by 1415. The reasons were a combination of local Roman and English politics as well as the schism. The wonder perhaps is not that there were few English at the curia but that there were so many present even at the end of the schism. The latter is an important reason why, against the odds, S Thomas's hospice survived.

[249] ASV, Reg. Av. 202, ff. 290v–91.
[250] *CPL*, VI, p. 38; G. Hennessy, *Novum Repertorium Ecclesiasticum Parochiale Londinense*, London 1898, pp. 18, 350. Newton did not obtain it until 1412.

Chapter 9

THE CAREER OF JOHN FRAUNCEYS

The career of John Fraunceys illustrates the problems of a *curialis* without sufficient backing from England. It also reveals in detail the working of the curia and how members used it. The role of proctors and the interactions of the members of the English group stand out too. It is rare to be able to investigate so fully a career spent largely in Rome with no personal papers to use; the good fortune that the deeds for his properties remain in the English College and that one of his cases involved William Swan means that a great deal can be reconstructed.

When Fraunceys first comes to notice he was enjoying royal patronage. The king presented him in May 1379 to Wolvesnewton church, Monmouth, in Llandaff diocese.[1] In February 1380 he became vicar of Aston Colvyle, in Coventry and Lichfield diocese, probably Aston in modern Birmingham, in the king's hands because of the confiscation of alien priories.[2] In May 1380 he was presented to the church of S Mary Moysi, in London, vacant for the same reason.[3] In 1381, called now king's clerk, he was exchanging this for the free chapel of Spargove, Somerset, in the diocese of Bath and Wells.[4] In 1384 the king ordered him to be given maintenance in the hospital of S Leonard, York.[5]

All this prefaced a curial career. By April 1388 he had gone to Rome,[6] where in November he was appointed abbreviator at the request of King Richard, whose clerk he was.[7] Thereafter he was exempted from royal customs,[8] and, still called king's clerk, allowed to sue for benefices, notwithstanding the statutes against provisors, in July

---

[1] Many details from Chitty and Jacob, 'Some Winchester College muniments', *EHR*, 49 (1934), pp. 1–13; *CPR 1377–81*, p. 346.
[2] *CPR 1377–81*, p. 439.   [3] *CPR 1377–81*, p. 497.
[4] *CPR 1377–81*. p. 609–10.   [5] *CPR 1381–5*, p. 366.
[6] *CCR, 1392–6*, p. 525.   [7] *CPL*, IV, p. 269.
[8] *CCR 1389–92*, p. 440, and see p. 573.

1389.[9] One then glimpses him in Rome. He was proctor (for the king) in the papal appointment of William Colchester to S Augustine's Canterbury, for the priory of Holy Trinity, London, in 1389, for Winchester and New College in 1389 and 1391 and for S Alban's in 1395.[10] He was William of Wykeham's proctor 'long and faithfully';[11] in 1389 at the outset of Boniface IX's pontificate he presented a roll about the bishop's colleges, his advice is in the margins.[12] Ralph Ergham, bishop of Bath and Wells between 1388 and 1400, entrusted him with letters to the pope and called him his friend.[13] He was the confidential messenger when the king was seeking advancement for John Prophet, keeper of the Privy Seal in about 1393.[14]

As abbreviator he was *familiaris domesticus continuus commensalis* of the pope, a resident member of the papal household. He may also have studied in the papal court university. It unclear where he received his degree but by 1400 certainly he was batchelor of civil law.[15] He thus seems to have had strong support from Richard II. But he probably expected support from Henry IV also. In 1407 among his 'maintainers' when he engaged in bitter legal dispute were said to be Robert Fraunceys, knight, and William Fraunceys, clerk.[16] Robert was probably of Foremark, Derbyshire, very important locally and favoured by Henry IV, constable of Castle Donnington in 1403 and a king's knight.[17]

But John Fraunceys probably did not make his peace with the new regime in 1399, which may explain why from then onwards he set about accumulating property in Rome, for which there is no evidence earlier. Those with whom he had dealings were of the better sort and the properties expensive. In 1399 he bought his first property, a palace in Parione, two-storeyed with a columned portico, with two adjoining houses, costing 309 gold florins.[18] What the Index of the college deeds in 1598 called a *turris et domunculae* in the Parione region were bought by Fraunceys in 1404 from the heirs of the Cardelli family.[19] Fraunceys' *turris* and houses were probably part of a complex of family property.[20] His property also included eleven pieces of vineyards and three pieces of

[9] *CPR 1388–92*, p. 84.
[10] Zutshi, *Original*, nos. 394, 397, 414, 431, for him as proctor and abbreviator.
[11] Chitty and Jacob, 'Some Winchester', p. 4.
[12] Chitty and Jacob, includes a photocopy.   [13] MS Bodley 859, f. 22v.
[14] Perroy, *Diplomatic Correspondence*, p. 236.   [15] *CPL*, V, p. 270.
[16] R. L. Storey, 'Clergy and common law', p. 400.
[17] Roskell, *History of Parliament, The House of Commons 1386–1421*, III, pp. 120–1.
[18] *m.* 151.   [19] *m.* 167, very faded but the dorse gives this information; see also *mm.* 5, 13.
[20] *m.* 167 where the names Johannes . . . Lelli Cardelli of Parione with consent of Johanna and Petrus *filiorum* . . . *olim Cardelli* are visible; see also *m.* 33.

land outside Porta S Angelo beyond Ponte Molle, in the village or *casale* of Falcone (*in loco qui dicitur Falcone,*) in the *proprietas* of S Eusthacio.[21]

Thus John Fraunceys by 1404 had established himself as an important holder of property in Rome and was having a successful career in the curia. He might have expected to achieve high ecclesiastical office in England but this did not happen and he was remarkably unsuccessful in accumulating benefices after 1400.

In April 1400 he obtained confirmation of the dates of his *motu proprio* (by the pope's direct orders) provisions to a series of benefices which he had clearly not yet obtained: canonries of Lincoln, York, Lichfield, London, Salisbury, Chichester and Southwell and a benefice with cure in Ely diocese.[22] In June he added another *motu proprio* confirmation of his collation to the canonry of Ilton in the cathedral of Wells.[23] In February 1402 he had *motu proprio* provision of the prebend of Masham in York, fulfilling an earlier expectative.[24] Early in 1403 he was litigating in Rome about Masham and about Charminster and Bere in Salisbury, when he also obtained an expectative in Lincoln and Salisbury[25] and, supported by Cardinal Carbone, the papal penitentiary, for canonries of York and Southwell.[26] In April 1404 he had provision for expectative prebends in Southwell and Beverley again.[27]

There is no evidence that he ever held any prebend in Beverley.[28] In York he encountered stiff opposition from Thomas de Stanley, whose provision dated 13 June 1402,[29] whereas Fraunceys had been provided on 16 February and he also had a royal pardon allowing him to circumvent the statutes against provisors.[30] The king, however, supported the treasurer of his household and Fraunceys gave up.[31] This is a classic example of a very valuable prebend which the curia considered reserved from the time of Robert de Stratton. The papal registers give, as the holder previous to Fraunceys, John Mowbray the auditor. The royal government however did not accept this reservation and a royal candidate carried the day.[32] Further defeats came over the prebend of Charminster and Bere in Salisbury, 1402–4,[33] and Combe in Salisbury in 1404.[34] In 1405 he lost a claim in Lincoln, where the canons admitted his rival with a royal title, though under protest, yielding:

---

[21] *m.* 125; for S Eustachio see Huelsen, *Le chiese*, p. 231.   [22] *CPL*, V, pp. 270–1.
[23] *CPL*, V, pp. 296–7.   [24] *CPL*, V, pp. 490–1.
[25] *CPL*, V, p. 523.   [26] *CPL*, V, pp. 523–4.
[27] *CPL*, V, pp. 616–17.   [28] Not in McDermid, *Beverley Minster Fasti*.
[29] Stanley, *CPL*, V, p. 491; Fraunceys, pp. 490–1.   [30] *CPR 1401–5*, p. 52.
[31] He mentions this in Arch. Seld. B 23, f. 44.
[32] Le Neve, *Northern*, p. 67; *CPR 1401–5*, p. 332.
[33] *CPL*, V, p. 523; Le Neve, *Salisbury*, p. 42.   [34] Ibid., p. 46.

because of the various dangers threatening them these days and because of loss of the temporal goods of their church and costs to the persons of the chapter and because of fear threatened on behalf of the king.[35]

In 1404 he lost the archdeaconry of Berkshire to Simon Sydenham who had a provision, a royal pardon and certainly the royal favour.[36]

After these disappointments, Fraunceys clearly hoped to be allowed to succeed in another attempt to obtain a provision. Thanks to Professor Storey the English end of the celebrated case about the prebend of Stillington in Yorkshire, disputed between 1405 and 1408, can now be studied in detail from the King's Bench rolls.[37] The Roman side, unusually, can be followed in the letter book of William Swan, proctor for the 'royal' candidate, Thomas Towton. Swan also preserved some theoretical arguments for use in the curia, together with discussion of why the case would be better conducted in the royal court. The case also gives invaluable insight into the political manoeuvring in the curia.

For purposes of achieving his end Fraunceys' English connections were just as important as his Roman status and his kinsman, Sir Robert Fraunceys, who acted for him in England, was a useful connection.[38] His opponent, however, was better placed. Thomas Towton was master of the hospital of S Nicholas, Pontefract and rector of Wath-upon-Dearne,[39] whose patron in the former was the Duchy of Lancaster and in the latter a kinsman (Sir Thomas Flemming) of Robert Waterton of Methley, Yorkshire.[40] In opposing Towton Fraunceys was in reality taking on the formidable Waterton, one of a family group who had made their fortunes supporting Henry IV. In 1399 Henry retained Robert for life and made him master of the royal horse. He was one of the custodians of Richard II, played an important part in the defence of the North against the Percies and was an executor of Henry's will.[41] Between 1406 and 1408 Swan was also doing business for Waterton and

---

[35] H. P. King, 'A dispute between Henry IV and the chapter of Lincoln', *Archives*, 4/22 (1959), pp. 81–3; Le Neve, *Lincoln*, p. 64.

[36] Le Neve, *Salisbury*, p. 10; *BRUO*, III, p. 1838, for Sydenham.

[37] Storey, 'Clergy and the common law', no. 17, pp. 394–401.

[38] Ibid., p. 395, note 324, p. 400; Given-Wilson, *Royal Household*, p. 288.

[39] For him see A. H. Thompson and C. T. Clay, *Fasti parochiales*, II, Yorkshire Archaeological Society, Record Series, 107 (1943), pp. 111, 112.

[40] R. Scrope, *A Calendar of the Register of Richard Scrope, Archbishop of York, 1398–1405*, 2 parts (= Borthwick Texts and Calendars. Records of the Northern Province 8, 11), ed R. N. Swanson, York 1981, 1985, II, p. 48; Storey, 'Clergy and common law', p. 395, fn 314 for Pontefract; Arch. Seld. B 23, f. 128v calls Towton *consanguineus* of Waterton and he may have been related to the Flemmings of Wath, see Roskell in next note. Waterton married Cecilia Flemming of Wath.

[41] Given-Wilson, *Royal Household*, p. 190, p. 312 note 132; Roskell, *History of Parliament, The Commons 1386–1421*, IV, pp. 785–7, esp. p. 785.

his wife, for Waterton's brother-in-law, Richard Flemming, soon to be bishop of Lincoln, and for Waterton's chaplain.[42]

The claims and counterclaims about the prebend were complicated and not always truthful but can be summarised as follows. Fraunceys had a papal expectative for a prebend of York, dated 2 January 1403.[43] He also had a royal pardon for a previous attempt at provision with licence to obtain prebends in York and Salisbury, covering Charminster, Masham and one other, dated 5 January 1404.[44] Both licence and pardons were at the request of cardinals.[45] Theoretically Stillington was in the gift of the archbishop of York, but not surprisingly Towton and Fraunceys gave rival accounts of its descent to them. Professor Storey has given these, from the case in the royal court. Fraunceys (and the curia) considered Stillington reserved because its holder, in 1375 Henry Wakefield, had become a bishop.[46] He had been followed by a cardinal, by another provisor and then by a cardinal deprived in the schism. This last was followed by Nicholas Feriby, said to be a papal sub-collector, considered a member of the curia.[47] Towton claimed the prebend first because it was in the king's hands when Alexander Neville was deprived in 1388, or as he put it to Henry IV 'in the hands of the king's progenitors'.[48] The evidence in Towton's favour for use in Rome said that Urban VI provided Feriby in 1379[49] but before he had been admitted properly by the dean and chapter Richard II confiscated Neville's *temporalia*.[50] In England, however, Towton claimed the prebend first in July 1404, but then, two days after Archbishop Scrope's execution in 1405, claimed again on the grounds that its then holder Thomas Walworth, Feriby's successor and a residentiary canon of York, who had been properly appointed when Neville had seisin of the prebend, had resigned and the temporalities were in royal hands, as Towton later pointed out to the pope.[51] Walworth may have been implicated in Scrope's treason and there may have been pressure by Towton.[52] Not surprisingly the second confiscation was not stressed to Rome. Towton was admitted to the prebend on 17 June 1405.[53]

---

[42] Arch. Seld. B 23, f. 37, Waterton refers to Flemming as his brother, and Flemming refers to Waterton likewise, f. 51v. cf. *BRUO*; see also f. 82v, from W. Hallsted, chaplain at Methlay.

[43] *CPL*, V, p. 523; and evidence of Fraunceys proctor before the King's Bench (K. B.)

[44] *CPR 1401–5*, p. 332 and K. B. evidence.   [45] Le Neve, *Northern*, p. 79.

[46] Storey, 'Clergy and common law', p. 395 and Towton's evidence there.

[47] R. N. Swanson, 'Papal letters among the ecclesiastical archives of York, 1378–1415', *Borthwick Institute Bulletin*, 1/4 (1978), pp. 165–93, esp p. 170; *BRUC*; *CPL*, IV, p. 262–3, Fraunceys evidence, Storey, 'Clergy and common law', pp. 398–9.

[48] Storey, 'Clergy and common law', p. 395.   [49] Above Swanson as note 47.

[50] Arch. Seld. B 23, f. 24; if the story was true it left no trace.

[51] Arch. Seld. B 23, f. 116.   [52] Storey, 'Clergy and common law', p. 395.

[53] Le Neve, *Northern*, p. 79

Scrope's rebellion probably provided Towton with a cast-iron case in England; in Rome it was another matter.

Towton's first inkling that Stillington was contested was Fraunceys' citation of him to Rome dated 6 August 1405, giving him 100 days to appear.[54] Towton later questioned the legality of this but meanwhile appointed Swan as proctor, asking him and another Yorkshire man, William Lovell, abbreviator, to act.[55] The case then pursued different courses in Rome and in England. In Rome, to which Towton insisted he was not allowed to come in person, the case was assigned to the bishop of Ferentino, Nicolas de Vincione, an auditor.[56] In England Towton proceeded under the statute against provisors of 1365.

After a preliminary hearing in Stillington, where Fraunceys appeared by proxy, the King's Bench heard the case from early 1406. The jury declined to believe Fraunceys' claim that he had had corporate possession of the prebend in Scrope's lifetime and awarded damages to Towton.[57] Fraunceys, however, proved contumacious, perhaps because he had a good case in Rome; the King's Bench rolls show him being summoned again in 1407 and being outlawed for non-appearance on 9 October 1407. On 30 October 1408 he finally surrendered and was pardoned.[58]

Towton relied very heavily for legal advice in England on an advocate of the court of York, Master Alan Newerk, bachelor of civil law, master of Sherburn Hospital, Durham area, a king's clerk[59] Another friend was Swan's colleague in Rome, Master Thomas Weston, who supplied advice and acted as go-between for Swan. Weston was a proctor of long-standing, and archdeacon of Durham.[60] At one point in the argument Newerk wrote a long letter to Towton explaining why it was much better for him to pursue his case in England where he had much greater chance of success,[61] but the case was in fact being pursued in Rome by Fraunceys, at first regardless of what happened in England.

After the first decision in Towton's favour in England Fraunceys and his supporters did not pay their fines, but, continuing the case in the

---

54 Storey, 'Clergy and common law', from Towton's evidence before KB.
55 Arch. Seld. B 23, f. 32v; f. 116v for legality.
56 Arch. Seld. B 23, f. 116v; see *CPL*, VI, pp. 66–7.
57 Storey, 'Clergy and common law', p. 395; see London, Lambeth Palace Library, Arundel Register, Canterbury, I, f. 150v, for writ to Arundel to collect 100s from Fraunceys's benefices for contempt of the statute, 12 July 1407.
58 The second part is contained in London, PRO, KB 27 590, membrane 18.
59 *BRUO*, II, pp. 1354–5; Scrope, *Calendar*, I, p. 42.
60 *BRUO*; Legge, *Anglo-Norman Letters*, nos. 13 (c1394), 208; Storey, *Langley*, pp. 165–6, 175, 222–3.
61 Arch. Seld. B 23, ff. 23v–24.

curia, were outlawed on 9 October 1407.[62] On 28 November Swan told Towton that Fraunceys was using the outlawry as part of his case in Rome. Swan suggested pressing on in England and consulting Master John Chaundler,[63] dean of Salisbury, who was immensely influential in the royal councils. Swan had by this time received money from Towton and secured legal representation. He suggested that Towton discuss the legal rights (*iura*) of both sides with Newerk. He also pointed out that it was expedient to have support from cardinals and others influential with the pope, suggesting particularly Antonio de Calvis, cardinal of Todi (*Tudertinus*). Swan had told de Calvis that Waterton would try to influence the king to give the cardinal the parish church of Shillington in Bedfordshire for which he had a provision.[64] De Calvis was of an influential Roman family, of Monti region, recently (12 June 1405) made a cardinal and probably important in the curia of Innocent VII, where local Roman problems loomed large.[65] Swan's book contains an interesting schedule of advice to de Calvis about what to include in a letter to Waterton, mentioning his work for Towton.[66] There was also a list of other influential people (not preserved) to whom Waterton was to write, with the suggestion that royal letters might also be sent to these.[67] Towton replied on 25 March,[68] whilst meanwhile Swan had been frantically writing to others to know why he had not heard.[69] Swan of course was following the curia from place to place.

Towton, whose letter probably arrived long after it was of use, sent royal letters and suggested presenting them to suitable recipients through Master Thomas Weston and the English ambassadors at the time in the curia, Sir John Cheyne and Henry Chichele. Swan was to consult Weston about the whole matter. In England, meanwhile, Towton was searching for information about the exact status of Feriby, since Swan had suggested that he might not have been a sub-collector and might have been deprived.

Before Swan received any letter he wrote again on 1 January 1408 describing a public consistory before the pope and cardinals (in Sienna) about 16 December 1407 where Fraunceys had pleaded that because of the outlawry he and several of his friends were reduced to beggary.[70]

---

[62] Storey, 'Clergy and common law', p. 395.   [63] *BRUO*, I, pp. 397–8.

[64] *CPL*, VI, p. 168, de Calvis is allowed in 1410 to exchange Shillington because though provided he has not yet obtained the church. There is no record of his earlier provision. In 1411 he was granted royal licence to obtain English benefices, *CPR 1408–13*, p. 290.

[65] Eubel, *Hierarchia*, I, p. 26; Esch, *Bonifaz IX*, p. 636, for the family; M. Souchon, *Die Papstwahlen in der Zeit des grossen Schismas. Entwicklung und Verfassungskämpf des Kardinalates von 1378 bis 1417*, 2 vols., Braunschweig 1898–9, repr. 1970, I, p. 75; *DBI*, 17, pp. 9–10, article by Gennaro.

[66] Arch. Seld. B 23, ff. 128v–129.   [67] Arch. Seld. B 23, f. 55.

[68] As last note.   [69] Arch seld B 23, ff. 48v, 49.   [70] Arch. Seld. B 23, ff. 43v–44.

The outlawry, he said, showed that Towton held papal rights and liberties in contempt and Fraunceys wanted York sent a *monitorium* ordering the Dean and Chapter to admit Fraunceys under pain of excommunication, suspension, interdict and monetary penalties. He was also trying to cite Towton personally. The pope (by now Gregory XII), had been favourable but because of the arguments of the lawyers had asked for further information. This had been given and he had then granted the personal citation. Swan also pointed out that Master William Lovell, whom Towton thought a friend, was now supporting Fraunceys; he had offered to fight Swan after the consistory, had called Towton a serf and expressed the hope that Waterton would be hanged, drawn and quartered as a traitor. This may express Lovell's attitude to Henry IV in the Scrope affair. Swan pointed out that it was more than ever necessary to have support from cardinals and influential people, suggesting Antonius Caetani, by now bishop of Palestrina, whom we have already met in John White's affairs and the pope's nephew Antonius Correr, bishop of Bologna, soon (May) to be a cardinal.[71] This new advice reflects very well changing influences in the curia.

Swan repeated the need for royal letters, including letters[72]

in which our lord the king enjoins and commands me to defend the case, which letters I can show to the lord pope and other lord cardinals, for because of this case several Englishmen even among my friends are moved against me and have informed the cardinals that I was against the status and advantage of letters apostolic and provisors.

He suggested that it might be expedient to allow Fraunceys to be verbally admitted to the prebend, making sure that a suitable protest was registered at the time. Swan had spoken several times with Cheyne and Chichele about the injury to the royal rights in this case but they would not act without royal letters. He also pointed out that cardinal Ugguccione (archbishop of Bordeaux) 'who is thoroughly English' (*qui est totus Anglicus*) was in the curia, so the king could also write to him. Uggucione had come to persuade Gregory to keep his oath to end the schism.[73] Swan summarised what might be said and suggested sending a precious jewel to the pope 'to have you in mind' (*ut vos habeat in mente*), and repeated the need to write to Correr. To stir Towton Swan pointed out that Fraunceys had written to the king and to Fraunceys' friend

---

[71] For these see Eubel, *Hierarchia*, I, pp. 26, 31.

[72] Arch. Seld. B 23, f. 43v: *in quibus idem dominus noster rex iniungat et michi mandet quod predictam causam defendam quas literas domino nostro pape et aliis cardinalibus ostendere valeam. Nam propter istam causam plures Anglici eciam ex amicis meis moventur contra me et informarunt dominos cardinales quod essem contra statum et commdum apostolicorum et provisorum.*

[73] Harvey, *Solutions*, pp. 137–8. 143–4.

Thomas Arundel, pointing out (what was true) that he had given up the prebends of Masham and Charminster because of royal letters[74] and so might be allowed to keep this. The king could perhaps be moved, even though it would be unjust, though Swan was sure that the king would not truly wish to give up his royal title thus. He also pointed out that Correr had a provision for the archdeaconry of Lincoln and another nephew, Gabriel Condulmaro, provision to the parish church of North-fleet, Kent.[75] Towton could write offering to work for them in return for help; 'bearing one another's burdens' (*alter alterius onera portans*), as Swan put it sententiously.

In a further letter, shortly afterwards,[76] Swan pointed out that Fraunceys should be overcome by the process in England if Towton persevered. In the curia the *monitorium* had been revoked and it appeared that Towton might win there also. Fraunceys was losing heart and Master Thomas Weston had thought of a formula of reconciliation. By 10 March 1408 Swan wrote that the case in Rome was suspended because Weston was negotiating peace.[77]

What 'peace' involved is unclear. In October 1408 Fraunceys surrendered, paid damages and was pardoned, giving up Stillington.[78] Towton subsequently wrote to Swan asking that, in view of the arrangement he and Fraunceys had made with Swan in London, he must now be surrogated by the pope into Fraunceys' rights. In the eyes of the curia and of church law, apparently, he and Fraunceys had exchanged benefices.[79] Le Neve shows Fraunceys resigning Stillington on 10 November 1408;[80] the same day he was admitted to Wath-upon-Dearne presented by Robert Waterton who had the advowson by then.[81] Towton had been reinstituted to Wath in July, having resigned it apparently when he thought he had obtained Stillington.[82] This looks like a temporary deal; Towton told Swan that he must be surrogated into Fraunceys' rights to the prebend or the deal would not work, adding that he was not obliged to pay first fruits 'because it is an exchange' (*causa permutacionis*)[83] and Bowet's register calls Fraunceys'

---

[74] Storey, 'Clergy and common law', p. 394 has the details.
[75] Le Neve, *Lincoln*, p. 7; *CPL*, VI, p. 113. There is no record of the provision to Northfleet, Hallum was its rector cf. *BRUO*, II, p. 854.
[76] Arch. Seld. B 23, f. 50v.   [77] Arch. Seld. B 23, f. 50v again.
[78] KB 27.590; *CPR 1408–13*, p. 27.
[79] *CPR 1408–1413*, p. 27; Towton to Swan, Arch. Seld. B 23, f. 54v.
[80] Le Neve, *Northern*, p, 79; York, Borthwick Institute (Bowet) Register 17, f. 15r/v.
[81] Thompson and Clay, *Fasti Parochiales*, II, pp. 111–12; York, Borthwick Institute (Bowet) Register 17, f. 15v.
[82] York, Borthwick Institute (Bowet) Register 18, f. 9.
[83] Arch. Seld. B 23, f. 54v; Thompson and Clay, *Fasti Parochiales*, II, p. 111–12.

appointment to Wath an exchange.[84] But Fraunceys probably resigned Wath almost at once, since Towton was re-admitted on 9 December, by the Archbishop himself, presented by Waterton,[85] so ultimately Towton held both benefices and was allowed to appropriate Wath to S Nicholas' hospital in 1410.[86]

Suggestive also is the information that in Rome Fraunceys' supporters were said to include, apart from Lovell, Edmund Eslake and Thomas Prys, who were in the curia and could not return to England until the case ended.[87] Prys was a proctor, later chaplain to pope John XXIII, so he may already have had a secure position.[88] According to Swan, Eslake was chaplain to Sir Robert Urswick,[89] and in Towton's last letter to Swan, where he talked about the surrogation, there is a further passage where he said that at York recently he and Eslake had agreed that Eslake was to have ten pounds yearly from Towton until he was promoted to a benefice of the value of twenty pounds a year, and that the abbot and convent of S Mary's York had promised him their next vacancy, for which Eslake, incidentally, had a provision.[90] Writing to Towton of the agreement in March 1408, Swan said it needed thinking over and discussing; Fraunceys had no right to the prebend 'but one may buy off unjust vexation and I believe it ought to be done, as long as it is not too expensive' (*nihilominus vexacionem iniustam redimere licet et crederem faciendum fore, dummodo non nimis sumptuose*).[91] So there were behind-the-scenes deals involved in the settlement, involving money.

This might seem a simple victory of royal over papal law; *praemunire* triumphant. To some extent, of course, this is correct, but not wholly, because the tergivations over Wath-upon-Dearne show that Towton had to satisfy the papal law before he could hold Stillington safely. It appears that, with the connivance of his patron Waterton and of archbishop Bowet, he resigned Wath in preparation for holding Stillington and was then allowed to hold it again so that he could fictitiously 'exchange' it with Fraunceys, to satisfy the papal court that a compromise rather than a defeat had happened. Exchanges are often very difficult to understand but this one has a strong feeling of fraud, as does the payment to Eslake.[92]

---

[84] Bowet Register, York, 17, f. 15r/v.

[85] J. Hunter, *South Yorkshire. The History and Topography of the Deanery of Doncaster in the Diocese and County of York*, 2 vols., London 1831, II, p. 71, if Torre, quoted here, is correct. See (Bowet) Register 18, f. 18 for William Eslak as vicar of Wath when it was appropriated in 1410.

[86] Thompson and Clay, *Fasti Parochiales*, II, p. 106; Zutshi, *Original*, no. 499.

[87] Arch. Seld. B 23, f. 50v.   [88] See above p. 167.

[89] Roskell, *History of Parliament. The Commons 1386–1421*, IV, pp. 693–6; son, pp. 695–6.

[90] Arch. Seld. B 23, f. 54v; *CPL*, VI, p. 90.   [91] Arch. Seld. B 23, f. 50v.

[92] R. N. Swanson, *Church and Society in Late Medieval England*, Oxford 1989, 1993, pp. 55–7.

The case shows how a proctor acted. The canvassing of supporters in the curia, both English and cardinals, was as expected, but Swan's grasp of the politics involved was very sure. He understood how dependent on English goodwill the pope was. 'You may take it as fixed that our lord the pope seeks to please our lord the king' (*Exhibeatis pro constanti quod dominus noster papa studet conplacere domino nostro regi*).[93] Newerk supplied much of the legal expertise, but Swan hired the legal experts locally: Johannes de Roma, as an advocate, and for proctors masters Willelmus Leo, [H]arthongus de Cappel and Petrus de Mera, the last a Flemming who rose high in the curia later,[94] 'and two others among the more powerful in the curia' (*et duos alios valenciores curie*).[95]

Advising that the king and others be induced to write to the pope, Swan thought it would be easy to arrange 'seeing that my lord Waterton can do much with our lord the king it does not seem difficult since you can have letters as often as you please' (*attenta quod dominus meus Waterton plura potest cum domino nostro rege non videtur difficile quoniam literas habere possitis tociens et quotiens vobis placeret*).[96] He gave exact instructions and explained that he needed copies, with information as to who was to get which letters: 'let it be placed on each letter, as is usual, whose letter it is and to whom it is directed thus: letter of the king directed to the pope or to such and such a cardinal' (*ponatur super eisdem literis ad partem, ut moris est, cuius sit litera et cui dirigatur sub hac forma videlicet litera regis directa pape vel tali cardinali*).

One can see the problems which arose because of the disarray of papal archives at this time. The answer to the question whether Feriby had been a sub-collector proved elusive. Swan asked the bishop of Volterra, Luigi Alliotti, collector in England from 1399 to 1406, who did not know,[97] 'but from his books left behind in London you can be fully informed about this' (*ex libris tamen suis London dimissis plene de predictis poteritis informari*). Swan had recently, he told Towton, been informed that Feriby had been deprived by the late cardinal *Iserniensis*, Cristoforo Maroni, but he could not find which prebend or benefice this concerned 'though I have hunted diligently, for the notary of the case is not now in the curia' (*licet diligenciam fecerim in perquirendo nam qui notarius eiusdem cause erat nunc non est in curia presens*).

The letters Swan preserved contained theoretical arguments both for and against the royal title to the benefice. Newerk, counselling

---

[93] Arch. Seld. B 23, f. 44.
[94] For de Mera: Harvey, *England, Rome*, p. 153; Leo: Schuchard, *Die Deutschen*, p.81 and *RG* III, col. 372. Hartungus Molitoris de Kappel: *RG*, III, cols. 141–2.
[95] Arch. Seld. B 23, f. 41v.   [96] Arch. Seld. B 23, f. 44.
[97] Arch. Seld. B 23, f. 41v; Favier, *Les finances*, p. 731.

Towton, advised that the quickest action was in the royal court where Towton had adequate remedy.[98] If Towton wished to pursue the case in Rome he would have to complete there and this would prejudice the royal court against him since he would be acting against the law of England. On the other hand the curia did not recognise a royal title contrary to apostolic constitutions. Towton would probably lose in Rome and the subsequent censures were formidable, as was the expense. The royal court was cheaper, no one could say he was litigating in Rome nor subjecting the royal title to the curia, which would render his claim invalid in England. The formula covering royal rights reads:[99]

the royal title is founded on the temporal right of the king's crown and it is wrong to subject that temporal right to litigation at the Holy See since in temporal matters the king recognises no superior on earth.

Newerk was confident that if Towton pressed the case in England his opponent would not continue in the curia and if Fraunceys did continue Towton could use a royal writ under pain of forfeiture for such contempt. 'I have often seen this', he added. He also said that the curia was slow, its penalties were worse than the royal ones and so, between two dangers, one should choose the lesser.

Newerk understood that the curia was objecting to the claim that the temporalities of York had fallen into the royal hands, which was a custom of the country, not strictly allowed by canon law. He defended this as an ancient custom long observed and tolerated by the pope. He likened the reservation by the king of benefices during an episcopal vacancy to papal reservations.[100]

Swan concurred with Newerk. In the letter which Swan suggested the king should write he included the following[101]

that our lord the king believes that our lord the sovereign pontiff does not wish to infringe the royal prerogatives and right of his crown nor the statutes of the kingdom produced by so many nobles, prelates and other magnates and important men nor to remove one single word of them, especially at the

---

[98] Arch. Seld. B 23, ff. 23v–25.

[99] Arch. Seld. B 23, f. 24; *titulus vero regius fundatur super iure temporali corone regis et illud ius temporale supponere dissensioni apostolice nephas est, cum rex in temporalibus non recognoscat superiorem in terris.*

[100] Arch. Seld. B 23, f. 25: *spiritualis consuetudo antiquissimis temporibus observata quam papa scit et tolleratur specialiter reservavit regi collaciones et concessiones temporalium sede episcopali vacante . . . nec est mirandum de tali reservacione quia consuetudo tanti temporis equiparatur privilegio . . . per talem consuetudinem cuius contrarii memoriam hominum non existit potuit rex querere tale ius reservacionis.*

[101] Arch. Seld. B 23, f. 44: *et quod dominus noster rex credit quod dominus noster summus pontifex non velit et presertim ad preces unius ligei sui regalia et ius corone sue ac statuta regni per tot proceres, prelatos et alios magnates seu satrapes salubriter edita infringere aut unico verbo tollere, sed ea pocius sustinere, canonizare, defendere et defensare.*

request of one of his own subjects, but rather to sustain, canonise, defend and protect them.

When Swan told Towton here that he could take it for granted that the pope was anxious to please the king, he was writing on 1 January 1408 when Gregory XII was still considered fairly favourably by the English court but certainly was in desperate need of English help.

In what was almost certainly the details of the appeal in the curia against Frounceys,[102] the royal practice of keeping benefices during vacancy was defended on the grounds that the king was the founder of all cathedrals. The royal reservation was compared, as we saw, to papal reservation. For the pope's benefit it was claimed that Towton, anxious to obey the pope's citation to Rome, his loyalty to the pope being much stressed, had begged the king for permission to leave England, but this had merely made the king angry and had been forbidden. Only very reluctantly had the king even allowed Towton to defend himself by proxy. Obviously when it suited Henry IV's subjects they knew how to defend his prerogatives.

Frounceys lost but probably not because Towton had a better case nor solely because he had the crown on his side. The time could not have been less propitious for pursuing a case in the curia. Frounceys' patron Carbone died on 18 June 1405.[103] Swan realised who the truly influential cardinals were and there is evidence of attempts to buy their favour. Correr did not obtain appointment to the archdeaconry of Lincoln,[104] but Robert Hallum had been rector of Northfleet, which presumably was regarded by the papacy as vacant in curia by his elevation first to York and then to Salisbury. In 1408 Arundel was trying to appropriate it and succeeded in the end.[105] This would have been known to Swan and would have provided a very good bargaining counter but both papal nephews of course soon became very unpopular because of the schism and there was no need to placate them nor the pope after early 1409. In 1411, however, De Calvis, who finally deserted Gregory XII and joined Pisa, was allowed a rare royal licence to hold English benefices, though it is not clear that he obtained any.[106] He certainly did not get Shillington.[107]

In the end the only prebend that Frounceys held was probably Combe Octava in Bath and Wells.[108] After this case we have one brief

[102] Arch. Seld. B 23, ff. 115v–16v.   [103] Eubel, *Hierarchia*, I, p. 25.

[104] *CPL*, VI, p. 113; Le Neve, *Lincoln*, p. 7.

[105] *CPL*, VI, pp. 133–4, 313; A. Hussey, ed. *Kent Chantries*, Kent Records 12 (1936), p. 117; and E. Holland, ed. *The Canterbury Chantries and Hospitals together with some others in the Neighbourhood in 1546*, Kent Records, 12, Supplement (1934), pp. 65–6.

[106] *CPR 1408–13*, p. 290.   [107] *CPL*, VI, p. 168.   [108] Le Neve, *Bath and Wells*, p. 30.

glimpse of him at work for John XXIII,[109] a record of his death in
1413[110] and that is all. His property must have come to the English
hospice but he does not figure as a noted benefactor. Everything
suggests that he never succeeded in making his peace with the English
regime after 1399 and therefore decided to make a career in Rome, not
a plan likely to bring honours in England and, in the state of the curia
after 1404, unlikely to produce much tangible fruit in Rome either.

[109] *CPL*, VI, p. 168.   [110] Le Neve, *Index*, p. 125.

Chapter 10

ADAM EASTON, AN ENGLISH CARDINAL: HIS CAREER

Adam Easton was the last Englishman to become a cardinal resident at the curia for about one hundred years. His career is therefore of great interest; he was a scholar rather than a politician, but both his rise to position and his subsequent career tell us a great deal about the curia in his day, particularly its cultural climate.

Easton owed his success to his own intelligence and to the notice of Simon Langham. He was probably born about 1330 (in 1378 he described himself as 'more than forty years old') and probably came from Easton in Norfolk,[1] since the majority of Norwich monks, as Easton became, were from the Norfolk estates of the priory.[2] We do not know when he entered the priory but 1348 would be a good guess.[3] Promising young monks like this, thought likely to rise in the monastery, were for some years sent to Oxford, where young Adam read theology.[4] We first hear of him there in 1352, when Bishop Bateman tried to recall him and another monk with books and plate from the convent.[5] It is not now clear what was going on, but Easton protested saying he had appealed to the pope. Whatever the trouble he stayed in Oxford.

---

[1] *BRUO*, I, pp. 620–1; *Dictionnaire de spiritualité, ascetique et mystique, doctrine et histoire*, IV/1, Paris 1968, article by L. J. MacFarlane, cols. 5–8; L. J. MacFarlane, The life and writings of Adam Easton, OSB, 3 vols., University of London PhD, 1955. I would like to thank Professor MacFarlane. 'More than forty': MacFarlane, 'An English account', p. 79. See also Sharpe, *A Handlist*, pp. 12–14; Greatrex, *Biographical Register*, pp. 502–3. I would like to thank Dr Greatrex for lending me notes and answering many queries and Professsor Sharpe for much support and help.
[2] N. P. Tanner, *The Church in Late Medieval Norwich, 1370–1532* (= Pontifical Institute of Medieval Studies, Studies and Texts 66), Toronto 1984, p. 25.
[3] R. B. Dobson, *Durham Priory, 1400–1450* (= Cambridge Studies in Medieval Life and Thought, 3rd series 6), Cambridge 1973, p. 61.
[4] J. Greatrex, 'Monk Students from Norwich Cathedral Priory at Oxford and Cambridge', *EHR*, 106 (1991), pp. 555–83.
[5] J. Lydford, *John Lydford's Book*, ed. D.M. Owen, Devon and Cornwall Record Society, new series 19(20) (1974/75), jointly with the Historical Manuscripts Commission, nos. 201, 202.

We know little about his student days. Thomas de Brinton, later a well-known preacher and bishop, with a distinguished career in Rome, was a contemporary.[6] In 1355/6 he and Easton, both students, were recalled to Norwich to preach for the vigil of the Assumption (14 August) and some time between 1357 and 1363 the prior of Norwich told the prior of students in Oxford that Adam was not returning to incept because he was needed in Norwich to preach and confute friars who were attacking the Black Monks.[7] This implies that Easton had become involved in the latest twist of the secular-mendicant quarrel, with Richard Fitzralph in Avignon attacking the friars, supported by the Black Monks in England.[8] One of the books Easton owned was William of S Amour's *Collectiones*, a defence of bishops against the privileges of friars.[9] When Easton was established in the curia, in June 1375, Norwich obtained a papal injunction, in which Simon Langham or Easton may have had a hand, to the four orders of friars in Norwich to stop attacking the house and to observe *Super Cathedram* and the council of Vienne, which were supposed to regulate relations between monks and friars.[10] Adam returned eventually to Oxford and was there in 1363–4; he incepted finally in about 1365, as 'master of divinity'[11].

A few exercises from this period give some idea of his intellectual concerns. As bachelor of divinity he lectured on Peter Lombard's *Sentences*; though the lectures do not now exist he referred to them in a (presumably post-doctoral) determination: 'as I show elsewhere in a lecture on the *Sentences*',[12] where he discussed references to the Trinity in the Old Testament. His *vesperies* before the doctorate exist in a Worcester Cathedral manuscript,[13] in which the bachelor responding was Master Nicholas Radcliffe, a contemporary Benedictine, but from S Alban's.[14] Later he, like Adam, became a notable opponent of Wyclif. The question which the pair discussed was whether all vows made to God must be kept.[15] Three determinations by Easton remain, two in

---

[6] See Greatrex, *Biographical Register*, pp. 487–8; Sharpe, *Handlist*.

[7] Pantin, *Chapters*, III, pp. 28–9; Oxford, Bodleian Library, MS Bodley 692, f. 116.

[8] See below pp. 227–8.

[9] Oxford, Bodleian Library, MS Bodley 151; the only printed version is *Opera Omnia*, Constance 1632, pp. 111–490.

[10] ASV, Reg. Av. 197, f. 134.

[11] NRO, Norwich Dean and Chapter Archives (DCN) 1/12/29, 1/12/30; 1/8/42, 1/1/49, 1/1/65, 1/4/35, 2/3/7, to which my attention was drawn by Dr Greatrex.

[12] Oxford, Oriel College, MS 15, f. 224; I thank Dr Richard Sharpe for drawing my attention to this MS.

[13] Worcester Cathedral, MS F 65, f. 21r/v, copy from MacFarlane thesis.

[14] *BRUO*, III, p. 1539.

[15] Discussion in MacFarlane, Thesis, II, pp. 102–14; transcript, III, pp. 2–6; for Radcliffe see Sharpe, *Handlist*, pp. 391–2.

the same Worcester manuscript, where he discussed Adam's vision of God in the state of innocence.[16] The third is anonymous but the title and *incipit De comunicatione idiomatum (incipit: Suppono primo cum doctoribus)* agree with that given by John Bale for a work of Easton and there is no reason to doubt this.[17] It discusses the divine and human nature of Christ and to what extent the properties (*ydiomata seu proprietates*) which apply to Him as God apply also to Him as man and vice versa. The final work, which may belong to this period since it is attributed to Adam Easton monk of Norwich but is incomplete in the only manuscript we have, is an explanation of certain astrological terms.[18] It includes an explanation of how planets affect fortunes. Statements about astrologers are contained in several works of Easton's; astrology seems to have been an abiding interest.[19]

On 20 September 1366 Easton was made prior *studentium* of Gloucester College, the equivalent of a modern dean of students,[20] the high point of a Benedictine monastic academic career, often followed by high office in the order or one's own monastery. Easton came to the notice, though we do not know how, of Simon Langham, archbishop of Canterbury. Langham would in any case have encountered the leading monks in Oxford because of his involvement in Canterbury College, if for no other reason, but he was also himself an ex-Westminster monk and abbot.[21]

Until this point in his career we can tell almost nothing about Easton's personality nor his talent. The surviving works are conventional. The most 'modern' authority quoted was Richard Fitzralph's *De questionibus Armenorum*, completed in Avignon in the 1350s and used by Easton to discuss the nature of Adam's vision of God.[22] The questions discussed: the state of innocence and human knowledge of God, were also preoccupying his contemporaries. There is nothing original here.

By the time Easton took his doctorate Brinton had left for Avignon

---

[16] Worcester, ff. 20v and 13r, see also S. L. Forte, A study of some Oxford schoolmen of the middle of the fourteenth century, with special reference to Worcester Cathedral MS F 65, University of Oxford B. Litt. 1947, I, p. 4, II, pp. 66–9, 103–4, 120.

[17] Oxford, Oriel College, MS 15, ff. 222v–24v; Cambridge, Emmanuel College, MS 142, ff. 135–136v. J. Bale, *Index Britanniae Scriptorum, John Bale's Index of British and Other Writers*, 2nd edn, eds C. Brett and J. P. Carley, Cambridge 1990, pp. 4–6.

[18] CCCC, MS 347, f. 163.

[19] See Vatican Library, MS, V, 4116, ff. 56–58v, for instance.

[20] Supplied by Dr Greatrex.

[21] W. A. Pantin, ed., *Canterbury College, Oxford*, 4 vols., Oxford Historical Society, new series 6, 7, 8, 30 (1946–50, 1985), IV, pp. 18–21; Langham in *BRUO*, II, 1095–7.

[22] K. Walsh, *A Fourteenth-Century Scholar and Primate. Richard Fitzralph in Oxford, Avignon and Armagh*, Oxford 1981, pp. 129–81 esp. p. 167, for date; Forte, Thesis, ed., p. 68 for the ref; J. I. Catto and T. A. R. Evans, *The History of the University of Oxford*, II, *Late Medieval Oxford*, Oxford 1992, p. 184.

with his prior.[23] In 1362 Brinton was made English penitentiary in the curia and was also proctor for his order.[24] He returned briefly to Oxford in 1364–6 to incept in canon law, returning to the curia in 1366. There he made a name as a preacher. Radcliffe, the younger contemporary, returned to S Alban's and about 1377 undertook, at the request of his abbot, the task of refuting Wyclif's ideas on dominion, for the benefit of the younger monks.[25]

Easton went to Avignon, probably finally in early summer 1369, accompanying Langham. He had made one journey there already, probably on Langham's behalf. In May 1368 he was sent from Avignon with a message to Edward III about papal taxation.[26] Langham was made a cardinal on 22 September that year.[27] Since the curia was temporarily in Italy he entered it at Montefiascone on 24 May 1369, presumably accompanied by Easton.[28] Adam was called Langham's *socius* when receiving on Langham's behalf the generous coronation gift which Gregory XI offered all cardinals.[29] Sometimes this is translated secretary but perhaps 'companion' in the Victorian sense better explains the implication.

Very little of Easton's (or Langham's) activities in the curia can be traced. Almost at once Langham was involved in the quarrels of Black Monks and seculars over whether Canterbury College, Oxford, was to be purely monastic. Sentence was given in favour of the monks and in May 1370 at Montefiascone Easton witnessed the order to execute the judgement.[30] He doubtless accompanied Langham when the curia returned to Avignon and then certainly was with Langham's legation to mediate between France and England which followed from early 1371 to about April 1373. Easton was in Paris in May 1371 and then at Freton in Utrecht diocese on 2 April 1372, witnessing Langham's request for procurations from England to cover the costs of his stay; presumably he came to Westminster Abbey with Langham in October 1371.[31] He was in contact with Ely Abbey in 1372.[32]

On return to Avignon Easton's activities are obscure until in 1375 he headed the legatees among the household members in Langham's will

---

[23] Pantin, *Chapters*, III, p. 61 note; Oxford, Bodleian Library, Tanner MS 342, ff. 109v, 110.

[24] Majic, 'Die apostolische Pönitentiarie', pp. 143, 147.

[25] London, BL MS Royal 6 D X, ff. 1–143v. The work deals only with Wyclif's *De civili dominio* I and makes no mention of the papal condemnation; see also Catto and Evans, *Oxford*, II, p. 206.

[26] *CPL*, IV, p. 27.

[27] Eubel, *Hierarchia*, I, p. 47; *The Anonimalle Chronicle 1333–1381*, ed. V. H. Galbraith, Manchester 1927, pp. 57–8.

[28] Eubel, *Hierarchia*, I, p. 21.   [29] ASV, Collect. 464, ff. 169v–72; 193r/v.

[30] Pantin, *Canterbury College*, III, p. 206, IV, pp. 28–9.

[31] Harvey, 'Langham', p. 23 with notes.

[32] Greatrex, *Biographical Register*, from a Cambridge MS.

in July, when he was both a beneficiary and an executor.[33] Langham was a major benefactor of Westminster and the monastery needed urgently to ship the goods home, so in October 1376 when the prior of Westminster arrived, Easton headed those *familiares* of Langham whom he consulted.[34] All this agrees with Easton's statement after Langham's death that he had been *capellanus commensalis* to Langham for about eight years (since 1368) and that with the cardinal he had faithfully laboured for the business of the Roman church.[35]

For a scholar one of the excitements of Avignon must have been its wealth of libraries, not least Langham's own which numbered about ninety books when finally sent to Westminster.[36] Langham's included not only standard works but also 'modern' controversy: refutations of the prophecies of Jean de Roquetaillade (Rupescissa), which had caused a great stir in Avignon just before Langham arrived, for example,[37] or collections of prophecies with Fitzralph's *De questionibus* and also his *De pauperie Salvatoris* which Easton later owned in one of the earliest complete editions.[38]

Easton made the most of these intellectual opportunities. He set about learning Hebrew, for which Avignon, with its famous learned ghetto, offered unrivalled opportunity. When, in about 1378, he presented his great work *Defensorium ecclesiastice potestatis* to the newly elected Urban VI in Rome, he explained that he had been studying the Book of Kings for about twenty years, implying that he had already begun the work in Oxford, but finally, beginning to fear that Jerome's translation was inaccurate, he studied Hebrew and translated for two years, with Jerome's text in one hand and the Hebrew in the other, with four Jewish teachers or expositors and a Jewish interpreter.[39] Almost certainly Easton's doubts arose from actual arguments with Jews. He may have composed a *De cessatione legalium*, which was criticised by Jewish scholars, presumably a typical treatise trying to prove that Christ had abrogated the Law of Moses, a theme dear to the hearts of many medieval Christian biblical scholars.[40]

---

[33] Widmore, *An History*, pp. 185–6.   [34] WAM, 9232.

[35] ASV, Reg. Av. 200, f. 74v.

[36] R. Sharpe et al., *English Benedictine Libraries. The Shorter Catalogues* (= Corpus of British Medieval Library Catalogues 4), London 1996, pp. 615–26.

[37] J. Bignami-Odier, *Études sur Jean de Roquetaillade*, Paris 1952; and see also M. Reeves, *The Influence of Prophecy in the Later Middle Ages. A Study of Joachimism*, Oxford 1969, esp. pp. 225–8; Sharpe, *Shorter Catalogues*, p. 620.

[38] Walsh, *Fitzralph*, pp. 472–3, on CCCC, MS 180, made for Easton; Sharpe, *Shorter Catalogues*, pp. 619, 621.

[39] V, 4116, f. 2; for learning Hebrew: G. Dahan, *Les intellectuels chrétiens et les juifs au moyen âge*, Paris 1990, pp. 239–70.

[40] V, 4116, f. 2.

Some traces of debate remain in *Defensorium*. *Episcopus*, the voice of orthodoxy (and Easton) cites psalm 71 (= 72) verse 2 (which reads in the Vulgate in part: *Deus iudicium tuum regi da, et justitiam tuam filio regis*; 'give to the king thy judgement, O God, and to the king's son thy justice'), referring it to Christ.[41] The Vulgate title for this psalm is *In Salomonem*. *Rex*, the secularist opponent, at once protests:

Here I resist you and exclaim as did lately Master Samuel de Doma, the leader of the Jews, because by the title of the Hebrew text of this psalm it seems that this psalm ought to derive its truth only from Solomon simply as a man and lately chief king of the Jews. The title in Hebrew is *le Salomone*, which means in Latin 'for Solomon'.[42]

Episcopus replies

I reply to you as I did then to the Jew: Let the psalm be read and if it can be verified about Solomon purely as a man and a king I agree with you and am convinced. If it cannot be explained thus, hold what the church holds.[43]

He expounded the next verses to show that they could not refer to Solomon, whose conquests were never as extensive as the text implied. Reminiscences of actual debate continued: 'If you object as did another Jew then . . .' and he even gave his own translation from the Hebrew of verse 16. Much of the content came from Nicholas de Lyra, who knew that some Jews and Christians thought the title of the psalm was 'For Solomon'. Lyra had also pointed out that the peace mentioned could not have referred to Solomon's time because as soon as the latter was dead the kingdom split. Such debates certainly occurred in Avignon but have seldom left actual traces. There is a tradition from the sixteenth century, by a scholar who owned a copy, that the result of Easton's study was a translation of the bible, excluding the psalms, from Hebrew into Latin.[44]

Easton was probably also employed at the curia as a theological consultant. When later he gave evidence about the election of Urban

---

[41] v, 4116, f. 316v; Dahan, *Intellectuels*, pp. 229–38, 270–307, with no mention of Avignon.

[42] v, 4116, f. 316v: *hic tibi resisto primitus et exclamo sicut nuper fecit magister Samuel de Doma precipuus Judeorum qui[a] per titulum textus hebrayici huius psalmi videtur quod iste psalmus de Salomone puro homine et rege nuper precipuo hebreorum debet capere veritatem et erat titulus ita dicit le Salomone in hebrayco quod ad Salomonem signat in latino.* I have not found this man's name among the many known Avignon Jews. For the community see B. Guillemain, *La cour pontifical d'Avignon (1309–1376). Étude d'une société* (= Bibliothèque des écoles françaises d'Athènes et de Rome 201), Paris 1962, pp. 642–53; Walsh, *Fitzralph*, pp. 158–60; G. Bruckner, An unpublished source of the Avignonese papacy, the letters of Francisco Bruni, *Traditio*, 19 (1963), pp. 368–70, esp. pp. 368–9.

[43] *Respondeo sicut feceram tunc Judeo: Legatur psalmus et si poterit verificari de Salomone puro homine atque rege tibi consencio et convintor et si non poterit sic exponi tene sicut tenet ecclesia.*

[44] See below p. 236.

VI he recorded that he and two other masters of theology had been commissioned by Cardinal Jacobus Orsini to examine the liturgy for the feast of the Transfixion of the Virgin, an early version of the later feast of the Seven Dolors.[45] Apparently an earlier attempt under Clement VI to establish this feast was renewed under Gregory XI. Easton was commissioned but reported to Orsini under Urban VI, only to be told that Urban was much too concerned with church reform to be interested.

Easton would have been kept by Langham until the latter died. The will brought him 200 florins, a horse, a bed with a cover and a cup.[46] But Langham's death forced Easton to reconsider his career. As a member of Langham's household he had permission to be absent from his monastery and immediately he needed to be in Avignon to help administer the will.[47] Quite soon, however, he must have decided to try to stay in the curia, since there is a petition from him granted by the pope in September 1376, asking to hold Langham's former benefice of Somersham in Huntingdon.[48] He had obtained the grace to choose his own confessor in 1375;[49] in 1377 he obtained permission to have a portable altar and to say mass in interdicted places.[50] All this suggests someone who has decided not to return as a monk to Norwich.

Langham's death broke up his household. Some members returned to England very soon. Thomas Southam, Langham's legal expert (*auditor*), a canon lawyer and the main executor of the will in Avignon, stayed on in a house in the city near the church of Notre Dame de Miraculis, on the modern rue Velouterie, providing a pied à terre for various Westminster representatives who came to pack Langham's books and household goods.[51] Probably in order to stay in Avignon, not resident in his archdeaconry of Oxford, Southam entered the University of Avignon in 1378[52] and did not follow the curia to Rome when the administration of Langham's will was finished. He was probably deterred by the schism, which made continuance of a curial career doubtful. William Colchester, from Westminster, stayed with him when Colchester came from Rome between 2 and 24 September 1378 'whilst awaiting greater stability of the curia' as Colchester's *compotus* for Westminster explained.[53] But by then Easton had gone to Rome, where he was a leading witness of the events of Urban VI's election and the outbreak of schism. Southam was in touch with Rome through the journeyings of his servant John Kentyf, a former *familiaris commensalis* of

[45] MacFarlane, 'An English Account', p. 84.   [46] Widmore, *An History*, pp. 185–6.
[47] Pantin, *Chapters*, III, no. 229.   [48] ASV, Reg. Av. 200, f. 74v.
[49] ASV, Reg. Av. 197, f. 182.   [50] ASV, Reg. Av. 201, f. 485v; Reg. Av. 202, f. 470.
[51] WAM, 9256B; 9223*.   [52] *CPP*, p. 544.   [53] WAM, 9256B.

Langham.[54] Kentyf's news cannot have been encouraging; by 1382 Southam was in England.[55]

Easton, however, with some others of Langham's former servants, followed the main curia,[56] very likely as an executor of Langham's will, since one of the cardinal executors was cardinal Aigrefeuille, who also followed it (and soon became heavily involved in the schism).

At the end of Gregory XI's pontificate Easton had also become concerned in recent controversies in England about John Wyclif. Following the quarrels about poverty which had concerned him at Oxford he would probably have heard whilst in England with Langham on the legation in 1371/2 about the discussion Wyclif was causing. There is a possible reference in *Defensorium* when *Episcopus* warned *Rex* 'in this matter I heard a notable master in theology arguing on your side', which caused him to worry about modern trends.[57] Writing when still in Avignon negotiating about Langham's goods, on 18 November, probably 1376, he asked Westminster for works of Wyclif.[58] He had heard, he said, that Wyclif had been attacking the Benedictine order. He requested Wyclif's *dicta* and *De potestate regali* in several chapters. Wyclif later complained that he had been reported to the curia:

A certain black dog . . . savaged the writings of others and especially in that his scribe wrote, lying, as another previous doctor had, that he (Wyclif) had said that all law is God and with this, elsewhere, that every creature has its own law . . . correspondingly the said Tolstanus or his whelps are said to have told tales to the Roman curia.[59]

Wyclif was clear that the copyist of the black dog was mistaken. It has often been assumed that the black dog was a black monk in England but it would fit well if he were Easton (*Estonus* miscopied *Tolstanus*) in the curia, relying on students in Oxford to copy snippets of Wyclif's lectures.[60] Easton was thus informed of Wyclif's ideas but first became alerted to Wyclif as an opponent of monks. The tone of the letter to Westminster suggests that he did not know Wyclif personally; 'a certain

---

[54] ASV, Reg. Av. 200 ff. 106v–107; WAM, 9256B.
[55] Wilkins, *Concilia*, III, p. 164 at Blackfriars' council.
[56] See below p. 196.   [57] V, 4116, f. 181.
[58] Pantin, *Chapters*, III, no. 229, pp. 76–7.
[59] See M. Harvey, 'Adam Easton and the condemnation of John Wyclif, 1377', *EHR*, 113 (1998), pp. 321–34; J. Wyclif, *Sermones*, ed. J. Loserth, 4 vols. (= Wycliffe Society), London, 1886–90, III *Super Epistolas*, pp. 188, 189.
[60] K. B. McFarlane, *John Wyclif and the Beginnings of English Nonconformity*, Aylesbury 1952, p. 79, identified *Tolstanus* with Easton. Professor Anne Hudson checked MSS for me and found that all use *Tolstanus*.

master John Wyclif' is not a reference even to a close acquaintance. Referring to the genesis of *Defensorium*, Easton wrote:

there came to the ears of the pope news about new material on a certain matter previously dealt with by the determination of a certain well-known doctor. The material as reported touched not only a great part of the spiritual rights of the church but also temporal rights . . . I, present in the curia, and called to decide the matter, inflamed with zeal for the worship of God and the honour of the apostolic see . . .[61]

wrote this work. In other words he must have been involved in the curial investigation preceding Gregory XI's bulls condemning Wyclif issued on 22 May 1377.[62]

Gregory had come back to Rome with some of the curia in January and went to Anagni in late May. On 7 November he returned to Rome where he died on 27 March 1378. Easton witnessed the events during the controversial conclave which elected Urban VI. In evidence he talked of a house in Anagni which he had caused to be repaired, presumably when Gregory first went there.[63]

The two sets of evidence by Easton shed much light on the curial circles in which he moved. The first statement was collected on 9 March 1379. Easton's was one of five testimonies taken for the ambassador of the king of Aragon by Bishop Alfonso of Pecha, in the curia trying to achieve the canonisation of Bridget of Sweden. Bridget had died in 1373 and a group of enthusiasts in the city after her death promoted her cause, led by Alfonso who moved into her entourage in 1368 and was also the main editor of her *Revelations*. Bridget's daughter Katherine and Adam Easton were the other chief enthusiasts. Alfonso, like Easton, was a supporter of Urban VI and produced an early defence of him. When the king of Aragon sent a representative to Rome in March 1379 to investigate Urban's election, Alfonso collected evidence, the first three testimonies being his own, Katherine's and Easton's.[64]

Easton gave evidence again in November 1379.[65] In this he talked about discussions before the conclave and evidently was largely talking to *familiares* of cardinals. He considered himself on particularly easy terms with Aigrefeuille, coming to the cardinal's house for a talk after a

---

[61] V, 4116, f. 2 r/v: *nova contencio perstrepebat in auribus domini nostri pape de novellis opinionibus materie prius tacte per cuiusdam doctoris notabilis determinacionem, que materia sicuti reportatur non solum ecclesie spiritualium sed eciam temporalium interimere magnam partem.*

[62] Walsingham, *Chronicon angliae*, pp. 173–81, with the list of condemned propositions pp. 181–3. See also Harvey, 'Wyclif', Appendix.

[63] MacFarlane, 'An English account', p. 85.

[64] Ibid., p. 79; E. Colledge, '*Epistola solitarii ad reges*: Alphonso of Pecha as organiser of Birgittine and Urbanese propaganda', *Medieval Studies*, 18 (1956), pp. 19–49, esp pp. 22, 36.

[65] MacFarlane, 'An English account', pp. 81–5.

meal, 'as I was often wont to do on other occasions',[66] and even once spending a night so the cardinal could next morning present him to the new pope to make his reverence and commend him. Presumably, if Easton was speaking the truth, the relationship existed because Aigrefeuille was one of Langham's executors. Aigrefeuille acknowledged the familiarity in 1386:

he replied that he knew the said master Adam well and he was quite familiar with him.

but did not recall presenting him to the new pope; if he had done so it was at Adam's own request. He had certainly not invited Easton to his house for the night which was not his practice.[67]

Presumably because of Aigrefeuille Easton also knew Roger Foucault, dean of St Emilion, the cardinal's companion in the conclave,[68] later sent by the dissident cardinals to spread anti-Urban propaganda in England. Foucault later gave testimony very hostile to Urban and to English support for his cause.[69] Easton spoke English to the Gascon Foucault and represented him in 1378 supporting Urban and asking Easton to further his candidacy for the church of Bordeaux.

Likewise through Langham Easton knew, though evidently less well, cardinal Corsini (*Florentinus*).[70] He knew the new pope Bartolomeo Prignano also, so Aigrefeuille thought his chances of favour excellent.[71] He also remained in contact by letter with Petrus de Monteruc, cardinal of Pamplona, the main cardinal executor of Langham's will, still in Avignon.[72] In addition he talked of eating with cardinals Petrus de Luna and Jacobus Orsini.[73]

The impression is of a man living the normal life of the curia. He may have been a monk but there is no evidence that he lived in a monastery. He was coming and going to meals with cardinals and was present at the papal enthronement and coronation as well as attending a mass when the cardinals were present. He claimed to have seen some diplomatic documents and to have been regarded by fellow *curiales* as having knowledge of, as well perhaps as influence in, England.

Urban VI's controversial election was on 8 April 1378. Easton's evidence was that of an observer, not close enough to any cardinal to have been a *socius*. All his information about voting decisions came

---

[66] Ibid., p. 83: *sicut sepe alias consuevi.*
[67] ASV, Arm 54/16, f. 133; Gayet, *Le grand schisme*, II, p. 71, 72.
[68] ASV, Reg. Supp. 47, f. 130v.   [69] Harvey, *Solutions*, pp. 22–4.
[70] MacFarlane, 'An English account', p. 85: *offerens se pro me multa facere penes dominum nostrum papam ob reverenciam domini mei mortui cardinalis.*
[71] MacFarlane, 'An English account', p. 83.
[72] Ibid., p. 83: *statim scripsi ad dominum Pamplonensem.*   [73] Ibid., p. 84.

second hand. But he was obviously hoping to obtain something from the new pope and it was normal to present a gift for the pope's accession. This may have been the moment when Easton presented his *Defensorium* to Urban. Its preface stated that it was presented to the pope; there was no hint of any schism yet, so we may assume presentation before 20 September 1378 when Clement VII was elected as Urban's rival. The work had been a very long time gestating; Easton talks of twenty years' consideration of the Book of Kings,[74] so to use a new papal reign to present a powerful defence of a very high doctrine of the papacy made perfect sense.[75]

Easton's loyalty was eventually rewarded. On 21 December 1381 Urban created him cardinal,[76] somewhat unexpected but readily understood given the depleted state of the college. He was however obviously not Urban VI's first English choice. In the first promotion, of September 1378, when twenty-five cardinals replaced the deserters, he named the bishop of London, William Courtenay.[77] The latter was a much more likely candidate: a high-born political prelate with a well-known reputation for both orthodoxy and toughness.[78] He, however, turned it down, ostensibly because the Londoners did not want to lose him, but probably because during a minority and a schism he did not want to leave England.[79]

Easton thus owed his rise to Langham first and then to schism. There is little evidence that he was ever an influential political figure in the curia or in England. He did not figure prominently in the calculations of English politicians dealing with the curia. His activity as a cardinal under Urban left little trace in Rome, though material for Urban VI's reign is notoriously sparse there in any case, nor in England, where one might expect more. He exchanged money in 1382, but after that his finances remain unclear.[80] He acted as a sort of special protector for the English Benedictines. In April 1383 he obtained a papal bull empowering their presidents to enforce the reforming constitutions of Benedict XII but we know about this only because it was stolen.[81] He also won the good opinion of the chronicler of Bury S Edmund's because he intervened in favour of a free election for the abbey; probably acting as a mediator in the quarrel involving Edmund Bramfield.[82]

---

[74] See p. 192.   [75] See p. 213.   [76] Eubel, *Hierarchia*, I, p. 24.
[77] Ibid., p. 24.
[78] For the man *BRUO*, I, pp. 502–4; J. H. Dahmus, *William Courtenay, Archbishop of Canterbury, 1386–1396*, University Park, Pa and London 1966, pp. 39, 72, 188–9; Eubel, *Hierarchia*, I, p. 24 for the cardinalate.
[79] *Calendar of Letter Books. Letter Book H*, pp. 116–17; Walsingham, *Historia anglicana*, I, p. 382.
[80] *CCR 1392–6*, p. 521.   [81] Pantin, *Chapters*, III, no. 233.
[82] Arnold, *Memorials of S Edmund's Bury*, III, p. 135.

Easton must have been a member of the consistory which condemned Nicholas Hereford, the supporter of Wyclif who had appealed to the pope against Courtenay in June 1382 and fled to the curia in July.[83] The only account of this, in Knighton's Chronicle, reads as if based upon a document. Hereford presented his conclusions before a consistory; they were condemned as heretical and he was imprisoned, but was released by rioters while Urban was in Nocera, returning to England in 1385. Courtenay imprisoned him again in 1387. Knighton wrote that several magnates (*plures magnates*) petitioned Urban for his release in Rome but it is unclear who these would be. There was no mention of Easton but he must have taken part in the consistory and would of course be among those best qualified.

The only other activity of Easton's which has left a little trace in the records concerned the canonisation of Bridget of Sweden. Bridget died in Rome in July 1373. Before Gregory died (March 1378) her *Revelations* had been presented to the pope and an examination by theologians instituted. By 15 January 1378 the process was progressing very well; twice the canonisation had been requested in consistory.[84] According to the *Acta and Processus*, (the official account of the evidence given by witnesses), the third request was made in the church of S Maria in Trastevere by William, bishop of Achonry (*Acatensis*) master of the sacred palace,[85] that is William Andrew.[86] The date must be after Gregory's death, since Andrew was appointed to replace someone who had joined Clement VII and may not have become master until his predecessor definitively deserted on 15 July 1378. He was certainly master by 14 November 1379 and by November 1380 was in England.[87] Gregory's death meant that Bridget's process had to recommence. The *Revelations* were presented again to Urban VI and according to Juan de Torquemada (much later), the pope committed their examination to Cardinal Orsini, the cardinal of England (Easton), John of Legnano and Alfonso de Pecha.[88] It is uncertain whether these were successively commissioned. Easton could not have been called the

---

[83] Catto, *History of Oxford*, II, p. 214–17, 225; *Knighton's Chronicle 1337–1396*, ed. G. H. Martin, Oxford 1995, pp. 280–2.

[84] S. Ekwall, *Vår äldsta Birgittavita och dennas viktigastes varianter* (= Kungl. Vitterhets Historie-och Antikvitetsakademien, Historika series 12), Lund 1965, pp. 126–7, 128–9 for two letters about these propositions, though p. 128 suggests another speaker.

[85] Collijn, *Acta et processus* p. 4: *Guilelmus Acatensis*. For his predecessor Nicolas de S Saturnino, OP, see Eubel, *Hierarchia*, I, p. 26 and Seidlmayer, *Die Anfänge*, p. 303.

[86] *BRUO*, I, p. 36.

[87] He gave evidence on Urban's election, Harvey, *Solutions*, pp. 17–18; he was in England in November 1380, see *CPR 1377–81*, p. 553.

[88] C.-G. Undhagen, 'Une source du prologue (chap. 1) aux *Revelationes* de Sainte Brigitte par le Cardinal Turrecremata', *Eranos* 58 (1960), pp. 214–26, esp. p. 233; see helpful chronology in

cardinal of England before 1381, but he might have been involved from 1378 as a skilled theologian. As we have seen, he was already working with Orsini, who died in 1379.[89] John of Legnano died in 1383.

The engagement of Andrew and Easton is very significant for the spread of Bridget's cult in England. Furthermore Bridget's daughter Katherine in 1377 considered the cardinal of Poitiers and cardinal Aigrefeuille as special supporters. Aigrefeuille's relations with Easton have been examined and Andrew mentioned discussing the election of Urban with him too.[90]

According to the *Defensorium* Easton intended to continue scholarly work, promising a refutation of Ockham,[91] but if this ever existed it is now lost. Urban's curia cannot have been conducive to quiet study but we know little about Easton's role. He must have fitted uneasily among much more political fellow-cardinals and when he did become more visible it was as a spectator rather than an activist.

He was never wealthy, though he defended the possession of wealth by clerics.[92] When he was appointed cardinal priest there was already a holder of the 'title' church of S Cecilia but by March 1382 he was referred to by that title, so he must by then have been holding the church.[93] At appointment Easton held Somersham, inherited from Langham, upon whose fruits he must have lived until promoted.[94] In 1381 most probably Urban also provided him to the archdeaconry of Shetland; theoretically he was holding this at the time of his deprivation in 1385.[95] In fact he had a rival in Walter de Buchan and never enjoyed any revenue. Then on 4 March 1382 he had provision to the deanery of York, replacing Anglic Grimaud, a supporter of the anti-pope.[96] He was certainly holding this at the time of his deprivation. Finally he claimed the archdeaconry of Wells, probably by 'inheritance' from Langham,[97] but there is no evidence that he drew revenue. Thus Somersham and York gave him extra of income, coupled with any

A. Jonsson, *Alfonso of Jaen. His Life and Works, with critical editions of Epistola Solitarii, Informaciones amd Epistola Servi Christi* (= Studia Graeca et Latina Lundensia 1), Lund 1989, p. 108.

[89] Eubel, *Hierarchia*, I, p. 22   [90] See above p. 197 for Easton's acquaintance.

[91] V, 4116, f. 348.

[92] Quotations in M. Harvey, 'Adam Easton and pseudo-Dionysius', *Journal of Theological Studies*, new series 48 (1997), pp. 77–89, esp. p. 88.

[93] York, Borthwick Institute (Neville), Register 12, f. 12, when appointed dean; Eubel, *Hierarchia*, I, p. 23, with no date. Caraffa, *Monasticon Italiae*, I, p. 48, for the community attached to the church.

[94] See p. 194.

[95] D. E. R. Watt, *Fasti ecclesiae Scotticanae medii aevi ad annum 1638* (= Scottish Record Society, new series 1), Edinburgh 1969, pp. 261–2.

[96] Le Neve, *Northern*, p. 7.

[97] Perroy, *Diplomatic Correspondence*, no. 214B. Le Neve, *Bath and Wells* does not include him but there is a gap before 1385.

payments from his share of benefice taxes (services). He was not well placed for garnering lucrative benefices in England and certainly had no strong 'party' in the curia.

Urban's behaviour became increasingly erratic As has been seen, to enforce his demands on Charles of Durazzo he went to Naples and found himself under arrest. Though he came to an agreement with Charles, Urban rightly did not trust him and took refuge in Nocera in 1384.[98] At that point some cardinals decided that a way out of the impasse was to subject the pope (whom they perhaps thought insane) to rule by committee. In January 1385 Urban found out because cardinal Orsini, one of the plotters, was advised that he had better tell the pope before someone else did. On 11 January therefore when the cardinals arrived for the usual consistory, the pope had six arrested, including Easton. Urban was sure that Durazzo was privy to the intrigue but his excommunication led to the siege of the pope in Nocera, from where he was rescued by dissident Neapolitans in Genoese galleys on 5 July. Meanwhile, however, he tortured the plotters to extract confessions. Dietrich of Niem later recalled the horror (they were hauled up on pulleys) and Easton vowed to Bridget that if he survived he would promote her canonisation with all his might.[99] Even Urban admitted that the greatest extent of Easton's guilt was that he knew but did not reveal the plot.[100] Nonetheless the pope took him with the rest, in chains, when he left Nocera upon an appalling journey, vividly described by the German *curialis* Gobelinus Persona.[101] The curia did not reach Genoa until September. There was an abortive attempt to rescue the cardinals early in 1386[102] and when Urban finally left Genoa on 16 December only four plotters were still alive, one of them Easton. The others had been murdered.

Easton owed his life to his comparative innocence and to pressure from the English government and Benedictines. England was one of the most important allies of the Roman popes in the schism; Niem asserted that Easton was finally released 'at the supplication of Richard, king of England', explaining that by the time the curia reached Genoa (Sep-

---

[98] See p. 39.
[99] Niem, *De Scismate*, pp. 79, 83–5, 92–5; Persona, *Cosmidromius*, pp. 99, 120, 121–2, Oxford, Bodleian Library, MS Hamilton 7, f. 248, from Easton's letter to the nuns of Vadstena, printed by J. Hogg, 'Cardinal Easton's letter to the abbess and community of Vadstena', *Studies in S Birgitta and the Brigittine Order*, 2, *Analecta Cartusiana*, 19 (1993), pp. 20–6, with letter ed. from a Lincoln Cathedral MS, pp. 24–5.
[100] Persona, *Cosmidromius*, p. 100; confessions later published by H. Simonsfeld, 'Analekten zur Papst und Konzilien geschichte', *Abhandlungen der hist. Classe der königlichen Bayerischen Akademie der Wissenschaften*, 20/1 (1893), pp. 1–56, esp. pp. 41–5.
[101] Persona, *Cosmidromius*, pp. 110–16.   [102] Ibid., p. 120.

tember 1386), Easton was merely under house arrest, in the custody of a French camera clerk, but only as a poor monk, in other words no longer a cardinal. Royal letters show that he was without his benefices (although Boniface IX denied it), allowed merely to eat in Urban's hall without access to his friends or his order.[103] Several letters on his behalf have been preserved. The earliest, from the king, probably from 1385 and dated 3 December, explained that English people at the curia had told the king that Easton had been deprived, tortured and imprisoned, as he still was, though there was a strong suggestion that he was innocent. His hitherto blameless life, his University career, his fidelity to crown and pope were all recalled to support a pardon. The pope was assured that the cardinal had the backing of the king and magnates.[104] Oxford University, writing while Easton was still imprisoned, emphasised his learning and the compassion which the Holy See should exercise.[105] The General Chapter of the Benedictines wrote to the same effect about the same time.[106] When he was then released but not wholly rehabilitated, the king requested full reinstatement.[107] The Benedictines sent John Welles to the curia after July 1387 to work for this and the English presidents sent Easton a copy of their letter to the pope, asking if they could help in any other way. They would, they said, have written earlier had they thought their letters could reach him.[108]

The phrasing of this last suggests that probably by mid-July 1387 (if that is its date), Easton was at liberty, though not yet restored to his benefices nor to his cardinalate.[109] Further reason for believing this is his role in the recognition of the new feast of the Visitation of the Virgin. Promotion of this feast was a particular concern of John of Jenstein, archbishop of Prague, who in the summer of 1386 asked Urban VI to recognise it as a feast for the universal church. Consideration was not surprisingly delayed by the troubles in the curia but when Urban regained Rome late in 1388 serious study began.[110] Urban

---

[103] Niem, *De Scismate*, p. 103; Perroy, *Diplomatic Correspondence*, no. 96, referring to earlier letters, asking for release from prison.

[104] BL Add. MS 48179, ff. 8v–9r, with alternative version f. 9r/v.

[105] BL Add. MS 48179, ff. 9v–10, undated.

[106] BL Add. MS 48179, f. 10r/v; CCCC, MS 358, f. 92.

[107] Perroy, *Diplomatic Correspondence*, no. 96.

[108] J. Raine, ed., *Historical Papers and Letters from Northern Registers*, RS, 61 (1873), pp. 423–5 CCCC, 358, f. 92; BL Add. MS 48179, f. 10v.

[109] Fodale, *Ladislao*, p. 175, has lengthy quotations.

[110] For what follows I have relied on Polc, *De origine festi visitationis*. I have also used the manuscript referred to there, Wroclaw I F 177, ff. 120–3, 129v, 134r/v. See also Polc, 'La festa' passim.

commissioned six theologians for discussions,[111] including Easton and Edmund Bramfield, by then master of the sacred palace.[112] Their task was to consider the suitability of the feast and its proposed liturgy, composed by John of Jenstein in a rough style. They first debated before Urban himself and then their conclusions were given to other theologians and discussed by cardinals in a private consistory. Finally on 8 April 1389 Urban held a solemn consistory at which Bramfield preached, asking for the feast to be recognised.[113] Urban then announced agreement and also proclaimed the Jubilee Year for 1390. Thus by the end of Urban's reign Easton was sufficiently rehabilitated to function as a respected theologian. It seems, however, that he thought very seriously about returning to Norwich, hardly surprising under the circumstances. The Norwich account rolls have several items for 1389 suggesting that he shipped books home via Bruges, though there is no evidence that he followed them, even briefly.[114]

Easton was not restored to his cardinalate, however, until Boniface IX became pope on 9 November 1389. By 18 December Adam was again called cardinal priest of S Cecilia[115] and at once began to function as a full member of the college. Only about three weeks after Boniface's coronation the pope was referring English petitions to his judgement, though John Fraunceys said that Easton thought this was only when the pope wanted an excuse not to grant them.[116] In other words he had no political power either in the curia or in England.

He was, however, still respected as a theologian. John of Jenstein came to Rome for the Jubilee for a few weeks in March 1390 and whilst there urged Boniface to complete the arrangements for the Visitation, which as yet had neither a day nor a universally recognised office. Boniface commissioned four cardinals, including the cardinal of England, Easton.[117] They considered eight possible offices, including Jenstein's, one by the master of the Dominican Order and Easton's. The Bohemian historian of these events said that after debate for three hours they finally told Jenstein that in his liturgy some points were doubtful, some of his scansion was poor and that he had used some unknown words. This, the writer thought, stemmed from Easton, determined to

---

[111] Wroclaw, f. 123r/v, printed Polc, 'La Festa', pp. 163–4; extracts also Polc, *De Origine*, pp. 78–9, 110, 114, 120.
[112] *BRUO*, I, pp. 275–6; R. L. Storey, 'Papal provisions', pp. 82–8.
[113] Wroclaw, ff. 123–9 for speech.
[114] Norwich RO, DCN 2/1/17;1/2/23; 1/1/65, all for 1389/90; Greatrex, *Register*, for extracts.
[115] Souchon, *Papstwahlen*, II, p. 273.
[116] Chitty and Jacob, 'Some Winchester College muniments', pp. 5, 8: said Fraunceys *ut dicit idem quando papa non vult expedire aliquam supplicationem tunc signat informet se cardinalis Anglie*.
[117] R. W. Pfaff, *New Liturgical Feasts in Later Medieval England*, Oxford 1970, pp. 40–61.

promote his own work and blacken everyone else's. Easton's was in fact chosen and under the title *Accedunt Laudes* became the most popular Visitation liturgy, though never the only one.[118] One of his hymns presents the feast as an antidote to schism.[119] Professor Strohm thinks that he may also have written a famous motet *Alme Pater*, about Neapolitan ingratitude and the sufferings at Nocera, though in view of Urban's treatment of Easton this seems improbable, even as an exercise in flattery.[120] The same Bohemian historian credited Easton with a series of homilies on the Magnificat in honour of the feast,[121] and at least one of the miracles which Jenstein associated with it was attested by him.[122]

From December 1389 Easton also began to fulfil his vow to Bridget when under torture; the commission for her canonisation re-started. By 13 August 1380 all the hearings about her personal life had already finished, but the turbulent events of the schism prevented anything else.[123] Once restored to Rome Urban allowed the work to proceed and on 8 April 1389 announced his intention of canonising her.[124] But the pope then died (15 October 1389) so the process was not completed until the next reign. Finally Bridget was canonised on 7 October 1391.

An offshoot of the canonisation was Easton's *Defence* of Bridget, his second most substantial work. Easton sent it to Alfonso of Pecha and to the nuns of Vadstena.[125] The immediate context was the publication of a work hostile to Bridget, which can now only be re-constructed from Easton's reply, completed by 9 February 1390, the date of his covering letter.[126] This *Defence* was almost certainly produced after the death of Urban, since in the covering letter he is evidently dead and Bridget not yet canonised.[127] The occasion was to answer an attack on Bridget issued in Perugia by an unknown opponent who may have been a

---

[118] G. M. Dréves, *Analecta hymnica medii aevi*, 24, Leipzig 1896, pp 89–94; Dréves, 52, ed. C. Blume, Liepzig 1909, pp. 47–51, compares Easton with Jenstein.

[119] See p. 00.

[120] R. Strohm, *The Rise of European Music 1380–1500*, Cambridge 1993, pp. 17, 19 from the so-called Fountains Fragments in BL Add. MS 40011B (printed in full in P. M. Lefferts, *The Motet in England in the Fouteenth Century* (= Studies in Musicology 94) Ann Arbor 1986, pp. 348–9.). Strohm is wrong about Easton's degree of freedom at the time.

[121] Polc, *De origine*, p. 104.

[122] V. J. Koudelka, 'Raymond von Capua und Böhmen,', *AFP*, 30 (1960), pp. 206–26, esp. p. 218 note 38.

[123] Jonsson, *Alfonso*, p. 80.   [124] Ibid., p. 82.

[125] See letters prefacing the work in MS Hamilton 7, f. 248r/v.

[126] The date 9 February is given in the Uppsala MS C 819. 1390 is arrived at because Urban VI is dead and Alfonso is thought by Easton to be still alive, whereas he died in August 1389, which Easton may not yet have heard.

[127] See pp. 220–22. I quote always from Bodleian Library MS Hamilton 7 but have also looked at Uppsala C 819.

theologian trained in Paris, since at one point Easton says 'I send him back to Straw Street in Paris to learn to solve his own argument' (*remitto eum ad vicum straminum Parisius ut addiscat proprium solvere argumentum*).[128] That Perugia was the source is no coincidence. There were Fraticelli there in 1367/8 and Alfonso de Pecha had contacts. He lived with a group of Observant Franciscans in Perugia when he first left Jaen. Clearly there were arguments among the Minorites in Perugia about the status of reform; the connection of the hermit centres with Alfonso would have given ammunition to their enemies.[129]

The rest of this story is provided by the Vadstena *Diarium* and in an account by a Vadstena monk, Laurentius Romanus. Boniface IX agreed to canonise Bridget; the ceremony occurred on 7 October 1391.[130] On that morning all the bells in Rome rang, the great chapel in the papal palace was hung with draperies, strewn with sweet-smelling herbs and lit with innumerable candles. The pope preached about Bridget's life and virtues, accepting the findings of his commission. He offered generous indulgences to all present and to all who visited the church of S Lorenzo in Panisperna, where the new saint was buried. On a subsequent day the pope said a mass of the new saint in S Peter's, at which the three cardinal commissioners, including Easton as subdeacon, presented the offerings along with brothers from Vadstena.[131] The same day the cardinal of Ostia, Philip Alençon, leader of the commissioners, held a grand banquet in his house and the cardinal commissioners showed the relics of S Bridget in S Lorenzo's church.[132] The banquet caused Laurentius the monk from Vadstena great wonder, especially when a pie set before Adam Easton, the senior cardinal present, opened and birds flew out(!)[133] Next day each cardinal received a relic of the new saint and one was sent to Richard II.[134]

Easton was thus fully restored as a leading theologian by 1390. He was, however, by no means restored to his benefices. The English considered him deprived of all benefices from January 1385. He lost S Cecilia. In April 1389 his was one of the cardinals' titles regarded as

---

[128] Hamilton 7, f. 235.

[129] M. Sensi, 'Alfonso Pecha e l'eremitismo Italiano di fine secolo XIV', *Rivista di storia della chiesa in Italia*, 47 (1993), pp. 51–80.

[130] *Diarium Vadstenense. The Memorial Book of Vadstena Abbey*, ed. G. Gejrot (= Studia Latina Stockholmiensia 33), Stockholm 1988, nos. 58 (pp. 124–5), 59, 60, 61 (p. 126); Laurentius Romanus, *Lars Romares berattelse om dem heiligar Birgittas kanonisering*, ed. K. Karllson, Stockholm 1901.

[131] *Diarium*, nos. 62, 63; Laurentius Romanus, p. 10.   [132] *Diarium*, no. 64.

[133] Laurentius Romanus, p. 12.

[134] Ibid.; F. R. Johnston, 'The English cult of S Bridget of Sweden', *Analecta Bollandiana*, 103 (1985), pp. 75–93, esp. pp. 75–80 but with no mention of this.

vacant.[135] When in 1385/6 Richard II wrote to the pope he called Adam 'the cardinal of Norwich' whereas writing to Boniface IX he gave him the title S Cecilia.[136] Pope Boniface tried to persuade the royal council that he had not truly been deprived, but only with partial success.[137] The problem was that those now holding the benefices were very influential and not to be disturbed without considerable problems for the king, raising the question of the pope's right to provide. Richard II (or those advising him, some holding the offending benefices) considered that the king had done quite enough for Easton in supporting his release. Attempts to oust current holders were rank ingratitude. From Easton's and the pope's, view-point of course the income was vital; Boniface IX was notoriously short of cash and could probably do little to help Easton otherwise. The cardinal's attempts to recover his losses show how weak he was in England.

Somersham had fallen into the hands of someone who had exchanged it with John Boore, dean (chief chaplain) of the king's household chapel.[138] The deanery of York had gone to Edmund Stafford, keeper of the privy seal, elected to the position on 10 July 1385.[139] The archdeaconry of Wells went first to Andrew Baret, a papal auditor, but from 1391, when the pope began to support Easton's attempts to recover it and it probably became too difficult for a *curialis* to retain, the king gave it to Nicholas Slake, a household clerk, which Richard regarded as recovering his right.[140] Easton was litigating in the curia about these from 1391, backed by a papal declaration that Urban had not deprived him of them,[141] despite increasingly acrimonious letters from Richard, prompted no doubt by Easton's English rivals, reminding him that his actions were against English law and the royal rights, to persuade him that he would do better to make friends of his English opponents.

Before 5 August 1396 Easton had resigned his (never very realistic) claim to Shetland.[142] Almost certainly he retained Somersham, despite a royal letter reminding him of his allegiance to the king and the rights of the crown.[143] Edmund Stafford, however, retained the deanery of York and Slake the archdeaconry of Wells.[144] Several English suppliants of

---

135 ASV, Arm. 29/1, ff. 83v–84.
136 Perroy, *Diplomatic Correspondence*, no. 96, pp. 63–4.   137 *CPL*, IV, p. 279.
138 Perroy, *Diplomatic Correspondence*, no. 213.
139 Ibid., nos. 211, 212; Le Neve, *Northern*, p. 7.
140 Le Neve, *Bath and Wells*, pp. 13–14; Perroy, *Diplomatic Correspondence*, no. 214B; Given-Wilson, *The Royal Household*, pp. 175–6.
141 *CPL*, IV, p. 279.   142 Watt, *Fasti*, p. 262.
143 Perroy, *Diplomatic Correspondence*. no. 214; *CPR*, 1396–9, p. 262.
144 Le Neve, as above notes 139, 140.

the papacy suggested the employment of Easton, known to want his benefices back, to obtain favours in Rome.[145] Easton maintained a bitter correspondence with Stafford and temporarily had Ralph Ergham, bishop of Bath, placed under ecclesiastical censure, though the king pointed out to the pope that Ergham and Easton had been contemporaries in Oxford.[146]

Stafford's correspondence with Easton is illuminating. Stafford was elected dean of York in July 1385 and the king ratified his estate in April 1392, signalling that Easton's counter-claim was not to be allowed. Stafford wrote both to the pope and Easton in November 1392, sending the letters with the returning papal nuncio Damian de Cataneis, who had been negotiating about the anti-papal legislation of 1390.[147] To the pope Stafford pointed out that the king wanted his promotion, presumably to a bishopric.[148] Rather cynically he enlisted Easton's help in this, on the understanding no doubt that promotion would leave his benefices vacant. Evidently Easton had insisted that Stafford should try to influence Slake to come to an agreement about Wells. Slake informed Stafford that the king intended to write to Easton in a manner which ought to content the cardinal. If he was not content, Stafford promised to do what he could.[149] This cannot have been much comfort, especially as Boniface IX was taking a very hard line with the king and in 1393 parliament toughened the benefice legislation with the statute of *praemunire*.[150] Easton reacted badly; the next letter to him from Stafford was in April 1395 when Stafford had finally obtained the bishopric of Exeter and could sign himself 'bishop elect'.[151] The messenger who brought the news had told Stafford that Easton had laboured on his behalf with the pope for the bishopric. Stafford acknowledged that bitter words had passed between them but thanked Easton very warmly for his efforts. Nothing of substance was said about Easton's own concerns, however, because, said Stafford, the archbishop of Canterbury's own clerk, John Montagu, was working in the curia and an answer was expected any day. In other words, nothing happened. Roger Walden, a chapel clerk, later king's secretary and from 1396 treasurer, an intimate of Richard's, soon appeared as dean of York.[152]

[145] Bodley 859, ff. 18v–19, from Stone to the king suggesting he pressure Easton to pressure Baret.

[146] Perroy, *Diplomatic Correspondence*. p. 248, notes to numbers 214A–B; Bodley 859, ff. 24v–25: *nuper in scolis eiusdem cardinalis consortem.*

[147] Perroy, *L'Angleterre*, pp. 323–4, 331 for the occasion; Edinburgh, MS Laing 351A, f. 143, to pope, 29 November, f. 153v to Easton, 1 November.

[148] Perroy, *Diplomatic Correspondence*, no. 164 for letter from the king.

[149] Laing 351A, f. 153v: *facio quod incumbit.*   [150] Perroy, *L'Angleterre*, pp. 331–6.

[151] Laing 351A, f. 45v; Perroy, *Diplomatic Correspondence*, notes to 215, p. 249.

[152] Le Neve, *Northern*, p. 7; Given-Wilson, *Royal Household*, pp. 179–80.

It proved more profitable for Easton to hunt for new benefices. In December 1389 from the new pope he had provision at the latter's direct command (*motu proprio*) to the provostship of Beverley Minster, but there seems no doubt that he could not make this good. His rival, Robert Manfield, had a royal grant and eventually held the benefice.[153] In April 1392 Easton was admitted, with a papal endorsement of the exchange, as rector of Hitcham in Suffolk, in return for which he surrendered the prebend of Yetminster Secunda in Salisbury cathedral to John of Ilkilington.[154] It is unclear when he had acquired Yetminster; there is a predecessor with a royal grant in 1388. Boniface IX also gave him Bishop Wearmouth rectory, Durham, another former Langham benefice, but he failed to obtain possession. Despite confirmation (probably in 1393) he was still litigating at his death.[155] In November 1390 he had provision of a canonry with expectation of a prebend in Lisbon, and also the prebend of Aylesbury in Lincoln cathedral.[156] He never obtained the Lincoln prebend.[157] In the same month he was given reservation of the Basilian priory of S George de Trocolo in Sicily but renounced it again in August 1391, 'doubting the validity of the provision'.[158] On 19 November 1393 he was given *motu proprio* provision of the church of S John de Rabhia, Lamego, in Portugal with a canonry and prebend in the secular collegiate church of S Martin de Cedosecca, Porto.[159] These were vacant because the previous holder was a Cistercian with no right to hold a benefice. Easton had rivals for these benefices, however, and may not have held them.[160] On 7 October 1394 he received *motu proprio* provision of a canonry of S Severin, Cologne, with the church of Hasselt in the diocese of Liège, vacant because his recently dead *familiaris* Theodoric Bukelden had held them.[161] In April 1396 he exchanged Hasselt for S Alban's, Cologne.[162] Finally in September 1396 he had provision of the priory of S Agnes, Ferrara, a Benedictine house.[163] It is impossible to be sure whether he

---

153 *CPL*, IV, pp. 343, 459–61; Leach, ed. *Memorials of Beverley Minster*, II, pp. lxxxi–iii; McDermid, *Beverley Minster Fasti*, p. 10, note 30.
154 Le Neve, *Salisbury*, p. 102; *CPL*, V, p. 80; *CPR*, 1396–9, p. 80; Ratification of exchange, Despenser Register, Norwich Record office, DN Reg/3/6, f. 163v.
155 *CPL*, IV, p. 468.   156 *CPL*, IV, p. 335.   157 Le Neve, *Lincoln*, p. 25.
158 S. Fodale, ed., *Documenti del pontificato di Bonifacio IX (1389–1404)* (= Fonti per la storia di Sicilia, 5) Palermo 1983, nos. lvii,lviii, lix, cxxxviii.
159 ASV Suppliche, 104A, ff. 77v–8; printed in A. de Sousa Costa, ed., *Monumenta Portugaliae Vaticana: Supplicas dos pontificados dos papas de Avinhao Clemente VII e Bento XIII e do papa de Roma Bonifacio IX*, II, Braga 1970, p. 391, no. 14 and note.
160 ASV, Reg. Suppliche 104A, f. 150.   161 ASV, Reg. Suppliche 104A, f. 174v.
162 *CPL*, IV, p. 536; for the other party Godfrey Bothorn or Bochorn see *RG*, II, cols. 104, 347, 356.
163 *CPL*, IV, pp. 536–7.

in fact held any non-English benefices. At his death in September 1397 he was still attempting to make good a provision to the archdeaconry of Dorset in Salisbury Cathedral which he had claimed since at least 1396 and was disputing with Michael Cergeaux, chancellor of Canterbury.[164]

As a cardinal Easton must always have had a household but we know nothing of it until he was restored under Boniface IX. In September 1394 he obtained the papal privilege that members of his household could be non-resident in their benefices.[165] In the absence of a will, however, it is not easy to add to the information from the papal letters, such as it is.

At the end of his life Easton's *camerarius*, in charge of the whole household, even keeping a list of his benefices, was Roger White, priest of York diocese, who said in 1400 that he had also been Easton's confessor.[166] Ieuan Trefor, noted above as a Rota auditor, was also auditor of Easton, that is his chief legal adviser.[167] Very likely he was taken under Easton's wing when he first arrived in 1390.[168]

The other Englishmen attached to Easton's household were *familiares*, so that their exact role, even whether they were living in the household, is sometimes uncertain. Richard Benet, priest of Norwich diocese, litigating in December 1391 for the position of perpetual vicar of Walpole, was supported by Easton who said he was *familiaris suus domesticus commensalis* meaning certainly resident in the cardinal's house but nothing more.[169] John Skendelby, in 1394 litigating about the vicarage of Mitford, Northumberland, died at the apostolic see by 5 January 1394. He had won his suit but Easton, whose *familiaris* he was (*familiaris* only, not more), advised him not to persist, and he did not demand execution of the sentence.[170] John Ingelwood who succeeded to Skendelby's claims, was also called *familiaris* by Easton. The only other English household member was Richard Possewich, son of Richard the Irish *cursor* who had come with his family from Avignon in 1379. In July 1392 Richard Possewich, junior, of Avignon, at the petition of Easton, described as *familiaris continuus commensalis* (thus certainly living with the cardinal), was granted provision of the canonry of Saggart in Dublin, void by the death of Hugh Arlam at the curia in

---

[164] Le Neve, *Salisbury*, p. 8; *CPL*, V, pp. 205–6.

[165] ASV, Reg. Suppliche. 104A, f. 77v.

[166] ASV, Reg. Lat. 82, ff. 114v–5: *ut asseris confessor et camerarius*; *CPL*, V, pp. 338–9.

[167] ASV, Reg. Lat. 32, ff. 160–2: *qui capellanus noster et causarum palacii apostolici ac delecti filii Ade tit. S. Cecilie cardinalis auditor et familiaris erat.*

[168] Perroy, *Diplomatic Correspondence*, nos. 110, 127; and see pp. 136–7.

[169] ASV, Reg. Lat. 25, ff. 150–1.

[170] ASV, Reg. Lat. 31, f. 221: *et eius inherendo obsequiis eisdem sentenciis execucione non demandatis.* *CPL*, IV, p. 472.

the lifetime of Gregory XI and never filled by Urban VI.[171] This was Hugh Arlam who had lived in the housing complex or *livrée* of Simon Langham in Avignon and therefore was well known to Easton.[172] On 25 October 1394 the same young man, still described by Easton as a continual familiar, was given reservation of a canonry and prebend of S David's and Llandewi-Brefi, vacant because Trefor had now been promoted to S Asaph.[173] Possewich probably made this good.[174] Finally in July 1397 Easton resigned in his favour the rectory of Hitcham. The young familiar was said to be in his twenty-first year (thus he must have been sixteen when he first entered the household), and this document dispensed him to hold a benefice under age, holding a canonry of S Georgio in Velabro in Rome, with a definitive sentence in his favour for Saggart, in addition to the Welsh provision, and provision in the church of S Servatius, Liège, which he would resign if he obtained Hitcham.[175] In April 1399 his estate was ratified as parson of Hitcham and he was pardoned in England for having obtained it by papal provision without royal licence.[176]

The others called *familiares* of Easton were not English. His *cubicularius*, in charge of the daily needs of his household, in 1396 was John Gammen, appointed to the chapter of S Mary, Cologne.[177] Rupert of Hokelhem was called *familiaris continuus commensalis* in June 1397.[178] Merely *familiaris* were Hidebrand Lobeke clerk of Meeseberg in 1391,[179] Peter Rembold, dead by October 1396 and Johannes Iselhorst, dead by the same time, with Utrecht benefices.[180]

He supported others: in 1391 Thomas Walkyngton for provision of Sherburn, Durham, where the connection was probably via the Durham Benedictines, and William Chesterton, priest of Norwich, to hold in plurality, where the Norwich connection may explain his backing.[181] Another similar petition was in 1394 for William Gylcon, a priest of Dublin for an Irish archdeaconry, granted *motu proprio pro cardinali de Anglia* by Boniface IX.[182] Easton may also have patronised Henricus Dezier de Lattuna, probably cantor of the papal capella in 1378, and composer of Visitation music under Urban VI. He came to

---

[171] ASV, Reg. Lat. 13, ff. 46v–48; *CPL*, IV, pp. 381–2; Arlam was dead by 26 January 1378, D. Williman, The Right of Spoil of the Popes of Avignon, 1316–1415, *Transactions of the American Philosophical Society*, 78/6 (1988), p. 146.

[172] Harvey, 'Langham', p. 22.   [173] ASV, Reg. Lat. 32, ff. 160–2; *CPL*, V, p. 475.

[174] Le Neve, *Welsh*, p. 82.   [175] ASV, Reg. Lat. 49, ff. 165v–166; *CPL*, V, p. 80.

[176] *CPR 1396–9*, pp. 528, 536.   [177] ASV, Reg. Lat. 41, f. 4; *RG*, II, col. 630.

[178] ASV, Reg. Lat. 49, fols. 155–157; *RG*, II, col. 1030.

[179] ASV, Reg. Lat. 16, f. 259; *RG*, II, col. 527.

[180] ASV, Reg. Lat. 39, ff. 277–8; *RG*, II, cols. 630, 674.

[181] *CPL*, IV, pp. 379, 420.   [182] ASV Reg. Suppliche 104A, f. 29v.

Italy with the curia under cardinal Corsini and ended in the chapel of Boniface IX, but there is a gap in his career, or in our records, which service for Easton could have filled.[183]

Unlike Langham's, however, Easton's household never became a centre for the patronage of Englishmen at the curia. Among the interconnections of the English in the courts of Urban VI and Boniface IX it is remarkable how few had close connections with him. His importance depended much more upon intellectual achievements than upon political power. His household none the less shows how a group could alert one another to vacancies; the succession to Arlam's benefices for instance or Easton's care for Richard Possewych and also his own succession to his *familiares*. This group did not act as executors for each other. For Saggart in 1392 Possewich had Richard Young, canon of Lincoln, the auditor, who would be in the curia, with John Griffin, bishop of Leighlin and Richard Caron, canon of Dublin on the spot in Ireland. In 1394 for Llandewy-Brefi, he had Trefnant, bishop of Hereford, another former auditor, Richard Wych, canon of Salisbury,[184] and the bishop of Tuy, a resident in the curia.[185] Wych was again an executor for Possewyche in 1397 for Hitcham, with the prior of Norwich, doubtless well-known to Easton, and Pierre du Bosc, the Gascon bishop of Dax, the curial representative, and a friend of the English much used in forwarding correspondence; sent by the pope in 1398 to obtain more favourable conditions for provisors.[186]

Adam Easton died on 15 August 1398.[187] He was buried in Rome in his titular church of S Cecilia where his tomb, which still exists, has been subject to some controversy.[188] It has been moved to its modern position against a wall, whereas it used to be free standing. Experts consider it very fine; it is therefore galling that very little is known about its commissioning or date. In the absence of a will we do not know Easton's executors, but the style of the tomb is English rather than Italian. This could be the tomb which Ghiberti saw being carved in S Cecilia on his first trip to Rome, probably before 1416. A further puzzle is that Easton's books did not return to Norwich, to which we

---

[183] Information kindly supplied by John Nardas, K. Hanquet and U. Berlière eds., *Lettres de Clément VII 1378–9* (= *AVB* 12, *DRGS* 2), Rome 1930, no. 153, p. 47; Gastout, *Suppliques d'Urbain VI*, pp. 310–11, 231; Strohm, *European Music*, p. 19.

[184] *BRUO*, III, p. 2101.   [185] Eubel, *Hierarchia*, I, p. 501, note.

[186] Perroy, *L'Angleterre*, pp. 346–7, 419–20.   [187] Eubel, *Hierarchia*, I, p. 24

[188] For the details see J. Gardiner, *The Tomb and the Tiara. Curial Tomb Sculpture in Rome and Avignon in the Later Middle Ages*, Oxford 1992, pp. 130–2; R. Krautheimer, *Lorenzo Ghiberti*, Princeton 1970, p. 284; *Lorenzo Ghibertis Denkwürdigkeiten (I Commentarii)*, ed. J. von Schlosser, 2 vols., Berlin 1912, I, p. 62.

may suppose he left them, until 1407.[189] Possibly the delay was a combination of trouble in Rome and the collection of *spolia* by the papacy.[190] It certainly suggests that Norwich did not find it easy to recover what seems to have been a very large library.

[189] See p. 222.   [190] For books as *spolia* see Williman, *Bibliothèques ecclésiastiques*.

Chapter 11

ADAM EASTON'S IDEAS AND THEIR SOURCES

Adam Easton's reputation both in England and the curia depended on his theology. As a leading pro-papalist at the outbreak of the schism his ideas and their sources were important. The breadth of his reading, compared for instance with that of his contemporary from Oxford days, Nicholas Radcliffe, on some of the same subjects, is impressive, reflecting in part the greater availability of libraries in Rome and Avignon and a wider experience.[1]

His greatest work, *Defensorium ecclesiastice potestatis* (which for clarity I shall refer to as *De ecclesiastica potestate*), probably originated in debates in Oxford about the origins of dominion, followed by further exploration of the question in Avignon, finally quickened by the advent of Wyclif. Easton supplied expertise for the bull against Wyclif and this colours the last section of the book.[2]

The extremely long and very discursive work traces the development of dominion from its origins in the heavenly hierarchy, through its arrival on this earth, with a discussion of Adam before and after the Fall, then a history of human beings and their politics until the coming of Christ and finally dominion in the Christian era. The whole defends a very high doctrine of papal power; throughout priests had dominion over everyone else. Easton took his model from pseudo-Dionysius, thought by all fourteenth-century scholars to be Dionysius the Areopagite, converted by S Paul, 'the greatest doctor of the church after the apostles' as Easton put it.[3] The central theme therefore is power and illumination pouring out from God as the central Hierarch, mediated through a series of lesser Hierarchs in the angelic world, to the created world, with its corresponding hierarchies.

Rex, the lay representative, begins by defending kingship as prior to

---

[1] For Radcliffe see Catto and Evans, *The History of Oxford*, II, p. 184, 235, 228–30, 234–5.

[2] Above p. 195; M. Harvey, 'Easton and the condemnation of Wyclif', pp. 321–34.

[3] V, 4116, f. 33v; quoted Harvey, 'Easton and pseudo-Dionysius', pp. 77–89.

priesthood. Easton, whose views are represented by *Episcopus*, counters by proving that kingship is properly used only of rule over created things, so the kingdom given to Christ had a beginning in time, though no end.[4] He disassociated the word *rex* from the idea that kings coerce, or create. God first brought the world into being and then organised its government. God brings into being, keeps in existence and brings to completion, a very Dionysian view.[5]

Episcopus then tackled the nub: all *principatus* depends on its exemplar, the Trinity.[6] The angelic hierarchy had levels of rule, to guide those below to perfection and this hierarchical rule should be reflected at the next, earthly, level.[7] Kingship as we know it, with death penalties and suchlike, was the result of sin. If the state of innocence had lasted God would have given full dominion of the world to created man but in the state of lapse kings had only such dominion as they needed.[8] The divine exemplar radiated light to illuminate creation, bringing it to perfection.[9] Thus guidance, conservation and so on would have been needed even had creation not fallen, whereas punishment only became necessary because of the Fall.[10]

Episcopus insisted that God was always sacred, therefore *sacerdos* and priestly power was eternal but the kingdom of God implied rule over creation and therefore began with created things.[11] All power came from God, although evil rulers had power by God's permissive will only. True power from God implied having his grace but all rule in some sense had a sacred aspect.[12]

All offices should be based on the divine exemplar according to their position in the hierarchy; those with a higher end being higher offices.[13] A higher end could only be reached with God's grace; the end which God intended for mankind could only be grasped by revelation and offices were needed to minister this.[14] Kings could not make laws leading men to their eternal happiness.[15] Just as body was subordinate to spirit, so bodily or earthly offices were subordinate to spiritual.[16]

Episcopus condemned any notion of two equal powers as contrary to scripture and the order of the universe, quoting among others John of Salisbury's *Policraticus*,[17] insisting that priests presided over the whole of humanity, when *Rex* argued that they could not correct temporal faults.[18] *Rex* countered that priests who concentrated on spiritual ends

---

4 All quotations from *De ecclesiastica potestate* are from v, 4116, unless otherwise stated; f. 22r/v.
5 f. 26r.   6 f. 28r/v.   7 f. 29r/v.   8 f. 30v.   9 f. 34.   10 f. 35v.
11 f. 67.   12 f. 68r/v.   13 f. 70.   14 f. 71v.   15 f. 73v.   16 ff. 74–5v.
17 ff. 76v–7; John of Salisbury, *Policraticus*, ed. C. C. J. Webb, 2 vols., Oxford 1909, Book v, chapters 2, and 3.
18 f. 78v.

would be less diverted into corporal concerns,[19] but *Episcopus* insisted that everything ultimately pertained to the final end; there was only one end.[20] The first book ended by arguing that there should be one supreme earthly power, a priest who would not rule *politice*, because his institution involved more than human power:

such a vicar would be instituted by God to make all people show him the due, acceptable cult meriting eternal life (*talis enim vicarius a deo institueretur ad faciendum totum populum exibere sibi cultum debitum et acceptum et vite eterne meritorium.*)[21]

Part two placed *Summus sacerdos* in the angelic hierarchy.[22] His task was to purge men of ignorance, to illuminate and to perfect in morals. A very wide-ranging discussion, including debate about why angels fell,[23] established that there was a hierarchy with a *Summus sacerdos* among the angels.[24] The angelic and ecclesiastical hierarchies were compared,[25] with a section on the role of cardinals.[26] *Episcopus*, with a long description of national guardian angels, maintained that angels ruled the world.[27] Remaining strife and faction were explained by human free will.[28]

Episcopus argued that had the state of innocence lasted human hierarchy would have been based on angelic models.[29] 'Bible history' showed that with aid from angels Israel tried at first to base its rule on these, with kings as priests. Most other groups did not, although the presence of Melchisedech, priest and king, showed that some did.[30] Once the Law had been given everything was subordinate to the priesthood.[31] When kings were introduced, because of sin (*ratione peccati*), they were extorted from God by the wicked people.[32] Easton considered that priests in the Old Testament world had ultimate power and originally were also kings.[33]

Angels had no coercive power,[34] except such as God allowed them for the good of those ruled.[35] The levels of earthly hierarchy were discussed as reflecting this, with the pope at the head and lesser ranks, from cardinal downwards, below.[36] Kings and princes were at the lowest level.[37]

Part three re-asserted the need for priesthood in the state of innocence, since priesthood was any honour to God, offering of sacrifice or God-given power, to lead men to God.[38] Adam, Abel and Moses were thus priests. In the state of innocence there would have

---

[19] f. 89. [20] f. 91v. [21] f. 94v. [22] f. 95r/v. [23] f. 99v.
[24] ff. 99v–109. [25] ff. 109–10. [26] ff. 110v–12v. [27] ff. 113–14v. [28] f. 118r/v.
[29] f. 125. [30] ff. 126v–27v. [31] ff. 127v–28. [32] ff. 128v–29. [33] f. 131v.
[34] f. 132. [35] f. 133r/v. [36] ff. 134v–36v. [37] ff. 136v–37. [38] f. 137.

been inequality, since natural capacities vary.[39] Even without the Fall some humans had more capacity, so Adam had a more perfect soul and therefore the capacity to instruct, especially in holy things.[40] The need for illumination, purgation and perfecting existed just as in the angelic hierarchy. All the knowledge humans required for this world and the next was given to Adam.[41] Discussing Adam's knowledge, Easton envisaged a world with 'sacraments' and ceremonies, with music, songs and a hierarchy of sacred persons to lead all to God, with a supreme priest, lesser priests and laity.[42]

Rex then asked why positive laws are needed.[43] *Episcopus* considered law given so that humans knew the will of their lord. In the natural state, of innocence, laws, whether about grammar or worship of God, would have been passed to the young.[44] Writing would have been unnecessary because memory would have been perfect. Hebrew would have been the sole language. In a discussion about the best kind of rule: aristocracy, democracy etc.[45] *Episcopus* noted that even without the Fall kings would have been needed for counsel and as leaders, whereas afterwards they punished the delinquent;[46] subjection of man to man results from sin.[47]

Here *De civili dominio* of John Wyclif was introduced by *Rex*, to condemn the use of civil dominion by the church.[48] On appointment to office in the state of innocence,[49] *Episcopus* asserted that the power came from God, exercised with human prudence; he defended the need for rulers even then, because human arrangements would follow the heavenly model.[50] *Episcopus* however insisted that ecclesiastical office did not originate from prudent human choice but from God, who appointed the first chief priest. The notion that the *valentior pars* of humans should appoint priests, was heresy from *Defensor pacis*,[51] in contradiction to the heavenly model of hierarchy.[52] *Episcopus* considered election of rulers as always best.[53] Though in the state of innocence *rex* and *sacerdos* would be the same, *sacerdos* would delegate to suit local conditions. After Christ the pope ought to combine temporal and spiritual rule,[54] because Adam was priest, king and emperor and Christ, his heir, gave this inheritance to his vicar.[55]

When *Rex* protested that if this were true no king would have a true title to his office, *Episcopus* insisted that Adam passed his title to one person.[56] The Judges and Moses were in fact kings, although not ruling *civiliter*; the essence of human kingship was government and conserva-

---

[39] f. 138v.   [40] f. 140r/v   [41] f. 141v.   [42] ff. 141v–51v.   [43] f. 156.
[44] ff. 156v–57.   [45] ff. 157v–59v.   [46] f. 160.   [47] f. 162.   [48] f. 162v.
[49] f. 165.   [50] f. 165v.   [51] f. 167r/v.   [52] ff. 167v–68.   [53] ff. 168–70.
[54] f. 171v.   [55] f. 171r/v.   [56] f. 172r/v.

tion, not to be *dominus*. The oppression associated with *rex* was not God's original plan. Kings resulted from sin (I Sam. 8 vv. 8–9).[57] In the state of innocence, therefore, royal power was subsidiary to pastoral care; ideally the various rulers were subordinated to each other, depending on their final goal. Certainly there was no equality, though all men were equal in essence.[58]

In the state of innocence civil laws existed for information, goods were in common, as in a monastery where student theologians had books set aside for them from the common stock.[59] *Episcopus* warned *Rex* against the pestiferous ideas of clerics who urged kings to greed, in particular one such (Wyclif, the view is his), giving kings power over clerical wealth.[60] In the state of innocence some who were naturally servile would gladly have served others otherwise gifted.[61] A discussion followed concerning whether grace was needed for true dominion.[62] Episcopus thought it uncertain that Adam had dominion merely because he was in grace.[63] Ultimately Adam did not lose everything by sin and *gratia gratificans* was insufficient cause for dominion, contrary to the view of Fitzralph.[64] After the Fall God gave dominion both to sinners and just. Adam did not lose his dominion by his fall.[65] It was possible to have *conplacencia* after the Fall which then gave just temporal dominion.[66] *Episcopus* denied that *proprietas* existed before the Fall,[67] but also Wyclif's contention that there would have been no civil acts,[68] only civil acts which excluded others. As to superfluity,[69] some would have had more but there would have been no poor.[70]

The fourth book discussed the view (involving considerable repetition), that in the fallen state the earthly offices should as far as possible follow those of the state of innocence.[71] Borrowing from Hugh of St Victor,[72] Easton contended that even under the law of nature there were in effect sacraments[73] and a continuous line of high priests from the time of Adam which functioned by the passing on of the wisdom known before the Fall.[74] Therefore some men always remembered some of the truths known before the Fall.[75] Reason became more blinded as time passed, so God gave a law to show what was and was not sin, gradually teaching men what they needed.[76]

Not surprisingly, *Episcopus* considered that the *Summus sacerdos*

---

[57] ff. 173v–74v.   [58] f.176v.   [59] f. 179.
[60] f. 181; J.Wyclif, *De Civili Dominio*, ed. J. Loserth, 4 vols. (= Wyclif Society), London 1886–90, I, p. 186, which, f. 181v, is said by *Episcopus* to be *De Iure* by Wyclif.
[61] ff. 184v–85v.   [62] ff. 185v–87.   [63] f. 187v.   [64] ff. 192–93v.
[65] f. 194r/v.   [66] f. 196.   [67] f. 196v.   [68] f. 197r/v.   [69] f. 200v.
[70] f. 202.   [71] f. 205v.
[72] Hugh of S Victor, *De sacramentis*, PL, 176, cols. 173–613.   [73] f. 210.   [74] f. 211v.
[75] f. 212v.   [76] f. 213r/v.

appointed by God in the postlapsarian state had supreme jurisdiction both temporal and spiritual.[77] The *Summus sacerdos* illuminated by God passed to the rest the positive laws needed to ordain men to their end.[78] *Episcopus* considered that law must fit man's end, which was supernatural, and Aristotle was simply wrong to argue that the people make the law.[79] To think men are 'free' is to be blinded by sin.[80]

When *Rex* again denied that the priest could use coercion in temporal matters, *Episcopus* said he was falling into the errors of Marsilius and a certain modern master (Wyclif).[81] Only after the flood was temporal rule (thought of in very Dionysian terms as God ruling through mediators), truly legitimate.[82] It is evident that *Episcopus* considered that, in a sense, coercion always involved some injustice;[83] in the end the rule of anti-Christ would arrive, stronger than all except Christ.[84] The ideal temporal rule was *imperium protectivum ad nutum sacerdocii*.[85]

Considering Adam's *dominium* after the Fall, *Episcopus* concluded that, despite expulsion from Paradise and labour, he retained his previous *dominium*, though limited in its use.[86] *Episcopus* admitted that private property after the Fall was a very vexed question.[87] He quoted Fitzralph's *De pauperie salvatoris* and a new master (Wyclif), to show varying views about its origins and legitimacy.[88] He formally denied Wyclif's view that civil dominion was sin; it was introduced after the Fall to remedy corrupt nature.[89] *Proprietas* was allowed by Christ, though sharing in common was nearer perfection.[90] A discussion followed about use, proprietary right and *dominium*.

A *Summus sacerdos* with universal jurisdiction, even over gentiles, was necessary, though not all doctors agreed and the power of the Law was much disputed.[91] The rule of *Summus sacerdos*, choosing lesser officials for instance, showed that the priest had full power.[92] Wyclif's view that judges (or aristocracy) would be the best rulers was, said *Episcopus*, well expressed but should apply to the *Summus sacerdos*.[93] God originally gave power to the *Summus sacerdos* and never revoked it, though many doctors, including Alexander of S Elpidio and Augustine of Ancona

---

[77] ff. 214–15.   [78] f. 218.
[79] f. 218v, quoting Aristotle's *Politics*, book 6, chapter 2, book 3, chapter 7.   [80] f. 220v.
[81] ff. 222r/v, 224v, 230v; Marsilius of Padua, *Defensor pacis*, ed. C. W. Previté-Orton, Cambridge 1928, Distinctio. 2, chapters 8, 9, 30.
[82] f. 232r/v.   [83] ff. 240v–42.   [84] f. 242.   [85] f. 242v.   [86] ff. 244v–45.
[87] ff. 245v–46v.
[88] ff. 247–48v, see Harvey, 'Easton and the condemnation', passim, for Wyclif.
[89] f. 252r/v.   [90] ff. 254–55v.   [91] ff. 264–67   [92] ff. 268–71v.
[93] f. 272v, from *De civili dominio* I, pp. 192–3.

denied this about the Old Testament.[94] For *Episcopus* kings existed to act as intermediaries for the coercive power of priests. Royal power was not necessary but was a punishment, by divine permission, not divine will.[95]

Defensorium was a magisterial sweep over many subjects being debated in the Schools, and several of its diversions show Easton's own stance on questions only tangentially related to the main point. Concerning the origin of punishment, for instance, *Rex* raised free will, divine punishment and suffering. *Episcopus* explained Augustine's view that the mass of mankind was predestined to damnation and that some would be saved by God's mercy, but when *Rex* found this too harsh, *Episcopus* agreed, though explaining that the majority of doctors agreed with Augustine.[96] He added that pseudo-Dionysius did not, since he assumed that God was moving all humans to their supernatural end and that those who followed God's movement must receive his grace. All humans were assumed to have this instinct of the spirit. *Episcopus* did not think that all were predestined to damnation, nor that all would be saved.[97] It was possible to resist God's prompting.

Not surprisingly *Rex* then asked what difference baptism made. *Episcopus* insisted that after it only sin freely committed condemned one; before baptism was invented grace was still offered to all. *Rex*, however, was troubled that God might simply reject him, but *Episcopus* reiterated that everyone had the possibility of persevering in grace.[98] He agreed with Dionysius that God sent illumination to every creature; only a defect of the creature, by refusal, prevented illumination from producing its effect.[99] When *Rex* introduced examples where Augustine asserted that God damned some humans, Easton firmly replied:

Although Augustine spoke vary variously on this point in different works, I think that what you have said was his opinion (*Licet beatus Augustinus in isto puncto in diversis opusculis satis varie sit locutus, reputo quod predicta quam recitas opinio sua fuit*).[100]

and Easton disagreed, outlining a very optimistic view of the wide availability of salvation. He disagreed that only the predestined are saved,[101] and was unwilling to ascribe to God illness or natural disaster, attributing these to God's permissive will or sometimes to natural causes, though they could be educational. Eclipses or conjunctions of the planets could not cause men to act.[102] He discussed these before the Fall, suggesting, for instance, that thorns would have existed without

---

[94] f. 275r/v; for the authorities quoted here see below pp. 226–7.   [95] ff. 281v–83.
[96] ff. 38v–39v.   [97] f. 41v.   [98] f. 44v.   [99] ff. 45–7v.   [100] f. 51.
[101] f. 53r/v.   [102] ff.56–7v.

injuring, eclipses would then have been harmless; certainly even now the latter could not predict the final judgement, a supernatural event.[103]

Since the world was deteriorating steadily, *Rex* wondered how this could be if the first Hierarch was in fact in charge but *Episcopus* considered individual tribulation was God's correction and education.[104] Bishops, like the first Hierarch, were illuminators and purgers,[105] bridges between Christ and mankind. *Sacerdos* implied *sacer docens*.

Another important digression involved consideration of the earliest kingdoms, including discussion of the legitimacy of the kingdoms of infidels, where Innocent IV's view was debated, whereby land never occupied could be taken by Christians but not land already occupied.[106] The power of the pope over infidels and Jews was discussed, though *Episcopus* did not endorse all Innocent's views. He then discussed rule by conquest,[107] with consideration of the origins of several great empires and their justness or unjustness, using a mixture of scripture and Augustine as his main sources.[108]

The only other work of true importance which Easton wrote was the Defence (*Defensorium*) of Bridget.[109] We only know the complaints about Bridget from Easton's replies, which were given in forty-one articles. A critic had argued that Christ could not have dictated Bridget's Rule for nuns, as its prologue stated; thus Bridget's probity was questioned. The gross style was criticised and the critic thought that at least it should be corrected before the work was approved by the Holy See. He also considered that the rule and prayers contained doctrinal errors and doubted that a woman could receive true revelations. The Brigittine liturgy or *Lectiones*, which Bridget said were dictated by Angels, contained falsehoods; the writer criticised the way Bridget dealt with the messages she said she had received. There followed detailed doctrinal criticisms of individual readings and prayers, finding fault with Bridget's belief in the Immaculate Conception of the Virgin and her understanding of the Incarnation, of angels, of free will and in general accusing her of over-emphasising devotion to the Virgin.

Easton refuted these point by point. The adversary had evidently quoted verbatim from the *Regula salvatoris*,[110] *Sermo angelicus*,[111] and

---

[103] f. 58.   [104] ff. 60–2.   [105] f. 64.

[106] f. 233 and see in general J. Muldoon, *Popes, Lawyers and Infidels. The Church and the Non-Christian World, 1280–1550*, Liverpool 1979, esp. chapter 2, pp. 29–48.

[107] ff. 235v–37.   [108] f. 237–39.   [109] Above p. 204.

[110] Oxford, Bodleian Library, MS Hamilton 7, f. 229, from Bridget, *Opera minora*, I, *Regula salvatoris*, ed. S. Eklund (= Samlingar utgivna av Svenska Fornskrift-sällskapet, series 2, Latinska skrifter 8/1), Lund 1975, p. 102; f. 231v, p. 210.

[111] Hamilton 7, f. 234, *Opera minora*, II, ed. Eklund (= same series as note 110, 8/2) Upsala 1972,

Orationes,[112] and Easton repeated the extracts discussing them in detail. Perhaps the most interesting part for modern historians is the consideration of the role of women and their worthiness to receive special revelations. In his *De ecclesiastica potestate* Easton made statements rather scornful of women's intellects,[113] but although he was not much more flattering here, he believed that they had often received special revelations, giving examples like Matthew 28 (vv. 1–7) where the first message of the resurrection was given to women. Bridget was clearly of exemplary religious life; not surprisingly Christ spoke to her. Easton believed in Bridget as a prophet and that her prophesies had been fulfilled. In general, however, women had only a domestic role in the church; they were not permitted to teach publicly but could certainly speak.

In the common course of things women are not strong in wisdom . . . according to common law the man rules the woman and not vice versa . . . in common law woman is fragile, imprudent, subject and not authorised to teach publicly as a doctor in the church . . . but she can teach at home (*sapientia vero non viget in mulieribus de communi cursu . . . de iure communi vir regit mulierem et non econtra . . . de iure communi mulier est fragilis, imprudens, subjecta, et de iure communi inabilis ad docendum publice tamquam doctor in ecclesia . . . sed domestice posset docere*).[114]

The grossness of Bridget's style was defended by Easton; nuns were not sufficiently well-educated to understand anything very subtle! 'Nuns and women are weak in understanding and unskilled at grasping the subtleties of the law of God' (*moniales seu mulieres sunt imbecilles intellectu et rudes ad capiendum subtilia legis dei*).[115]

Evidently only men could be true theologians. Easton argued, however, that many women had had visions and had been prophetesses; he refused to limit Revelation to the scriptures alone, as his adversary apparently wished to do.[116] He also pointed out that S Pachomius'

---

pp. 75 and 75–6; f. 234v–235, p. 75; f. 235r/v, p. 77; f. 236, p. 81; f. 236v, p. 83; f. 237, p. 85; f. 237v–8, p. 87; f. 238v–9, pp. 89–91; f. 239–40, p. 91; f. 243r/v, p. 95; f. 243v, p. 128; f. 243v–244, p. 129; f. 244r/v, p. 122–4.

[112] Hamilton 7, ff. 245v–46, from *Opera minora*, III, *Quattuor orationes*, ed. S. Eklund, Stockholm 1991, p. 72, section 28; f. 246r/v, p. 73, section 31, ff. 246v–47, pp. 86–7, section 83; ff. 247v–48, p. 90 section 95.

[113] Quoted in Harvey, 'Easton and pseudo-Dionysius', p. 85.

[114] Hamilton 7, f. 232.   [115] Hamilton 7, f. 231.

[116] Hamilton 7, f. 233; see also R. Ellis, 'The visionary and the canon lawyers: papal and other revisions to the *Regula salvatoris* of St Bridget of Sweden,' in R. Voeden, ed., *Prophets Abroad. The Reception of Continental Holy Women in Late Medieval England*, Woodbridge 1996, pp. 71–90, esp. pp. 76, 78.

Rule was said to have been dictated by Christ; why not therefore Bridget's?[117]

Article 12 onwards contained detailed discussion of the texts and their presentation. Easton evidently knew a considerable amount about Bridget's account of how the various Revelations had been delivered, defending her scrupulous offering of them to her confessors.[118] He then discussed various uses of words about the Virgin, comparing, for instance, her description of the Virgin as having supreme excellence with that of pseudo-Dionysius in the *Celestial Hierarchy*.[119] In general he maintained that Bridget's words were in conformity with scripture.

The adversary had claimed that Bridget was promulgating predestination, particularly when discussing fallen angels, but Easton defended her strongly. He likewise strongly defended the orthodoxy of her belief in the Immaculate Conception of the Virgin, quoting in its favour miracles connected with the feast, determinations by Benedictines and the writings of master Peter Aureol, OFM, the first writer (1314–15) of a thoroughly scholastic text on the question.[120]

To have written as he did Easton must have had access to a large library. Some of it was his own. In 1389/90, when very probably he was thinking of returning to Norwich from his sufferings in Rome, the monastery paid for the shipping of his books, or some of them, from Flanders (via Bruges, one supposes).[121] But there is no evidence that he followed and in 1407 (ten years after his death) six barrels of his books came to Norwich from Rome, with a royal order allowing importation.[122] The barrels reached Norwich and carriage was paid.[123] They were then incorporated into Norwich library but only nine can now be identified by their distinctive red markings, as Dr Neil Ker showed many years ago.[124] Not all have a note saying that they were Easton's.

Those with a press mark and an inscription saying that Easton gave the book, are Cambridge, Corpus Christi College, 74, Berrengarius Bitterensis, *Inventarium iuris canonici*, a vast early fourteenth-century volume, which gives evidence of much use. It would have been a useful

---

[117] Hamilton, 7, f. 233v. [118] Hamilton 7, f. 234v, article 14.

[119] *Sermo angelicus*, p. 75; perhaps from Pseudo-Dionysius, *The Complete Works*, trans. C. Luibhead and P. Roem et al. (= Classics of Western Spirituality), Mahwah, NJ 1989, *CH*, chapter 4, 181A.

[120] Hamilton 7, ff. 239–40; H. Graef, *Mary. A History of Doctrine and Devotion*, 2 vols., London 1963–5, I, pp. 302–4.

[121] NRO DCN 2/1/17; 1/2/23; 1/1/65. [122] *CCR 1405–9*, p. 299.

[123] DCN 1/12/41.

[124] N. R. Ker, *Books, Collectors and Libraries. Studies in the Medieval Heritage*, ed. A. G. Watson, London 1985, pp. 243–72. This version is essential because it contains later material.

reference book for a non-expert, giving an index of canon law.[125] A second is Bodleian Library, Bodley 151, a fourteenth-century copy of William of S Amour's *Collectiones*, a trenchant defence of the power of bishops against the friars.[126] Thirdly there is Cambridge, Corpus Christi College, 180, a fourteenth-century copy of Richard Fitzralph's *De pauperie Salvatoris*, with an inscription of Easton's ownership at folio 88 and his name on the back inner cover.[127] This extremely important volume contained the last book, eight, which was evidently added.[128] This suggests that either Easton himself added it or, possibly, that the book was Langham's.[129] It has abundant signs of use. There is no evidence that Easton actually had the book made but the hand is English.[130] A further volume is Avignon, Bibliothèque de la Ville 996, Bernardus de Gordonio, *Lilium medicinale* a medical text-book, written between 1303 and 1305 by Bernard, who lectured on medicine in Montpellier.[131] Like several other Easton books it has been corrected, with additions in the margin where there were omissions.

There are also books with a Norwich pressmark, in sequence with the other Easton books and therefore probably his, identified by Dr Neil Ker. These include Balliol College, 300b, John of Salisbury's *Policraticus*, with corrections which may be in Easton's own hand, where the Norwich ascription can only be read by ultra-violet light;[132] Cambridge University Library, Ii. 1. 21, a twelfth-century volume of Origen *De vitiis Levitici, de ritu sacrificiorum* with plenty of evidence of use;[133] Gg. 6. 3., a composite volume of fourteenth-century astrological tables, some based on Oxford;[134] Ii. 3. 32, a mid twelfth-century copy of pseudo-Dionysius, *Hierarchia*, with an inscription at f. 126v in a French hand of the fourteenth or early fifteenth century. At f 58v is a hand definitely English. The inscription suggests that the manuscript belonged to Cardinal Androin de la Roche, who bought it in Paris. He died in 1369. It may have belonged thereafter to Langham and then Easton.[135] Another Norwich book is Cambridge University library Kk.

---

[125] Ker, *Books*, p. 260, no. 50; could it have been Langham's? See Sharpe, *Shorter Catalogues*, p. 623.

[126] Ker, *Books*, p. 261, no. 51; SC 1929.   [127] Ker, *Books*, p. 261, no. 52.

[128] f. 90, called *De Mendacitate* (see heading at f. 89v).

[129] See Walsh, *Richard Fitzralph*, pp. 472–3; Sharpe, *Shorter Catalogues*, p. 621.

[130] Pace Walsh, p. 472.

[131] Ker, *Books*, p. 271, note to p. 261, line 9.The inscription attributing it to Easton's gift to Norwich is f. 1; for the author, L. E. Demaitre, *Doctor Bernard de Gordon: Professor and Practitioner* (= Studies and Texts 51, Pontifical Institute of Medieval Studies), Toronto 1980, pp. 51–9, with MS at p. 186, but wrongly dated.

[132] Ker, *Books*, p. 264 no. 83a and note p. 272.   [133] Ibid., no. 81.   [134] Ibid., no. 82.

[135] Harvey, 'Easton and pseudo-Dionysius', pp. 79–80, for details; there is no reference to one in Langham's library.

2. 8. thirteenth-century glosses on the gospels of Matthew and Mark.[136] Norwich certainly owned Cambridge, S John's College, 218 (I. 10) David Kimchi, *Sepher Ha-shorashim*, a book of roots, in Hebrew.[137] This is the second half of Kimchi's *Miklol*, a bible dictionary given to S John's in 1740 by T. Baker, but probably owned by Robert Wakefield, the reader in Hebrew who was a fellow in the 1520s and whose hand appears in it.[138] The connection with him makes the ascription of ownership to Easton more likely, since he knew about Easton's Hebrew studies and owned an Easton work.[139]

To complete the information about libraries we need to discover what sources Easton used, particularly in his *De ecclesiastica potestate* and what research tools he had. He was very explicit about sources, though like all medieval writers he did not reveal all he used and was not above disguising his real source.

De ecclesiastica potestate was Easton's great work, started as an attack on all the major supporters of the most dangerous idea of his time: that state was superior to church. As pointed out above, he adopted the framework presented by pseudo-Dionysius, of whom he was an eager, careful and accurate user, using the version in the volume known as *Compellit me*, a text from the University of Paris, but probably also used in Oxford. It had pseudo-Dionysius' basic text and also the glosses of 'Maximus', John the Scot and John the Saracen as well as that of Hugh of St Victor.[140] Though Easton owned a copy of John the Scot's translation with an apparatus of glosses now in Cambridge University Library (MS Ii 3 32), a twelfth-century collection of the whole of Dionysius' works in the 'T' version, there is no evidence that he used this for his *Defensorium*.[141]

Apart from pseudo-Dionysius, the list of traditional authorities was large, some certainly cited at second hand but some of the more unusual actually used. In addition Easton quoted many more 'modern' works, including of course some Wyclif.

Easton had read the *Summa* of Alexander of Hales, which was quoted repeatedly. It was completed after Alexander's death in 1245 by some of his pupils. Easton evidently had the whole work, perhaps from the papal library,[142] since he quoted from every part, including sections said to be

---

[136] Ker, *Books*, p. 264, no. 80.   [137] Ibid., no. 83.

[138] See note in the annotated catalogue in the college library. I must thank the college librarian for help with this volume. For Wakefield, Emden, *A Biographical Register of the University of Oxford AD 1501–1540*, Oxford 1974, pp. 599–600.

[139] Below p. 236.   [140] Harvey, 'Adam Easton and pseudo-Dionysius', pp. 77–89.

[141] The MS is discussed in Harvey, 'Adam Easton and pseudo-Dionysius', pp. 79–80.

[142] F. Ehrle, *Historia bibliothecae Romanorum pontificum tum Bonifatianae tum Avenionensis*, 2 vols., Rome 1890, 1947, I, p. 324, for one in 1369.

in the third part or the beginning of the fourth, which are not included in the Quarrachi edition.[143] Traceable quotations are correct, sometimes verbatim.[144] He did not always agree with Hales. He considered that the moral rules in the state of sin would also have applied in the state of innocence, whereas Hales thought there would have been change.[145] Easton did not agree with Hales either that Job and those of his age were not subject to priestly rule.[146] His argument required priests in charge from the beginning.

The main work of Augustine quoted was *De civitate dei*, with references to almost every part and strong evidence that Easton knew it well.[147] Langham owned a copy.[148] All other mentions of Augustine were single references to works, often biblical commentaries which may come from glosses.[149]

Aquinas was quoted much less. There are references to the *Commentary on the Sentences* and the *Summa theologiae*. Where traceable the references are exact and often a section of text is quoted, usually a sign that Easton had in fact read the work.[150] These would have been readily available to Easton in Avignon in Langham's library.[151]

There were a few references to S Bernard, not suggesting any close

---

[143] Alexander of Hales, *Summa theologica*, 4 vols. Quarrachi 1924–48; References V, 4116, ff. 143v, 164v, 241v, 251v, 261v, 264, 266v, 275, 282v, 283v, 289.

[144] V, 4116, f. 261v, from Book III, part II, inq. 3, tract. I, qu. I, no. 260 (vol. IV, pp. 369–70); f. 275, from Book III, part II, inq. 3, tract. 2, sect. 2, tit. I, c. 5, no. 415 (vol. IV, pp. 611–12).

[145] V, 4116, f. 143v, quoting *Summa*, Bk III, pars II, inq. 2, qu. 3, no. 247 (vol. IV, p. 348).

[146] V, 4116, f. 264, quoting Book III, part II, inq 3, tract. I, qu. I, no. 261 (vol. IV, pp. 370–2).

[147] V, 4116, Book I c. 8,quoted, f. 189v; Book III c. 4, f. 236; Book V, many chapters, ff. 17, 20v, 21, 38v, 165, 187, 236v, 237v, 238, 238v; Book VII, c. 32, f. 209v; Book X, c. 4, f. 238v, c. 5, f. 148v, 149; Book XI, f. 162; Book XII, c. 10 f. 242; Book XIV, c. 1, f. 142; Book XV, c. 6, f. 226, c. 17 ff. 223, 231v, c. 18, f. 337, c. 20, ff. 169, 336v; , Book XVIII, f. 304v, c. 12, f. 238, cc. 18, 22, f. 231v; Book XIX, c. 14, ff. 161v, 162, 244, c. 15, ff. 162, 244v, cc. 16, 17, f. 214, 244.

[148] Sharpe, *Shorter Catalogues*, p. 620.

[149] ff. 144v, 150, *Contra Faustum*; ff. 246v, 335v on John; f. 260, on ps.98 v. 6; ff. 280v/81, on I Kg, c. 10; f. 224v:*in libro primo de mirabilibus (sacre scripture)*; f. 38v *Enchiridion*; f. 43, on Malachy; ff. 139, 153, 162,163v, on Genesis (*ad literam*); f. 161 on I Cor.15v45; f. 335 on prophecy; letter 30 (?3); f. 186v, *Ad Macedonium*; f. 265, Questions on the Old and New Testament; f. 336, Sermon on the Epiphany.

[150] Aquinas, *Summa theologiae*, ed. P. Caramello, 4 vols., Turin and Rome, 1948–50. Refs V, 4116 f. 152: *Summa*, I, q.100, art. 2 (pp. 480–2), where Easton quotes Aquinas' refutation of Anselm, with the segment of Anselm which Aquinas gives; f. 162: from *Summa* I, q. 96 art. 4 (p. 472), exact quotation including Aquinas' refs. to Aristotle Politics and I Peter 4 . The MS gives Augustine ref. as *De civitate dei* book XI but it is from Aquinas and is Augustine book XIX; f. 235v: II/i q. 100 art. 5 (Caramello ed. II, p. 471), an exact quotation.; f. 234v II/2 q. 10, art. 10 p. 74, the scripture refs. at f. 234 are from Aquinas; f. 249v: II/2, q. 76 (recte q. 66), arts 1 and 2. exact quotation (Caramello, ed. II, p. 347); f. 264, ref. not exact quotation to II/I, q. 98 (Caramello ed. II, pp. 456–61).

[151] Sharpe, *Shorter Catalogues*, pp. 617, 621, 622, 623.

study except of *De consideratione*[152] which Langham owned.[153] Perhaps not so surprisingly there were a few references to Robert Grosseteste: *De preceptis*,[154] Grosseteste on pseudo-Dionysius, but only a single reference,[155] and *dicta*.[156]

Quotations from canon lawyers did occur: for instance in considering the rights of infidels, from Hostiensis in his *Summa*, which was in Langham's library, on *De foro competenti* and on the emperor and pope in *Qui filii sunt legitimi*.[157] Easton likewise quoted Innocent III's letter to the Greek Emperor *Solite benignitatis affectum*.[158] In general, however, he was deeply distrustful of law and lawyers.[159] When referring to the problem of 'the fear that might attack a constant man' in the election of Urban, he referred to violence or fear 'speaking in conformity to scripture' rather than law.[160] The passage on fear in his Berengarius has been annotated, perhaps by Easton himself.[161]

In the course of *Defensorium* he cited almost all the current well-known polemical works on ecclesiastical power. Some, however, played very little part in his thinking. Dante's *De monarchia* for instance was cited, probably the first example of its use by an Englishman, but close examination shows that Easton was largely refuting book three with only one other reference, from the very beginning.[162] There seems no doubt that Easton had read book three very carefully. Where it was not cited exactly his paraphrases were very exact.[163] No doubt *De monarchia* was well known in Avignon.

Other writers who took part in the same set of debates were referred to in *Defensorium*, for instance Augustinus of Ancona and James of Viterbo but there are no extensive quotations from these and one may assume that Easton did not know them well.[164] In two cases a view of

---

[152] V, 4116, ff. 323, 324,347, referring to Book IV, c. 4, on 'Put up thy sword into its sheath', and f. 360v on Peter. f. 136v refers to B. on the Canticles.

[153] Sharpe, *Shorter Catalogues*, p. 624.

[154] R. W. Southern, *Robert Grosseteste. The Growth of an English Mind in Medieval Europe*, Oxford 1986. For ref. V, 4116, f. 143v.

[155] Southern, *Grosseteste*, pp. 200–3; V, 4116, f. 296v, on chapter 9 of Celestial Hierarchy.

[156] Southern, *Grosseteste*, p. 331 index; V, 4116, f. 186v, *in dictis suis* on Matt. 5 v 20; ff. 191, 193 on giving.

[157] For the man J. A. Brundage, *Medieval Canon Law*, London and New York 1995, p. 58; with refs; and pp. 163–4, 214; V, 4116, ff. 277v, 295v; Sharpe, *Shorter Catalogues*, p. 624.

[158] On Innocent, V, 4116, ff. 275r/v, 276v.   [159] See below p. 229.

[160] Macfarlane, 'An English account', p. 82.   [161] Noted by Macfarlane, Thesis, I, p, 46.

[162] *De Monarchia*, ed. G. Vinay, Florence 1950; V, 4116, f. 299v: *Dans in libro suo de Monarchia Mundi in principio*, where the reference is to I/2 p. 8.

[163] References: V, 4116, ff. 293, 293v–4, from III, c. 6 p 226, f. 294, from III c. 4 p. 210, c. 8, pp. 232, 236, c. 9, pp. 238, 240; f. 294v from III, c. 6, p. 226; ff. 294v–5, from III, c. 12, p. 258; f. 323 from III, c. 9, p. 238; f. 325 from III, c. 8, p. 236; f. 360, from III, c. 10 p. 250.

[164] Augustinus, V, 4116, f. 275v; James of Viterbo, f. 297. For Augustinus see M. Wilks, *The Problem of Sovereignty in the Later Middle Ages*, Cambridge 1963. For James see *De Regimine*

theirs was linked with views of Alexander of S. Elpidio, discussed below,[165] and in another place Augustine of Ancona was said to share a view on dispensations (false according to *Episcopus*) with Wyclif.[166]

Easton was well read in the quarrel between pope John XXII and the Emperor in which Ockham and Marsilius of Padua became involved and he intended to devote a whole book to refuting Ockham's *Dialogus*.[167] In the present work he refers to many writings on the poverty controversy, including the various pronouncements of John XXII: *Ad conditorem, Cum inter nonnullos* and *Quia vir reprobus*.[168] He refers in general terms to the arguments of Louis, king of the Romans, against the papacy.[169] He had certainly read *Defensor pacis*,[170] though he made little of it here, using it largely to show that Wyclif shared its heretical ideas.[171]

Of the other literature of the controversy between *regnum* and *sacerdotium* Easton had evidently read Alexander de S Elpidio's *De ecclesiastica potestate* [172] Alexander was prior general of the order of Hermits of S Augustine, and bishop of Melfi, writing 1320–6.[173] Easton had read him with care and quoted at some length from tract two, chapters 8 and 9.[174] He certainly did not always agree with Alexander, expressing clear disagreement several times. Alexander (and others) held that in the Old Testament temporal power was supreme. Easton thought this contrary to scripture.[175] *Rex* supported Alexander's view with exact references and quotations,[176] but *Episcopus* would not accept.

Easton had read some of Richard Fitzralph's writings. His use of these is extremely interesting because not only did he own *De pauperie salvatoris* but Langham also had one (perhaps the same book) and Easton or Langham was so interested that he bothered to have copied the last

---

Christiano, ed. H-X. Arquillière, Paris 1926. Augustinus was in the papal library in 1369, Ehrle, *Historia*, I, p. 338.

[165] As previous note.   [166] v, 4116, f. 326: *in libro suo De ecclesiastica potestate*.

[167] v, 4116, ff. 348, 349v, he intended to devote the first part of book six to this.

[168] M. Lambert, *Franciscan Poverty. The Doctrine of the Absolute Poverty of Christ and the Apostles in the Franciscan Order 1210–1323*, London 1961, pp. 230–5, 235–40, 242; B. Tierney, *Origins of Papal Infallibility, 1150–1350. A Study on the Concepts of Infallibility, Sovereignty and Tradition in the Middle Ages* (= Studies in the History of Christian Thought 6), Leiden 1972, pp. 171–204.

[169] v, 4116, f. 345v.   [170] *Defensor pacis*, ed. C. W. Previté-Orton, Cambridge 1928.

[171] Full discussion, with references in Harvey, 'Adam Easton and the condemnation', pp. 326–7.

[172] Printed J. T. Rocaberti, ed., *Bibliotheca maxima pontificia*, II/vii, Rome 1698; for one belonging first to cardinal Anglic Grimoard and then to his nephew (1378), now Paris, Bibl., Nat. Lat. 4230, Ehrle, *Historia*, I, p. 526, note 1196. See also M-N. Julien de Pommerel and J. Monfrin, *La bibliothèque pontificale à Avignon et à Peñiscola, pendant le grand schisme d'occident et sa dispersion*, 2 vols. (= Collection de l'école française de Rome 141) Rome 1991, II, p. 942.

[173] H. J. Sieben, *Die Konzilsidee des lateinischen Mittelalters (847–1378)*, Paderborn 1984, p. 321.

[174] v, 4116, ff. 289v, 297, 343v, 349. Quotations from Rocaberti, *Bibliotheca*, II/vii, pp. 17, 23, 24, 27.

[175] v, 4116, f. 275v.   [176] v, 4116, f. 289v, from Rocaberti, *Bibliotheca*, II/vii, pp. 17, 23, 24.

book (VIII).[177] Easton's quotations suggest very careful reading, but there were exact references only up to book VI,[178] unless some of the later references, without books, came from the last part. He did not always agree with Fitzralph, though he was always very respectful: 'the sublime doctor lately archbishop of Armagh', 'the venerable man the excellent doctor lately archbishop of Armagh'.[179] But on the crucial point about dominion by grace Easton disagreed.[180] *Rex* pointed out that some argued that man had *dominium* because of the grace of God *per gratiam gratum facientem*. *Episcopus* replied that he knew this was indeed the view of excellent theologians, including to some extent Fitzralph, but that scripture did not agree. Grace did not give dominion; it was not the cause.[181] The only other Fitzralph work certainly quoted was *De questionibus Armenorum* to which there was a reference, without, as far as I can see, any deep knowledge.[182] Already at Oxford Easton was quoting both these, and he had been in Oxford when Fitzralph first published *De pauperie* there in 1356–7, but he would have had access to better copies in Avignon. Langham owned one.[183]

Easton maintained an interest in secular/mendicant quarrels and thus probably first became interested in Wyclif, who was presented to him first, probably by informants from Oxford, as an enemy of monks and their property, inordinately supporting royal power against the church. The evidence from *De ecclesiastica potestate* is quite clear. He knew well book one of *De civili dominio* which he quoted directly and paraphrased accurately throughout. For the rest, by the end of *De ecclesiastica potestate* he had lists (probably *dicta* supplied from Oxford), of offensive and heretical statements by Wyclif in other books of the same work.[184] There is no evidence that he knew other works of Wyclif. By the end of the book refutation of Wyclif's ideas had begun to dominate the argument.

---

177 Langham: Sharpe, *Shorter Catalogues*, p. 621. Easton: Walsh, *Fitzralph*, pp. 472–3 The manuscript is now Cambridge, CCCC 180. Ed. R. L. Poole, books I–IV, in J. Wyclif, *De dominio divino* (= Wyclif Society), London 1890, pp. 257–476.

178 V, 4116, f. 27, from pp. 285, 285–6; f. 30, quotation from chapter III, p. 281, lines 1–4, f. 186v, exact quotation from p. 345, and 347; f. 247, quotation from Book IV, chapter 3, p. 440, lines 12–24; f. 251, quotation from Book III, chapter 27, p. 419, lines 8–12; f. 314 quotes Book V, chapter 1; ff. 337, 351v quote book VI.

179 V, 4116, ff. 30, 193v.   180 V, 4116, f. 193v.

181 V, 4116, f. 193v: *scio quod hec fuit opinio patrum theologorum precipuorum videlicet venerabilis viri et domini doctoris eximii nuper Archiepiscopi Armacani que in hac materia sequitur in parte opinio predicta.*

182 V, 4116, f. 328v; there is an edition by J. Sudoris, *Summa de questionibus Armenorum*, Paris 1511.

183 See Walsh, *Fitzralph*, pp. 472–3. For Easton's use in Oxford see in his disputation with Radcliffe, cf. edition by Forte, Thesis, p. 104, quotation from *De questionibus Armenorum*, Book I, chaps 1–6; Book 14, chap. 14; see also reference to *De pauperie*, Forte, Thesis, p. 121; Sharpe, *Shorter Catalogues*, p. 619.

184 All the details are discussed in Harvey, 'Easton and the condemnation'.

They were still not wholly dominant, however. He found time to read some very modern work by John of Legnano. The earliest reference[185] was to a view from John's book *De antichristo* where John maintained that Nebuchadnezzar had no right to rule the Jews but was a tyrant. Easton disagreed and said that this was contrary to Augustine.[186] Later, in answer to *Rex*, who put forward Wyclif's view that the *Summus sacerdos* could not have *plena potestas* because this would totally subject all law to the pope,[187] *Episcopus* quoted John's lectures on the chapter *Novit, de judiciis*[188] (the constitution by which Innocent III said he could proceed against the king of France, *ratione peccati*) and in his book *De somnio* where he dealt with *de mundi unico principatu*. Easton said that he could not fully agree with John (especially, it seems, with John's views on the primacy of canon law) but he did agree in thinking that the pope could abolish laws and that the jurisdiction of the emperor derived from the pope.

John of Legnano was a famous doctor of both laws, teaching in Bologna from 1352.[189] He was a notable supporter of Urban V, journeying to Rome in 1368 to meet the pope. Easton might have met him then and he and Easton were jointly used by the pope from 1378 to examine the case for canonising Bridget of Sweden.[190] The *Somnium* and *De principatu* were produced in 1372 as part of the pope's quarrel with Bologna. John took the pope's side, backing papal law and proving that the pope's power was necessary and superior. Easton's references to John, who later became one of the most fervent early supporters of Urban VI, were deeply respectful: 'the venerable and devout doctor John of Legnano'; 'Lord John of Legnano, my especial and reverend lord'.[191] John discussed monarchy on a pseudo-Dionysian basis, just as Easton did, with the heavenly bodies ruled by the *primum mobile* and in

[185] V, 4116, f. 239v.   [186] In *De civitate Dei*, presumably.   [187] V, 4116, f 332.
[188] X, 2,1,13.
[189] See M. C. De Matteis, 'Profilo di Giovanni da Legnano' in O. Capitani, ed. *L'università a Bologna. Personaggi, momenti e luoghi dalle origini a XVI secolo*, Bologna 1987, pp. 157–71; Capitani, 'Giovanni da Legnano e lo scisma', *Conciliarismo, stati nazionali, inizi dell'umanismo. Atti del XXV convegno storico internationale, Todi 9–12 October 1988*, ed. O. Capitani, Spoleto 1990, pp. 29–46. The text of *Somnium* I have used is in V, 2639, ff. 247–69v, described by S. Kuttner and R. Elze, *A Catalogue of Canon and Roman Law Manuscripts in the Vatican Library*, II (= Studi e testi 328), Vatican 1987, pp. 206–10; see also G. Ermini, 'Un ignoto tratto *De Principatu* di Giovanni da Legnano', in *Studi di storia e diritto in onore di Carlo Calisse*, III, Milan 1940, pp. 421–46, reprinted in G. Ermini, *Scritti storico-giuridici*, ed. O. Capitani and E. Menesto, Spoleto 1997, pp. 165–88; see also there pp. 7–43, 44–55, further on his life and work. G. M. Donovan and M. H. Keen, 'The *Somnium* of John of Legnano', *Traditio* 37 (1981), pp. 325–45; J. P. McCall, 'The Writings of John of Legnano, with a list of manuscripts', *Traditio*, 23 (1967), pp. 415–37.
[190] See above p. 199.
[191] V, 4116, f. 239v: *venerabilis doctor devotus*; f. 332 *reverendus dominus meus et specialiter singularis* .

turn the angels ruling earth. In earthly monarchy everything flowed from the church 'so that all are dependent [on the *principatus* of the church] as tributaries from an original source'.[192] John also defended the Donation of Constantine[193] and moderate use of possessions, just like Easton.[194] Probably therefore Easton was sharing in a curial discussion of dominion, not solely arguing with English opponents.

Easton set out to learn Hebrew in order to be sure that the Vulgate did not contain errors, as his Jewish opponents contended.[195] He almost certainly met them in Avignon, where there was a famous and learned Jewish community, startling to an English scholar, as we know Brinton was startled and dismayed, who could not have met anything like this at home.[196] It would have been impossible to learn Hebrew at Oxford or in the University of Avignon.[197] It was possible, however, to make a show of 'Hebrew' learning by using previous work.[198] Comments on the Books of Kings, which most especially interested Easton, containing 'rabbinical' ideas, were known from the ninth century and were incorporated (under Jerome's name) into the *Glossa ordinaria*.[199] Easton, however, was not alone in welcoming more contact; others also learned Hebrew in Avignon.[200] The only remaining evidence for his studies is in the *De ecclesiastica potestate*. It is of three kinds: direct translation from Hebrew, usually to show that Jerome is misleading but sometimes to prove that the Vulgate translated the *sententia* (real meaning) even if the translation was not literal; references to Jewish views; and evidence of participation in discussions. In the existing manuscripts no attempt was made to write Hebrew script; transliteration into Latin letters was always given and must, I think, have been used by Easton. I therefore use it here.

An example of his understanding of the language is discussion of the

---

[192] v, 2369, f. 259v: *sic in terrestri monarchia totus principatus mundi dependet a principatu ecclesie . . . ut omnes sint inde dependentes sicut rivuli a fonte originali.*
[193] v, 2639, ff. 261–4v.
[194] v, 2639, f. 262; for Easton's ideas see Harvey, ' Easton and the condemnation', p. 330.
[195] v, 4116, f. 2.
[196] For some details see: M. Harvey, 'Preaching in the curia', pp. 299–301.
[197] B. Altaner, 'Die Durchführung des Vienner Konzilsbeschlusses uber die Errichtung von Lehrstuhlen für orientalische Sprache', *Zeitschrift für Kirchengeschichte* 52 (1933), pp. 226–36, esp. pp. 230–1, 235.
[198] Pseudo-Jerome, *Questiones on the Book of Samuel*, ed. and intro. A. Saltman (= Studia Post-Biblica, 27), Leiden 1975, pp. 23–58; B. Smalley, T*he Study of the Bible in the Middle Ages*, 3rd rev. edn, Oxford 1983, pp. 329–55.
[199] Saltman intro. as above note 198 and R. Loewe, 'Hebrew books and Judaica in Medieval Oxford and Cambridge', from J. M. Shaftesley, ed., *Remember the Days. Essays on Anglo-Jewish History presented to Cecil Roth* (= Jewish Historical Society of England), London 1966, pp. 23–48, esp. p. 33.
[200] G. Bruckner, 'An unpublished source', p. 368–9.

word translated *sacerdos* by Jerome, *cohen* in Hebrew. *Rex* contended that this should be translated *ministerium*, with *cohen gadol* translated *ministerium magnum*.[201] This would have implied inferiority, so that priests were inferior to kings. Episcopus replied with the Vulgate psalm 109 (= 110) verse 4, which Jerome translated as: *Tu es sacerdos in eternum secundum ordinem Melchisedech*.[202] He pointed out that the Hebrew had *tu cohen*, implying that the ministry was pleasing to God. Where the Bible referred to Melchisedech (Genesis chapter 14, verse 18) the Hebrew called him *rex Salem et cohen*, that is minister, *ad Deum supremum*. Jerome therefore was correct in translating the word as *sacerdos*.

Some direct translations from the Hebrew were apparently by Easton himself, though the best were from the psalms, which he is not supposed to have translated. For instance, when *Rex* tried to give earthly kingship a pedigree from eternity by quoting psalm 73 (= 74) verse 12: *Deus autem rex noster ante secula operatus est salutem in medio terre*, *Episcopus* countered by saying that God can only be called king from the beginning of the created world. The psalm text did not support his opponent:

since the Hebrew text reads thus, word for word: 'and God my king from the beginning working his salvation within the earth'

adding, 'and this can well be explained "from the beginning of the world"'.[203] Easton was not using Jerome's *Psalterium iuxta Hebraeos* to achieve this.[204]

Some ideas certainly came from Nicholas de Lyra but there is enough to show that on some matters Easton was thinking out problems for himself. On psalm 73 verse 12 Lyra said that *rex* could be taken as God but not *rex ab eterno* because 'king' denotes a subject creature; or the text could mean *ante secula*, meaning a long time. In the discussion about Melchisedech Easton was joining Lyra in the latter's argument with the Jewish scholar Rashi, discussing what *sacerdos* might mean.[205]

---

[201] V, 4116, f. 19v.

[202] V, 4116, f. 20; Dahan, *Les intellectuels*, pp. 502–3 for this as a polemical text.

[203] V, 4116, f. 20 *quoniam textus ebraycus habet sic de verbo ad verbum: et deus rex meus a principio operans salvaciones infra terram . . . et bene potest exponi a principio mundi*; *Biblia Sacra cum Glossa Ordinaria*, 6 vols., Douai and Antwerp 1617, ps 73 at *Deus autem* partly De Lyra. See A. Kleinhans, 'Nicolaus Trevet, OP, *psalmorum interpres*', *Angelicum*, 20 (1943), pp. 219–36, esp. p. 223. Trevet used Jerome, see Oxford, Bodleian Library, MS Bodley 738, f. 131, but Easton's latin differs.

[204] *Sancti Hieronymi Psalterium iuxta Hebraeos*, ed. H. de Sainte-Marie (= Collectanea Biblica Latina 11), Rome 1954, at the relevant psalms; R. Loewe, 'The medieval Christian Hebraists of England. The *Superscriptio Lincolniensis*', *Hebrew Union College Annual*, 28 (1957), pp. 205–52.

[205] H. Hailperin, *Rashi and the Christian Scholars*, Pittsburg 1963, pp. 77–81 for Rashi and 198–223 for Lyra on this subject.

Easton knew the views of Jewish scholars. Of course he quoted Rashi and derived much of what he quoted from De Lyra, who had done more than any other to make Rashi known in the West, but in some places Easton knew, without De Lyra telling him, that a view was from Rashi. For instance he quoted Judges chapter 2 verse 1, saying that the angel from Galgol was Phineas the priest:

who was called the angel of the Lord because of the fervent zeal for the law of the Lord which he had and this is what Rabbi Solomon says in the beginning of the second chapter of the book of Judges.[206]

Lyra supplied the main point here but did not use Rashi's name nor discuss the meaning of Phineas' name as Easton did.

The other Jew cited is David Kimhi.[207] Easton said, for instance, that he derived the translation of *cohen* as *ministerium* from Kimhi.[208] *Episcopus* argued that according to the Mosaic law kings had no power over priests, who were a separate caste. He quoted Leviticus chapter 27 verses 28–9, where the Vulgate read (in part):

Omne quod Domino consecratur, sive homo fuerit sive animal . . . non vendetur nec redimi potest . . . et omnis consecratio quae offeretur ab homine non redimetur.

which the sixteenth century translated (Rheims):

anything that is devoted to the Lord, whether it be man or beast . . . shall not be sold neither may it be redeemed . . . and any consecration that is offered by man may not be redeemed.

Easton said the word here translated *consecratio* was the Hebrew *herem*, which, according to Rabbi David meant destruction or removal, 'because it is given to God and destroyed for human use'.[209] Even though at Leviticus 27 Lyra had a long exposition of *herem*, Easton probably was relying on Kimhi here.

He was aware that the two Jewish scholars did not always agree and was able to discuss their disagreements in a way quite unlike anything in contemporary English scholarship. On Genesis chapter 3 verses 17–18, where the Vulgate read *maledicta terra in opere tuo* (cursed is the earth in thy work) Easton, perhaps following De Lyra, insisted that the Hebrew

---

[206] V, 4116, f. 274v: *qui vocabitur angelus domini propter ferventem zelum legis domini quem habebat et sic dicit Rabi Salomon in principio secundi capituli super librum judicium; Biblia Sacra,* Judges I, at *ascendit.*

[207] For the man F. E. Talmage, *David Kimhi: the Man and the Commentaries* (= Harvard Judaic Monographs I), Cambridge(Mass) and London, 1975; Talmage, 'R. David as polemicist,' *Hebrew Union College Annual,* 38 (1967), pp. 213–35.

[208] V, 4116, f. 15v.

[209] V, 4116, ff. 181v and 300: *quia datur ad deum et destruitur ab usu humano. Biblia Sacra,* at *omne quod domino.*

read *maledicta terra propter te* (cursed is the earth because of thee).[210] Where the Vulgate continued *in laboribus commedes ex ea*, (in labours shalt thou eat thereof) the Hebrew, according to Rabbi David, should be translated *in tristitia* (in sadness). The reason was 'because the word *osebb*, according to Rabbi David, means both sadness and anger'. This translation suited Easton's because he believed with De Lyra that before the Fall men would have cultivated the earth without wearisome labour. He noted, however, that 'according to Rabbi Solomon it signifies labour and Jerome and the Targum say this also'.[211]

Similarly to prove that royalty was superior to priesthood *Rex* quoted first the Vulgate of Exodus chapter 19 verses 5–6:[212]

eritis michi in peculium de cunctis populis: mea est omnis terra. Et vos eritis michi in regnum sacerdotale et gens sancta (in the Rheims translation: 'you shall be my peculiar possession above all people: for all the earth is mine. And you shall be to me a priestly kingdom and a holy nation').

and then the text continued with Easton's own translation, replacing *peculium* with either *in proprium* (for my own) or *in thesaurium* (as a treasure) according to Rabbi David, or *in amicabilitatem* (for friendship) according to Rabbi Solomon. He quoted Kimhi to show that the Hebrew word was *segulla*, which means *proprium* and added, almost certainly from De Lyra, 'and thus it is made pleasing to God according to the explanation of the Targum and Rabbi Solomon'.[213] Therefore, according to Easton, verse 6 should read *eritis regnum ministrantes deo* (you will be a kingdom ministering to God) He added that although some Jews and De Lyra take the word *hatohanym* for princes or elders, Jerome's *sacerdotale* was correct.

One should not over-emphasise the extent of Easton's Hebrew learning. Some views which he called Jewish came from the *Glossa ordinaria*, for example the notion that in the state of innocence all first-born sons would have been priests, which was the *Glossa*, quoting Jerome on Genesis chapter 14, verse 18.[214] But he continued:

---

[210] V, 4116, f. 185; the Authorised Version follows the Hebrew as Easton. *Biblia Sacra*, at *maledicta terra*.

[211] *quia hoc vocabulum osebb secundum Rabbi David est commune ad tristitiam et iram. Secundum Rabbi Salomen signat laborem et sic tenet Jeronimum et Targum.*

[212] V, 4116, f. 66.

[213] *et sic fit amicabilitas Deo secundum exposicionem Targum et Rabi Salomon. Biblia Sacra*, Exodus 19 at *Eritis michi* and *et vos*.

[214] V, 4116, f. 154: *omnes primogenitos a Noe usque ad Aaron pontifices fuisse.* See Hailperin, *Rashi*, p. 336, note 496, for De Lyra; *Biblia Sacra*, Genesis 14 v. 18 at *at vero* for Jerome; Dahan, *Intellectuels*, pp. 289, 294 for other sources.

but another point of view says that in the state of innocence the first priests ordained for governing the people were chosen by Adam . . . whence Adam was a priest as well as a monarch.[215]

This is not De Lyra.

Discussing psalm 8 verses 6–7, where the Vulgate read:[216]

minuisti eum paulo minus ab angelis; gloria et honore coronasti eum; et constituisti eum super opera manuus tuarum (thou hast made him a little less than the angels, thou hast crowned him with glory and honour and hast set him over the work of thy hands).

he took this to refer to Christ but gave his own translation:

textus hebraycus habet sic: minuisti eum modicum de deo, gloria et honore coronatus eum et facies dominari eum in operibus manuum tuarum (the Hebrew text says: thou hast made him little less than God, thou hast crowned him with glory and honour and made him to have dominion over the works of thy hands).

He continues:

Although some Jews take *elohym* here to mean angels, as Jerome seems to do, I do not see that this is correct according to the actual words of the text.[217]

Lyra had referred this psalm and verse to Christ. Possibly Easton knew Kimhi's commentary on the psalm, where Kimhi certainly took *elohym* to mean angels.[218] As we have seen there is also evidence that Easton actually debated with Jews, probably in Avignon.[219]

Easton thus took trouble to check for accuracy his text and its translation. This was fairly unusual in the late fourteenth century; Wyclif was not capable of any such scholarly exercise. On the other hand the *De ecclesiastica potestate* does not suggest that he had advanced very far in his Hebrew studies.[220] Much of his discussion of individual words could have come from De Lyra; in only two years he could not have become very expert. Nevertheless few contemporaries were even aware of the problems discussed and almost none knew about Jewish scholarly debates, as Easton knew the problem concerning *sacerdos*, for

---

[215] V, 4116, f. 154: *sed alia opinio dicat quod in statu innocencie sacerdotes primi pro gubernacione populi ordinari per Adam electi fuissent . . . unde Adam fuit sacerdos similis et monarcha.*

[216] V, 4116, f. 22r/v; this is not Jerome.

[217] *licet aliqui hebrei ibi capiunt elohym pro angelis, sicut videtur Jeronimus facere, non video quod hoc sit conveniens propriis verbis textus.*

[218] David Kimhi, *The Commentary of David Kimhi on the Book of Psalms*, trans. A. W. Greenup, London 1918, p. 66.

[219] In Trevet's commentary *paulo minus a Deo* is simply assumed, Bodley 738, f. 17, *sub verbo.*

[220] Dahan, *Intellectuels*, pp. 238–70, esp. p. 265 for reference to Easton, though little evidence that Dahan has read him.

instance.[221] What stands out is how a stay in Avignon had allowed him to meet Jewish scholars whom normally Englishmen never encountered, thus forcing him, if only a little, to broaden his mind.

Easton was not, however, a very broad scholar. His vision of the church, its rule and its development was so entirely biblical (including in 'biblical' the use of pseudo-Dionysius) that he had, by modern standards, a very defective historical sense and though he considered that up to the Incarnation humans were learning and changing, afterwards everything was 'given' and static, so that his notions about church organisation were governed entirely by the way he saw the New Testament and not at all by a reading of history. Apart from Augustine and Jerome, there is little evidence of a reading of the Fathers and no genuine historical sense when talking of the development of institutions.

Easton's works continued to have a minor influence after his death. His minor scholastic exercises of course, remain in single copies or at most two, but the *De ecclesiastica potestate* came to Norwich, from where presumably it was copied for S Alban's under John Whethamstede and given an index.[222] Whethamstede depended on it in the 1440s for some of his knowledge of polemics about the papacy, probably relying on Easton for references to Dante's *De monarchia*, and to James of Viterbo.[223] Whethamstede may also have discovered Alexander de S Elpidio from Easton,[224] and perhaps too Augustinus of Ancona; there was a copy of the latter with an index in S Albans, made at Whethamstede's command; perhaps his reading of Easton prompted its production.[225]

In mid century the *De ecclesiastica potestate* enjoyed a brief revival. The existing manuscripts date to that period and the original, given by Easton to Urban VI, is lost. That currently in the Vatican library (Vat Lat 4116) states that it was begun in 1431 by brother Nardellus of Naples, when Martin V was still pope (he died on 20 February) and completed in 1432 on the feast of the conversion of S Paul (25 January).[226] It belonged to cardinal Jordanus Orsini (died 1438) and

---

[221] Walsh, *Fitzralph*, pp. 159–60 for comparable information about Fitzralph.

[222] M. Harvey, 'John Whethamstede, the pope and the general council', in *The Church in Pre-Reformation England: Essays in Honour of F. R. H. DuBoulay*, ed. C. M. Barron and C. Harper-Bill, Woodbridge, 1985, pp. 108–22, esp. p. 118; Sharpe, *Shorter Catalogues*, pp. 567, 570, 582, 584.

[223] Harvey, 'Whethamstede', pp. 117, 118.   [224] Ibid., p. 116.   [225] Ibid., p. 116.

[226] V, 4116 f. 364: *Explicit liber primus defensorii ecclesiastice potestatis qui fuit inchoatus ad scribendum per me fratrem Nardellum de Neapoli anno domini mccccxxxi pontificatus domini Martini pape V. Et fuit finitus per me supradictum fratrem Nardellum anno domini mccccxxxii de mense Januarii x ind. in die conversionis sancti Pauli tempore pontificatus domini pape Eugenii divina providencia pape iiij nacione Veneti Amen.*

came from his library to that of Nicholas V.[227] There is another copy in Seville, in the Biblioteca Columbina (57–1–7) which is probably of the same approximate date. The third copy in the National Library, Madrid (738) says in its explicit that it was copied in 1455 from the Roman one by John Lichtensfelser, clerk of Bamberg, rector of the German Campo Santo in Rome and formerly *scriptor* and *familiaris* of pope Nicholas V, for Cosmas of Monseratto, archdeacon of S Lawrence, Tarragona, prior of Saragossa (*Sedis Cesaraugustine*), master of theology, datary and confessor to Calixtus III.[228] The *Office for the Visitation* exists in many manuscripts, since it was probably the most popular of all the pre-reformation Offices. It was certainly being used in England by 1421 when a monk of Vadstena copied it there.[229] By the late fifteenth century, however, Easton's name had been lost from it and when Jakob Wimpfeling criticised its barbarous style (*magnam rusticitatem et insipidissimam compositionem*) he did not know the author.[230]

Early in the sixteenth century a very few scholars continued to realise that Easton had been learned in Hebrew. Robert Wakefield, the leading Hebrew scholar in England, was made lecturer in Hebrew in S John's College, Cambridge about 1520, funded from John Fisher's chantry. He taught Hebrew to Fisher among others. Fisher seems to have been an important influence in persuading Henry VIII to found the first University lectureship in Hebrew and in obtaining Wakefield to fill it.[231] Wakefield, as we saw, probably owned Easton's volume of David Kimhi.[232] He also said that he had owned, until stolen, Easton's translation of the Bible (except for the psalms) from Hebrew to Latin. He used it with Easton's preface as evidence of Easton's view that the text of the Hebrew Bible had not been corrupted by the Jews, a common charge among medieval scholars, including Nicholas de Lyra.[233] *De*

---

227 A. Manfredi, *I codici latini di Nicolo V. Edizione degli inventari e identifcazione dei manuscritti* (= Studi e testi 359), Vatican City 1994, pp. 494–5, no. 795.

228 I have not seen this MS. Explicit from *Inventario general de manuscritos de la biblioteca nacional*, 13 vols. so far, Madrid 1956 onwards, II, no. 738.

229 MS Uppsala C 621, ff. 13–36. I have not seen this.

230 R. Donner, *Jabok Wimpfelings Bemühungen um die Verbesserung der liturgischen Texte* (= Quellen und Abhandlungen zur mittelrheinischen Kirchengeschichte 26), Mainz 1976, pp. 70–9; the work is *Castigationes locorum in canticis ecclesiasticis et divinis officiis depravatorum*. Joannes Schottus, Strasbourg 1513, which Professor Anne Moss very kindly looked at for me in Wolfenbuttel (124.b.Quod (4)), quotation from p. bv.

231 Sharpe, *Handlist*, pp. 575–6; J. K. McConica, *English Humanists and Reformation Politics under Henry VIII and Edward VI*, Oxford 1965, pp. 132–4; J. Rex, *The Theology of John Fisher*, Cambridge 1991, esp. pp. 58–9; Wakefield's career is also sketched in *BRUO*, 1501–40, pp. 599–600.

232 Above p. 224.

233 R. Wakefield, *Syntagma de Hebreorum Codicum Incorruptione, c.* 1530 (Pollard and Redgrave 24946), f. Hii.

ecclesiastica potestate makes it clear that Easton's reasons for learning Hebrew had included this charge and that his studies proved that it was untrue.[234]

Almost certainly Easton and his colleague William Andrew, played a large part in spreading the cult of Bridget to England, though the stages are now hard to trace. The sending of relics to Richard II was probably important. But Easton's lack of political influence in England coupled with the vicissitudes of the papal court so soon after his death, which probably delayed the return of his books to Norwich, meant that his major ideas, included in his great defence of ecclesiastical power, had little influence on England in the early fifteenth century and were probably never known to more than a handful of scholars. Nothing could better illustrate the damage done by the Great Schism than this example of the comparative waste of a lifetime of scholarship by a man who might have made an important contribution to biblical and anti-Wyclif studies but was largely forgotten by the next generation. By 1420 work such as his was already a little old-fashioned in Rome, beginning to be overtaken by more stylish (and ultimately more learned) Renaissance scholarship and by the debates about conciliarism. In England his great work was probably not sufficiently broad in its attack on Wycliffite ideas to be helpful to opponents of lollardy.[235] Support for church wealth against greedy lay rulers and for authoritarian papal power were not likely to be found very helpful in the English church in the early fifteenth century which was wooing the secular power for its help against the Lollards!

---

[234] V, 4116, f. 2.
[235] It would be worth comparing his work with the *Doctrinale* against the Lollards of Thomas Netter of Walden, which I have not yet done.

CONCLUSION

The history of the English in Rome between 1362 and 1420 has turned out to be more than the history of English institutions in the city, although they supply information about Englishmen which the curial records do not. There was clearly an English presence in Rome which was not closely connected to the curia. The English in the upper echelons of the papal curia were still not very involved in the two hospices when the papacy returned from Constance but by then the institutions were already more clerical and destined to become almost wholly so.

The origin of the English foundations was lay initiative, based on the desire of merchants and artisans to have a centre for charity and prayer for their souls, including in some cases care in old age, which would also serve pilgrims. The founders seem to have resided in Rome because it looked like an expanding market where English enterprise might compete with the Italians. Both the pilgrim market and more general trade seem to have been the targets. As far as one can tell, this lay enterprise succeeded only until about 1404; until then several lay men played an important part in the hospices, the second of which was founded only in 1396. After 1404 the state of Rome, the politics of the schism and probably the downturn in trade seem to have been responsible for a downturn also in the numbers of laymen coming to settle in Rome, or certainly coming to play a leading part in the English group. Of known officers of the hospice of S Thomas after 1420 even some of the men called 'lay' had posts in the papal court.[1]

The English presence at the papal curia, however, was rather different. Here the curia in Avignon held comparatively few English people and the largest concentration, the household of Simon Langham, was neither very distinguished, with a few exceptions including Adam Easton, nor did it survive the cardinal's death in 1376.

---

[1] John Ely was a sergeant at arms (see above p. 125).

Conclusion

The move to Rome, followed by the schism, however, gave the English a chance which they took. This is the only period with substantial numbers of English Rota auditors, including some of leading English canonists and the only resident English cardinal for one hundred years. Again, however, the numbers did not survive the vicissitudes of the schism and the problems of trying to follow the curia on its perambulations. The situation was worsened by the 'benefice policy' of the English government; the regular defeat of members of the curia by royal claimants and of provisors by royal law after 1406 cannot have been encouraging. An ambitious clerk would do much better in England when intriguing about his desired benefices. The surprising fact is probably that English institutions in Rome actually survived the period from 1406, but survive they did, even if S Chrysogonus' was probably insecure from 1420 onwards. Probably survival depended on having kept their legal records intact and thus still being able to prove ownership of a substantial group of fairly closely related properties in what is now via Monserrato as well as rentable property elsewhere. There had apparently been continuity of government, and the main buildings were intact, even if some of the contents had been looted. There were also officials to greet the newly returned curia. Even if there was much to do in Rome itself, the English hospices were ready to greet the new pope and his entourage.

But the new regime was very different from that during the schism. Martin V was a Colonna and owed debts from the previous era; in the curia appointees from the past had to be accommodated. Almost all the officials from the Pisan obedience obtained posts in Martin V's bureaucracy and the majority of them were Italians. This was the beginning of Italian dominance in the curia, which had led by the third quarter of the fifteenth century to a predominantly (though never entirely) Italian bureaucracy in Rome.[2] Once most of the offices were for sale, the number of Italians increased, since it was easier for Italians to raise the necessary funds locally. The English benefice legislation was also against Englishmen in Rome.

But the intervening period had been a brief flowering of enterprise abroad, when for a short time it looked as if English merchants and then English members of the papal entourage might establish themselves with a base in Rome and with a significant English presence in the curia. That they never did so on the scale of Italians in English centres like Southampton is as significant as that they tried.

---

[2] Details in Partner, *The Pope's Men*, pp. 8–12.

BIBLIOGRAPHY

MANUSCRIPT SOURCES

AVIGNON

Archives de Vaucluse: H Ste Praxède d'Avignon 55, no. 73; 58 no. 39; 8 G. 44 Ste Agricole
Bibliothèque de la Ville: 996

CAMBRIDGE

College Libraries: Corpus Christi, 74, 180, 347, 358, Emmanuel, 142, S John's, 218 (I. 10)
University Library: Gg. 6. 3; Ii. 1.12; Ii. 3. 32; Kk. 2. 8

DURHAM

Dean and Chapter: Muniments: Register II; Misc. Ch. 1357; Loc. X: 42
Library: MS C IV 25

EDINBURGH

University Library: Laing 351A

KENT

Archive Office, Maidstone: DRb/Art./6 (Bottlesham Register); Rochester Consistory Court, I and II

LONDON

British Library: Add. MS 48179; Cotton Cleop. C IV, Cleop. E II, Faust. C V; Vitellius F II; Royal 6 D X, 9 E VIII, 9 F I
Guildhall: Commissary Court of London, Register of Wills 9171/2
Lambeth Palace Library: Arundel Register, Canterbury
Public Record Office: Prob. 11/2a and /3; KB 27. 590
Westminster Abbey Muniments: 9223*, 9232, 9233, 9256B

Bibliography

NORWICH

Record Office: Norwich Dean and Chapter Archives, 1/1/49, 65; 1/12/29, 30; 1/2/ 23; 1/4/35; 1/8/42; 2/1/17; 2/3/7; Diocese of Norwich, Reg./3/6 (Despenser)

OXFORD

Bodleian Library: Arch. Seld. B 23; Lat. Th. d. 10; Bodley 151, 692, 738, 859; Hamilton 7; Tanner 342;
College Libraries: Balliol 300b; New College 179, 214; Oriel 15

ROME

Archivio Capitolino: Fondo Notarile Sez I, 649/4–14; 650/1; 785/1–11; 785bis/1–3;
Archivio di Stato: Collegio dei Notai Capitolini, 270, 848;
Collegio di S Maria dell'Anima: Instr. Litt. B. tom. 1;
Venerabile Collegio Inglese: *Libri* 232, 272, 277, 1598; *Membrane* 1–203; Scritture 117(2)

SEVILLE

Biblioteca Columbina 57–1–7

UPPSALA

University Library: C819

VATICAN CITY

Biblioteca Apostolica Vaticana: Archivio della Chiesa di S Angelo in Pesharia, 1/ 1–25; Archivio Capitolare di S Pietro, Censuali, 4; Vat. Lat. 2639, 2664, 4116, 6330;
Archivio Segreto Vaticano: Arm. 29/1–3; Arm. 31/36; Arm. 54/16; Collectanea, 357, 358, 464, 465; Reg. Av. 173, 180, 185, 197, 200–4; Reg. Lat. 13, 16, 25, 31, 32, 39, 41, 49, 82, 110, 127, 132; Reg. Suppl. 47, 49, 104A

WORCESTER

Cathedral: F. 65 (transcript only)

WROCLAW

IF 177

YORK

Borthwick Institute: York Registers 12 (Neville), 14 (Arundel), 17, 18 (Bowet)

PRIMARY PRINTED SOURCES

Alen, J., *A Calendar of Archbishop Alen's Register*, ed. C. McNeill, Dublin 1950.
Alexander of Hales, *Summa theologica*, 4 vols., Quarrachi 1924–48.

Bibliography

Alexander of S Elpidio, *De ecclesiastica potestate*, in Rocaberti, J. T., *Bibliotheca maxima pontificia*, II/vii, Rome 1698.

Alfonso of Jaen, *Epistola Solitarii; Informaciones* and *Epistola Servi Christi*, in Jonsson, A., ed., *Alfonso of Jaen. His Life and Works, with Critical Editions of Epistola Solitarii, Informaciones and Epistola Servi Christi* (Studia Graeca et Latina Lundensia 1), Lund 1989, pp. 117–71, 177–9, 185–203.

The Anonimalle Chronicle 1333–1381, ed. V. H. Galbraith, Manchester 1927.

Aquinas, T., *Summa theologiae*, ed. P. Caramello, 4 vols., Turin and Rome 1948–50.

Arnold, T, ed., *Memorials of St Edmund's Abbey*, 3 vols., *RS*, 96 (1896).

Astalli, P., *Il protocollo notarile di Pietro di Nicola Astalli*, ed. I. L. Sanfilippo (= Codice diplomatico di Roma e della regione romana 6), Rome 1989.

Bale, J., *Index Britanniae Scriptorum. John Bale's Index of British and Other Writers*, 2nd edn, eds. C. Brett and J. P. Carley, Cambridge 1990.

Biblia sacra cum glossa ordinaria, 6 vols., Douai and Antwerp 1617.

Blume, C. see Drèves, G. M.

Boileau, E. (or Boyleau), *Le livre des métiers*, ed. R. de Lespinasse and F. Bonnardot (= Histoire générale de Paris), Paris 1879. Another edition in *Reglemens sur les arts et métiers de Paris . . . connus sous le nom du Livre des métiers d'Étienne Boileau*, ed. G.-B. Depping (= Documents inédits sur l'histoire de France, series 3/iv), Paris 1837.

Bridget, *Birgitta of Sweden. Life and Selected Revelations*, ed. M. T. Harris, trans. A. R. Kezel, Mahwah, NJ 1990.

The Revelations of S Birgitta, ed. W. P. Cumming, EETS, original series 178 (1929).

Revelationes, Book VII, ed. B. Bergh (= Samlingar utgivna av Svenska Fornskrift-sällskapet, series 2 Latinska skrifter 7), Uppsala 1967.

Opera minora, I, Regula salvatoris ed. S. Eklund (series as previous entry, 8/1), Lund 1975.

Opera minora, II, Sermo angelicus, ed. S. Eklund (series as previous entry, 8/2), Uppsala 1972.

Opera minora, III, Quattuor orationes, ed. S. Eklund, Stockholm 1991.

The Liber Celestis, I, Text, ed. R. M. Ellis, *EETS*, original series 291 (1987).

Brinton, T., *The Sermons*, ed. M. Devlin, 2 vols., Camden Society, 3rd series 85, 86 (1954).

Bruni, L., *Leonardi Bruni Arretini epistolarum libri VIII*, ed. L. Mehus, 2 vols., Florence 1741.

Bubwith, N., *The Register of Nicholas Bubwith, Bishop of Bath and Wells, 1407–1424*, ed. T. S. Holmes, 2 vols., Somerset Record Society 29, 30 (1913, 1914).

Burns, C., 'Sources of British and Irish history in the *Instrumenta Miscellanea* of the Vatican Archives', *AHP*, 9 (1971), pp. 7–141.

Calendar of Close Rolls, Richard II, Henry IV, London 1902 onwards.

Calendar of Entries in the Papal Registers Relating to Great Britain and Ireland. Papal Letters, ed. W. H. Bliss and J. A. Twemlow, London 1893 onwards.

Calendar of Entries in the Papal Registers. Petitions, I, ed. W. H. Bliss, London 1896.

Calendar of Letter Books Preserved Among the Archives of the Corporation of the City of London at the Guildhall, 1275–1498, Books A-L, ed. R. R. Sharpe, London 1899–1912.

Calendar of Patent Rolls, Richard II, Henry IV, London 1901 onwards.

Calendar of Select Pleas and Memoranda of the City of London Preserved Among the Archives of the Corporation of the City of London, 1323–1482, ed. A. H. Thomas (1–4) and P. E. Jones (5–6), 6 vols., Cambridge 1926–61.

Bibliography

Calendar of Signet Letters of Henry IV and Henry V, 1399–1422, ed. J. L. Kirby, London 1978.

A Calendar of Wills Proved and Enrolled in the Court of Hustings, London, II, *1358–1688*, ed. R. R. Sharpe, London 1890.

Caputgallis, F. de, *Un notaio romano del trecento. I protocolli di Francesco di Stefano de Caputgallis (1374–1386)*, ed. R. Mosti, Rome 1994.

Chichele, H. *The Register of Henry Chichele, Archbishop of Canterbury, 1414–1443*, ed. E. F. Jacob, 4 vols., CYS, 42, 45–7 (1938–47).

Chrimes, S. B. and Brown, A. L, *Select Documents of English Constitutional History*, London 1961.

Collijn, I., ed., *Acta et processus canonizacionis Beate Birgitte* (= Samlingar utgivna av svenska Fornskrift-sällskapet, Series 2, Latinska Skrifter 1), Uppsala 1924–31.

Dallari, U., ed., *I rotuli dei lettori, legisti e artisti della studio bolognese dal 1384 al 1799*, 4 vols. (= Deputazione di storia patria per le provincie di Romagna, 1. Dei monumenti istorici pertinenti alle provincie della Romagna, series 2), Bologna 1888–1924.

Dante Alighieri, *De monarchia*, ed. G.Vinay, Florence 1950.

David Kimhi, *R. David on the First Book of Psalms*, trans. R. G. Finch, London 1919.

The Commentary of David Kimhi on the Book of Psalms, trans. A. W. Greenup, London 1918.

Davies, J. S., ed., *An English Chronicle of the Reigns of Richard II, Henry IV and Henry V*, Camden Society, original series 64 (1856).

Diarium Vadstenense, The Memorial Book of Vadstena Abbey, ed. G. Gejrot (= Studia Latina Stockholmiensis 33), Stockholm 1988.

Dreves, G. M., *Analecta hymnica medii aevi*, 24, Leipzig 1896; 52, ed. C., Blume, Leipzig 1909.

Egidi, P., *Necrologi e libri affini della provincia romana*, 2 vols. (= Fonti per la storia d'Italia, 44, 45), Rome 1908, 1914.

Fasciculi zizaniorum magistri Johannis Wyclif cum tritico, ed. W. W. Shirley, RS 5 (1858).

Fitzralph, R., *Summa de questionibus Armenorum*, ed. J. Sudoris, Paris 1511.

De pauperie Salvatoris, Books I–IV, ed. R. L. Poole, in Wyclif, J, *De dominio divino* (= Wycliffe Society), London 1890, pp. 257–476.

Fleming, N., 'A Calendar of the Register of Archbishop Fleming', ed. H. J. Lawlor, *Proceedings of the Royal Irish Academy* 30 C, no. 5 (1912), pp. 94–190.

Fodale, S., *Documenti del pontificato di Bonifacio IX (1389–1404)*, (= Fonti per la storia di Sicilia 5), Palermo 1983.

Gastout, M., ed., *Suppliques et lettres d'Urbain VI (1378–1389) et de Boniface IX (cinq premières années 1389–1394)*, (= AVB, 29: DRGS, 7), Brussels and Rome 1976.

Gatti, G., ed., *Statuti dei mercanti di Roma*, Rome 1885.

Gayet, L., *Le grand schisme d'occident*, 2 vols., Florence and Berlin 1889.

Gessler, J., ed., *Le livre des mestiers de Bruges et ses derivés*, Bruges 1931.

Ghiberti, L., *Lorenzo Ghibertis Denkwurdigkeiten (I commentarii)*, ed. J. von Schlosser, 2 vols., Berlin 1912.

Goioli, A., *Il protocollo notarile di 'Anthonius Goioli Petri Scopte' (1365)*, ed. R. Mosti, Rome 1991.

Gregory XI, *Lettres secrètes et curiales du Pape Gregoire XI (1370–78) intéressantes les pays autres que la France*, ed. G. Mollat (= Bibliothèques des écoles françaises d'Athènes et de Rome), Paris 1962.

Guillaume de S Amore, *Opera Omnia*, Constance 1632.

Bibliography

Hallum, R., *The Register of Robert Hallum, Bishop of Salisbury, 1407–1417*, ed. J. M. Horn, CYS, 72 (1982).

Hanquet, K., ed., *Suppliques de Clément VII, 1378–79*, (= *AVB* 8, *DRGS* 1), Paris 1924.

Hanquet, K. and Berlière, U., *Lettres de Clément VII 1378–9 (AVB* 12, *DRGS* 2), Rome 1930.

Harvey, M., 'Some documents on the early history of the English hospice', *Venerabile*, 30 (1994), pp. 39–43.

Henry IV, *Royal and Historical Letters*, ed. F. C. Hingeston, 2 vols., *RS*, 18 (1860, 1965).

Hoborch, G., ed., *Decisiones*, Mainz 1477 (= London, BL, IB 214).

Holland, E. L., *The Canterbury Chantries and Hospitals together with some others in the Neighbourhood in 1546*, Kent Records, 12, Supplement (1934).

Hugh of S Victor, *De sacramentis*, *PL*, 176, cols. 173–613.

Hussey, A., ed., *Kent Chantries* Kent Records 12 (1936).

Infessura, S., *Diario della città di Roma di Stefano Infessura, scribasenato*, ed. O. Tommasini (= Fonti per la storia d'Italia 5), Rome 1890.

James of Viterbo, *De regimine christiano*, ed. H.-X. Arquillière, Paris 1926.

Jerome, *Sancti Hieronymi psalterium iuxta Hebraeos*, ed. H. de Sainte-Marie (= Collectanea Biblica Latina 11), Rome 1954.

Johannes Nicolai Pauli, *I protocolli di Johannes Nicolai Pauli, un notaio romano del' 300 (1348–1379)*, ed. R. Mosti (= Collection de l'école française de Rome 63), Rome 1982.

Johannes Paulus Antonii Goyoli, in R. Mosti, 'Un protocollo del notaio romano Johannes Paulus Antonii Goyoli' (1377), *Archivio della società romana di storia patria*, 117 (1994), pp. 119–69.

John of Salisbury, *Policraticus*, ed. C. C. J. Webb, 2 vols., Oxford 1909.

Kemp, M., *The Book of Margery Kemp*, ed. S. B. Meech and H. E. Allen, *EETS* 217 (1940).

Knighton, *Knighton's Chronicle, 1337–1396*, ed. G. H. Martin, Oxford 1995.

Laurentius Romanus (or Lars Romares), *Lars Romares berattelse om dem heiligar Birgittas kanoniserung*, ed. K. Karllson, Stockholm 1901.

Leach, A. F., ed., *Memorials of Beverley Minster. The Chapter Act Book of the Collegiate Church of St John of Beverley, AD 1286–1347*, 2 vols., SS, 98, 108 (1897, 1903).

Lee, E., *Descriptio urbis. The Roman Census of 1527* (= Biblioteca del cinquecento 32), Rome 1985.

Legge, M. D., *Anglo-Norman Letters and Petitions from All Souls MS 182* (= Anglo-Norman Texts 3), Oxford 1941.

Lespinasse, R. de., *Les métiers et corporations de la ville de Paris*, III (in three parts), Paris 1886–97.

Lombardo, M. L. ed., *Camera urbis. Dohana minuta urbis liber introitus 1422*, Rome 1963.

Lugano, P. L., *I processi inediti per Francesca Bussa dei Ponziani (Santa Francesca Romana) 1440–1453*, Studi e testi 120 (1945).

Lunt, W. E. and Graves, E. B., eds., *Accounts Rendered by Papal Collectors in England 1317–1378*, Philadelphia 1968.

Lydford, J., *John Lydford's Book*, ed. D. M. Owen, Devonshire and Cornwall Record Society, new series 19(20), (1974/5), jointly with Historical Manuscripts Commission.

Bibliography

Macfarlane, L., 'An English account of the election of Urban VI, 1378', *BIHR*, 26 (1953), pp. 79–85.

Marsilius of Padua, *Defensor pacis*, ed. C. W. Previté-Orton, Cambridge 1928.

Mascall, R., *Registrum Roberti Mascall, episcopi Herefordensis, 1404–1416*, ed. J. H. Parry, CYS, 21 (1917).

Mone, G., *The Episcopal Registers of the Diocese of St David's 1397–1518*, ed. R. F. Isaacson and A. Roberts, 3 vols. (= Cymmrodorion Record Series 6), I, *The Register of Guy Mone, Bishop of St David's 1397–1407*, London 1917–20.

Nagl, F.-X., *Urkundliches zur Geschichte der Anima in Rom* (= Römische Quartalschrift für christliche Alterthumkunde und für Kirchengeschichte, Supplementheft 12), Rome 1899.

Nelis, H., ed., *Suppliques et lettres de Clément VII (= AVB* 13, *DRGS* 3), Rome 1934.

Nicolaus Johannis Jacobi, in R. Mosti 'Un quaderno superstite di protocollo del notaio romano Nicolaus Johannis Jacobi, 1391', *Archivio della società romana di storia patria*, 116 (1993), pp. 153–75.

Niem, Dietrich of, *De scismate*, ed. G. Erler, Leipzig 1890.

Nemus unionis, vol. IV of *De scismate. Historiae Theodorici de Niem qua res suo tempore durante gestae exponuntur*, ed. S. Schardius, Basel 1566.

Liber Cancellariae Apostolicae vom Jahr 1380 und der Stilus Palatii Abbreviatus, ed. G. Erler, Leipzig 1888.

Pantin, W. A., ed., *Canterbury College Oxford*, 4 vols., Oxford Historical Society, new series 6,7,8,30 (1946–50, 1985).

Chapters of the English Black Monks. Documents Illustrating the Activities of the General and Provincial Chapter, 3 vols., Camden Society, 3rd series 45, 47, 54 (1931–7).

Paulus Nicolai Pauli: R. Mosti,'Due quaderni superstiti dei protocolli del notaio romano Paulus Nicolai Pauli (1361–2)', *Mélanges de l'école française de Rome, moyen âge/temps modernes*, 96 (1984), pp. 777–844.

Perroy, E., ed., Richard II, *The Diplomatic Correspondence of Richard II*, Camden Society, 3rd series 48 (1933).

Persona, G., *Cosmidromius*, ed. M. Jansen, Münster in W. 1900.

Polychronicon Ranulphi Higden Monaci Cestrensis, ed. J. R. Lumby, 9 vols., *RS*, 41 (1865–86).

Porta, G., ed., 'Anonimo romano', *Cronica*, Milan 1979.

Pseudo-Dionysius, *The Complete Works*, trans. C. Luibhead and P. Roem, et al. (= Classics of Western Spirituality), Mahwah, NJ, 1989.

Pseudo-Jerome, *Quaestiones on the Book of Samuel*, ed. and intro. A. Saltman (= Studia Post-Biblica 27), Leiden 1975.

Raine, J., ed., *Historical Papers and Letters from Northern Registers*, RS, 61 (1873).

Historians of the Church of York and its Archbishops, 3 vols., RS, 70 (1886).

Re, E., *Statuti della città di Roma*, Rome 1880.

Register of Freemen of the City of York, I, *1272–1558*, ed. F. Collins, SS 96 (1897).

Repertorium Germanicum:

I, *Verzeichnis der in der Registern und Kameralackten Clemens VII von Avignon vorkommenden Personen, Kirchen und Orten des deutschen Reiches, seiner Diözesen und Territorien. 1378–94*, ed. E. Göller, Berlin 1916.

II, *Verzeichnis etc Urbans VI, Bonifaz IX, Innocents VII und Gregors XII . . . 1378–1415*, ed. G. Tellenbach, Berlin 1933.

Bibliography

III, *Verzeichnis etc . . . Alexanders V, Johannes XXIII und des Konstanzer Konzils, 1409–1417*, ed. U. Kühne, Berlin 1935.

Riley, H. T., *Memorials of London and London Life in the XIIIth, XIVth and XVth Centuries*, London 1878.

Rotuli Parliamentorum ut et Placita et Petitiones in Parliamento, 6 vols., London 1767–77.

Rotulorum Patentium et Clausarum Cancellariae Hiberniae Calendarium, I/1, London 1828.

Royce, D., ed., *Landboc sive registrum monasterii Beatae Mariae Virginis et Sancti Centelmi de Winchelcumba*. 2 vols., Exeter 1892.

Rymer, T., ed., *Foedera, Conventiones et Literae*, 3rd edn, 10 vols., The Hague 1739–45 (I quote the photo-reprint of 1967, citing the earlier edition from its margins).

The Saint Alban's Chronicle, ed. V. H. Galbraith, Oxford 1937.

Salimei, A., *Senatori e statuti di Roma nel medioevo*, I, *Senatori (1144–1447)*, (= Biblioteca storica di fonti e documenti 2), Rome 1935.

Schäfer, K. H., ed., *Die Ausgaben der Apostolischen Kammer unter den Papsten Urban V und Gregor XI (1362–1377)*, (= Vatikanische Quellen zur Geschichte der päpstlichen Hof- und Finanzverwaltung, 1316–1378), Paderborn 1938.

Schiavo, A. P., *Il diario romano di Antonio di Pietro dello Schiavo*, ed. F. Isoldi (= Rerum Italicarum Scriptores 24/5), Bologna 1917.

Schwarz, B., *Regesten der in Niedersachsen und Bremen überlieferten Papsturkunden, 1198–1503* (= Quellen und Untersuchungen zur Geschichte Niedersachsens im Mittelalter 15), Hannover 1993.

Scrope, R., *A Calendar of the Register of Richard Scrope, Archbishop of York 1398–1405*, 2 parts (= Borthwick Texts and Calendars. Records of the Northern Province 8, 11), ed. R. N. Swanson, York 1981–5.

Segre, A., ed., 'I dispacci di Cristoforo da Piacenza procuratore mantovano alla corte pontificia (1371–1383)', *Archivio storico italiano*, 5th series 43 (1909), pp. 27–95; 44 (1909), pp. 253–326.

Sellers, M., *The York Mercers and Merchant Venturers 1356–1917*, SS, 129 (1918).

Sharpe, R., *English Benedictine Libraries. The Shorter Catalogues* (= Corpus of British Medieval Library Catalogues 4), London 1996.

Sheppard, J. B. ed., *Literae Cantuarienses*, 3 vols., RS, 85 (1887–9).

Simonsfeld, H., 'Analeckten zur Papst und Konziliengeschichte', *Abhandlungen der hist. Classe der königlichen Bayerischen Akademie der Wissenschaft*, 20/1 (1893), pp. 1–56.

Sorbelli, A. ed., *Il Liber Secretus Juris Cesarei dell'università di Bologna*, I, *1378–1420* (= Universitatis Bononiensis Monumenta 2), Bologna 1938.

Sousa Costa, A. de., ed. *Monumenta Portugaliae Vaticana: Supplicas dos pontificados dos papas de Avinhao Clemente VII e Bento XIII e do papa de Roma Bonifacio IX*, II, Braga 1970.

Stafford, E., *The Register of Edmund Stafford (AD 1395–1419): an Index and Abstract of its Contents*, ed. F. C. Hingeston-Randolph, London and Exeter 1886.

Staglia, L., *Il protocollo notarile di Lorenzo Staglia (1372)*, ed. I. L. Sanfilippo (= Codice diplomatico di Roma e della regione romana 3), Rome 1986.

Stevenson, E., *Statuti dell' arte dei merciai e della lana di Roma*, Rome 1893.

Stow, J., *Annales or General Chronicle of England*, London 1631.

Stretton, R. de, *The Registers or Act Books of the Bishops of Coventry and Lichfield, Book 4*, ed. R. A. Wilson, William Salt Archaeological Society, new series 10/2 (1907); *Book 5*, same edn, same series 8 (1905).

Supino, P., ed., *La Margarita cornetana. Registro dei documenti*, Rome 1969.

246

Bibliography

Swanson, R. N., 'Papal letters among the ecclesiastical archives of York, 1378–1415', *Borthwick Institute Bulletin*, 1/4 (1978), pp. 165–93.

Swayne, J., *Register*, ed. D. A. Chart, Belfast 1935.

Testamenta Eboracensia, SS 4, 30, 45 (1836, 1855, 1864).

Trefnant, J., *Registrum Johannis Trefnant, Episcopi Herefordensis, 1389–1404*, ed. W. W. Capes, CYS, 20 (1916).

Tuccia, N, della, *Cronaca di Viterbo*, ed. I. Ciampo (= Documenti di storia italiana 5), Florence 1872.

Usk, A., *The Chronicle of Adam of Usk, 1377–1421*, ed. and trans. C. Given-Wilson (= Oxford Medieval Texts) Oxford 1997.

Villani, M., *Cronaca*, in Villani, G., M. and F., *Chronache di Dino Compagni e di Giovanni, Matteo e Filippo Villani*, One vol. in two parts, Padua 1841, part II.

Villani, G., *Nuova cronica*, 3 vols., ed. G. Porta, Parma 1990–1.

Wakefield, R., *Syntagma de hebreorum codicum incorruptione, c.* 1530 (Pollard and Redgrave 24946).

Walsingham, T., *Chronicon angliae*, ed. E. M. Thompson, RS, 64 (1874).

Historia anglicana, 2 vols., ed. H. T. Riley, RS, 28 (1863).

Waltham, J., *The Register of John Waltham, Bishop of Salisbury 1388–1395*, ed. T. C. B. Timmins, CYS, 80 (1994).

Wells: *Calendar of the MSS of the Dean and Chapter of Wells*, 2 vols. (= Historical Manuscripts Commission), London 1907, 1914.

The Westminster Chronicle 1381–1394, eds. L. C. Hector and B. F. Harvey, Oxford 1982.

Wilkins, D., ed., *Concilia magnae Britanniae et Hiberniae*, 4 vols., London 1737.

William of S Amour, *Opera Omnia*, Constance 1632.

Williman, D., *Bibliothèques ecclésiastiques au temps de la papauté d'Avignon*, I, Paris 1980.

Wimpfeling, J., *Castigationes locorum in canticis ecclesiasticis et divinis officiis depravatorum*, Johannes Schottus, Strasbourg 1513.

Wyclif, J., *De civili dominio*, ed. J. Loserth, 4 vols. (= Wyclif Society), London 1886–90.

De dominio divino, ed. R. L. Poole (= Wyclif Society), London 1890.

Sermones, ed. J. Loserth, 4 vols. (= Wyclif Society), London 1886–90.

Wykeham, W., *Wykeham's Register*, ed. T. F. Kirby, 2 vols., Hampshire Record Society (1896–9).

Zutshi, P. N. R., ed., *Original Papal Letters in England, 1305–1415* (= Index Actorum Romanorum Pontificum ab Innocentio III ad Martinum V Electum 5), Vatican City 1990.

SECONDARY SOURCES

Allmand, C., 'A bishop of Bangor during the Glyn Dwr revolt, Richard Young', *Journal of the Historical Society of the Church in Wales*, 23 (1986), pp. 47–56.

Altaner, B., 'Die Durchführung des Vienna Konzilsbeschlusses über die Errichtung von Lehrestuhlen für orientalische Sprache', *Zeitschrift für Kirchengeschichte*, 52 (1933), pp. 226–36.

Altaner, B., 'Zur Kenntnis des Hebräischen im Mittelalter', *Biblische Zeitschrift*, 21 (1933), pp. 288–308.

Armellini, M., *Le chiese di Roma*, 2 vols., Rome 1942.

Aston, M., *Thomas Arundel. A Study of Church Life in the Reign of Richard II*, Oxford 1967.

Bibliography

Aylmer, G. E. and Cant, R., *A History of York Minster*, Oxford 1977.

Bailey, M., 'Historiographical essay: the commercialisation of the English economy, 1086–1500', *Journal of Medieval History*, 24 (1998), pp. 277–311.

Barron, C. M., and Sutton, A. F., eds., *Medieval London Widows*, London 1994.

Bignami-Odier, J., *Études sur Jean de Roquetaillade*, Paris 1952.

Blair, J. and Ramsay, N., *English Medieval Industries. Craftsmen, Techniques, Products*, London and Rio Grande 1991.

Blouin, F. X., et al., *Vatican Archives. An Inventory and Guide to Historical Documents of the Holy See*, New York and Oxford 1998.

Borland, C. R., *A Descriptive Catalogue of the Western Medieval Manuscripts in Edinburgh University Library*, Edinburgh 1916.

Bradshaw, H., *Collected Papers*, Cambridge 1889.

Brentano, R., *Rome before Avignon. A Social History of Thirteenth Century Rome*, New York 1974.

Bridge, J. C., 'Two Cheshire soldiers of fortune of the xivth century: Sir Hugh Calveley and Sir Robert Knolles', *Journal of the Chester Archaeological Society*, 14 (1909), pp. 111–231.

Britnell, R. H., *Growth and Decline in Colchester 1300–1525*, Cambridge 1986.

'The new bridge', in *Traffic and Politics. The Construction and Management of Rochester Bridge AD 43–1993*, eds. N. Yates and J. M. Gibson, Woodbridge 1994, pp. 43–59.

Broise, H., 'Les maisons d'habitation à Rome aux xve et xvie siècles: les leçons de la documentation graphique', in J. C. Maire-Vigueur, ed., *D'une ville à l'autre. Structures matérielles et organisation de l'espace dans les villes européenes (XIIIe–XVIe siècles)*. (= Collection de l'école française de Rome 122), Rome 1989, pp. 609–29.

Brown, A., 'London and North West Kent in the later Middle Ages. The development of a land market', *Archaeologia Cantiana*, 92 (1976), pp. 145–55.

Brown, A. L., 'The Latin letters in MS All Souls 182', *EHR*, 87 (1972), pp. 565–73.

Bruckner, G., 'An unpublished source of the Avignonese papacy. The letters of Francesco Bruni', *Traditio*, 19 (1963), pp. 349–70.

Brundage, J. A., *Medieval Canon Law*, London and New York 1995.

Campbell, B. M. S., Galloway, J. A., Keene, D., and Murphy, M., *A Medieval Capital and its Grain Supply. Agrarian Production and Distribution in the London Region c. 1300* (= Historical Geography Research Series 30), London 1993.

Capitani, O., ed., *L'università a Bologna. Personaggi, momenti e luoghi dalle origini a XVI secolo*, Bologna 1987.

Capitani, O., et al., eds., *Conciliarismo, stati nazionali, inizi dell'umanismo. Atti del XXV convegno storico internazionale, Todi 9–12 Ottobre, 1988*, Spoleto 1990.

Caraffa, F., ed., *Monasticon Italiae*, I, *Roma e Lazio*, Cesena 1981.

Scritti in onore di Filippo Caraffa (= Biblioteca di Latium 2), Anagni 1986.

Carbonetti Venditelli, C., 'La curia dei *magistri edificarum urbis* nei secoli xiiie e xive e la sua documentazione', in E. Hubert, ed., *Rome au XIIIe et XIVe siècles* (see below under ed.), pp. 3–42.

Carocci, S., 'Baroni in città. Considerazioni sull'insediamento e i diritti urbani della grande nobiltà', in E. Hubert, ed., *Rome aux XIIIe et XIVe siècles* (see below under ed.), pp. 140–66.

Baroni di Roma. Dominazioni signorili e lignaggi aristocratici nel duecento e nel primo trecento (= Istituto storico italiano per il medioevo. Nuovi studi storici 23 or Collection de l'école française de Rome 181), Rome 1993.

Bibliography

Carus-Wilson, E. M., *The Medieval Merchant Venturers*, 2nd edn, Oxford 1967.

Carus-Wilson, E. M., and Coleman, O., *England's Export Trade*, Oxford 1963.

Catto, J. I. and Evans, T. A. R., eds., *The History of the University of Oxford*, I, *The Early Oxford Schools*, Oxford 1984.

Catto, J. I. and Evans, T. A. R., eds., *The History of the University of Oxford*, II, *Late Medieval Oxford*, Oxford 1992.

Cerchiari, E., *Capellani Papae et Apostolicae Sedis. Auditores causarum Sacri Palacii Apostolici seu Sacra Romana Rota ab origine ad diem usque 20 Septembris 1870*, 4 vols., Rome 1919–21.

Charles, B. D. and Emanuel, H. D., 'The library of John Trefnant, Bishop of Hereford 1389–1404', *The Journal of the National Library of Wales*, 6 (1949–50), pp. 355–60.

Chastel, A. and Vallet, G., eds., *Le palais Farnese* (= École française de Rome), 2 vols. (one in two), Rome 1980–1.

Chitty, H., and Jacob, E. F., 'Some Winchester College muniments', *EHR*, 49 (1934), pp. 1–13.

Churchill, I. J., *Canterbury Administration*, 2 vols., London 1933.

Clough, C. H., ed., *Profession, Vocation and Culture in Late Medieval England. Essays Dedicated to the Memory of A. R. Myers*, Liverpool 1982.

Cobban, A. B., *The King's Hall within the University of Cambridge in the Later Middle Ages* (= Cambridge Studies in Medieval Life and Thought, 3rd series 1), Cambridge 1969.

Cokayne, G. E., *The Complete Peerage*, various eds, 2nd edn, 13 vols., London 1910–40.

Colledge, E., '*Epistola solitarii ad reges*. Alphonso of Pecha as organiser of Birgittine and Urbanese propaganda', *Medieval Studies*, 18 (1956), pp. 19–49.

Corbo, A.-M., 'I legati "pro anima" e il restauro delle chiese a Roma tra la seconda metà del XIV secolo e la prima metà del XV', *Commentari*, 18 (1967), pp. 225–30.

Cullum, P. H., 'Vowesses and female lay piety in the province of York, 1300–1530', *Northern History*, 32 (1996), pp. 21–41.

Cutolo, A., *Re Ladislao d'Angio-Durazzo*, 2 vols., Milan 1936–44.

Dahan, G., *Les intellectuels chrétiens et les juifs au moyen âge*, Paris 1990.

'La connaisance de l'Hébreu dans les corrections de la Bible du XIIIe siècle', in *Rashi 1040–1990. Hommage à Ephraim E. Urbach. Congrès européen des études juives*, ed. G. Sed-Rajna, Paris 1993, pp. 567–78.

Dahmus, J. H., *William Courtenay, Archbishop of Canterbury 1381–1396*, University Park, Pa and London 1966.

D'Amico, J. F., *Renaissance Humanism in Papal Rome. Humanists and Churchmen on the Eve of the Reformation*, Baltimore and London 1983.

Darby, M., John Philipot. A 14th Century London Merchant. MSc for the University of London, 1976.

Davies, R. G., 'Richard II and the church in the years of "tyranny"', *Journal of Medieval History*, 1 (1975), pp. 329–62.

'Alexander Neville, archbishop of York, 1374–1388', *Yorkshire Archaeological Journal*, 47 (1975), pp. 87–101.

'After the execution of Archbishop Scrope. Henry IV, the papacy and the English episcopate, 1405–8', *BJRL*, 59 (1976–7), pp. 40–74.

'The episcopate and the political crisis in England, 1386–8', *Speculum*, 51 (1976), pp. 659–93.

Bibliography

'The Anglo-papal concordat of Bruges, 1375. A reconsideration', *AHP*, 19 (1981), pp. 97–146.

Davies, R. R., *The Revolt of Owen Glyn Dwr*, Oxford 1995.

Delaruelle, E., Labande, E.-R. and Ourliac, P., *L'église au temps du grand schisme et de la crise conciliaire, 1378–1449* (= A. Fliche and V. Martin, Histoire de l'église 14), 2 vols., Paris 1962.

Demaitre, L. E., *Doctor Bernard de Gordon, Professor and Practitioner* (= Studies and Texts 51, Pontifical Institute of Medieval Studies), Toronto 1980.

De Matteis, M. C., 'Giovanni da Legnano e lo scisma', in O. Capitani, ed., *Conciliarismo*, above, pp. 29–46.

'Profilo di Giovanni da Legnano', in O. Capitani, ed., *L'università a Bologna*, above, pp. 157–71.

Dictionnaire de spiritualité, ascetique et mystique, doctrine et histoire, 16 vols., Paris 1937–95.

Dizionario biografico degli Italiani, 49 vols. so far, Rome 1960 continuing.

Dobson, R. B., *Durham Priory, 1400–1450* (= Cambridge Studies in Medieval Life and Thought, 3rd series 6), Cambridge 1973.

'Beverley in conflict. Archbishop Alexander Neville and the minster clergy 1381–8', *Medieval Art and Architecture in the East Riding of Yorkshire*, ed. C. Wilson, *Proceedings of the British Archaeological Association Conference*, 9 (1983), pp. 149–64.

'The authority of the bishop in late medieval England: the case of Archbishop Alexander Neville of York, 1374–88', in Dobson, *Church and Society in the Medieval North of England*, London and Rio Grande 1996, pp. 185–93.

Dolezalek, G., 'Questiones motae in Rota: Richterliche Beratungsnotizen aus dem Vierzehten Jahrhundert' (= Monumenta Juris Canonici, series C, Subsidia 6), *Proceedings of the Fifth International Congress of Medieval Canon Law*, Vatican 1980, pp. 99–114.

Donner, R., *Jakob Wimpfelings Bemühungen um die Verbesserung der liturgischen Texte* (= Quellen und Abhandlungen zur mittelrheinischen Kirchengeschichte 26), Mainz 1976.

Donovan, G. M. and Keen, M. H., 'The *Somnium* of John of Legnano', *Traditio* 37 (1981), pp. 325–45.

Edler, F., *Glossary of Medieval Terms of Business. Italian Series*, Cambridge, Mass., 1934.

Ehrle, F., *Historia bibliothecae Romanorum pontificum tum Bonifatianae tum Avenionensis*, 2 vols., Rome 1890, 1947.

Ekwall, S., *Vår äldsta Birgittavita och dennas viktigastes varianter* (= Kungl. Vitterhets Historie- och Antikvitetsakademien, Historiska series 12), Lund 1965.

Ellis, R., 'Flores ad fabricandum . . . coronam': an investigation into the uses of the Revelations of St Bridget of Sweden in fifteenth-century England', *Medium Aevum*, 51 (1982), pp. 163–86.

'The visionary and the canon lawyers: papal and other revisions to the *Regula salvatoris* of St Bridget of Sweden', in Voeden, ed., *Prophets Abroad* (see below), pp. 71–90.

Emden, A. B., *A Biographical Register of the University of Oxford to 1500*, 3 vols., Oxford 1957–9.

A Biographical Register of the University of Cambridge to 1500, Cambridge 1963.

A Biographical Register of the University of Oxford 1501–1540, Oxford 1974.

Erler, G., *Dietrich von Nieheim (Theodoricus de Nyem). Sein Leben und seine Schriften*, Leipzig 1887.

Bibliography

Erler, M. C., 'Three fifteenth-century vowesses', in Barron, C. M. and Sutton, A. F., eds., *Medieval London Widows* (above), pp. 165–83.

Ermini, G., 'Un ignoto tratto *De Principatu* di Giovanni da Legnano', in *Studi di storia e diritto in onore di Carlo Calisse*, III, Milan 1940, pp. 421–46.

Scritti storico-giuridici, eds. O. Capitani and E. Menesto, Spoleto 1997.

Esch, A., 'Bankiers der Kirche im Grossen Schisma', *QFAIB*, 46 (1966), pp. 277–398.

Bonifaz IX und der Kirchenstaat, Tubingen 1969.

'Das Papstum unter der Herrschaft der Neapolitaner: die führender Gruppe Neapolitaner Familien an der Kurie während des Schismas 1378–1415', in *Festschrift für Hermann Heimpel zum 70. Gebürtstag*, ed. J. Fleckenstein et al., 3 vols. (= Veröffentlichungen des Max-Planck Instituts für Geschichte 36), II, Göttingen 1971, pp. 713–800.

'Florentiner in Rom um 1400. Namenverzeichnis der ersten Quattrocento-Generation', *QFAIB*, 52 (1972), pp. 476–525.

'Die Zeugenaussagen im Heiligensprechungsverfahren für S Francesca Romana als Quelle zur Sozialgeschichte Roms im frühen Quattrocento', *QFAIB*, 53 (1973), pp. 93–151.

'Simonie-geschaft in Rom 1400. "Kein papst wird das tun, was dieser tut"', *Vierteljahrschrift für Sozial- und Wirtschaftsgeschichte*, 61 (1974), pp. 433–51.

'Das Archiv eines lucchesischen Kaufmanns an der Kurie, 1376–87', *Zeitschrift für historische Forschung*, 2 (1975), pp. 129–71.

'La fine del libero commune di Roma nel giudizio dei mercanti fiorentini. Lettere romane degli anni 1395–1398 nell'archivio Datini', *Bulletino dell'istituto storico italiano per il medio evo e archivio muratoriano*, 86 (1976–7), pp. 235–77.

Eubel, C., *Hierarchia catholica medii aevi*, I, Munster 1913.

Fasoli, G., 'Richerche sulla legislazione antimagnatiza nei communi dell'alta e media Italia', *Rivista di storia del diritto italiano*, 12 (1939), pp. 86–133, 240–309.

Favier, J., *Les finances pontificales à l'époque du grand schisme d'occident 1378–1409* (= Bibliothèque des écoles françaises d'Athènes et de Rome 211), Paris 1966.

Fodale, S., *La politica napoletana di Urbano VI*, Rome 1973.

Forte, S. L., A study of some Oxford Schoolmen of the middle of the fourteenth century with special reference to Worcester Cathedral MS F. 65, University of Oxford B. Litt., 1947.

Fryde, E. B., Greenway, D. E., Porter, S. and Roy, I., *Handbook of British Chronology*, 3rd edn, London 1986.

Galbraith, V. H., 'John Seward and his circle. Some London scholars of the early fifteenth century', *Medieval and Renaissance Studies*, 1 (1941–3), pp. 85–104.

Gardiner, J., *The Tomb and the Tiara. Curial Tomb Sculpture in Rome and Avignon in the Later Middle Ages*, Oxford 1992.

Gennaro, C., 'Mercanti e bovattieri nella Roma della seconda metà del trecento (da una ricerca su registri notarili)', *Bulletino dell'istituto storico italiano per il medio evo e archivio muratoriano*, 78 (1967), pp. 155–203.

Gilkaer, H. T., *The Political Ideas of St Birgitta and her Spanish Confessor Alfonso Pecha* (= Odense University Studies in History and Social Sciences 163), Odense 1993.

Girgensohn, D., 'Wie wird man Kardinal? Kuriale und auskuriale Karrieren an der Wende des 14 zum 15 Jahrhundert', *QFAIB*, 57 (1977), pp. 138–62.

'Kardinal Antonio Caetani und Gregor XII in der Jahren 1406–8: vom Papstmacher zum Papstgegner', *QFAIB*, 64 (1984), pp. 116–226.

Bibliography

Given-Wilson, C., *The Royal Household and the King's Affinity. Service, Politics and Finance in England, 1360–1413*, New Haven (Conn.) and London 1986.

Gnoli, U., *Topografia e toponomastica di Roma medioevale e moderno*, Rome 1939.

Graef, H., *Mary. A History of Doctrine and Devotion*, 2 vols., London 1963–5.

Greatrex, J., 'Monk students from Norwich Cathedral Priory at Oxford and Cambridge', *EHR*, 106 (1991), pp. 555–83.

Biographical Register of the English Cathedral Priories of the Province of Canterbury, c. 1066–1540, Oxford 1997.

Guillemain, B., 'Citoyens, juifs et courtisans dans Avignon pontificale au XIVe siècle', *Bulletin philologique et historique du comité des travaux historiques et scientifiques* (1961), pp. 147–60.

La cour pontificale d'Avignon (1309–1376). Étude d'une société (= Bibliothèque des écoles françaises d'Athènes et de Rome 201), Paris 1962.

Gwynn, A., 'Ireland and the English nation at the council of Constance', *Proceedings of the Royal Irish Academy*, 45C (1940), pp. 183–233.

Gwynn, A. and Hadcock, R. N., *Medieval Religious Houses, Ireland*, Bristol 1970.

Hailperin, H., *Rashi and the Christian Scholars*, Pittsburg 1963.

Haren, M. J., 'Social structures of the Irish church. A new source in papal penitentiary dispensations for illegitimacy', in Schmugge et al., *Illegitimität*, below pp. 207–26.

Harriss, G. L., *Cardinal Beaufort. A Study of Lancastrian Ascendancy and Decline*, Oxford 1988.

Harvey, M., 'England and the Council of Pisa: some new information', *Annuarium Historiae Conciliorum*, 2 (1970), pp. 263–83.

Solutions to the Schism, A Study of Some English Attitudes 1378–1409 (= Kirchengeschichtliche Quellen und Studien 12), St Ottilien 1983.

'John Whethamsted, the pope and the general council', in *The Church in Pre-Reformation England. Essays in Honour of F. R. H. DuBoulay*, ed. C. M. Barron and C. Harper-Bill, Woodbridge 1985, pp. 108–22.

England, Rome and the Papacy, 1417–1464. The Study of a Relationship, Manchester 1993.

'Preaching in the curia: some sermons by Thomas Brinton', *AHP*, 33 (1995), pp. 299–301.

'The household of Simon Langham', *JEH*, 47 (1996), pp. 18–44.

'Adam Easton and pseudo-Dionysius', *Journal of Theological Studies*, new series 48 (1997), pp. 77–89.

'Adam Easton and the condemnation of John Wyclif, 1377', *EHR*, 113 (1998), pp. 321–34.

Haslop, G. S., 'Two entries from the register of John de Shirburn, abbot of Selby, 1369–1408', *Yorkshire Archaeological Journal*, 41 (1963–6), pp. 287–96.

Hasted, E., *The History and Topographical Survey of the County of Kent*, 12 vols., Canterbury 1797–1801.

Hayez, A-M., 'Les bourgs avignonnais du XIVe siècle', *Bulletin philologique et historique (jusqu'au 1610) du comité des travaux historiques et scientifiques*, Paris 1977 (for 1975), pp. 77–102.

Heimpel, H., *Dietrich von Niem (c. 1340–1418)*, Münster 1932.

Hennessey, G., *Novum Repertorium Ecclesiasticum Parochiale Londinense*, London 1898.

Herlihy, D., 'The Tuscan town in the Quattrocento: a demographic profile', *Medievalia et Humanisticia*, new series 1 (1970), pp. 81–109.

Bibliography

Herlihy, D., *Opera Muliebria. Women and Work in Medieval Europe*, New York etc., 1990.

Hoberg, H., 'Die Rotarrichter in den Eidregistern der apostolischen Kammer von 1347–1494', *QFAIB*, 34 (1954), pp. 159–69.

Hofmann, W. von, *Forschungen zur Geschichte der kurialen Behörden vom Schisma bis zur Reformation*, 2 vols. (= Bibliothek des kgl. Preussischen historischen Instituts in Rom. 12 and 13), Rome 1914.

Hogg, J., 'Cardinal Easton's letter to the abbess and community of Vadstena', *Studies in S Birgitta and the Brigittine Order*, 2, *Analecta Cartusiana*, 19 (1993), pp. 20–6.

Höjer, T., *I studier Vadstena klosters och Birgittinordens historia*, Uppsala 1905.

Holmes, G., 'Florentine merchants in England 1346–1436' *Economic History Review*, 2nd series 13 (1960), pp. 193–208.

'How the Medici became the pope's bankers', in *Florentine Studies*, ed. N. Rubenstein, London 1968, pp. 357–80.

The Good Parliament, Oxford 1975.

'Florence and the Great Schism', in G. Holmes, ed., *Art and Politics in Renaissance Italy. British Academy Lectures*, Oxford 1993, pp. 19–40.

Hoshino, H., *L'arte della lana in Firenze nel basso medioevo. Il commercio della lana e il mercato dei panni fiorentini nei secolo XIII–XV* (= Biblioteca storica toscana 21), Florence 1980.

Hubert, E., *Espace urbain et habitat à Rome du Xe siècle à la fin du XIIIe siècle* (= Collection de l'école française de Rome 135), Rome 1990.

'Économie de la propriété immobilière des établissements religieux et leurs patrimoines au XIVe siècle', in Hubert, ed., *Rome aux XIIIe*, below, pp. 177–230.

'Gestion immobilière, propriété dissociée et seigneuries foncières à Rome aux XIIIe et XIVe siècles', in O. Faron and E. Hubert, eds., *Le sol et l'immeuble. Les formes dissociées de propriété immobilière dans les villes de France et d'Italie* (XIIe–XIXe siècles) (= Collection de l'école française de Rome 206), Rome 1995, pp. 185–205.

'Élection de sépulture et fondation de chapelle funeraire à Rome au XIVe siècle, donation et concession de l'espace sacré', in Parravicini-Bagliani, *La parrochia nel medio evo* (below), pp. 209–27.

Hubert, E., ed., *Rome aux XIIIe et XIVe siècles* (= Collection de l'école française de Rome 170), Rome 1993.

Huelsen, C., *Le chiese di Roma nel medio evo. Cataloghi ed appunti*, Rome 1927.

Hunnisett, R. F. and Post, J. B., eds., *Medieval Records Edited in Memory of C. A. F. Meekings*, London 1978.

Hunter, J., *South Yorkshire. The History and Topography of the Deanery of Doncaster in the Diocese and County of York*, 2 vols., London 1831.

Inventario general de manuscritos de la biblioteca nacional, 13 vols. continuing, Madrid 1956 onwards.

Jacob, E. F., *Essays in the Conciliar Epoch*, 2nd edn, Manchester 1953.

'To and from the court of Rome in the early fifteenth century', in Jacob, *Essays in Later Medieval History*, Manchester 1968, pp. 58–78.

Jewell, H., *Women in Medieval England*, Manchester 1996.

Johnston, F. R., 'The English cult of S Bridget of Sweden', *Analecta Bollandiana*, 103 (1985), pp. 75–93.

Jonsson, A., ed., *Alfonso of Jaen. His Life and Works, with critical editions of Epistola Solitarii, Informaciones and Epistola Servi Christi* (= Studia Graeca et Latina Lundensia 1), Lund 1989.

Bibliography

Jones, E. J., 'The authorship of the Continuation of the *Eulogium Historiarum*: a suggestion', *Speculum*, 12 (1937), pp. 200–2.

Jones, E. F., 'An examination of the authorship of the Deposition and Death of Richard II attributed to Creton', *Speculum*, 15 (1940), pp. 460–77.

Jorgensen, J., *Saint Bridget of Sweden*, 2 vols., London 1954.

Julien de Pommerel, M.-H. and Monfrin, J., *La bibliothèque pontifical à Avignon et à Peñiscola, pendant le grand schisme d'occident et sa dispersion*, 2 vols. (= Collection de l'école française de Rome 141), Rome 1991.

Katermaa-Ottela, A., *Le casetorri medievali in Roma* (= Commentationes Humanarum Litterarum 67), Helsinki 1981.

Kelly, J. N. D., *The Oxford Dictionary of the Popes*, Oxford 1986.

Ker, N. R., *Books, Collectors and Libraries. Studies in the Medieval Heritage*, ed. A. G. Watson, London 1985.

King, H. P., 'A dispute between Henry IV and the chapter of Lincoln', *Archives*, 4/22 (1959), pp. 81–3.

Kirby, J. L., *Henry IV of England*, London 1970.

Klapisch-Zuber, C., *Women, Family and Ritual in Renaissance Italy*, Chicago 1985.

Kleinhans, A, 'Nicolaus Trevet, OP, *psalmorum interpres*', *Angelicum*, 20 (1943), pp. 219–36.

Koudelka, V. J., 'Raymond von Capua und Böhmen', *AFP*, 30 (1960), pp. 206–26.

Krautheimer, R., *Lorenzo Ghiberti*, Princeton 1970.

Krautheimer, R., *Rome, Profile of a City 312–1308*, Princeton 1980.

Kuttner, S. and Elze, R., *A Catalogue of Canon and Roman Law Manuscripts in the Vatican Library*, 2 vols. (= Studi e testi 322, 328), Vatican City 1986–7.

Lambert, M., *Franciscan Poverty. The Doctrine of the Absolute Poverty of Christ and the Apostles in the Franciscan Order 1210–1323*, London 1961.

Landi, A., *Il papa deposto (Pisa 1409). L'idea conciliare nel grande scisma*, Turin 1985.

Lefferts, P. M., *The Motet in England in the Fourteenth Century* (= Studies in Musicology 94), Ann Arbor 1986.

Le Neve, J., *Fasti eccleiae anglicane*, rev. edn, various eds, 12 vols., London 1962 onwards.

Leyser, H., *Medieval Women. A Social History of Women in England 450–1500*, London 1995.

Lloyd, T. H., *The English Wool Trade in the Middle Ages*, Cambridge 1977.

Loewe, R., 'Hebrew books and Judaica in Medieval Oxford and Cambridge', in J. M. Shaftesley, ed., *Remember the Days. Essays on Anglo-Jewish History presented to Cecil Roth* (= Jewish Historical Society of England), London 1966, pp. 23–48.

Loewe, R., 'The medieval Christian Hebraists of England. The *Superscriptio Lincolniensis*', *Hebrew Union College Annual*, 28 (1957), pp. 205–52.

Louth, A., *Denys the Areopagite*, London 1989.

Lunt, W. E., *Financial Relations of the Papacy with England 1327–1534*, II, Cambridge (Mass.) 1962.

Maas, C. W., *The German Community in Renaissance Rome, 1378–1523* (= Römische Quartalschrift für christliche Altertumskunde und Kirchengeschichte, Supplementheft 39), Rome 1981.

Macfarlane, L. J., The life and writings of Adam Easton, OSB, 3 vols., University of London PhD, 1955.

McCall, J. P., 'The writings of John of Legnano, with a list of manuscripts', *Traditio*, 23 (1967), pp. 415–37.

Bibliography

McConica, J. K., *English Humanists and Reformation Politics under Henry VIII and Edward VI*, Oxford 1965.

McDermid, R. J. W., *Beverley Minster Fasti*, Yorkshire Archaeological Society, Record Series 149 (1993 for 1990).

McFarlane, K. B., *John Wycliffe and the Beginnings of English Non-conformity*, Aylesbury 1952.

England in the Fifteenth Century, Collected Essays, ed. and intro., G. L. Harriss, London 1981.

Maire-Vigueur, J. C., 'Les casali des églises de Rome à la fin du moyen âge (1348–1428)' *Mélanges de l'école française de Rome, moyen âge/temps moderne*, 86 (1974), pp. 63–136.

Majic, T., 'Die apostolische Pönitentiarie im 14. Jahrhundert', *Römische Quartalschrift*, 50 (1955), pp. 129–77.

Manfredi, A., *I codici latini di Nicolo V. Edizione degli inventari e identificazione dei manuscritti* (= Studi e testi 359), Vatican City 1994.

Maxfield, D. K., 'A fifteenth-century lawsuit: the case of St Anthony's Hospital', *JEH*, 44 (1993), pp. 199–223.

Montel, R., 'Les chanoines de la basilique de Saint-Pierre de Rome des statuts capitulaires de 1277–1279 à la fin de la papauté d'Avignon. Étude prosopographique', *Rivista di storia della chiesa in Italia*, 42 (1988), pp. 365–50; 43 (1989), pp. 1–49, 413–79.

Muldoon, J., *Popes, Lawyers and Infidels. The Church and the Non-Christian World, 1280–1550*, Liverpool 1979.

Nicholas, D., *The Later Medieval City, 1300–1500*, London and New York 1997.

Nightingale, P., 'Monetary contraction and mercantile credit in later medieval England,' *Economic History Review*, 2nd series 43 (1990), pp. 560–75.

A Medieval Mercantile Community. The Grocers' Company and the Politics and Trade of London 1000–1485, New Haven and London 1995.

Ninci, R., 'Ladislao e la conquista di Roma del 1408: ragioni e contraddizioni della diplomazia fiorentini', *Archivio della società romana di storia patria*, 111 (1988), pp. 161–224.

Palermo, L., *Il porto di Roma nel XIV e XV secolo. Strutture socio-economiche e statuti* (= Fonti e studi per la storia economica e sociale di Roma e dello stato pontificio nel tardo medioevo 2), Rome 1979.

Palermo, L., 'Banchi privati e finanze pubbliche nella Roma del primo rinascimento', in *Banchi pubblichi, banchi privati e monte di pietà nell'Europa pre-industriale*, 2 vols. (= Atti del convegno, Genoa 1991), *Atti della società ligure di storia patria*, new series 31 (105), (1991), pp. 435–59.

Paravicini-Bagliani, A. and Pasche, V., *La parrochia nel medio evo. Economia, scambi, solidarità* (= Italia sacra. Studi e documenti di storia ecclesiastica 53), Rome 1995.

Parks, G. B., *The English Traveller to Italy*, I, *The Middle Ages to 1525*, Rome 1954.

Partner, P., *The Lands of St Peter. The Papal State in the Middle Ages and the Early Renaissance*, London 1972.

The Pope's Men. The Papal Civil Service in the Renaissance, Oxford 1990.

Passigli, R. and Temperini, L., see under Temperini.

Passigli, S., 'Geografia parrochiale e circonscrizioni territoriale nei secoli XII–XIV: istituzione e realtà quotidiana', in Hubert, *Rome aux XIIIe e XIVe siècles*, pp. 45–77.

255

Bibliography

Perroy, E., *L'Angleterre et le grand schisme d'occident. Étude de la politique religieuse d'Angleterre sous Richard II, 1378–1399*, Paris 1933.

Petrucci, E., 'Pievi e parrochie del Lazio nel basso medioevo: note e osservazione', in *Pievi e parrochia*, 1 (36), pp. 892–1017, see below.

Pfaff, R. W., *New Liturgical Feasts in Later Medieval England*, Oxford 1970.

'The English devotion of St Gregory's Trental', *Speculum*, 49 (1974), pp. 75–90.

Pievi e parrochia in Italia nel basso medioevo (sec. XIII–XV), 2 vols. (= Italia sacra. Studi e documenti di storia ecclesiastica 36, 37), Rome 1984.

Polc, J. V., *De origine festi visitationis B V M* (= Corona Lateranensis 9A), Rome 1967.

'La festa della Visitazione e il giubileo del 1390', *Rivista di storia della chiesa in Italia*, 29 (1975), pp. 149–72.

Prerovský, O., *L'elezione di Urbano VI e l'insorgere dello scisma d'occidente* (= Miscellanea della società romana di storia patria 20), Rome 1960.

Quaglioni, D., 'The legal definition of citizenship in the late Middle Ages', in Mohlo, A., Raaflaub, K.,and Emlen, J., eds., *City States in Classical Antiquity and Medieval Italy*, Stuttgart 1991, pp. 155–67.

Reeves, M., *The Influence of Prophecy in the Later Middle Ages. A Study of Joachimism*, Oxford 1969.

Renouard, Y., *Les relations des papes d'Avignon et des compagnies commerciales et bancaires de 1316 à 1378* (= Bibliothèque des écoles françaises d'Athènes et de Rome 151), Paris 1941.

Rex, J., *The Theology of John Fisher*, Cambridge 1991.

Robinson, J. A., 'Simon Langham, Abbot of Westminster', *Church Quarterly Review*, 66 (1908), pp. 339–66.

Robinson, J. A. and James, M. R., *The Manuscripts of Westminster Abbey*, Cambridge 1909.

Rodocanchi, E., 'Les couriers pontificaux du quatorzième au dixseptième siècle', *Revue d'histoire diplomatique*, 26 (1912), pp. 392–428.

Rorem, P., *Pseudo-Dionysius: a Commentary on the Texts and an Introduction to their Influence*, New York 1993.

Roskell, J. S., Clark, L. and Rawcliffe, C., *History of Parliament. The House of Commons 1386–1421*, 4 vols., Stroud 1992.

Ruddock, A. A., *Italian Merchants and Shipping in Southampton 1270–1600* (= Southampton Record Series 1), Southampton 1951.

Rusconi, R., *L'attesa della fine. Crisi della società, profezia ed apocalisse in Italia a tempo del grande scisma d'occidente (1378–1417)*, (= Studi storici 115–118), Rome 1979.

Sanfilippo, I. L., 'I protocolli notarile romani del trecento' *Archivio della società romana di storia patria*, 110 (1987), pp. 99–150.

Sayers, J. E., 'Proctors representing British interests at the papal court, 1198–1415', in Kuttner, S., ed., *Proceedings of the Third International Congress of Medieval Canon Law* (= Monumenta Iuris Canonici, series C, subsidia 4), Vatican City 1971, pp. 143–63.

'Canterbury Proctors', *Traditio*, 22 (1966), pp. 311–45.

Schmidlin, A. J., *Geschichte der deutschen Nationalkirche in Rom, S Maria dell'Anima*, Freiburg in Br. 1906.

Schmugge, L. and Wiggenhauser, B., *Illegitimät im Spätmittelalter* (= Schriften des historischen Kollegs, Kolloquien 29), Munich 1994.

Schmugge, L., Hersperger, P. and Wiggenhauser, B., *Die Supplikenregister der päpstlichen*

Bibliography

Pönitentiarie aus der Zeit der Pius II (1458–64), (= Bibliothek des deutschen historishen Instituts in Rom 84), Tübingen 1996.

Schuchard, C., *Die Deutschen an der päpstlichen Kurie im späten Mittelalter (1378–1447)* (= Bibliothek des deutschen historischen Instituts in Rom 65),Tübingen 1987.

'*Defectus natalium* und Karriere am römische Hof. Das Beispiel der Deutschen an der päptslichen Kurie (1378–1471)', in Schmugge et al., *Illegitimät*, pp. 149–70.

Schulte, J. F. von, *Geschichte der Quellen und Literatur des kanonischen Rechts*, 3 vols., Stuttgart 1875–89.

Schwarz, B., *Die Organisation kurialer Schreiberkollegien von irhrer Enstehung bis zur Mitte des 15. Jahrhunderts* (= Bibliothek des deutschen historischen Instituts in Rom 37), Tubingen 1972.

'L'organizzazione curiale di Martino V ed i problemi derivanti dallo scisma', in M. Ciabo et al., eds., *Alle origini della nuova Roma. Martino V (1417–1431)* (= Nuovi studi storici 20), Rome 1992, pp. 329–45.

'*Abbreviature officium est assistere vicecancellario in expeditione litterarum apostolicarum.* Zur Entwicklung des Abbreviatorenamtes vom grossen Schisma bis zur Grundung des Vakabilistenkollegs der Abbreviatoren durch Pius II', in E. Gatz, ed., *Römische Kurie, kirchliche Finanzen, vatikanisches Archiv. Studien zu Ehren von Hermann Hoberg*, II, Rome 1979, pp. 789–823.

Seidlmayer, M., *Die Anfänge des grossen abendländischen Schismas* (= Spanische Forschungen aus der Görresgesellschaft, Series 2/5), Münster 1940.

Sensi, M., 'Alfonso Pecha e l'eremitismo Italiano di fine secolo XIV', *Rivista di storia della chiesa in Italia*, 47 (1993), pp. 51–80.

Sharpe, R., *A Handlist of the Latin Writers of Great Britain and Ireland before 1540* (= Publications of the Journal of Medieval Latin 1), Turnhout 1997.

Sieben, H. J., *Die Konzilsidee des lateinische Mittelalters (847–1378)*, Paderborn 1984.

Small, C. M., 'The district of Rome in the early fourteenth century, 1300–1347', *Canadian Journal of History*, 16 (1981), pp. 193–213.

Smalley, B., *The Study of the Bible in the Middle Ages*, 3rd rev. edn, Oxford 1983.

Somerville, R., *History of the Duchy of Lancaster*, 2 vols., London 1953.

Souchon, M., *Die Papstwahlen in der Zeit des grossen Schismas. Entwicklung und Verfassungskämpf des Kardinalates von 1378 bis 1417*, 2 vols., Braunschweig 1898–9, repr. 1970.

Southern, R. W., *Robert Grosseteste. The Growth of an English Mind in Medieval Europe*, Oxford 1986.

Spufford, P., *Handbook of Medieval Exchange* (= Royal Historical Society, Guides and Handbooks 13), London 1986.

Steel, A., *Richard II*, Cambridge 1941.

Storey, R. L., *Thomas Langley and the Bishopric of Durham*, London 1961.

'Clergy and common law in the reign of Henry IV', in Hunnisett and Post, *Medieval Records in Memory of C. A. F.Meekings*, above, pp. 341–408.

'Papal provisions to English monasteries', *Nottingham Medieval Studies*, 35 (1991), pp. 77–91.

'Gentlemen bureaucrats', in Clough, ed., *Profession, Vocation*, above, pp. 90–117.

Strohm, R., *The Rise of European Music, 1380–1500*, Cambridge 1993.

Swanson, R. N., 'Archbishop Arundel and the chapter of York', *BIHR*, 54 (1981), pp. 254–7.

Church and Society in Late Medieval England, Oxford 1989, 1993.

Bibliography

Tacchella, L., *Il pontificato di Urbano VI a Genova (1385–1386) e l'eccidio dei cardinali*, Genoa 1976.

Talmage, F. E., 'R. David as polemicist', *Hebrew Union College Annual*, 38 (1967), pp. 213–35.

David Kimhi. The Man and the Commentaries (= Harvard Judaic Monographs 1), Cambridge (Mass.) and London 1975.

Tanner, N. P., *The Church in Late Medieval Norwich, 1370–1532* (= Pontifical Institute of Medieval Studies, Studies and Texts 66), Toronto 1984.

Temperini, L, 'Fenomeni di vita communitaria tra i penitenti Francescani in Roma e dintori', in Pazelli, R. and Temperini, L., eds., *Prima manifestazioni di vita communitaria maschile e femminile nel movimento franciscano della penitenza (1215–1447)* (= Commissione storica internazionale TOR), Rome 1982, pp. 603–53.

Temple-Leader, G. and Marcotti, G., *Giovanni Acuto (Sir John Hawkwood). Storia d'un condottiere*, Florence 1889.

Theseider, E. D., *Roma dal commune di popolo alla signoria pontificia, 1252–1377* (= Storia di Roma 11), Bologna 1952.

Thompson, A. H. and Clay, C. T., *Fasti Parochiales*, II, Yorkshire Archaeological Society, Record series, 107 (1943).

Thomson, J. A. F., 'The "well of grace": Englishmen and Rome in the fifteenth cenutury', in Dobson, R. B., ed., *The Church, Politics and Patronage in the Fifteenth Century*, Gloucester 1984, pp. 99–114.

Thomson, W. R., *The Latin Writings of John Wyclif* (= Pontifical Institute of Medieval Studies. Subsidia Medievalia 14), Toronto 1983.

Thrupp, S., *The Merchant Class of Medieval London*, London 1948.

Thurston, H., 'The rosary', *The Month*, 96 (1900), pp. 403– 18, 513–27.

'A history of the rosary in all countries', *Journal of the Society of Arts*, 50 (1901), pp. 261–76.

'Genuflexions and Aves', *The Month*, 127 (1916), pp. 441–52, 546–59.

Tierney, B., *Origins of Papal Infallibility 1150–1350. A Study on the Concepts of Infallibility, Sovereignty and Tradition in the Middle Ages* (= Studies in the History of Christian Thought 6), Leiden 1972.

Tout, T. F., *Chapters in the Administrative History of Medieval England*, 6 vols., London 1920–33.

Trexler, R. C., 'A medieval census: the *Liber Divisionis*', *Medievalia et Humanistica*, 17 (1966), pp. 82–5.

'Rome on the eve of the Great Schism', *Speculum*, 42 (1967), pp. 489–509.

The Spiritual Power. Republican Florence under Interdict (= Studies in Medieval and Reformation Thought 9), Leiden 1974.

Undhagen, C.-G., 'Une source du prologue (chap. 1) aux *Revelationes* de Sainte Brigitte par le cardinal Turrecremata', *Eranos*, 58 (1960), pp. 214–26.

Veale, E., *The English Fur Trade in the Later Middle Ages*, Oxford 1966.

Venerabile: 'The English Hospice in Rome', *Venerabile* (Sexcentenary issue), 21 (1962).

Victoria County History, ed. W. Page et al., London 1903 onwards, as *The Victoria History of the County of . . .* followed by name of county and volume.

Voeden, R., ed., *Prophets Abroad. The Reception of Continental Holy Women in Late-Medieval England*, Woodbridge 1996.

Voci, A. M., 'Giovanni I d'Angio e l'inizio del grande scisma d'occidente. La doppia elezione del 1378 e la proposta conciliare', *QFIAB*, 75 (1995), pp. 178–255.

Bibliography

Walker, S., *The Lancastrian Affinity*, Oxford 1990.

Walsh, K., *A Fourteenth-Century Scholar and Primate. Richard Fitzralph in Oxford, Avignon and Armagh*, Oxford 1981.

'The Roman career of John Swayne, Archbishop of Armagh, 1418–1439. Plans for an Irish hospital in Rome', *Seanchas Ardmacha*, 11/1 (1983) pp. 1–21.

Watt, D. E. R., *Fasti ecclesiae Scotticanae medii aevi ad annum 1638* (= Scottish Record Society, new series 1), Edinburgh 1969.

Weisheipl, J. A., *Friar Thomas D'Aquino. His Life, Thought and Works*, Oxford 1974.

Weiss, S., 'Kredit europäischer Fürsten für Gregor XI. Zur Finanzierung der Rückkehr des Papsttums von Avignon nach Rom', *QFIAB*, 77 (1997), pp. 176–205.

Widmore, R., *An History of the Church of St Peter, Westminster*, London 1751.

Wilks, M., *The Problem of Sovereignty in the Later Middle Ages*, Cambridge 1963.

Williams, G., *The Welsh Church from Conquest to Reformation*, Cardiff 1976.

Williams, M. E., *The Venerable English College, Rome, 1579–1979. A History*, London 1979.

Williman, D., 'The Right of Spoil of the Popes of Avignon, 1316–1415', *Transactions of the American Philosophical Society*, 78/6 (1988), whole vol.

Winston-Allen, A., *Stories of the Rose. The Making of the Rosary in the Middle Ages*, Pennsylvania 1997.

Wylie, J. H., *The History of England under Henry IV*, 4 vols., London 1884–96.

Zutshi, P. N. R., 'Proctors acting for English petitioners in the chancery of the Avignon Popes (1305–1378)', *JEH*, 35 (1984), pp. 15–29.

INDEX

Index

Index

Bernardus de Gordonio, *Lilium medicinale*, 223
Bethlehem, bishop of, *see* Bottlesham, William
Beverley Minster, 36, 41, 139, 176, prebend of
S Martin in, 150; *see also* Shipdam; Easton,
benefices
Bible, Vulgate, accuracy of, 230, 236–7
exegesis of: Exodus, 233; *glossa ordinaria*, 230,
233; glosses on Matthew and Mark, 223;
Genesis, 231–3; Kings, book of, 192, 230;
Leviticus, 232; Matthew, 221; psalms: 8,
234; 71 (=72) 16; 73 (=74), 231; 109
(=110), 231; I Sam., 217
Black Death, 23; *see also* Rome
Black monks, *see* Benedictines
Bodisham, (Bottlesham?), Nicholas, Rota
auditor, 133–4, 138
Boileau, Etienne, *Livre des métiers*, 28
Bokenhull, John, OSB of Westminster, 162–3
Bolingbroke, Henry, *see* Kings of England,
Henry IV
Bologna, 22, 30, 52, 161, 229
University of, 134, 137, 147, 155
archbishop of *see* Innocent VII, Correr,
Anthonius
Bona, widow of Bucius Nucii, 113
Bondis, Martinus de, *speciarius*, father of Nicola,
81
Bondis, Bondi, Nicola de, 68–9, 80–1
Boore, John, dean of king's household, 206; *see
also* Easton, benefices, Somersham
Bordeaux, 197; archbishop of, *see* Ugguccione
Borgo, 49, 50
Bosc, Pierre du, bishop of Dax, 211
Bottlesham, William, OP, bishop of
Bethlehem, Llandaff, Rochester, 39–40,
75, 134, 138, 164, 170
Boulogne, Guy of, cardinal, 78
Bowet, Henry, auditor of the camera, bishop of
Bath, archbishop of York, 39–41, 47,
143–4, 156, 158, 160, 170, 182–3; *see also*
Morhay, John
Bramantis, Bramante, John, *cernitor*, 96–8,
122–3, 126; husband of Rosa Casarola,
q.v.
Bramfield (Bromfield), alias Halesworth,
Edmund, OSB, of Bury S Edmunds,
master of the Sacred Palace, 162–4, 170,
172–3, 198, 203
Brantingham, Thomas, bishop of Exeter, 75,
135
Braybrooke, Robert, bishop of London, 59,
140
Bremore, John, proctor and secretary to pope
52–3, 152–3, 160
Bridget of Sweden, saint, 15, 19–20, 162, 204
canonisation of, 196, 199, 201, 204–5, 229

cult of, in England, 200, 205, 237
daughter Katherine, 196, 200
works of: *Orationes*, 221; *Revelations*, 196,
222; *Regula Salvatoris*, 220; *Sermo Angelicus*,
220; *see also* Easton, *Defensorium* of;
Alfonso of Pecha
Bridgettines, of Vadstena, 204–5, 236; *see also*
religious houses, Rome
Diarium of, 205
Brinkley, John, 163
Brinton, Thomas (Brampton), penitentiary,
bishop of Rochester, 59–60, 75, 163, 164,
189–91, 230
Brisby, Richard, 128
Bristol, 129
Bromyard, John, OP, *Distinctiones*, 143
Bron, John, layman, 33
Bruges, 1, 5, 26, 48, 107, 128, 157, 203
Brugge, Alice, wife of Simon, 125
Brut, William, OSB, 43
Brygstok, John, layman, 33
Bubwith, Nicholas, 75
Buchan, Walter de, 200
Bucius Nannoli, widow of, daughter of
Paulucius della Torre, *murator*, 64
Bucius Nucii, *see* Bona
Bucius Thomaxi Valsarii, 118
Buckenhall, rector, *see* Tart, William
Buckingham, John, bishop of Lincoln, 75
Bukelden, Theodoric, *see* Easton, household
Bulgaminis, Torre de, 81
Bulgariis, John de, 64
bullion famine, 42, 48, 109, 170
Burstede, Roger, rector of S Olave, London,
101–2, 173
Bury S Edmunds, chronicler, 198
abbey of, *see* Bramfield, Edmund; Brinkley,
John; Timworth, John
Bussa family, *see* S Francesca Romana
Butrigarius, on the Codex, 142
Buyton, Henry, canon of Hereford, 37–8

Caetani, family, 80, 171
Caetani, Onoratus, 37
Caetani, or de Caetanis, Antonius de, cardinal
priest of S Cecilia in Trastevere, 80, 85,
171–2, 181
Cafagi, family, 117
Cafagi, Cafagni, Casagi, Cofagi, Jacobellus,
murator 11, 117–18, wife Joanna
Cafagi, Barthelutius, alias Marcille, brother of
Jacobellus, 118, wife Angela, son Paulus,
notary, 118
Cafagi, Johannes, 118
Cages, Michael, perhaps Cergeaux, q.v.,
advocate, 155

262

Index

Calais, 26, 107–8
calcolarius, see shoemaker
Calderini, Johannes, on *Decreta*, 142
Calveley (Calverley), Sir Hugh, 59–60
Calvis, Antonio de, cardinal of Todi, 180, 186
Cambridge, University, 159, 236; Chancellor
    of, 135, 146
    Colleges: King's Hall, 143, 146 (warden),
    152; S John's, 236; *see also* manuscripts;
    Trinity Hall, 134
Camera, papal, 78, 142–3, 164; auditors of,
    English, *see* Bowet, Henry
Camerino 10, 22
Campidoglio, 44
canon law, books on, references to, 134,
    142–4, 226–7, 229
Canterbury, archbishop of, *see* Arundel,
    Thomas; Chichele, Henry; Courtenay,
    William; Sudbury, Simon; Walden,
    Roger
    archdeacon, *see* Acciauoli
    auditor of, *see* Ryssheton, Nicholas
    court of, 155
Canterbury, S Augustine's abbey, *see* Preston,
    John, Colchester, William
Capo da Ferro, family 17; Ceccus 17, 116;
    Paulus Gorcii 17–18, 116
Caputgallis, Francesco di Stephano de, notary
    27
Carbone, Franciscus, cardinal, 171–2, 176, 186
Cardelli, family 175; Johannes 18
cardinals, 3, 26, 32, 37, 170–1, 178, 198
    camerarius of, *see* Minutoli
    households of, 196, English in, 165–7
Carleton, Richard, advocate, 155
Carlisle, bishop of, 151
Caron, Richard, 211
Carraciolo, Nicholas, cardinal, 36
casalenum, casilenum, casalina (building plot,
    building),18, 64, 72
Casarola, *see* Rosa
casella, 19
Castel S Angelo, 85
Castello, bishop of, *see* Popes, Gregory XII
Castle Donnington, constable of, *see* Fraunceys,
    Robert
Castrum Lariani, 68
Castrum Molaris, 68
Cataneis, Damian de, 207
Catterick, John, protonotary and referendary,
    146–8
Cattle owners, 21; *see* Ponzianis, de; *popolo*
cavalerius 11, 117
Cecchus de Romalis, 80–1
Cecchus de Spuchicha, 66; *see also* Angela, wife
    of

Cecchus Simonelli, 64
Ceccus Capo da Ferro, *see* Capo da Ferro
Cephus Latini, 65
Cergeaux, Sergeaux, ?Cages, Michael,
    advocate, 155, 209
cernitores, stirps ad cernendum farinas, 24, 57, 74,
    92, 95–9, 110
    English, in Rome, listed, 96
Cesena, massacre at, 31
Champneys, (Ciampenez), John son of
    William, of London, 21, 32, 35, 58, 91,
    116, 144
chancery, papal, 89, 146, 154; rules of, 161
Chandler, William, of York 10–11, 55, 91
Chandos, Sir Thomas, and wife Lucy, 102, 106,
    114
Chandos, Sir Roger, of Snodhill Wellington
    and Townhope, Herefordshire, 102
Charles of Durazzo, of Naples 38–39, 44, 201;
    see also Ladislas
Charlton, John, 36
Chaundler, John, 180
Chesterton, William, 210
Cheyne, Sir John, 62, 167–8, 172, 180–1
Cheyne, William, master usher, 165
Chichele, Henry, archbishop of Canterbury,
    46, 62, 147, 160, 167–8, 172, 180–1
Chichele, Robert, grocer, 48
Chichele, William, grocer, 48
Chichester, bishopric of, *see* Scrope, Richard;
    Rushook, Thomas
Chichester, cathedral of, *see* Doneys, John;
    Swan, William
Childe, Laurence, OSB, of Battle, minor
    penitentiary, 34, 154
Christofori, Angelus, Luccan, 37
Christofori, Johannes, brother of Angelus, 37
churches and parishes, of Rome 14–15, 110
    Chiesa Nuova, 67
    S Anastasia de Marmorata, 24
    S Angelo in Pescharia (*in foro piscium*), 50, 68,
    160
    SS Apostoli, 97, 122–3
    S Appolinare, 115
    S Benedict *Sconci*, 69
    S Caterina, 74
    S Cecilia, in Trastevere, cardinal's title, 78,
    81, 86
    S Cecilia de Turre Campi, 110
    S Chrysogonus, 15, 77, 86, 97
    S Croce, 111
    S Georgio in Velabro, *see* Possewich,
    Richard, junior
    S Giovanni in Ayno, 66, 118
    S Gregorio, 110
    S John Lateran, 76, 111

Index

Index

Index

Index

Index

houses, named, *see* Scottus Torre, Lo Cafaria, Lo Confesse; Bulgaminis, Torre de
Howden, Cecilia, 111, 125
Hugh of S Victor, 217, 224
Hundred Years War, 3, 5, 60–1, 108, 191
Hutyon, Hugo de, priest 18

Ilkilington, John of, 208
illegitimacy, 150–1
Ilperinis, Franciscus Andreotti de, 84
indulgences, 58–9, 74–5
Inglewood, John, 209
innkeepers, Inns of Rome, 22, 24, 27, *see also* hostalarius
Interdict, 35
Interminelli, 35
Ireland, 75, 150
Irish, 21, 30, 35, 57, 89–90, 91, 137, 150–1
Irland, Irlond, *see* Possewich
Irlond, John, 52; *see also* Possewich
Iselhorst, Johannes, 210
Iserniensis, *see* Maroni, Cristoforo
Ixworth, John, proctor, referendary, 62, 101, 159, 167–8

Jacobellus Cafagi, *see* Cafagi
Jacobellus Cole Lemmi, flour miller and wife, 27
Jacobellus Petri Spechi, 72
Jacobucius Homodei, widow of, *see* Perna
Jacobus de Pappazuris *see* Pappazuris
Jacobus Giacomini, Florentine, 35, 102–3, 106
Jacobus Guilelmi de Ferraria, *sutor*, 46, 66–7, 101, 106; Nonna, *puella sua*, 121
Jacobus Magaleoti, 114
Jacobus Rubei, 109
Jacobus, son of Robert, *cernitor*, 96
Jaen, *see* Alfonso of Pecha
James of Viterbo, 226, 235
Jenstein, John of, archbishop of Prague, 164, 202–4
Jerome, saint, 230, 233, 235; *psalterium iuxta Hebraeos*, 231; Vulgate of, 192, and *see* Bible, Vulgate, accuracy of
Jews, 192–3, *see also* Hebrew, study of
Joanna, queen of Naples, 37–8
Joannes Andreas, *Novella*, 142–3
Johanna de la Morte de *Gascognia*, daughter of Peter, widow of Guilelmus de Civita Vecchia, 92, 111, 123, 127
Johannes, German mercer, 88
Johannes Cardelli, *see* Cardelli
Johannes Cecchi de Leis 19, 73
Johannes de Roma, advocate, 184
Johannes de Suecia and wife Sabella, 83

Johannes Hugolini Bartholomei Johannis Gentilis, 112–13; son Jotius, 113
Johannes Jacomini (or Jacobini) Cecchi de Acula, 80
Johannes Ley or Lei, 84
Johannes Mei Gratiani Muti 12
Johannes Nardi Pichi or Picchi, 84
Johannes Nicolai Pauli, notary, 8, 11
Johannes Petri Cole de Pappazuris, *see* Pappazuris
Johannes Petri Percorarii, *see* Shepherd, John
Johannes Porfili, notary, 97
Johannes Pucii Berte, shoemaker, 68
Johannes son of Petrus, *Theotonicus*, 79–80, 102
John, English *romitus*, 30
John, son of Richard of Roger, 15, 68
John Apollinaris, alias Janni Croce, 99; *see also* Cross, John; Perna, widow of Andreas Mannus and daughter Anna
John servant of Rosa Casarola, 123
John son of Robert, 68
John son of the late William son of Thomas, 109
John son of William, goldsmith (*aurificus*), of Massingham Norfolk, 11, 24, 91, 93
John the English priest, 30
John the Englishman, *cernitor*, 96, 122–3
John the Saracen, 224
John the Scot, 224
Jordanus de Cappis, notary, father of Paula, wife of Petrus Viviani, 115
Jubilee of 1350, 3, 22, 27; of 1390, 42, 60, 77, 203
Julianus Johannes Lipi Alberti, citizen and merchant of Florence, 105

Kelleseye, William, or Clophill, 75–6, 127
Kelsey, Katherine, 76, 127
Kemp, Margery, 19–20, 129–30; servant of, 126, 129
Kentyf, John, 194–5
Kildare, bishop of, *see* Madock, John
Kimhi, *see* David Kimhi
King's bench, court, 163, 179
kings of England,
  Edward II, 43
  Edward III, 5, 150, 191
  Henry IV, 44, 47, 63, 138–40, 143, 152, 167, 169, 171–2, 175–8, 186
  Henry V, 147–8
  Henry VIII, 236
  Richard II, 5, 43–4, 63, 108, 135, 136–7, 150, 169, 174–5, 201–2, 205
Kirkeby, John, monk, 102
Knight, Roger (Chanyht), 83, 85, 105
Knighton, chronicler, 199

Index

Knolles (Knowleys) Sir Robert, 42, 59–61, 63
Knolles, Thomas, grocer, 48, 61, 62–3

Ladislas of Durazzo, son of Charles, 44–5,
    49–50, 52, 85–6, 89, 171
Lagier, Bertrand, cardinal, 17
Lampeter, see S David's, prebends
lanarolus, see woolman
Lanciarius Jannectolus Pauli Celebis, called
    Lomnencho, *speciarius*, 115
Langham, Simon, cardinal, 70, 103, 154, 162,
    188, 190–1, 194, 197–8, 200, 210
    library of, 192, 223, 225–8
    household of, 30, 32, 33, 36, 162–3, 165–6,
    172–3, 190–2, 194–5, 211, 238
Langley, Thomas, keeper of privy seal, later
    bishop of Durham, 137, 141, 147
Lattuna, Henricus Dezier de, see Dezier
Launce, John, 29, 48, 51, 52, 53, 128, 156–7,
    159, 167
Laurence, John, skinner, 157
Laurencius de Serromanis, see Serromanis
Laurencius Johannis Galerie, *ferurius*, 115
Laurentius Anthonii Lancetti Impona, notary,
    73
Laurentius Johannis Laurentii Johannis Canis, 78
Laurentius Romanus, Lars Romares, 205
Lars Romares, see Laurentius Romanus
Ledyard, Adam, jeweller, 28–9
Legnano, John of, 199–200, 229–30; *De*
    antichristo, 229; *De somnio*, 229; *Lectura* on
    Clementines, 142, 229
Lellus Baracta, 117
Lellus Cappa, 113
Lellus de Narnia, *ponderator*, 11
Lellus domini Johannis *cavalerii*, see Saracenis
Lenne, John, advocate, 155
Leo, Willelmus, proctor, 184
Leonardus Justi, 102
librata, see livrée
Lichtensfelser, John, 236
Liège, S Servatius, see Possewich, Richard,
    junior
Liège, diocese of, 144
Lincoln, John, alias Blyton, 51, 128
Lincoln, cathedral, prebends of, 176–7;
    archdeaconry of, 182, 186
Line Draper (Lynedraper), Henry, 60–1
Lisbon, 108
Little, see Parvus
Livre des Mestiers, 28
livrée, or librata, of cardinal, 36, 210
Llandaff, bishopric of, see Bramfield, Edmund;
    Rushook, Thomas, Bottlesham, William;
    Barret, Andrew; Tydeman of
    Winchcombe

Lo Cafaria, house, 23, 72
Lo Confesse, house, 45, 68–9, 72, 81, 124
Lobeke, Hildebrand, 210
loggiado, place called, 82
London, bishopric of, see Braybrooke, Robert,
    Courtenay, William; Walden, Roger
London, citizens of, 75, 91
London, William, OSB of Canterbury, 43
London, mentioned, 128
London, Holy Trinity, priory, 175
London,
    Faringdon within Ward, 29
    Lombard Street, 37
    Paternoster Row, 29
London, and wool trade, 25, 106–9
London jewellers 28–9
London merchants, 26, 47–8, 56, 63, 76, 91
London skinners, see skinners
Lopham, Dionysius, 62–3
Lougham, John, 100
Louis of Anjou 38, 42, 49, 85
Lovell, William, proctor, abbreviator, 45, 62,
    140–1, 149–52, 159, 179, 181, 183
Lucas Johannis, and wife Sabella, 84
Lucca, Luccans, 35–7, 40, 46, 52, 89, 107, 152
Luna, Petrus de, cardinal, see Popes, Benedict
    XIII
Lunt, William E., 42
Lyra, Nicholas de, 193, 231–4, 236

Mabiliota, daughter of Richard of Roger, 68
Macaranis, Laurencius de, *iurisperitus*, 80–1, 84,
    85–6; sons of, Stephanus and Franciscus,
    86
Macclesfield, John, 89
Machiotius Velli, 64
Madock, John, bishop of Kildare, 150
Magistri Stratarum, see Masters of the Streets
Maire-Vigueur, J-C, 78
Malesec, Guido de, cardinal of Poitiers, 200
Malgionis, Cecchus, 78
Malgionis, Alexius Cecchi, notary, 80, 84
Malpas, John, 75
Malpileis, family, Edificato Tucii de and
    Jacobus Edificatii, 18
Mandagout, Guillaume, 142
Manfield, Robert, 208
Mantel, William, with wife Alys, 18, 58,
    69–70, 74
manuscripts,
    Avignon, Bibliothèque de la Ville 996: 223
    Cambridge, CCC 74: 222; CCC 180: 223;
    S John's 218 (I.10), 224; University
    Library: Gg. 6. 3: 223; Ii. 1. 21: 223;
    Ii.3.32: 223–4; Kk 2.8: 223–4
    Madrid, National Library 738: 236

Index

Index

Index

proctor of, in England, *see* Newton, Robert
custos, 58; *see also* Shepherd, John;
  Thomasson, John; William son of Richard
houses, named, *see* Scottus Torre, Lo Cafaria
  Lo Confesse
S Tommaso de Yspanis, parish, in Arenula, 15
Sabbas Cole Galgioffi or della Fragna, 84;
  father Cola, also called Fragna, a miller, 84
Sabella wife of Johannes de Suecia, q.v.
Salibury, John of, *Policraticus*, 214, 223
Salisbury, 25, 91, 100
  cathedral of, 138
  dean of, *see* Chaundler, John
  archdeaconry of, 177
  archdeaconry of Dorset, 209
  prebends of: Charminster and Bere, 176,
    178, 182; Combe, 176; Yetminster
    Secunda, 209
Salmon, John, of Salisbury, with wife Elena,
  71, 91, 100, 115–16, 145
Sancta sanctorum, 76
Saoya, or Sagoia, Johannes Barberii de, son of
  Johannetta, 105; wife Leone and son
  Peter, 105
Saoya, Jacobus Johannis de, *laborator*, 105
Saracenis, de, family, 19
  Johannes 19, 69, 118
  Cecilia wife of Johannes 19
  Johannes Cole 19, 73; his wife Francesca 19,
    73; Anthonius, their son 19; Margarita, his
    grandmother 19
  Lellus *domini Johannis cavalerii or cabalerii*, 11,
    105, 117
  Nicolas, 20
Sauler, John, 101
Sauve Majeure, abbey, 164
Scala Celi, 76, 128
Scangialemosine, family, 84
  Johannes Antonius son of Cola, of Parione,
    79, 84
  Cola Dominici, 84
  Johannes Antonius son of Cola, 113
Schiavo, Antonio Pietro dello, chronicler, 50
Schism, Great, 1, 4, 34, 37, 42, 44–5, 49–50,
  78, 132, 142–3, 146, 152, 164, 172–3,
  178, 194–5, 203, 237
Schocho, Paulus dello, *see* Paulus
Scotland, Scots, 17, 57, 91
Scottus (Scotte) Torre, house, 17, 69, 116
Scriptors, 168
  see Fraunceys, John, Gilby, Nicholas; Niem
    Dietrich of
Scrope, Richard, Rota auditor, bishop of
  Chichester, bishop of Coventry and
  Lichfield, archbishop of York, 75, 133–5,
  138, 146, 147, 151, 178–9

Scrope, Henry, first baron Scrope, of Masham,
  135
Scrope, Sir Richard, 135
secretary, papal, English listed, 153
sergeant-at-arms, papal, *see* Ely, John and Grey,
  Thomas
Sergeaux, *see* Cergeaux
Sermones Parisienses, 142
Serromanis, Nicola, rector of S Stefano de
  Pigna, 110, 114
Serromanis, Paulus de, notary, 110–14
Serromanis, Laurencius de, canon of S Stefano
  de Pigna, 110, 114
Seven Dolors of the Virgin, feast of, 194
Seward, John, schoolmaster, 157
sheepowners, 25
Shepherd, John, alias John son of Peter,
  Pecorarii, *paternostrius*, 8, 10–11, 22, 55,
  58, 59, 64, 92–4, 113, 117, 127
Shepherd, Alice, wife of John, 10–11, 59, 93,
  130
Shillington, parish church, 180
Shipdam, John, advocate, 155, 163
shoemaker (*calcolarius*), 66, 68
shops, in Rome, 65, 66–7, 88, 126, 145
Sicilians, 23
Sienna, 23, 180
  University, 152
Simon, Symon, *mandatarius curie Anglorum*, 57,
  97
Simon de Anglia, advocate, 155
Simon son of John, *paternostrarius*, *see* Barber
Simon son of Simon, of Colchester, with wife
  Cecilia, 66, 69, 91, 105–6, 115, 117, 127;
  brother John, 91, 127
Simon son of the late Cecchus Nardi de Pupo,
  macallarius, 105
simony, 170
Skendelby, John, 209
skinners, of London, 156–8
Skirlaw, Walter, bishop of Durham, 150, 152
Slake, Nicholas, household clerk, 206, *see*
  Easton, benefices, Wells
socius, 191, 197
Solite benignitatis affectum, 226
Solomon, Rabbi, *see* Rashi
Solomon, 193
Somersham, *see* Easton, benefices of
Southam. Thomas, auditor of Langham, 33, 34,
  103, 194
Southampton, 25, 108, 239
Southfleet, church of S Nicholas, 156, 158
Southwell, 176
Spaniards, 23
Sparcha, Agnes, English, 125
Spargrove, Somerset, 174

275

Index

Sparo, Simon son of John, 11
speciarius, 113, 115
spolia, spoils, 212
Sporier, John, 33
Squares, in Rome
  Campo dei Fiori, 17, 69, 79, 80, 89, 113, 116
  del Fico, 67
  Farnese, 10, 17, 19, 64, 69, 82
  Navona, 6, 115
  Platea Judeorum, 50, 69, 74, 81
  Venezia, 97
SS Maria e Caterina, *see* churches and parishes,
  Rome
St Alban's, *see* Walsingham, Thomas
St Quinton, Anthony de, 41, 150
Stable, Staple, Steple, Adam, 59, 61, 107–8
Stafford, Edmund, bishop of Ely, then Exeter,
  58–9, 74–5, 151, 171, 206–7
Staglia, Lorenzo, notary 25
Stanchon, John, prior of S Peter, Newtown
  Trim, 144
Stanley, Thomas de, 176
Staple, 107–8
Stapleton, Peter, 40
Statius Manerii, Eustatius Manerii, Maneys, son
  of John, English, 42, 67–8, 69, 73, 92, 94,
  104–5, 109
Statutes
  Praemunire, 1353 and later, 5, 183
  Provisors 1351 and later, 5, 163, 168, 174,
  179, 185–6
Stefania, widow of Richard son of Roger, 32,
  45, 68–9, 71–2, 122, 124–5, 131; *see also*
  John son of; Mabiliota, daughter of;
  Vannotia, daughter of
Stempel, Tyderic, *cursor*, 145
Stirps, (*stirpa*) and variants, ?cleared area, 12, 57,
  65, 68, 70, 73–4, 79, 115; *see also cernitores*
Stone, Gilbert, 136, 138
Storey, Professor Robin, 177–8
Stow, John, chronicler, 7, 59, 107
Stratton, or Stretton, Robert de, Rota auditor,
  34, 133–4, 141, 155, 173, 176
Street, William, butler to the king, 37
Strickland, Walter, bishop of Carlisle, 140
Strohm, Reinhard, professor, 204
sub-collector, papal, *see* Feriby, Nicholas
Sudbury, Simon, archbishop of Canterbury, 74,
  135, 164
Sudbury, Thomas de, 133–5
Sulmona, *see* Popes, Innocent VII
Super cathedram, 189
Surnames, 7–8
sutor, sartor 24, 25–6
  English in Rome, listed, 99–100
Sutri, 18

Swan, family, of Hook Place, Southfleet, 158
Swan, Richard, senior, skinner of Southfleet
  and London, brother of William and John,
  156–8
Swan, Elena, and Christine Althon, daughters
  of Richard, senior, 156
Swan, Thomas, son of Richard, senior, 156–7
Swan, William, junior, son of William, 157
Swan, William, son of John, 157
Swan, Joan, wife of Richard, 156
Swan, Joan, wife of William, 156–8
Swan, John, brother of William and Richard,
  ?pewterer, married to Petronilla, 156–7,
  and Dionisia, 157
Swan, Thomas, father of William, 156
Swan, William, proctor, papal secretary,
  abbreviator, brother of Richard and John,
  8, 45, 46–8, 50–3, 57–8, 62, 82, 88–9,
  128, 153, 156–61, 167–9, 172, 177–86
Swan, Annette, sister of Richard
Swan, Joan and Elizabeth, daughters of
  William, senior, 157
Swan Joan, wife of William, 156–8
Swayne, John, proctor, abbreviator, papal
  secretary, archbishop of Armagh, 89–90,
  149–53, 168
Swetelers, Lubricus, 157
Sybbesdon, Robert, 36
Sydenham, Simon, 177
syndicus, 11
syndicus 11

Tailor, *see* sutor
Targum, 233
Tart, William, abbreviator, 149, 151, 166
Taylor, (Taylour, Simonis, Symonis, Symund),
  Walter, *cursor*, tailor, 21, 46, 66, 69,
  100–1, 106, 110, 121, 127, 145, 159; wife
  Christine, 100, 145
Taylor, John, 54
Taylour, Agnes, 69, 111, 125
Taylour, Thomas, 33
Tebaldeschi, Franciscus, cardinal 'of Rome', 32
Teramo. diocese, 144
Testacio, Testaccio, place called, 12, 88
Teste, (Head), family, 32, 117–18
Teste, Richard, 33, 100, 106, 110–11, 124,
  127
Teste, Sibilla, Sybilla, Sybil, wife of Richard,
  19, 33, 66, 69, 73, 88, 100, 105, 111,
  124–5, 131
Teyr, John, treasurer of Dublin, proctor,
  abbreviator, 41, 149–52, 168
Theodora niece of Johannes Gregorii, orphan
  daughter of Johannes Romani de Rubeis,
  114; *see also* Vivianus

Index

Index

Cambridge Studies in Medieval Life and Thought
Fourth Series

Titles in series

★ *Also published as a paperback*